Praise for *The Murder Room*:

"...tional, and surprisingly funny."
—*Kirkus Reviews*

"...stery fans would kill for entry to the Vidocq Soci-
..., the Philadelphia-based crime-probing organization Michael
Capuzzo describes in *The Murder Room*. Imagine the thrill of being
in the same room with some of the world's most resourceful detectives, coroners, profilers, polygraph experts, and forensic artists
when they're presented details of a particularly perplexing homicide
and challenged to put their formidable minds to solving it. If there's
not a movie in the works about this charmed circle of cold-casers,
someone is missing the boat."   —BookPage.com

"Compelling reading."   —*Booklist*

"The book is at once terrifying and satisfying."
—*The Philadelphia Inquirer*

"Novelists know to be wary of those slices of reality that are just too
outlandish to be transformed into the stuff of fiction. In the superb
and tantalizing *The Murder Room*, Michael Capuzzo dares readers
to believe the can-they-really-be-true? stories of the heartbreaking
cold cases that have been investigated by the forensic dream team
that is the legendary Vidocq Society. The once-forgotten crimes are
horrendous, each bigger-than-life detective more outrageous than
the next, and the circuitous paths they take to find long-delayed
justice are impossible to forget."
—Stephen White, *New York Times* bestselling author

"Brilliant forensic artist Frank Bender, a frequent star on *America's
Most Wanted*, joined forces with the ace sleuths at the Vidocq Society
to perform some of the most exciting detective work I've ever read in
The Murder Room."   —John Walsh, host of *America's Most Wanted*

"With impressive access and a powerful narrative presence, Michael Capuzzo delivers an intimate portrait of the greatest crime fighters of our time. *The Murder Room* is as addictive as the most inventive of thriller novels, but let us not forget that these are true stories; the monsters in this book are real, and so are the dedicated men who hunt them."   —Jason Kersten, author of
The Art of Making Money and *Journal of the Dead*

"*The Murder Room* is flat-out fantastic. Even better than *Close to Shore*, which is one of my all-time favorites. Capuzzo's new book treats murder and the investigation of it as not just a science but an art—strange, full of wonder, terrifying, and exhilarating. It is also an odyssey of true crime that lends true grace to the genre."
—Jeff Leen, *Washington Post* Pulitzer Prize winner
and author of *Kings of Cocaine* and *The Queen of the Ring*

Praise for *Close to Shore*

"Deserves a place among the adventure classics."   —*The New Yorker*

"A remarkable read . . . a flash photo of the moment when our fascination with sharks transformed from awe into mortal dread."
—*Entertainment Weekly*

"One of the ten best books of the year."   —*People*

"[Capuzzo's] deep and detailed research breathes life into the period. An absorbing page-turner."   —*The Miami Herald*

"Though *Jaws* capitalized on the series of 1916 shark attacks described in this book, Capuzzo's graceful, painstakingly researched account is even more compelling."   —*New York* magazine

"Gripping . . . thoroughly researched . . . fascinating."
—*The Denver Post*

Michael Capuzzo is the author of the *New York Times* bestseller *Close to Shore* and a former award-winning writer for *The Philadelphia Inquirer* and *The Miami Herald*. His stories have appeared in *Esquire*, *Sports Illustrated*, *Life*, and *Reader's Digest*. He lives in the Pennsylvania mountains.

THE
MURDER
ROOM

THE HEIRS OF SHERLOCK HOLMES
GATHER TO SOLVE THE WORLD'S MOST
PERPLEXING COLD CASES

MICHAEL CAPUZZO

GOTHAM BOOKS

GOTHAM BOOKS
Published by Penguin Group (USA) Inc.
375 Hudson Street, New York, New York 10014, U.S.A.

Penguin Group (Canada), 90 Eglinton Avenue East, Suite 700, Toronto, Ontario M4P 2Y3,
Canada (a division of Pearson Penguin Canada Inc.) · Penguin Books Ltd, 80 Strand, London
WC2R 0RL, England · Penguin Ireland, 25 St Stephen's Green, Dublin 2, Ireland (a division
of Penguin Books Ltd) · Penguin Group (Australia), 250 Camberwell Road, Camberwell,
Victoria 3124, Australia (a division of Pearson Australia Group Pty Ltd) · Penguin Books
India Pvt Ltd, 11 Community Centre, Panchsheel Park, New Delhi–110 017, India · Penguin
Group (NZ), 67 Apollo Drive, Rosedale, Auckland 0632, New Zealand (a division of Pearson
New Zealand Ltd) · Penguin Books (South Africa) (Pty) Ltd, 24 Sturdee Avenue, Rosebank,
Johannesburg 2196, South Africa

Penguin Books Ltd, Registered Offices: 80 Strand, London WC2R 0RL, England

Published by Gotham Books, a member of Penguin Group (USA) Inc.

Previously published as a Gotham Books hardcover edition

First trade paperback printing, June 2011

1   3   5   7   9   10   8   6   4   2

Gotham Books and the skyscraper logo are trademarks of Penguin Group (USA) Inc.

Capuzzo, Michael.
The murder room : the heirs of Sherlock Holmes gather to solve the world's
most perplexing cold cases / Michael Capuzzo.
p.   cm.
ISBN 978-1-592-40142-0 (hc)   978-1-592-40635-7 (pbk)
1. Murder—United States—Case studies.   2. Vidocq Society.   I. Title.
HV6529.C37 2010
363.25'95230973—dc22   2010005044

Printed in the United States of America • Set in Bembo • Designed by Elke Sigal

For Teresa

· CONTENTS ·

PART THREE
· THE VIDOCQ SOCIETY ·

PART FOUR
· BATTLING MONSTERS ·

PROLOGUE

THE PROFILER AND THE PRIEST

Hudson, Wisconsin, December 2004

The profiler would not shake hands with the priest. It was unacceptable, intolerable if he was to go in for the kill. And the profiler always went in for the kill. That was the thing that excited him most. It never ceased to enthrall him, even in retirement.

The priest had swept in, cassock whirling, smiling and pumping familiar hands, trailing an assistant "to puff himself up with more power," the profiler noted. The Father was a large man, commanding in his black garb; bearded, youthful face cracked in a welcoming Midwestern smile. Next to him the profiler seemed shrunken, emaciated, pale as a ghost. He coughed up a lung with each cigarette, at least three times an hour. He also was an atheist, sneering and quite cynical about the whole question. But that was not the point.

The point was moral standards must be upheld as a matter of honor, a point of manhood. The more immediate point was control, and the thin man would not let the psychopath acquire it, not for a moment. Each moment in life, he believed, was a choice: a step toward good or evil, dominance or submission, authenticity or falsehood. He did not tolerate the lesser choices. He did not tolerate those who crossed the line invading common decency. This made him a lot of enemies. He was proud to have enemies. "One should never apologize for being right," he said.

Now the big, fleshy hand near to God was outstretched toward the thin man in fellowship. The others, the sergeant and two detectives, were watching.

The profiler wrinkled his aquiline nose in disgust, "as if I was being offered a piece of dog shit." Swiftly he withdrew his hand and turned away. He was pleased to see a stricken look fleetingly cross the priest's face. Then, "composure returned like a sheen coating the hollow man."

It was always all about control. The profiler had instructed the detectives how to introduce him. No name, no city or rank, only "this is a man from out of town who is an expert on murder." Once the detective introduced the profiler as instructed, the thin man shook hands with the priest with Victorian courtesy, like the old-school gentleman he was. Then he sat in the corner, legs folded, lip turned in a sneer, quietly watching as the police asked the priest about the murders.

The police were no closer to an arrest than they had been that afternoon in broad daylight when the town was shocked from a century of innocence in such matters, unimagined and unimaginable, with the execution-style murder of two prominent citizens. The police had once had eleven suspects and now, two years later, had moved no further. The profiler studied the case file and chatted with the police for three hours before narrowing the eleven suspects to one. "It's the priest," he told the police. "Of course, I know you don't want it to be the priest. Nonetheless, it's the priest." The thin man had appeared on the front page of the small-town newspaper declaring he was "quite confident" the mysterious murders would soon be solved. "If I were the killer," he quipped, "I wouldn't buy any green bananas."

The police hadn't known what to expect when they presented the cold case in the nineteenth-century men's club in Philadelphia to the world's greatest detectives. The French flags, the walnut paneling, the chandeliers made them nervous. There was an immense, portly, bearded man with a huge head, a man of a thousand jokes they called the Grand Inquisitor; a slim, short, muscular artist, bald with a white goatee and dressed all in black, who saw dead people; and the gaunt profiler with the face of Poe. There were a hundred others, famous sleuths, the FBI agent whose movie double nails Hannibal Lecter in The Silence of the Lambs, *investigators of the RFK and Martin Luther King assassinations, too many to remember.*

They said they'd consider taking the case, possibly organize a team.

Then one man, the thin man, got off the plane alone.

And now he watched as the priest sat before him and fielded questions from the police with dignity and poise. The priest sat erect with his elbows on the table, his hands tented as if in prayer. The detectives asked him about the young boys. The priest sat back with umbrage; the mere suggestion was an insult. The detectives pushed harder, with names and dates, until the priest had to admit to sex with the young teenagers. But the priest told the police they badly misunderstood. He was not assaulting the boys. He was teaching them sex education.

There was quiet. A detective looked to the corner and asked if the profiler had any questions.

The thin man leaned forward and removed his glasses to stare at the priest. "To begin with, if I were in charge of this investigation, you would not be wearing that costume." He spat out the word "costume" as if it were something foul.

"I'm a priest twenty-four hours a day!" the priest objected.

The profiler gave the priest a merciless glare and scowled in deepening disgust. "Here, you are not representing the Roman Catholic Church. Here, in fact, what you're doing is representing a failed man."

The priest blanched and fell silent. The police resumed their questioning about the boys. The priest repeated his educational theory, his justifications. Of course, he got them drunk first; they were too ashamed of their bodies otherwise. Then he got them excited. But he didn't bring them to climax. He was teaching them responsible sexuality. It's not wrong to get a hard-on, it's wrong to use it.

The thin man's voice rose shrilly from the corner. "Ridiculous! You're a pervert!"

The police asked the priest to remove his cassock. It had been the profiler's idea. "With this sort of psychopath, we must do everything to rattle him." Indeed the priest seemed a smaller man after he pulled off the cassock and removed the undershirt beneath. The police compared the tattoo on his shoulder with one a witness described. It was a match.

As the priest pulled his undergarment back on, and then his cassock, the profiler stood and approached him, coming very close, and gave him a death stare. He kept staring, implacable, his eyes as cold and unrelenting as a night wind, until the priest looked down and away. Suddenly, the profiler's heart leaped in joy, though he kept his face expressionless as a smoothed stone.

The priest was crying!

"A tear of hatred slowly trilled down his cheek," the thin man noted. "It was quite lovely."

They were standing two feet apart, the man of law and the man of God. As the tear dissolved into the thick beard, the big man wiped it away, then looked up into the thin man's eyes with loathing and slowly hissed:

"God . . . damn . . . it!"

The thin man couldn't contain himself. He was grinning openly.

"Was it a thrill to hear this man of the cloth taking the name of the Lord in vain?" Indeed it was.

"I knew then the bitch was mine."

THE VOICE OF THE BLOOD

In the beginning of the world all hope was lost. But there were three men:

> The chieftain, the warrior, the shaman.
> The king, the knight, the wizard.

We tell these stories to survive. The story swirls in smoke, fabric, and music; spins in the winds of the gods and the vortex of DNA. Harvard University biologist E. O. Wilson calls such stories "The Voice of the Species"—the essential stories formed by the "epigenetic rules of human nature . . . the inborn rules of mental development."

This tale, the most enduring in the west outside the Holy Bible, was first written down more than eight hundred years ago. Between the years 1129 and 1151 a Benedictine monk who taught at Oxford translated into Latin, at his bishop's request, a series of ancient Celtic prophecies, *Prophetiae Merlini (Prophecies of Merlin)*. The monk then wrote *Historia Regum Britanniae (History of the Kings of Britain)*, pieces of which were handed down to him from the oldest written Welsh sources, the *Red Book of Hergest* and the *White Book of Rhydderch*. In these texts can be found fragments of the first historical record of King Arthur and the Knights of the Round Table.

The story, as told numberless times across the centuries, begins with the world in ruins. Crops wither, even the trees are dead, "tortured bones of a perished race, of monsters no mortal knows," the poet cries. The wounded king ails in his castle, powerless. The king cannot act without help; he needs two other men to embark on a journey, men of great and unique talents to complement his own.

Why we ceaselessly tell this story is a mystery. Scientists cannot explain why *Homo sapiens* must take in oxygen and release certain stories to live.

Philosophers say the ultimate source of the story is the eternal human need to find, in the words of Joseph Campbell, "the promise enshrined in the Mysteries since the beginning of the world." The prophets say it is our pathway through trials to the grace of God. A man of action might say the relevant point of more than a million years of human trial, error, and wisdom embedded in the story is entirely practical:

When the world breaks and needs fixing, the thing to do is find the right three men.

THE
MURDER
ROOM

PART ONE

·

THE MURDER ROOM

CHAPTER I

THE CONNOISSEURS OF MURDER

The great hall was filled with the lingering aroma of pork and mallard duck sausage as black-vested waiters appeared, shouldering cups of vanilla bean blancmange. Connoisseurs sat at tables between the hearths under glittering eighteenth-century chandeliers, chatting amiably in several languages. When the coffee arrived, a fine Colombian *supremo* steaming in its pots, the image of the corpse of a young man of uncommon beauty, lying on his back, materialized in the center of the room.

A gray winter light slanted into the hall, as the midday sun had sailed beyond the city, and the image on the large screen was crisp. The young man's blond locks were matted in a corona of dried blood, his sculpted cheekbones reduced to a pulp. The police photograph had been taken at night in a restaurant alley, and the surrounding scene was obscured in darkness. Yet the strobe light had thrown the young man's face into sharp relief. Out of the shadows of a distant southern night, the stark, wide-open eyes loomed over the room.

It was shortly before one o'clock in the afternoon, and the fifth and final course had been served to the connoisseurs of the Vidocq Society.

"My goodness," said a short-haired young woman in a red dress. Patting her mouth with a napkin, she excused herself from the table and, a hand over her mouth, hurried to the door. William Fleisher, a big man in a magnificent blue suit, *WLF* embroidered on his custom shirt, sadly shook his large, bearded head. "We need to do a better job screening guests," he said. Richard Walter, his gaunt cheekbones sunken in the wan light, glared at the departing figure. Frank Bender—clad in a tight black T-shirt and jeans, the only man in the hall not wearing a suit—whispered to the detective next to him, "Nice legs."

Fleisher shook his head in wonderment at the two eccentric, moody geniuses with whom he had thrown in his lot. His partners were criminologists without peer or precedent in his thirty years with the feds.

Forensic psychologist Richard Walter was the coolest eye on murder in the world. Tall and acerbic, he spoke with a clipped propriety that had earned him the moniker the Englishman from certain criminal elements. Walter had spent twenty years treating the most violent psychopaths in the state of Michigan at the largest walled penitentiary in the world, in Jackson, and at one of the toughest, the old Romanesque castle in Marquette on Lake Superior. His habit of peering over the top of his owlish black glasses and boring into the souls of inmates was known as the "Marquette stare," and it was a look to be avoided at all costs. He employed it to crack the façade of psychopaths. Walter was unsurpassed in his understanding of the darkest regions of the heart. In his spare time, moonlighting as a consulting detective, he was one of the small group of American criminologists who invented modern criminal profiling in the 1970s and '80s to battle serial killers.

At Scotland Yard, which used him on the most extreme murder cases, he was known as the "Living Sherlock Holmes"—an epithet that horrified him.

"Richard looks like Basil Rathbone in *The Hound of the Baskervilles*," Fleisher said. "He talks like him, he thinks like him."

"Whenever someone says *that*," Walter said, "I look away and wait for the moment to pass, as if someone has just farted."

Frank Bender was the most celebrated forensic artist working at that time, perhaps in history. The wiry ex-boxer was muscled and balding, with a Van Dyke beard and piercing hazel eyes. For the occasion, he wore long sleeves that concealed his Navy tattoos. Bender, who grew up in tough North Philadelphia with bullets hitting the row house wall, was high school–educated, blunt-spoken, happily sex-addicted, and a psychic—a gift he was shy about in the roomful of cops. But cops were awed by his ability to keep six or seven girlfriends happy as well as his wife, and to catch Most Wanted mass murderers with a sketchpad and scalpel.

"Frank," Walter liked to tease him. "You would have been burned at the stake in the seventeenth century. Now you'll just get shot in the back."

The tall, melancholy, deductive Walter and the manic, intuitive Bender were blood brothers and partners on major cases. A detective duo without precedent, the psychologist and artist were capable of penetrating secrets of the living and the dead. When they could stand each other.

Bender saw dead people; Walter was contemptuous of spiritualism. The artist counted his sexual conquests in the hundreds; the psychologist, divorced, shrank from the touch of man, woman, child, dog, and cat. Walter was the most orderly mind on a murder, Bender the most chaotic.

William Lynn Fleisher was the glue that held the three together—the one, friends said, "with a sail attached to the mast." The sartorial big man was the number two in charge of United States Customs law enforcement in three states, a world-class polygraph examiner and interrogator, a former FBI special agent, and an ex–Philadelphia beat cop. Fleisher was obsessed with the truth, had made himself a scholar of the history of truth-finding and an expert at distinguishing the truth from a lie. He used the polygraph to try to peer into the hearts of men to judge them, but really what he wanted to do was redeem them—both the criminals whose psychophysiological signs spiked with guilt, and their tragic victims whose suffering society forgot. The big man, it was said by his special agents, had gained a hundred pounds to make room for his heart.

Bender and Walter were the most astonishing investigative team Fleisher had ever seen, equal parts reason and revelation, when they turned their combustible gifts on a killer and not on each other, like a man trying to extinguish his own shadow. The stout federal agent was the administrator who allowed them to take shape and function in the world.

They had met that morning in Bender's hall of bones, where a legendary and especially terrifying mob hit man had been the force that first brought them together, bonded in their fierce and awkward way, to create a private club of forensic avengers. Fleisher was sipping coffee with Bender at the kitchen table when the thin man entered the warehouse studio, nose wrinkled in disapproval "at the cat smells and whatever else."

"Richard!" Bender shouted, pumping Walter's hand enthusiastically, yet careful not to give a manly hug. "Let me show you my new painting!"

It was an enormous, brightly colored oil portrait of one of his many girlfriends, rendered in paint as thick as cake frosting. It was an eight-foot frontal nude; from the left nipple dangled a real brass ring.

"Chrissie has the cutest little butt," Bender said quietly, smiling as if visited by a wonderful memory.

Walter stood with his nose upturned, which pushed his mouth into a frown, studying the painting for a long moment.

"It's smut, Frank," he declared, turning away. "Simple smut." Bender howled with delight, as if there was no greater compliment. Walter glared at him. "Frank, Jesus Christ, you're almost sixty years old, and you're behaving like a fifteen-year-old Bolivian sex slave houseboy! You're using sex as an antidote to depression. As I have tried to explain, at our age it is not healthy for one to live as if one is poised before a mirror ringed with stage lights. One day the lights will go out and you will look in the mirror and see nothing at all.

"Now I'll take some coffee, black, if it's not too much trouble," Walter added. "I'm not fussy, so long as it wasn't boiled with a head."

Now with Fleisher in the great hall, Bender and Walter greeted each other warmly. The three men radiated an energy that seemed to animate the room. The habitual sadness in Fleisher's brown eyes lifted like a mist as he looked proudly across the gathering. All morning forensic specialists from around the globe had been quietly arriving at Second and Walnut streets in Philadelphia. They had gathered as they arrived in the high-ceilinged Coffee Room and Subscription Room on the first floor of the tavern, where colonists had once discussed politics, trade, and ship movements over the latest magazines and Franklin's *Pennsylvania Gazette*. Fleisher had felt the heady buzz of reunited friends, peers, and rivals. But now as he studied the assembly of sleuths from seventeen American states and eleven foreign countries, he sensed that something special was happening. Each man and woman was more renowned than the next.

There was FBI agent Robert Ressler, tall and silver-haired, who had confronted Charles Manson, John Wayne Gacy, and more "serial killers," a term he coined, than anyone in history. He was accepting congratulations, and no small amount of teasing, for *The Silence of the Lambs,* the new hit movie featuring Hannibal "The Cannibal" Lecter being hunted by the FBI's Jack Crawford, a character based partly on Ressler. Ressler was never far from his cohort Richard Walter. They were two of the greatest profilers in the world.

Of equal distinction were the forensic pathologists. Their table included Dr. Hal Fillinger of Philadelphia, who had proven that the "Unicorn Killer," fugitive Ira Einhorn, had murdered his girlfriend Holly Maddux; Fillinger had arrived in his big white Cadillac with the "Homicide Hal" vanity plates. Next to him sat Dr. Richard Froede of Arizona, who would autopsy the remains of kidnapped CIA agent William Buckley, tortured, murdered, and dumped at a Beirut roadside by Islamic jihadists. Among the Philadelphia cops was Frank Friel, the former homicide captain who solved the 1981 assassination of mob underboss Philip "Chicken Man" Testa, immortalized in Bruce Springsteen's song "Atlantic City": ". . . they blew up the chicken man in Philly last night . . ." Fleisher saw noted investigators of the JFK and Martin Luther King assassinations, and a CIA friend who was leading the bureau's secret war on Afghanistan, sitting with a colleague, a young blond female "spook" who loathed to show her face in public, even here. At the French table, with the agents from Interpol in Lyon, sat the director of *Brigade de la Sûreté* in Paris, the French equivalent of the FBI. *Sûreté*, founded in 1811 by Vidocq, had been the very first state investigative agency, later inspiring the creation of the FBI and Scotland Yard.

The chamber on the second floor of the City Tavern was the historic Long Room, forty-four feet long and narrow with a soaring chapel ceiling, the first ballroom in the New World, where General George Washington had toasted his election to the presidency as cannons boomed across the city and Madeira glasses smashed. By modern standards it was austere, a pale green chamber with chair rails and candle sconces. But now it had been arranged to re-create the spirit of a second-floor chamber in Paris in 1833. In the upstairs room of No. 12 *rue Cloche-Perce*, Vidocq had run the first private detective agency in history, *Le Bureau des Renseignements* (Office of Information), seventeen years before the Pinkerton Agency was founded in the United States. It was the first room in history designed for a group of men to systematically deduce and brainstorm solutions to murder cases.

In the north corner of the room, overlooking the Delaware River, a bronze bust of Eugène François Vidocq rested on an oak pedestal. The wide, arrogant face was stippled in shadows from the heavy green drapes, beneath crossed French and American flags. In the room at No. 12 *rue Cloche-Perce*, in the flickering shadows of hissing gaslights, Vidocq and his men kept intricate records to track criminals' patterns. They discussed motive and modus operandi in greater detail than ever before in history. They made plaster casts of shoe impressions and studied bullets to link them to crimes. They worked under paintings of Damiens being quartered, John the Baptist losing his head, and Ravaillac being tortured. They were the first modern criminologists. Convinced of their superior knowledge of the criminal mind, Vidocq had chosen them from the ranks of ex-convicts, like himself.

Each of the men and women at the long tables wore a red-white-blue pin on their lapels—*Les Couleurs*, the colors of France, the signature of their status as Vidocq Society Members (VSMs). There were eighty-two VSMs, one for each year of Vidocq's life. It was the world's most exclusive club, open, regardless of race, sex, age, or national origin, only to the best detectives and forensic scientists on the planet. They had been called the greatest gathering of forensic detectives ever assembled in one room. "No police agency in the world has the luxury of this kind of talent," Fleisher said. *The New York Times* declared the Vidocq Society "The Heirs of Holmes." "This is not a gathering of a ragtag bunch of Baker Street Irregulars playing dutiful amanuensis to Sherlock Holmes's genius," the *Times* said. "Nor are they a bunch of good-natured Archie Goodwins, filling the role of narrator and legman to the sedentary but brilliant Nero Wolfe in the mystery novels of Rex Stout. . . . It is a group that collectively has hundreds of years of crime-solving experience."

The Vidocq Society's mission was simple and straightforward: As many as one in three murders in the United States went unsolved. It was a well of suffering scarcely known to the journalists who claimed crime was sensational and overblown, or the millions of Americans entertained nightly by it on TV. Murder was a scourge that had taken more than a million lives, more than most of the American wars ever fought in the twentieth century. Cops were overworked, departments underfunded; the criminal justice system favored the rights of criminals over victims. In a world that had forgotten its heroes, they resolved, by the light of a twelfth-century chivalric pledge, to hunt down murderers in cold cases, punish the guilty, free the innocent, and avenge, protect, and succor families victimized by murder. They resolved to work pro bono rather than swat a golf ball around in Florida or Arizona. They met on the third Thursday of every month; they were the Thursday Club. The eighty-two of them pledged themselves to their cause until death, when the rosette would be pinned on another man or woman chosen to fight for a better world.

The old Victorian brownstone on Locust Street in Philadelphia, headquarters of the Vidocq Society, was besieged with requests from around the world from cops and victims seeking an audience in the private chamber in City Tavern. A congressman who wanted to solve a murder in his family. A federal agent in Washington who needed another pair of eyes on the assassination of a woman agent in broad daylight while jogging. A young, small-town Tennessee cop overmatched by an elderly millionaire serial killer who moved from state to state killing his wives. But the Vidocq Society would not touch a case unless it was a murder, the victim had committed no crimes, and the case was at least two years old, officially a "cold case." "Our mission is to help the police at their request, working quietly in the background without fanfare, to act as an agent for justice," Fleisher said. In all cases, the society required the presence in the room of the municipal police officers, state or federal agents, or government prosecutors working on the cold case; families looking for vengeance became too emotional without official support. Yet in rare instances, when police corruption was suspected, an ordinary citizen was granted an audience before the Vidocq Society. This afternoon was one of those cases, when an ordinary citizen had earned an audience before the forensic court of last resort.

At one o'clock, Fleisher stood at the lectern and welcomed them from four continents to Philadelphia and the monthly convening of the Vidocq Society. Before lunch, he had led them in the Pledge of Allegiance, hand clamped over his heart, his voice the loudest in the room. He had introduced a pastor who asked that

God favor and guide their undertakings for justice. Now Fleisher loosened the room with a joke about their purpose, "to enjoy my great hobby, which is lunch." Then he reminded them somberly that their work was to speak for the dead who cannot speak for themselves. It was sacred work.

The essential method that Fleisher, Bender, and Walter had resurrected from the nineteenth century was deceptively simple: They had filled a room with detectives to unmask a crime of murder. Like Vidocq's ex-cons, though far more sophisticated, they had at their disposal the most advanced forensic tools of their age. Busboys swarmed out of the kitchen and swept away the last of the silver and china, carded the remaining crumbs from the white tablecloths. As the coffee was poured, the historic chamber was no longer the Long Room. It was the Murder Room, reborn.

At ten past one, Fleisher introduced Mr. Antoine LeHavre of Louisiana. A rotund man in his forties with dark hair and a gentlemanly manner, LeHavre wore a sports jacket and eyes burdened with woe. He stood at the lectern, slightly to the right of the gruesome image of his slain friend. There was an air of anticipation, as never before had an ordinary citizen presented to the Vidocq Society, alone.

LeHavre began by thanking the society for inviting him. "I know that you better than anyone else understand what I've been through," he said. "I just couldn't take it anymore. I couldn't do it anymore alone."

They had all seen enough cases to know the Murder Room was a place to walk far around, a step in life to bypass if you could. The chamber was invisible to a happy man. Agony lit the way. The room appeared to the suffering. They had seen his like before. He was one of the walking dead, zombified by the unsolved murder of a friend or loved one, a man willing to crawl to the end of the Earth to right a terrible wrong. But they saw something else as well, also well known among them: After four courses served hot, Antoine LeHavre was ready for revenge, served ice-cold.

CHAPTER 2

THE MAN WHO
GOT AWAY WITH MURDER

The killer got away with it—that's what he couldn't accept. The cops on the take didn't bother him anymore, though he hoped they would be punished. Nor did the blind coroner, the witnesses who saw nothing, the deaf and dumb DA. He'd forgiven them all, even the hit man who kept his address on file. Lastly his callow lawyer who said, Let it go—there's too much power against you. Let it go, Antoine. It's how the world works. It's the mob, for Chrissake. Which was a good point, an excellent point, except he couldn't let Paul Bernard Allain go.

Allain's bloodied face still shimmered in his dreams. His best friend was beaten to death right before his eyes, and he stood there helpless to pull him out of it. He couldn't sit now and watch Paul go all the way, slip into infinity, unredeemed.

The man who got away with murder was going to pay.

As strong as his feelings were, he didn't want revenge, only justice. Antoine LeHavre told his story simply and directly. He wanted to convey his gratitude for being granted an audience with the investigators, especially as a private citizen. He thanked Fleisher, who had said, "Don't worry, we'll solve it."

A respectful hush had fallen over the room as LeHavre stood at the lectern. The tall windows reduced the sounds of the city to a distant hum. On the sidewalk below, tourists walking to Independence Hall passed the old brick tavern at Second and Chestnut streets without a glance; once the grandest establishment in the New World, the City Tavern was an Enlightenment castle lost in time. As Fleisher stepped onto the wide-plank floor, he had fallen under the room's familiar spell. A history lover, Fleisher knew that Madison, Hamilton, Washington, and Franklin had dined here nightly during the Constitutional Convention, enjoying "a feast of Reason and a flow of soul." The Masons held their first secret rituals on the North American continent in this room.

As LeHavre began his presentation, Fleisher thought of the tavern's round pediment window, now obscured by taller buildings, which once commanded the New World harbor. It was the Masonic All-Seeing Eye that had blessed the colonies with the benediction *Annuit Coeptis,* "God is favorable to our undertakings." He silently prayed that God was still watching.

LeHavre was a furniture manufacturer in Louisiana, a civic leader. In the middle of June seven years earlier, he had taken a dozen of his employees, including Allain, a valuable office manager and a friend, to a minor-league baseball game under the lights. Afterward, they all repaired to a restaurant-bar. There Allain had become inebriated, and, out of character, made a small scene. The last LeHavre saw of him alive, he was being led out a side door by a bouncer. It all happened with a surreal speed. By the time LeHavre located Allain, he witnessed the end of a struggle in which two bouncers beat the young man unconscious. He never regained consciousness. LeHavre had been stunned and confused. Allain had no enemies. He was a young man with a wife and two young children, a churchgoer. The police and a series of private eyes were no help. His best guess was that it was a tragic misunderstanding: Allain, who was rarely inebriated and couldn't handle it, had acted out and the bouncers overreacted and killed him. He suspected the police and DA had stonewalled the investigation at the request of the bar owners, who had well-known ties to the mob.

LeHavre was giving the presentation he had provided to the

police, who had feigned interest seven years earlier. The second slide was even more gruesome: a close-up of the side of Allain's head, severely battered, leaking what appeared to be cranial fluid. Murmurs swept the tables. Fleisher felt his own indrawn breath, the familiar welling behind the eyes. He couldn't help himself: The view of a young man's corpse always reminded him of the yearnings and lost promise of his own youth.

The Vidocq Society had become famous for cracking cases with its freewheeling style of investigation. Now, with a nod from Fleisher, it began.

"Has any DNA testing been done?" Fleisher asked.

"No," LeHavre said. "Blood and hair samples were lost before there was a chance to do any testing."

"What do you mean, lost?" asked a Navy intelligence officer.

"There's a receipt for the samples in the evidence locker. But the samples disappeared. The DA has refused to look into it."

"Have you tried to exhume the body?" Bender asked.

"Yes," LeHavre replied. He was awaiting a ruling on his petition to do just that.

At the tables, the detectives shifted and rustled as they studied the police file and coroner's report. Ressler, the famed FBI agent, leaned over to whisper to Homicide Hal, the white-haired dean of Philadelphia coroners, and Homicide Hal nodded. Walter and Bender kept their own counsel.

The room was silent, "like an ocean drawing back," Walter recalled. As the last round of coffee was poured, the questions came in a burst, from forensic odontologists and medical examiners, explosives and firearms specialists, FBI, DEA, IRS, forensic anthropologists, ritual-murder experts, and psychiatrists.

"Did the bouncer and Allain have a prior relationship?" asked an NYPD homicide detective.

"No," LeHavre said.

During the fight, Allain's body had slammed against a door in the bar, splattering it with blood. "Do you still have the door? Have tests been run on it?"

"No," LeHavre said. The door was repainted. Tests were never conducted on it, to his knowledge.

"How have you documented the bar's connection to the mob?"

He hadn't, but it was well known in the business community.

"How long had you known the victim?"

"I met him when I hired him nine years ago."

"Were you drinking with him that night?"

"No. I was at a table with other friends and employees."

"What was your relationship?"

"He was one of my best employees. He came to me without a college education. We hire MBAs out of Vanderbilt and Tulane, but Paul made himself into one of the most capable managers I've ever had. He was exceptionally bright and dedicated, a natural leader."

The grilling continued for half an hour. As the questions and answers volleyed back and forth, LeHavre came alive. He seemed to sense the society's real interest and a burden lifting. His whole manner had changed; in place of stoic resignation his face brightened, his answers grew more detailed and energetic. After years of carrying the investigative load by himself, stonewalled by the police, he stopped in the middle of the questioning to openly thank the Vidocq Society again. "Frankly, after all this time going it alone, I'm overwhelmed at the level of interest and support."

This was a common response to the society's efforts, although stoic law enforcement officers seldom expressed it aloud. Fleisher, right in front of LeHavre at the head table, sat beaming.

By 2 P.M., the men and women at the tables began to rustle in their chairs. Fleisher looked conspicuously at his wristwatch, and looked up and signaled to LeHavre that the session was over.

The VSMs had agencies to run, their own private cases to work, planes to catch. If members were interested enough to form a "working group" to dig deeper into the case, that would come later.

Fleisher joined LeHavre at the lectern. "Thank you for coming," he said. "We hope we've helped provide Mr. LeHavre with some new leads, taken the case a way down the path toward justice. As you know, he has no official help from law enforcement, so if any of you are interested in taking this further, you know where to find me." He grinned. "Meanwhile, we'd like to give you this small token of appreciation for appearing before the Vidocq Society—the very first tool of deduction." He opened a small, polished wooden box and held up a wood-handled magnifying glass. For an instant the curved glass blazed with light.

Fleisher put the glass back in its box as the VSMs were standing to leave. "Everybody, wait," he called out. "Frank has something else."

Everyone sat down as Bender stood, his pure line of black emphasizing his bald head and white goatee, and waited a bit impatiently for it to be over, although they knew the forensic artist wouldn't take long. While his partner Richard Walter possessed an arch, erudite, verbose style, Bender was known to be brutally plain and blunt-spoken, true to his Philadelphia row house roots. The muscular artist lowered his head, his eyes disappearing in shadows under the heavy brow, raised his arm to the front of the room, and pointed directly at LeHavre.

"I know who killed Allain," he said evenly. "You did. For my money, you're the murderer."

An uproar swept the room. Fleisher stood and called for order. LeHavre's face drained of color, but he said nothing. Then all eyes turned to Walter, the blade of a man in a blue suit, as he walked to the front of the gathering and asked for silence.

"Ladies and gentlemen," he said, "I might be wrong, OK, but I haven't been wrong since 1949." Tittering laughter, a lone guffaw. Walter turned and stared at LeHavre. "My impetuous friend may jump to wild, unsupported conclusions on occasion, but as it happens, in this instance Frank Bender is indeed quite right—you, sir, are quite clearly a psychopath." The profiler removed his spectacles, revealing small blue eyes set in a baleful stare.

Walter coolly described the presenter as a classic murdering personality who had sex with his employee before he killed him.

LeHavre stood at the podium, his face a blank mask, and said nothing.

The first clue, Walter calmly noted, was that he detected "a grand, slightly overinflated presence in our guest. I picked up what I considered to be a covered, macho effeminate voice, just that clip of language that made me raise my eyebrow and look up at him, notice him as it were, in a new way." Walter arched his left eyebrow for emphasis.

"Studying the photographs of the young man who is the victim in this case, as it happens a young and very handsome man, it became clear to me the nature of the friendship the two men enjoyed, at least for a time. It was clearly a biblical alliance—the young, handsome man and the older, powerful but less attractive boss—and the whole issue of jealousy had come into play. And of course in these situations the guy who is the boss controls the money."

Walter looked up at the chandelier as if in contemplation. "Now then, many times in such relationships, as one observes them," he said, "you kiss the hand you dare not bite. But such relationships are notoriously unstable, especially in the homosexual realm. Almost always there comes a time where the young one is unfaithful, untrue, or goes in search of a new alliance, and what we have is punishment coming back—if this guy can't have him nobody's going to have him."

"This is outrageous," LeHavre said softly, to no one in particular. He gathered his materials and began to move toward the door.

"You see, it never made sense that a bouncer or bouncers had killed Allain," Walter went on. "What's in it for them? Bouncers don't kill people; they throw them out of bars.

"Mr. LeHavre, for the pleasures of power and control, has thrust himself into the police investigation for years," he added. "He believes he's smarter than anyone." He smiled. "He enjoys playing that dangerous game of catch-me-if-you-can. Today we have witnessed an arrogant and vainglorious attempt to brag to a roomful of cops.

"You see, the first rule of murder is the murder isn't over until the murderer says it is . . . and you, sir, are attempting to extend the pleasure of murder by exploiting all of us here today. At that, you have failed. You are not smarter than any of us. You are bright but an underachiever, for which the triumph of murder compensates."

At the door, LeHavre turned back and said, "You have no proof of this, of any of this, none whatsoever. You'll be hearing from my lawyer."

Walter spoke over the top of his glasses. "You must have enjoyed it whilst it lasted."

"Poor guy didn't even get his magnifying glass," Fleisher said as he left the room with his partners. "What did I tell you? I told you it was a case that merited attention," he added, a huge smile creasing his beard. Bender grinned and Walter glared at his partners.

"Another Vidocq Society lunch," Bender said, "another murder solved."

Fleisher said he was uncomfortable with his partners' attack on LeHavre. "I don't see the evidence for it," he said.

"You may want to rethink it, Bill," Walter said. "The guy didn't get his jollies this time. The urge is insatiable. If he can't stimulate himself sufficiently with memory, he'll kill again."

CHAPTER 3

THE KNIGHTS OF THE CAFÉ TABLE

After lunch, the VSMs exited the eighteenth-century tavern and hurried across the narrow and cobbled streets, making connections to Arizona, England, Egypt, France, and beyond; Fleisher, Bender, and Walter walked to a coffee shop on the corner. "Murder will out," Chaucer wrote in *The Canterbury Tales*. "This is my conclusion." But real life, Walter was fond of saying, was never so easy.

"That's bullshit!" Fleisher said to his partners as heads turned to their small table. "LeHavre is an innocent man until we prove otherwise. It'll take a lot more than intuition to convince the police." The big man's bearded face was flushed; in political infighting as during interrogations he was an overwhelming and mercurial force, bully, teddy bear, jokester, loyal friend, withering skeptic, con man, tickling feather—a needle poking for truth until it bled.

Vidocq Society cases were chosen by the founders in consultation with the society's board of directors. The board included an assistant U.S. attorney, a naval intelligence officer, the security director of Sun Oil Company, an Alcohol, Tobacco, Firearms, and Explosives agent, a Philadelphia homicide detective, and an English professor specializing in Shakespeare and literary analysis of bomb threats and suicide notes. But Fleisher was board president as well as commissioner. He had masterfully steered through a quarter century of federal bureaucracy; no case went forward without his blessing.

Bender's balding head reddened as it did when his paranormal revelations were questioned, which was almost always among world-weary cops. "Bill, I know the killer was LeHavre," Bender said. "I know it. Remember our first meeting, in the old Navy yard, this guy got up and spoke and I said, 'He's a Russian spy. I can feel it.' And I was right!"

Fleisher rolled his eyes, while Walter peered down his horn-rimmed glasses at the artist as if appraising a new species. "Frank, in this case you may be right, but keep your day job. There's no structure to your thinking. You're like a fart in a bathtub!" The thin man snorted with derision as Bender's crimson deepened. Fleisher laughed and slowly shook his head.

Fleisher marveled at the forces that brought them together, and constantly threatened to tear them apart. By combining his partners' deduction and intuition with his own leadership and investigative skills, they formed a tripartite Great Detective with skills seldom found in one man.

"Richard is our Sherlock Holmes," Fleisher said with genuine admiration. "He has the greatest deductive ability I've ever seen. As for Frank, only God can explain the things he does. Me, I'm just a fat Jewish kid who grew up reading true-crime comics and dreaming of being a detective."

It was fitting, Fleisher thought, that the idea of the great American detective was born in Philadelphia, just a few miles from where they sat—in a brownstone off Spring Garden Street, where Edgar Allan Poe, in 1841, created the first detective story, "The Murders in the Rue Morgue," and the first fictional detective— C. Auguste Dupin.

It was a new character type, which Poe is said to have borrowed from the life of Vidocq, whose memoirs, allegedly ghost-written by his friend Balzac, were an 1829 bestseller on both sides of the Atlantic. The new type was a darkly eccentric, deductive genius who outsmarted the police. Dupin possessed "a peculiar analytic ability. . . . He seemed, too, to take an eager delight in its exercise. . . . He boasted . . . with a low chuckling laugh, that most men, in respect to himself, wore windows in their bosoms, and was wont to follow up such assertions by direct and very startling proofs. . . ." This was Vidocq's life, and the inspiration for Sherlock Holmes and all fictional sleuths to follow.

It was an archetype made flesh in Richard Walter.

"You have to be on your game to beat me, Frank, and Bill," Walter said. "If you knock us off our feet we'll walk on our knees. If you knock us off our knees we'll walk on our balls—and our balls have calluses."

Now Fleisher scowled at his partners.

"There's a reason a case is cold for many years. This isn't TV. You need the family support, police commitment, the political winds blowing your way," he said, counting them off on the fingers of a raised hand. "You need investigative brilliance—and you need luck. You got about one out of five in this case."

Walter glared at Fleisher. The psychologist and federal agent complemented each other well, but their differences could be sharp along a philosophical fault line. Walter considered Fleisher a brilliant lawman but naïve about the nature of evil; Fleisher admired Walter's cold eye for evil, yet the thin man's Machiavellian view of human nature oppressed Fleisher's generous heart and hopes for redemption for all men.

Typical Fleisher, Walter thought now, utterly conventional.

Walter looked over at Bender, who seemed to have entirely forgotten about the case, his attention having drifted elsewhere. Bender was brooding over his espresso, his light hazel eyes in the middle distance, where laughter sounded at a table of young women. Fleisher, following his partner's eyes, quipped, "If I ever stop getting excited about that, shoot me." Bender returned from his reverie and chuckled.

Walter, with his uncompromising, antiquated code of honor, considered Bender a knight of opposite color—a man who honored little but his own desires, with nearly sociopathic cunning. Yet together Bender and Walter saw around corners that other detectives, Fleisher included, did not. It was the impish Bender, a wizard with the gift of seeing the past and the future, who had brought the three men together and ever conspired to bust them apart. Bender was narcissistic, manipulative, well named; he bent rules and time, the boundaries of the grave and the connubial bed. "Frank," Walter said, "is a shit stirrer. He thinks our motto is 'One for all and all for one, and that's me!'"

But nothing happened without Bender, or Walter, or Fleisher. No case went forward without accord between the three. Now they reminded themselves that they couldn't solve every case. They had no formal subpoena, arrest, or investigative powers; their goal was merely to offer advice and counsel to the police and victims of crime who needed it. "If we help move a case along, we've done our job," Fleisher repeated. In fact, wasn't the idea originally to be a social club for detectives? To have fun?

By the time they had reached the grounds in their cups, Walter and Bender had decided that Antoine LeHavre, if he had indeed done it, was free to get away with murder as far as they were concerned.

PART TWO

·

FOUR BOYS

CHAPTER 4

A LITTLE CHILD SHALL LEAD THEM

On Saturday, February 23, 1957, a cold rain spattered a lonely country road on the northern edge of Philadelphia, falling on a field of brush and vines slowly claiming an old cardboard box behind the tree line. Inside the box lay a small blue-eyed boy of perfect tapered form, naked and laid out with his arms by his side like a forgotten boy-king of Egypt. His sarcophagus was a J. C. Penney box of corrugated cardboard, three feet long and eighteen inches wide, marked FRAGILE, HANDLE WITH CARE. Great and prolonged care had been taken.

The boy had been washed and groomed and wrapped in a coarse Navajo blanket as if ritually prepared for the next life. His hair was roughly chopped, his fingernails trimmed with a loving touch. His life had been extinguished in an ancient ritual designed to harvest his innocence and beauty by inflicting on him the greatest of cruelties. These were the abominable mixing of love and tenderness with betrayal, torture, and terror, culminating in the horror of his murder, which alone provided the climax for the killer or killers.

The ritual was often confused with Satanism but bowed to neither God nor the devil. In the soft landscape of eastern Pennsylvania in the middle of the Eisenhower 1950s, no one had a clue what the signs meant. The boy was scarred with deep cuts and bruises from head to toe.

He was only three feet, four inches tall. But he was too long for the box, and had been curled into the little cardboard coffin to fit. His head peeked out the open end, sightless eyes fixed on the sky. Moles tunneled under the wild grass that sprouted around the boy. Mice and insects rustled nearby in the underbrush, sensing the seeping blood.

He lay only fifteen feet from the road, but remained unseen. The narrow one-lane road was mostly quiet. The field was a last wild green patch surrounded by city, by hospitals and police stations and thousands of suburban homes. But the surrounding fields had changed little since colonial horses thundered and hounds bayed their call over the Fox Chase Inn. Now and again an automobile tunneled on the road south through the mist to Verree Road, past the woods and fields to the Verree house, still standing, once invaded by the British. Then the road fell quiet again.

It was a remote grave, carefully chosen.

It was warm for February but the rain cut with a raw chill. The land was hushed in an attitude of waiting. There had not been much snow for years but the big storms were coming. The oceans were spinning the thirty-year cycle. Climatic changes that would turn the 1960s into the snowiest decade in a century were already in the air.

The boy was decomposing very slowly in the cold. The animals had not gotten to him yet. Clouds fled; sun dried the eyes and little face. Night came and went. Orion the hunter glittered in the south, Jupiter was bright. The field fell dark and quiet, the boy's lips white as the moon sailing with the winter stars. The sun rose without warmth. There was no movement left in him except gravity drawing his blood downward in his body.

That Saturday, city people whirred north to a city park with a creek Audubon had admired more than a hundred years earlier. A priest turned in to the quiet Good Shepherd Home for "wayward girls," deep in the field across the street. In the afternoon John

Stachowiak was bicycling by to play basketball at a Catholic church gymnasium, when suddenly he left his bike by the tree line and walked into the field.

He was nervous but excited. Stachowiak was eighteen years old, the son of Polish immigrants who spoke little English, and he was a trapper. He kept nineteen muskrat traps in the woods and field; he lived nearby, they were easy to check. But he hadn't even set them and the season was almost over. He had been afraid for weeks to set the traps since his older brother discovered a body hanging on the limb of a tree in the nearby woods. The pale dangling man haunted his nightmares. So did the memory of his mother and father when the Philadelphia patrolman came to the house to take a report from his brother about the suicide. Refugees from the Soviet police state, they trembled as if it were Stalin's dreaded NKVD, who'd snatched many of their friends in the night, never to be seen again.

The dense undergrowth stretching back from the tree line by the road was perfect cover for small game. But the teenager was startled and upset. Two of his muskrat traps were set! Who would have fooled with his traps? Combined with the suicide, the lonely field gave him an eerie feeling. He was about to leave when he saw a long rectangular box in a tangle of vines. The field was a dumping ground, and he was curious to see what was in it. He grabbed it on one end and pulled it upright, but it was heavy and he put it down. Walking around it, he looked into the open end for a long moment. He decided not to play basketball that day. Stachowiak rushed home determined not to tell his brother, his parents, or anyone what he had seen near the woods of the hanging man. He didn't want the police to return and terrify his family.

Two days later, on the afternoon of Monday the 25th, Frank Guthrum, a junior at LaSalle University, was taking the country road home from classes when he pulled over and parked by the tree line. Guthrum was an older student, in his midtwenties, who'd had trouble adjusting to student life. Two weeks earlier, on February 11, he'd braked for a rabbit that ran in front of his car and into the field. On a whim, he followed the rabbit into the under-brush. He lost sight of the rabbit but found two steel traps and decided to set them. Now it was 3:15, still light enough to see what had been caught in the steel jaws.

He was disappointed to find the traps empty. But about fifteen feet from the road, at the intersection of two footpaths, was a curi-osity, a long cardboard box snared by the underbrush. Guthrum leaned down and saw the small head, white as porcelain, the limp figure wrapped in a blanket.

A doll. A big doll. He looked again at the bruises on the small head, the chopped blond hair.

Not a doll.

Guthrum hurried home. That evening he told his brother, who was a priest, what he had seen, but he decided not to call the police. He didn't want to get involved, and the police were already watching him. They'd recently accused him of being a Peeping Tom, pretending to chase rabbits in the woods in order to spy on the "wayward girls" in the Good Shepherd Home across the street. The last thing he wanted was close questioning about the box.

The next morning, Tuesday the 26th, Guthrum was driving to school when he heard on the car radio that police were searching for possible kidnap victim Mary Jane Barker, four years old, miss-ing from Bellmawr, New Jersey. Bellmawr was just across the river from Philadelphia. When he got to school he sought advice from two faculty advisers, then spoke with his brother again. The priest said, "You know what you have to do." At 10:10 A.M., he called the police.

The Philadelphia Police Department was headquartered in the French Empire stone edifice of City Hall, with the stone relief of Moses the Lawgiver glowering over the judicial entrance. But despite the antiquated rooms the force was among the most mod-ern in the country. Patrolmen drove red 1955 Chevrolet paneled wagons, among the first heavy-duty cruisers designed especially for police.

Sergeant Charles Gargani took Guthrum's call in the homicide bureau, then ordered a radio message broadcast to all the red cars: ". . . investigate a cardboard box in the woods of Susquehanna Road, across from the girls' home. Could be a body inside, or could be a doll . . ."

Patrolman Sam Weinstein was skeptical and annoyed as he trudged into the muddy field through the cold rain. A stout man with a square head and broad nose, Weinstein was a streetwise rookie cop, thirty years old with a wife and two kids. He'd already made his name in the department as a tough guy, quick to use his fists. Weinstein had seen combat in the Pacific in World War II. His father had been murdered when he was in the womb. His mother died when he was a toddler. He'd been raised in South Philadelphia by an uncle and aunt who were Lutheran but kept his dead mother's wish to raise him Jewish. Weinstein had a surly attitude nobody liked unless he was on their side.

Ahead he saw patrolman Elmer Palmer, a fellow rookie, and called out a friendly greeting. But Palmer was standing quietly by the lopsided cardboard box, his face broken.

Weinstein looked in the box and was staggered. He'd seen enough suffering and death for three lifetimes, but he'd never seen a murdered child. Few cops had in Philadelphia in the 1950s. Murder happened to adults, at the hand of someone they knew— jealous spouse, ex-partner. The rare body in a field was a gin-smelling hobo, an old drifter.

Two homicide detectives joined the group around the body, in their dark overcoats and fedoras, accompanied by Dr. Joseph Spelman, the city's chief medical examiner. More detectives and street cops arrived, and a captain sent the uniforms into the field in their shiny wet raincoats, kicking the underbrush for evidence. Seventeen feet from the body, they found a men's blue Ivy League cap, size 7⅛.

The ambulance pulled up, and Weinstein volunteered to take the boy out of the box. He lifted the small corpse gingerly.

"Bruises, all up and down," Dr. Spelman said. Bruises and cuts too deep for a child to get falling off a bicycle, he said. Deep bruises around the head looked like thumbprints from an adult trying to steady the child for a haircut. It was a violent beating all right, but the medical examiner said he'd need the autopsy to determine cause of death.

Weinstein held the boy, instinctively trying to shield him from the rain. Suddenly he felt anger surging through him. He looked at Palmer and saw the same fury in his friend's eyes: *Whoever did this should burn in hell.*

But Weinstein couldn't imagine who would do such a thing. None of them could. The detectives were speculating that a mother or father, poor and pushed to the edge, had lost control during a bath and had been surprised trying to give the only burial they could afford. The dead boy somehow represented something beyond their grasp.

Criminals were changing. Everything was changing. Philadelphia had watched Pat Boone sing at President Eisenhower's inaugural ball the month before, and next month thousands of fans would crowd an Elvis Presley concert in Philadelphia. Everywhere the old order was dying, the new being born. The month before, the actor Humphrey Bogart, an icon of traditional masculinity, had died in Los Angeles the same week the Wham-O company made the first Frisbee for a new and liberated generation. Powerful new currents were upwelling, like an ocean turning over. Freedom and authenticity were the watchwords of the coming Age of Aquarius. Old injustices were being addressed, old boundaries smashed, deep longings unleashed.

Killers were exploring new freedoms, finding deeper and more authentic selves, too.

The patrolman looked into the small blue eyes, the dull orbs reflecting his own, and was overcome by a sadness tempered by thoughts he couldn't explain. "I saw so much pain and terror there," he said. The little face seemed to cry out to him. "Why did this happen? Why would someone do this to me?"

His eyes met Palmer's again with shared emotion: *We'll get the S.O.B., no matter what it takes.*

But who was the S.O.B.? What was the answer? Weinstein was a proud man, and it was difficult for him to admit, "I don't have an answer for that." He sensed he might never have the answer; it was beyond him. He felt shattered.

The ambulance door slammed shut, and Weinstein looked up at the gray February sky and the rain falling over the field.

CHAPTER 5

COPS AND ROBBERS

The first boy put nickels in the chrome slot and sighed with pleasure as the small glass door opened on a slice of pie. His father turned the crank of the ornate chrome "liquid machine," and coffee streamed from a dolphin's head copied from a Pompeian fountain. Dinner with his father at the Horn and Hardart in Philadelphia, America's first fast-food restaurant, was a special treat.

The Automat is cool, he thought. It was a dazzling display of modern technology as impressive to him as the transistor radio and his father's electric watch. A clean, orderly glass palace of meat loaf and macaroni and cheese, the Automat inspired an Irving Berlin theme song, "Let's Get Another Cup of Coffee." His dad whistled it during the Great Depression, and now it was the jingle for the TV show *Father Knows Best.*

William (Billy) Fleisher looked forward to Saturday all week long. Saturday mornings in 1957 he went shopping with his mother. But later in the day he got to be with his father, ride with him in the big 1953 Buick sedan to pick up the early edition of the Sunday papers. His father was Dr. Herbert Fleisher, a Navy dentist who came back from the war and opened dental offices in the Nash Building. His father was brilliant, a tall, dark-haired, handsome man who was a double for the actor Robert Taylor. Billy saw him as Lancelot opposite Ava Gardner as Guinevere in the 1953 movie *Knights of the Round Table*. Herbert Fleisher was named "Philadelphia's Best-Dressed Man" by the *Bulletin*. Nearly everybody read the *Bulletin,* and everybody respected Herbert Fleisher. Billy wanted to be just like him.

His father sat across from him in his suspenders and spats, reading the Sunday *Bulletin*. Billy had his favorite frizzled beef and creamed spinach. His father was six foot three; Billy was five foot three and had five more inches to go.

"You're behaving like a bum," his father said.

Billy cringed as if from a blow, but he loved to listen to his father. His father talked about his important friends at the Celebrity Room. Lawyers. Politicians. Entertainers. Horseplayers. Bookmakers. Craps players. The nightclub was owned by his good friend and patient, the beautiful showgirl Lillian Reis, "Tiger Lil." Tiger Lil's boyfriend was famous gangster Ralph "Junior" Staino, ringleader of the famous K & A gang, from right here in Kensington and Allegheny in Philadelphia, the classiest burglary outfit in the country. They wore suits and ties on their jewel jobs.

Tiger Lil was accused of masterminding the $478,000 heist of Pottsville coal baron John B. Rich, but was found innocent after the star witnesses against her drowned and died in a car explosion. She had nice teeth, his father said.

"You're acting like a loser," his father said.

His mother, Esther, often told him what his father said when she told him she was pregnant, a joke they loved at the club. "You have a son and daughter, what do you want now?" His dad responded, "I'd prefer a German shepherd."

Billy was a mistake after Ellis and Gloria. Ellis was six foot three, too, tall and handsome and smart like his father. "You take after my grandmother," his father said. She was four foot eleven.

His father was right. He was a punk. "You're an embarrassment to me," his father said. Billy was a poor student, always talking back, always getting into fights. He didn't do the things the other kids did. He didn't follow the Phillies, didn't read school books or watch TV. He hated *Leave It to Beaver*. His father didn't take him to temple services. He didn't have any interests except reading detective magazines.

On Saturday mornings before his mother took him to the market, he played with his cousins Mark and Glenn. "We'd play until we ended up beating each other up, go out and throw firecrackers on someone's stoop, shoot a match gun at an ant colony, that kind of thing." His cousins were his only friends. *I could eat nickels and shit out quarters all day and nobody would like me,* he thought.

The sidewalk was dark as they walked to the Buick. There were shadows in the city even at night, deeper shadows in alleys and the recesses of doors. When Billy was younger, his mother would scare him by saying, "Seymour Levin will get you if you don't behave!"

Seymour Levin was a fat pimply kid with glasses who used to live in the neighborhood, and everyone was still afraid of him. On January 9, 1949, the sixteen-year-old Levin went with twelve-year-old Ellis Simons to see *A Night at the Opera* at the movies, then brought his friend home to play with his chemistry set. Ellis took one look at it and said, "I have better test tubes at home." Seymour was very fond of his chemistry set. They got in a fight and test-tube glass was everywhere. Seymour got a kitchen knife, made Ellis undress, sodomized him, and then stabbed him more than fifty times through the heart and face and back and all over his body. He tied Ellis's hands and feet with laundry cord and dragged the body through the house and backyard and dumped it behind the garage.

Seymour could get out of jail at any time.

The police said there was not a drop of blood left in Ellis Simons's body.

Billy's mother was cool to him, but not uninvolved like his father.

That Saturday, she left him alone in the Penn Fruit Company market. She went down one of the aisles to do the shopping, leaving him standing there. Billy knew horror stories of what happened to kids left alone at markets. The famous one was Steven Damman, whose mother left him with a stick of licorice to watch the baby at a Long Island grocery store; when she came out the stroller and the baby were there, but Steven and his licorice were gone, and never seen again.

Billy wasn't afraid. He was older than Damman and could take care of himself, and he loved the trip to the market. He'd lose himself savoring the perfumed air of apples, pears, oranges, and potatoes stacked high on the counters; he'd forget where he was. It was "the greatest smell in the world" because it reminded him of his grandfather Sol, Philadelphia's largest potato and onion wholesaler. Billy's grandfather was his best friend, an oasis of love and safety.

Sol's full name was Solomon Tredwell, but everyone called him "Smiling Jim, the Potato King." Sol was a gregarious character who had taken the nickname "Smiling Jim" from a handsome Philadelphia mounted policeman who patrolled the city's parks. He figured the policeman's popularity would shine like a halo over him and his business. "My grandfather loved the police," Billy said, "and he loved me. A policeman couldn't leave his warehouse store without a free five-pound bag of potatoes."

Now the boy's eye caught a poster on a wall near the front of the store. It intrigued him; from a distance it looked like a portrait of three heads. He walked toward it and, up close, froze in fear.

A ghostly, shrunken face stared at him with lifeless blue eyes.

It was a pale, bloodless face—the face of a dead boy. On either side of the ghastly face were profile photographs of the child; the side of the head, like the face, was blistered in bruises and cuts. But the emotionless blue eyes held him fast.

He looked at the eyelids, frail and broken as the crushed wings of a butterfly. PHILADELPHIA POLICE DEPARTMENT, INFORMATION WANTED, the poster said. The print underneath said the unknown child had been brutally murdered and found two weeks ago in the woods of Fox Chase. Police were looking for the boy's name, and his killer. NOTIFY HOMICIDE UNIT, DETECTIVE HEADQUARTERS, CITY HALL, PHILADELPHIA, AT ANY TIME, DAY OR NIGHT, IN PERSON OR TELEPHONE, MUNICIPAL 6-9700.

For an instant the left eye seemed to glow yellow.

Billy had never seen a dead person. He hadn't heard the prayer to the Blessed Judge of Truth, the rabbi's wisdom that men were mortals and can't understand, can only accept God's will. His father had not prepared him; no one could have prepared him. Death whispers uniquely to each man, but its overture to Billy was beyond the understanding of midtwentieth-century adults, no less a child. In the limpid eye he had seen a glimpse of the darkest evil known to humankind.

The boy lay on a cold metal table in the city morgue. Outside the windowless chamber the night was dark and bitterly cold, but now the boy was bathed in warm bright light. The medical examiner measured him at forty inches long, thirty pounds. He looked so small.

Bill Kelly prepared his inks, rollers, and clean white paper. As the police department's principal fingerprinter, he was one of death's numberless attendants. He was trained to stoically touch the cool flesh of the dead, but this boy looked just like the fingerprinter's four-year-old son. His little feet fit into Kelly's palm. The fingerprinter bowed his head and quietly asked the Blessed Mother for strength and guidance.

The head of the Philadelphia police identification unit, Kelly was twenty-nine years old, a tall Irishman and devout Roman Catholic with shining blue eyes that reflected compassion rather than mirth. The fingerprinter was a devoutly religious man who believed children were a gift from God. He was a father of two with a third on the way; he and Ruth Ann dreamed of having as many as the Almighty would provide. To feed the extra mouths he was picking up work as a wedding photographer, a joyful interlude between corpses.

On closer inspection, Kelly saw the boy was painfully thin. University of Pennsylvania anthropologist Wilton Krogman, one of the world's foremost experts on human anatomy, known by the FBI as "the bone detective," examined him with his young assistant

Bill Bass (who would later found the Tennessee "Body Farm" to study decomposing human remains for law enforcement). Krogman calculated the boy had nearly the height of a four-year-old but the weight of a two-year-old. That meant starvation, malnutrition. X-rays of the legs showed scars on the long bones from halted growth. The boy had suffered in ill health for at least a year.

Kelly's heart clenched as he inked the tiny hands and feet, then pressed the prints onto the clean paper. He believed in God but if He indeed tipped the wing of every sparrow in flight, what was the purpose of this?

Kelly saw other things with a cop's eyes. The terrible cuts and bruises on the head and all over the body. The skin of one hand and foot withered from water immersion, the "washerwoman's effect." The narrow head looked like it had been squeezed, like an overripe melon. These were things Kelly, a civilian on the force, preferred not to contemplate. But he knew in his heart he was in the presence of evil—proof the devil existed as surely as did God.

From his humble prayers the comfort came to him that the boy could be hurt no more in his life. He was in heaven. All Kelly could do was help redeem his soul with a name. A name would cut a powerful trail to the murderer, a killer who would be judged in this life as well as the next. Neither task was his. But never had Kelly's work seemed so important.

A few miles away that evening, Remington Bristow, the dark-haired, craggy-faced son of an Oregon undertaker, sat at home smoking a Lucky Strike over the broadsheet pages of the *Bulletin*. The headline leaped out at him: BODY OF BOY FOUND IN BOX IN FOX CHASE. The story seared him with regret. His second daughter, Rita, was a lovely healthy girl, but his first daughter had died twelve years ago from sudden infant death syndrome. Annie Laurie had been three months old. Annie was buried in California, and he had never stopped missing her. Fortunately, he thought, the case would quickly be solved. A heartbroken parent or guardian would come forward as soon as the evening newspapers, TV, and radio reported the corpse had been found. He was scheduled for the midnight-to-eight shift at the medical examiner's office, where he worked as an investigator.

The boy would be identified by the time he got to work.

But Bristow was surprised when he arrived at the morgue at midnight. Nobody had come forward to claim the boy. He was assigned to cases of the deceased whose surnames began with letters at the end of the alphabet, including U. The boy was his, classified "Unknown."

It was ancient history, but Chief Inspector John Kelly knew Philadelphia had a bad reputation on big child death cases. The police had bungled the case of the first child kidnapping in America, the most famous crime of its day, the impact of which was still felt. Four-year-old, flaxen-haired Charley Ross vanished from in front of his mansion in July 1874, when two men lured him into a buggy with candy. Christian Ross raced to the police station, but the sergeant told the father not to worry, the two men were enjoying a "drunken frolic." The kidnappers demanded $20,000 for Charley's safe return in twenty-three illiterate letters grimly warning of the boy's annihilation: *". . . you wil hav two pay us befor you git him from us, and pay us a big cent to . . ."* On police advice, the father didn't respond to the letters, and "Little Charley" was never seen again. The story was a sensation in the county's three penny newspapers, and thereafter American parents warned their children, "Never take candy from a stranger."

Suffering a "bereavement sharper than death," the Ross family spent the next sixty years and a fortune in vain trying to find the boy.

Now, as the newspapers topped one another with daily headlines trumpeting police defeats—BEATEN CHILD IN BOX STILL UNKNOWN, MISTAKEN FOR DOLL, CLUE TO SLAIN BOY PROVES FALSE—Chief Inspector Kelly was determined to identify the boy and punish his killer, at whatever cost. He launched the largest police investigation of a child's death in the city's three centuries.

An urgent Teletype bulletin was sent to police departments in all forty-eight states. The FBI was brought in. The American Medical Association mailed descriptions of the boy's surgical scars, on the groin area, to all its members asking if they recalled performing the surgery. None did.

The homicide bureau dressed the boy in a suit that once fit a detective's son and propped him up lifelike for police and media photographs. Detectives traced the bassinet box to the J. C. Penney store in Upper Darby, Pennsylvania, and interviewed eleven of the twelve purchasers of that model. They learned the men's blue Ivy League cap found near the boy had been created by a seamstress in South Philadelphia, and tracked down all the men who'd purchased the cap. The Indian-pattern blanket was traced to one of three textile mills, then the thread was lost. Fingerprinter Kelly was dispatched to as many hospitals as he could drive to looking for a match of newborn footprints on file. Nothing came of it.

After days of little progress, the chief inspector ordered the largest police force ever assembled in the city, including new academy recruits, to comb twelve square miles around the crime scene. Three hundred men brought tons of possible evidence back to the department, including a dead cat wrapped in an old shirt. Three hundred neighborhood doors were knocked on, more than six hundred neighbors interviewed. All 773 white families who had moved into the city that month were questioned, not a scrap of useful information gleaned.

Nothing.

Long Island New York cops drove down to the morgue to see if it was Steven Damman, whose mother, Marilyn, told the story of his 1955 abduction in *The Saturday Evening Post*. It was too late for Marilyn; her husband divorced her, quit his Air Force career, and fled to Iowa and took up farming. He never forgave his wife for leaving the child alone for ten minutes. Damman was about the same age and weight, also had blond hair and a little scar on his chin. But the Philadelphia boy's kidneys were a markedly different size, and Damman had a big freckle on his right calf. It wasn't Steven Damman.

A Marine said it was a lost brother, one of his eighteen siblings; all eighteen proved to be alive and well. Angry ex-wives and ex-husbands swore it was their child, murdered by the dastardly "ex." Mothers-in-law denounced vile sons-in-law. Hundreds of letters poured in from the seamy underground of the American family; each was checked. ("I know my sister must have had an illegitimate baby, and she's the kind that would kill it.")

Nothing.

Detectives got excited studying a photograph of refugees from the Hungarian Revolution of 1956, fleeing the Soviet conquest. A boy in the photograph was the mirror image of the dead boy. Hadn't Krogman deducted likely European ancestry from the narrow face and high forehead? After an exhaustive manhunt, Philadelphia police found the Hungarian refugee child happily playing in a North Carolina backyard.

Detectives thought it had to be the Dudleys. The itinerant carnival couple admitted to starving to death six of their ten children as they followed the Big Top, casually dumping two bodies in Lake Pontchartrain near New Orleans, others along a West Virginia highway and in a Lakeland, Florida, mine. Detectives almost felt sorry for them while interviewing the disorganized man and his hapless wife, and had to remind themselves they were human beasts. Yes, they'd passed through Pennsylvania in February 1957. No, the boy in the morgue wasn't theirs.

Nothing.

The comforting smell of potatoes had disappeared.

Billy was held fast by the unblinking gaze of the dead boy. It was horrid, the ghastly yellowish face like a bruised gourd with hollowed-out eyes. His heart was pounding, his hands clammy with sweat.

The eyes were a well into which he was falling, falling into blackness with no one to catch him.

His mother returned and put a hand on him, broke the spell. She quietly drove him home in the Buick through the gray

February afternoon. He did not tell her what he had seen and felt. But something had changed in him. His tongue grew sharper around his parents, and bitterly sarcastic. He found friends, but while other high school cliques formed around sports or drama, his gang "didn't care about anything but drinking and having sex . . . I was white-collar Jewish hanging out with tough, blue-collar Italians." He began drinking and smoking. He stayed small but his fights now were more violent, with bigger kids.

He was one of the smallest kids around, the fastest runner, wiry and nasty and chin-out tough, a wiseass with an answer for everything.

Billy was no longer entertained by kicking over anthills. He got a BB gun, and when he was fifteen, he aimed the gun at the backside of another boy and pulled the trigger. The shot grazed the boy's butt. The kid squealed like a stuck pig. It was hilarious! Billy roared with laughter.

As he grew older, he grew angrier.

The police came to his house, a five-bedroom split-level, and talked to his father. They were tired of pulling the doctor's youngest out of scrapes, and now this. How could this happen in such a nice neighborhood, to such a good family?

Billy was still laughing. "It was just a BB gun." He grinned. "So I shot him in the ass, big deal. I was just trying to graze him."

The police were not amused. Billy was "just a kid," but teenage ruffians were no longer seen in the nostalgic, "boys will be boys" light of earlier generations.

FBI director J. Edgar Hoover declared youth crime, the new scourge of "juvenile delinquency," to be a national emergency brought on by family disruptions from the war and a general decline in morals. Parents fretted over traditional values under assault from rock music, materialism, and movies like James Dean's *Rebel Without a Cause*. A Roper Organization survey showed Americans were more worried about youth crime than open-air atomic testing, school segregation, or political corruption.

Something was wrong, very wrong, with the sons of the new

affluent America. William Heirens, from a wealthy suburban Chicago family, had collected guns at thirteen, was accepted to the prestigious University of Chicago, and became a serial killer at seventeen, scrawling in lipstick on the mirror of one of his three victims, "Stop me before I kill again!" Seymour Levin was no longer simply the neighborhood bogeyman. Psychologists said he was an example of the new, especially depraved breed known as "constitutional psychopathic inferiors"; CPIs were human monsters nobody understood, except they shared insatiable resentments and no conscience. This new generation was more violent and depraved than Al Capone's shooters and the worst criminals of the 1920s and '30s.

Billy's struggles in school intensified. He was spending all his time holed up in the basement reading detective comic books. His teachers frowned upon this; it was extremely troubling in a young boy. Detective comic books were thought to be a major cause of juvenile delinquency, a theory made popular by German-American psychiatrist Fredric Wertham, a disciple of Freud. His 1954 best seller, *Seduction of the Innocent,* led to U.S. congressional hearings to censor the comic book industry. Wertham said that comic books filled with sex and violence turned boys into murderers.

But Billy was obsessed with cops and robbers. His favorite book was *The Great Detectives,* the true-life adventures of the dozen most famous sleuths in history. He admired Scotland Yard detective Robert Fabian, the "Protector of the Innocent"; Treasury agent and Capone nemesis Elmer Lincoln Irey, "The Man Who Couldn't Be Fooled." But he was especially fascinated by the flamboyant Eugène François Vidocq of nineteenth-century Paris, "The Magician of Disguise."

Vidocq was a baker's son born in 1775 in the south of France, survived the French Revolution as a teenager, just escaped a beheading, and during the reign of Napoleon Bonaparte became the lawman hero of Paris, the swashbuckling "father" of modern criminology.

Even more interesting to Billy, Vidocq had been a rowdy, fearless teenager nicknamed *le Vautrin,* "Wild Boar." He'd killed a man at thirteen, robbed his parents at fourteen to leave home and eventually join the Army, where he fought constantly. In the Army Vidocq defeated fifteen men in duels, killed two, and deserted after striking an officer. But nothing stopped him. Vidocq was a notorious killer, con man, highwayman, prison-breaker, womanizer, and spy before turning himself into the mirror of all Western detectives. Billy was taken by one of history's great figures of transformation and redemption.

At seventeen, college was out of the question for Billy. He planned to join the Army, where he could "get in fights all the time and get away with it." In the future, he saw himself facing two choices: "I'll either go to jail or become a cop."

Billy's favorite TV show was *The Detectives Starring Robert Taylor.* It starred his father's look-alike Matt Holbrook as police captain, leading three brave detectives standing for truth and justice in a large, unnamed city. The three detectives spent all of their time tracking murderers, thieves, and other lawbreakers. They were all passionate in their search for truth—a truth they could believe in.

They were all good friends.

CHAPTER 6

THE MAN WHO SAW DEAD PEOPLE

The second boy balled his fist, cocked the bicep he had been developing for just this moment, and swung a roundhouse uppercut that crashed into his father's skull. That's how he'd imagined it. He'd pumped iron at age fifteen for just this moment. He was rippling with new muscles and confidence, determined his father would never hit him again without consequence. He was relieved when the old man backed down—he had never wanted to strike his father, and now he would never have to.

Now we can love each other like a father and son should.

Growing up in the tough Philadelphia river ward, Frank saw a headline in the *Bulletin* about the child found in a box in Fox Chase, only four or five Philadelphia neighborhoods to the north. He noticed a poster of the dead boy. But he didn't have the luxury of thinking about anything but his own survival.

At fifteen he was a supremely gifted artist. His teachers whispered enviously about his talent. Strangely though, the city kid was obsessed with Norman Rockwell. Rockwell's paintings of an idyllic small-town America on the covers of *The Saturday Evening Post* were Frank's windows to another world. That world was tangible and close. Frank's neighborhood was only a few miles up the Delaware River from the landmark Curtis Publishing Company building in Philadelphia, where the *Post* was published, overlooking

Independence Hall. He loved the Rockwell covers: Father in his best suit happily watching Mother serve a Thanksgiving turkey on a white tablecloth to a rosy-cheeked, all-American family; the runaway boy on a diner stool, all his belongings on the end of a stick wrapped in red cloth, seated next to the blue-suited cop; the baseball umps calling the game for rain.

They were happy images, and he preferred them all to the images of his own life: his father going off to work in the factory and coming home smelling of the machines he fixed; his father descending to the basement to hand-sew the big canvas sails for rich men's yachts. Lying in bed at night listening to the gunshots fly, hearing and *feeling* one slamming the side of his brick row house. His father drinking too much and hitting him. His father hitting and hitting and hitting him.

He'd dreamed of hitting his dad back all those years. Each hit forced the boy's anger one level higher until it was ready to explode. He'd lifted weights, carefully planning The Punch that would set things right and release the anger once and for all. He was amazed when his father gave him new respect, and he could concentrate on his gifts, his entrance to that other world.

Frank had extraordinary powers and gifts. He was not a student of English or mathematics. He didn't have a graceful mind, but a mind full of grace. The hands to draw, paint, and sculpt the beauty around him, the eye to see. He started drawing in art classes when he was five years old and had never stopped. And he seemed to possess a third eye, a talent that even when young he knew not to talk about. Sometimes it seemed he could see past and future. Yet with all his abilities, the boy's anger persisted.

As a high school sophomore, Frank won a gold medal in a citywide student art exhibit at a Gimbels department store. In a dream scenario for a young artist, his work was discovered by Walter Stuempfig, a notable realist painter of the midtwentieth century whose oils were compared to Edward Hopper and the Old Masters. Stuempfig offered Frank $5 for his painting and encouraged him to seek a scholarship at the Pennsylvania Academy of the Fine Arts, the famed school that graduated Thomas Eakins and Mary Cassatt, where Stuempfig had taught for forty years. But Frank, touchy as a water moccasin, grew angry when he never saw the $5 from Stuempfig. Then some of his exhibited paintings were never returned to him, and in a fury he swore off the academy, an art scholarship, and the art world entirely. "I wanted to do art, but I didn't want it hanging on someone's wall." He escaped into the Navy, where, aboard ship, he discovered he had his father's mechanical talents but obsessively sketched the men he worked with in the engine room.

Back home two years later, facing poverty, he landed a job as a commercial photographer at George Faraghan's studio at Nineteenth and Arch. Slim with light hazel eyes and curly blond hair, Frank was an artist with the rugged body of a lightweight boxer, a photographer of models and a model himself. He also had a lust for life and an intuitive grasp of the art of seduction. Women threw themselves at him like confetti.

He modeled for the *Philadelphia Inquirer* fashion section hanging out the window of his own 1947 Plymouth with girls hanging all over him; in *Reader's Digest* he dressed as a horned devil posing as the checkout boy for a Miss America contestant.

"I was like a kid in a candy shop. Plus I'd meet girls in bars and other places. I had sex constantly. I never really tried at it, to be honest. Single women, married women, they picked me up as often as I picked them up; it was all chemistry. I had sex in a lot of cars."

The blond photographer offered a full service to models: composites, head shots, and zipless sex. One day, bored, he wrote down all his trysts on a pad of paper, recalling all the bodies if not the names. He'd had sex with 165 different women. He was twenty-six years old.

Shortly after making The List, a friend introduced him to Jan Proctor, seventeen years old, a slim, pretty, blond go-go girl who'd run away from home in the suburbs and was living alone in the city. Jan had a child, baby Lisa, but didn't know who the father was. When she'd left home, she'd stolen all the money in her father's wallet and left Lisa for her parents to raise.

Now she wanted to stop hustling drinks as a stripper and become a model; she needed a composite. She was smart, sassy, and had grown up in the same neighborhood as Frank, in the riverside row houses of old blue-collar Kensington.

Frank was in love.

It was 1968, the summer of love, and "Jan was wild," Frank recalls. "She was into everything—sex, drugs, you name it." Wild enough, he figured, to satisfy his gargantuan sexual appetite.

They married a year later on Halloween as a lark, egged on by a friend. Halloween was the perfect day to consummate their hell-raising lifestyle. After the church wedding, the reception started at the notorious 7A bar in Kensington, birthplace of the city's legendary K & A burglary gang and a block from serial killer Gary Heidnik's future "House of Horrors." It ended with the cops chasing the booze-laden wedding party around the tombstones at Laurel Hill Cemetery, where Frank had moved the party out of sentiment. He'd once dug graves for his uncle. To memorialize his marriage, he painted an eerie Gothic scene of the sexton's cottage at night fronted by snow-dusted tombstones.

Marriage to Jan was a stabilizing influence. They had a child, Vanessa, and bought a dilapidated warehouse that had been a butcher's shop and meat market in the nineteenth century. Frank never stopped having affairs during this period of domestic bliss, but he had a lot fewer of them. "After I got married, it wasn't that many women." As he matured, his conquests evolved from weekly trysts with faceless strangers to several good friends. "Any affairs I had were with girls, women, who believed in me like I believed in them; we supported each other. It wasn't like a one-night stand. Jan said it was like I was bonding with my good friends, bonding with sex. She always encouraged me to have a girlfriend or two. She always liked to be able to spend some time by herself. She'd want me out of the house for a few days." Jan insisted only that

Frank bring his prospective girlfriends by the house for drinks and her blessing. "Jan would say, 'I like her, bring her by anytime,'" Frank said. "I would never bring a woman into the house that Jan didn't get along with."

She didn't even mind when Frank brought home Ella, a tall, buxom blonde, younger than Jan, as his art assistant. Ella in time also became Frank's accountant, business manager, Girl Friday— and girl Tuesday night, when she made love like clockwork in the artist's house. "Jan really likes Ella," Frank explained. "She'd say, 'Why don't you and Ella go down to the shore for a couple of days?'" Jan seemed relieved to find such a steady, capable woman to help satisfy her husband's voracious career and sexual needs. For her part, Ella respected Jan's role as the queen of the household and Frank's wife. But she was bitterly jealous of the many lesser girlfriends.

But real life intruded quickly into the newlywed romance. Jan's parents dropped her daughter Lisa, now six years old, on the Benders' stoop with all her clothes and medical records and said, "She's yours. We're getting a divorce." Now "the biker momma and go-go girl was the ultimate mother," Frank said. "She put her heart and soul into raising the kids and taking care of the house." But with two children to feed on a modest freelance photographer's income, the family was broke all the time.

Frank began to study at night to recover his art career, taking free evening classes at the Pennsylvania Academy, paid for by the Veterans Administration. He studied painting and drawing with the renowned artist Arthur DeCosta, who urged him to do some sculpting to better understand the human form. It would help all his creative work. But Frank struggled with sculpting facial proportions. The academy didn't offer free night classes in anatomy, and he couldn't afford to pay for day classes, so he reached out to his friend Bart Zandel, who fingerprinted corpses at the city morgue. Frank offered to shoot a model's composite for one of Zandel's favorite strippers if the fingerprinter would give him a tour of the morgue. Zandel agreed.

Frank arrived at the two-story morgue on University Avenue with a sketch pad and calipers in his knapsack. He was excited. He would learn anatomy by studying the human body up close, flesh, bones, and organs revealed, much as his hero Michelangelo once did. Banned by sixteenth-century church authorities from working with dead bodies, Michelangelo procured a key from a friend to the church basement morgue, and spent nights with a candle and a butcher knife studying how the body was assembled.

But as soon as Zandel began leading him through the windowless rooms filled with a cold, sickly sweet air, Frank knew he'd made a terrible mistake.

All around him, bodies on metal tables were grotesquely swollen by disease, shorn by knives and bullets, smashed in automobile accidents, devoured by animals and all the forces of time and decay. He saw a man in the autopsy room who had been hit by a train that cleanly sliced him in two across the thighs. He lifted the white sheet from one gurney and stared openmouthed. In place of a woman's corpse were three suitcases. The woman, apparently murdered, had been carved up and scattered along the New Jersey Turnpike in the luggage, which held all her remains. There was nothing left of her to put on paper.

In the autopsy room, Frank stared at a torso that was propped high on a block—the breastplate had been removed, the ribs cut. He gawked as an assistant medical examiner plunged his hand deep into the chest cavity and, while feeling around, turned and winked at Frank. The place was surreal.

This is no place for an anatomy lesson, he thought.

But he was fascinated by a body on a gurney in the storage room, toe tag number 5233. It was an unidentified white woman in her fifties, heavyset with dyed hair, a murdered Jane Doe. Her badly decomposed body had been found on October 16, 1977, dumped in a field near Philadelphia International Airport, wearing a herringbone suit, a white blouse, and three bullets in the brain. Frank studied her closely. Her skull was shattered on one side by gunshots; a mass of dried blood and dark blond hair was plastered around the wound. Neither her fingerprints nor missing-person bulletins came up with a match.

It looked like a professional hit. Zandel saw a mass of ruined flesh.

"This is one we'll never solve," he said. "Who knows what she looks like?"

But Frank saw something else—a face round and sagged with age, narrow nose, thin lips. He sensed tranquillity about the eyes.

"I know," he blurted out. "I know what she looks like."

Dr. Halbert Fillinger, the assistant ME who had winked at Frank, overheard the comment and approached. It was his case, Fillinger said, and he figured they'd never get an identity.

"Did you say you know what this woman looks like?"

"I do," Frank said. "I see a face in the skull."

Fillinger stared appraisingly at the blunt young man. "Have you ever done forensic art?"

Frank shook his head. "I don't even know what the word 'forensic' means."

"Well, you must try." As they chatted for a few minutes, Fillinger complained that TV shows like the new hit drama *Quincy, M.E.* starring Jack Klugman as a Los Angeles assistant medical examiner gave a false impression of cases quickly solved and tied up in a Christmas bow. The truth was, many cases went nowhere, often because of lack of identity.

"If you can get me an identity, we may also find her killer. Would you like to help us do that?"

Frank replied that he would.

"We can't pay you anything."

"That's OK."

Fillinger challenged him to "show me what she looks like."

"I've never completed a sculpture in my life," Frank said. At the academy they discarded their half-completed clay sculptures at the end of each class. "But I'll do it."

"Good. Come back at midnight Friday. I'll be on the grave-yard shift."

It took Frank eight hours. After measuring the skull and drawing a rough outline of the face on the sketch pad in the morgue,
he consulted artist friends and his academy sculpture teacher on
techniques. Working nights, he shaped a clay bust over the bones,
made a plaster mold of the bust, painted the face, and crowned
the head with a dark blond wig. "I saw every feature of her face,"
he said. "And how the form of one part of her face flowed into
all the other forms." He brought the head into the morgue that
Friday after midnight.

The Philadelphia police had never used a forensic sculpture,
but they distributed a photo of Frank's bust of the murdered Jane
Doe to the Philadelphia media, and published it in a missing-
person flyer sent widely to East Coast police departments.

Corpse number 5233 remained in the morgue, with no one
to mourn or bury her. A New Jersey philanthropist offered her
own cemetery plot so the "poor soul" wouldn't end up in a pau-
per's grave. But five months later, a New Jersey detective studying
missing-person reports noticed a "remarkable" similarity between
the bust of a woman in a Philadelphia Police Department circular
and the photo of a woman reported missing by Chicago police.

Anna Mary Duval, sixty-two, had left via Chicago's O'Hare
Airport on October 15, her family told the police. They didn't
know where she was going, and she never returned. Now authorities quickly confirmed that corpse 5233 found dumped at the Philadelphia airport was indeed the woman who'd boarded the plane
in Chicago. Police still were unable to determine what drew her to
the City of Brotherly Love, where she knew no one, or who had
killed her and why. But Anna Mary Duval had been identified, sad
as her story was, thanks to Bender's artistic vision.

Fillinger was stunned. The police had used sketch artists for
years, with little success. Here was a full three-dimensional head
sprung from the imagination of a high school–educated kid who
didn't know what "forensics" meant. Bender had been touched by
a gift neither he nor anybody else could fully explain.

Frank had his first ID and his first newspaper headlines. Within days, other police departments around the country began asking him to produce busts of unidentified murder victims.

He was a natural. His wife was immensely proud of him, and it was a new income source. But the work was ghoulish, especially with two young daughters in the house. Heads were always popping out of shoeboxes and beer coolers. The worst part was the horrific odor of the cooking craniums, or the thought of them swarming with flesh-stripping beetles. Once, when bugs came flowing out of their old Hotpoint stove, Jan opened it to find the skull of an unknown sailor from the Russian ship *Corinthus*. Frank figured half an hour would dry it out enough to apply clay. "Frank!" she screamed. "Come take this fucking head out of the oven and go visit your mother." It was a story they loved to tell.

She didn't know what "forensics" meant either. Spooked by her husband's new vocation, Jan went to the library to research forensic art, and was proud to learn that esteemed European sculptors were doing the same thing.

She wrote "Forensics" on a piece of paper and taped it to their refrigerator.

CHAPTER 7

SHADES OF THE DARK KNIGHT

In the eastern foothills of the Cascade Range, 150 miles from Seattle, is a view of a town nestled between two rivers and the high walls of the mountains like the dawn of the world. Down in the valley along the wide river are apple orchards and vineyards soaked in an arid, sunny climate like the Bordeaux region of France; Main Street is lined with shops. New to the town's 6,882 families was a bumper crop of Granny Smiths, until a large man came walking down the hill calmly carrying a screaming child drenched in blood.

It was autumn, with the smell of wood-smoke and ripening apples in the air and all the lawns on Eleventh Street neat and tended by the sidewalk where the boy struggled and cried against the man's shirt trying to escape. The boy was about five or six, but the wide arms held him as effortlessly as a bushel of new fruit. Suddenly the man stopped on the sidewalk, grinned, and with no visible effort crushed the boy to his chest. The child fell silent and limp.

Richard Walter was twelve years old and chubby, sitting in the passenger seat of his mother's car, a 1954 Dodge, as it climbed the hill. His mother, Viola, was driving him home from school when she slowed down and pulled over to the curb where the man and boy stood.

When they got close, the man started to cry.

"Get in!" she commanded him. "I'll take you to the hospital."

Sheepishly, the big man obeyed, climbing in the backseat with the bloody child.

Accelerating the car, Viola Walter looked in the rearview mirror and made eye contact with the boy.

"Sonny, tell me the truth. What did he do to you? Did he hurt you?"

The child whimpered.

"Tell me. I won't let him hurt you."

"My daddy beat me." The child was sobbing.

This is interesting, Richard thought. He was turned to the backseat, unsmiling, quietly studying the man and the boy as intently as he would an ant farm. They reached the hospital. While the boy was rushed to the ER, Viola Walter told the county sheriff's deputy about the man, who had fled.

"Son," the deputy sheriff said to Richard. "I need you to come with me and help me find him. Let's go."

Cool, Richard thought.

Richard raced through the night in the sheriff's car and helped the deputy identify the man for an arrest. He followed the court case in the newspapers and learned the father had twisted both his son's arms until they broke, then tried to break the boy's legs but couldn't manage it. The man was a sadist; he *enjoyed* it.

Richard had helped to apprehend his first psychopath.

Really cool, he thought. "It was awful, of course, but quite fascinating."

Until that moment, he'd felt like an alien set down in the remote valley. He was distant from his father, Irvin, a stern German American who was the service manager for Sugg's Tire Service for thirty-five years. He had two sisters and two brothers, one who became a truck driver. He was the only one of the five Walter children who disliked sports. Richard was a musical genius, gifted at piano with a voice like an angel. Given a chance to attend the big apple festival, he preferred *La Traviata*.

It was his mother who taught him that behind the façade of the sleepy all-American town lay a grand opera. Viola Walter was a housewife, a formidable, cunning, uncanny woman. Neighbors called her instead of the police.

One evening after dinner a young woman in town called Viola in a panic. Her husband was sitting in his easy chair with a loaded handgun instead of the evening newspaper in his lap. He wouldn't give up the gun and was threatening to shoot himself, growing louder and angrier as the night wore on.

"Can you come over?"

Viola Walter stormed into the living room, snatched the loaded gun from the man's hand and demanded, "What the hell do you think you're doing?" For the next half hour she berated him for his selfishness in frightening his wife who loved him so and lectured him on his blindness to the beauty and preciousness of life. The couple, childless at the time, went on to have children and grandchildren who, years later, at the man's funeral in old age, thanked Viola in their eulogies for making their family possible. It was one of three suicides she was credited with preventing.

Intrigued by crime and criminals, Richard went to study psychology at Michigan State University. A haughty, brilliant student, he set a school record by completing eleven courses in one semester, seven more than the usual load, with a near-perfect 3.8 grade point average because "one must have challenges." He discovered his gift of seeing into the heart of darkness in his Shakespeare class, where he belittled the professor for suggesting that Hamlet fretted and delayed avenging his father's murder because he was a conflicted, skeptical modern man. "As it happens, Hamlet is quite psychopathically brilliant, and plays the fool while passively controlling all the action in the play until his final revenge. I would have done it exactly the same way!"

In 1975, after a job as a clinical psychologist at the prestigious Cedars-Sinai Medical Center in Los Angeles fell through, he worked for a time at the Los Angeles County morgue under medical examiner Thomas Noguchi, who had handled the autopsies of Marilyn Monroe, Janis Joplin, John Belushi, Robert F. Kennedy, and Sharon Tate.

To be able to study hundreds of bodies, to immerse himself in the awful ways people die and are killed, he had to remain stoic, in total control of his emotions. One morning, he got a phone call with news—his father had died. He hung up and got dressed, put on his tie, and went to work. He went to a meeting on schedule. During a break from the meeting, out of the blue, a woman asked what his father did for a living. Walter said evenly, "Oh, he died." She was taken back. "I'm so sorry. When?" He answered calmly, "This morning, about two hours ago." They all finished the meeting. He went back to his desk in the lab. That night, he looked in the mirror and was shaken by the cold eyes staring back at him. He felt nothing. "That was pretty scary."

He learned the lesson that his mentors in criminal investigation would later drill into his brain: "Whoever fights monsters should see to it that in the process he does not become a monster," as Friedrich Nietzsche wrote. "And if you gaze long enough into an abyss, the abyss will gaze back into you."

Walter began to obsessively collect antiques, grand, beautiful pieces from nineteenth-century France and China, "to remind myself there are beautiful things in the world."

But he was hooked by the gory world of the morgue. He decided to spurn the more prestigious field of clinical psychology to become a prison psychologist. "There is high snobbery in the psychological world, and prisons are supposed to attract the dullest, the biggest drones, the most stupid," he said. "That may or may not be true, but I'm going to do what I want, what is most fun for me, what satisfies my needs. Listening to neurotic housewives discuss their cats' puberty won't do it for me."

In May 1978, he took a job in the frozen Upper Peninsula of Michigan as a psychologist at the old prison at Marquette, a Romanesque castle on Lake Superior with five-foot-thick stone walls. The castle housed all the most violent prisoners in Michigan in one place.

Winter had eight hours of daylight and fourteen feet of snow. For recreation, locals sat in a lakefront restaurant eating Cornish meat pies and watching the towering shards of lake ice break up as iron freighters came and went. Walter thought he had never seen such a gloomy, desolate place in his life.

The warden gave him his schedule. Each day he would see six appointments. Murderers, rapists, pedophiles, sadists, and serial killers. Men whose crimes had landed them in prison, and whose crimes in other prisons—stabbing a guard, gouging out a fellow inmate's eye with a spoon, leading a riot—had landed them in the toughest prison of all.

They'd mostly be psychopaths, far more cunning than Wall Street lawyers. They would try to charm, beguile, or frighten him. They would try to convince him they'd found Jesus; threaten to strangle him, cut out his heart and piss on it, eat his kidneys. They'd tried to shock him: The man who'd stapled his children's eyelids open, then urinated into them. The repeat child molesters who preyed on hundreds. Plato said that there were only a few ways to do good, but countless ways to do evil. He would hear all of them.

He would take it all in with a cold stare. His job was to judge whether a man was irredeemable, filled with demons that were a danger to him or to others, or whether a man's better angels could be called forth. He had to judge them correctly every time; lives were at stake. It was a daily contest of wills.

Some would be bright and impressive with good families and high IQs; others were tattoo-inked creatures who gave people the shivers just to look at them.

He'd tell them, "Let's be clear. The reason you are in prison is your neighbors don't want you to break into their house and rape the cat."

His office was a small rectangle with concrete-block walls,

an old wooden desk and old steel filing cabinet, a wooden chair for clients. There was a single picture on the wall—a flower. A window that looked out on the iron-ore port, one of the coldest, snowiest, and darkest places in the United States.

"Perfect," he said.

"What a terrible job," a friend said. "Did you say you moved from Los Angeles?"

"It'll be grand," he said.

It was the ideal laboratory to study evil.

· CHAPTER 8 ·

GUARDIANS OF THE CITY

The community room at the First Federal Bank building at Castor and Cottman streets in northeast Philadelphia was crowded with Philadelphia and New Jersey cops, all Jewish cops.

Federal agent William Fleisher, one of the foremost Jewish cops in the Philadelphia region, stood to introduce the evening's presenters on cold-case murder investigation. It was the monthly meeting of the Shomrim, Hebrew for "guardians," the national association of Jewish police officers. Jewish cops had to stick together: "Kike" was still a sinister noun in police departments. As president of Shomrim's Philadelphia chapter, Fleisher fought discrimination against men or women who were passed over for promotions in the tribal culture of police departments only because they belonged to the tribe of Abraham.

Fleisher was the assistant special agent in charge of U.S. Customs in Philadelphia, one of the most powerful federal agents in the Mid-Atlantic, responsible for criminal and drug law enforcement at the ports, airports, coastlines, and inland borders of three states. He commanded an $8 million budget, a hundred personnel, and sixty-five special agents in the Philadelphia field office, plus satellite offices in Pittsburgh, the Pennsylvania capital of Harrisburg, Wilmington, Delaware, and field agents in New Jersey. He had the equivalent federal rank of a full-bird colonel.

By that evening in 1984, Fleisher was a legend in the annals of federal officers. After two years in the Army—where hard-nosed first sergeant John Baylin "turned me into a man; it was the best mistake I ever made"—he'd returned home to Philadelphia and earned a sociology degree from Temple University, hoping to impress his father, a Temple alum. His father didn't seem impressed. After college he fulfilled a dream and was hired as a Philadelphia police officer, one of his hometown's "finest." His father still didn't seem impressed.

After three years as a patrolman and corporal, he joined the FBI as a special agent and made a name for himself as a fearless mob investigator in Boston, Detroit, Philadelphia, and New York. He became a renowned polygraph examiner and interrogator. Fleisher talked to everyone—pimps, hookers, politicians, door-men—and could wheedle information from anybody. He was a chameleon: friendly uncle, ruthless inquisitor, stout best friend, wise rabbi, comic. Once he went undercover on a Caribbean cruise as a stand-up comedian—and sent the crew to jail with smuggling convictions.

He transferred to Customs as a special agent in Philadelphia because Customs agents had more freedom to choose where they wanted to live, and Fleisher and his wife, pregnant at the time with their first child, wanted to raise their family back home. After a three-year assignment in Washington, D.C., the promotion to the powerful job as Assistant Special Agent in Charge in Philadelphia was a triumphant return to his hometown. He lived across the river in a five-bedroom split-level in Cherry Hill, New Jersey, and occasionally did Tuesday-night stand-up at the Holiday Inn. On the surface, life was good.

Yet as he accumulated substantial government power, Fleisher had greatly expanded to meet it. At fifty years old, the once-slim FBI agent had become a corpulent man behind a desk, all five feet and eight and a half inches, and 250 pounds splendidly wrapped in Italian suits under the penumbra of a great Old Testament beard. He carried himself flamboyantly with a gold Montblanc pen in the shirt pocket embroidered *WLF*, a pinkie ring (like the beloved Jewish men of his childhood), a gourmand's appetite, and street-wise wit. Fleisher's weight worried his doctor and his wife. But the big man's regret was that his large stomach prevented him from carrying his Smith & Wesson .38 Chief's Special next to his groin, cowboy style, as he had as a brash young FBI agent, twenty years and a hundred pounds ago.

He was still holding on to the dreams of youth. The comic book and TV stories of detectives, modern knights-errant, that inspired him as a boy still animated him. He'd joke about it. "I never wanted to be a government bureaucrat. I always wanted to devote my life to the battle of good versus evil." But he meant it.

His dreams deferred had left him with a deep and unknowable sadness that could erupt to the surface in the field, paralyzing him.

As a baby-faced rookie patrolman in 1968 in tough West Philadelphia—ridiculed on the streets as too small, too soft, too Jewish—he'd answered a radio call of a toddler fallen from a second-story window at Fifty-second and Market streets. He rode with the boy in the back of the patrol wagon to the ER, but the ER doctor was having trouble reviving the boy. Suddenly a cry burst from the baby's lips, and the doctor smiled and said, "This little guy's gonna be all right." The child was fine but Fleisher started crying and couldn't stop. His partner had to lead him out of the hospital, crying for joy, "But I thought he was going to die!"

Billy wept at the scene of a murdered child, just the same over the arrest of a mob hit man. He wept when the other white officers branded a black colleague a "nigger," shouting at them that he was a good man. The baby-faced cop insisted he'd read the Bible, the Torah, the Koran, and heard the Upanishads were no different—it was clear the battle for justice was in the heart; each soul was precious. "The great religions teach us," he said through tears, "that the loss of one soul affects us all."

Whispers started to follow him. Crier. Social worker. *Too soft.* "I may be a short, fat, Jewish detective," he later roared at critics, "but I'm the toughest short, fat, Jewish detective you've ever seen."

Now the roomful of Jewish cops buzzed as Fleisher stood. He was one of them. He had a mezuzah in his doorpost protecting his house from the evil of the world with the blinding light of the one God. They loved him. It didn't matter that Fleisher had hugged the Saudi state police in Riyadh after teaching them the polygraph, saying in tears, "I have read the Koran, and there is nothing between us. We share the same God." Or that he considered himself a Christian, too. His wife was Catholic, and they'd hung a portrait of Jesus near the mantelpiece next to an idyllic photograph of two swans on a lovely pond. When friends asked him about it, he said, "That's Michelle's. I call that 'Two Swans Getting Ready to Fuck'"—whereupon Michelle would cry, "Bill!"

"As for Jesus, yo, what can I tell you?" he added. "He was the first good guy in history."

That was Fleisher. A character. A mensch. Crazy enough to try to love the world. Other cops said he'd gained a hundred pounds to accommodate his heart, that immense heart filled with longing.

"Ladies and gentlemen," he said to the members of Shomrim, "many of us know Hal Fillinger, the great Philadelphia medical examiner. But it's a first chance for a lot of us to meet Frank Bender, the brilliant forensic artist who's making headlines solving murder cases with the Philadelphia Police Department.

"Fillinger discovering Bender one day in the Philadelphia morgue," he added, "is the forensic equivalent of Lana Turner being discovered in Hollywood at Schwab's Drugstore."

Fleisher had shaken hands with Bender for the first time only minutes earlier. He had been impressed by the artist's buoyant energy. But now as Bender stood and began to narrate the slide show of his forensic work, he was stunned by the artist's uncanny ability.

He showed the bust of Anna Duval, the first murder victim he helped identify. From the gallery of the dead, the face of Linda Keyes also looked out at the room. Her unidentified skeleton had been found on a hilltop in Slatington, Pennsylvania; Bender's bust ran in the Allentown *Morning Call,* and a man who lived 250 miles away in Salisbury, Pennsylvania, recognized his daughter Linda, missing for two years. Another bust led to the solving of a murder on North Leithgow Street in Philadelphia—the street Bender grew up on, just a few blocks from his house.

The case that touched Bender most deeply was a young black woman whose skeleton was found in a wooded area near a high school football field in North Philadelphia after being raped and murdered and dumped a year earlier. The frilly Ship 'n' Shore—brand blouse found near the bones inspired Bender to sculpt her looking up as if to an imagined future beyond the grim neighborhood. When "the Girl with Hope," as he called her, was exhibited at the Mütter Museum in Philadelphia, a niece recognized Rosella Atkinson, who had disappeared, leaving behind a two-year-old daughter, and brought Rosella's mother, who looked at the plaster face and wept.

VIGIL FOR DAUGHTER ENDS IN MUSEUM, the *Philadelphia Inquirer* headline read.

After Bender's speech, Fleisher went up and congratulated him warmly. The two men made enthusiastic plans to meet for lunch. Bender was eager to develop his forensic career through the connections of one of the most powerful federal lawmen in the Mid-Atlantic states. Fleisher was openly awed by the artist with paranormal crime-fighting abilities. "It's sacrilegious for a veteran investigator to think this way," he said, "but what he does goes beyond science and rationalism. Frank is the ultimate secret weapon for law enforcement."

That first lunch led to a weekly ritual. The federal agent from the suburbs and the libertine Center City artist formed an unbreakable bond: Both men used suffering at the hands of their fathers as fuel for a fiery passion for justice. Fleisher was outraged by victims who were raped or murdered by criminals and then by the system; Bender was furious at cops who gave up on cases he was still passionate about, like the young woman whose skeleton was found enclosing the tiny skeleton of her unborn child in an abandoned Bucks County whiskey distillery. He had done a bust and his own investigation and was convinced it was a murder and he could name the killer, but authorities lacked the political will to care. Over sandwiches and coffee, Fleisher and Bender asked themselves a simple question: People were suffering, the bad guys were winning, and somebody had to do something.

Why not them?

CHAPTER 9

COLD EYES FROM THE PAST

The big man, wide and squat, moved powerfully down the cracked and broken city sidewalk, 250 pounds in a hurry. His expansive white shirt was soaked through with sweat, and his jacket flapped, revealing a Walther PPK .380 handgun. The air reeked of garbage and urine; the stench of melting tar trailed his black brogans. He was gasping for breath but moving like a bull that would not be stopped.

It was nearly one hundred degrees at midday, the hottest month in Philadelphia history, and William Fleisher wondered for the hundredth time what brought him obsessively into the bowels of the city, why he left the cool, ordered hallways of the U.S. Custom House for the steaming end of South Street, where chaos ruled.

He passed an old wino, and three homeless men sharing a flattened box in some shade, skeletal dogs feeding in a pile of garbage. Criminals along with the whole human race stagnated in the heat, waiting for dark. He was armed, and remained vigilant. A slasher was stalking poor neighborhoods. Four women, ages twenty-eight to seventy-four, had been stabbed to death and mutilated in a frenzy that recalled Jack the Ripper, their torsos carved open. That summer of 1986, "serial killer" was a new and terrifying term in the United States; Philadelphians in particular spied the dim corners of their old city with fears once unimaginable.

Two miles from his office at the Customs House, the nineteenth-century storefront sagged in the darkness. Once the Victorian butcher shop of a prosperous neighborhood, it now shadowed drug dealers and addicts drifting by in a dank river breeze. Old newspaper, long faded by the sun, covered the storefront windows. The green door appeared abandoned, except for two small signs: PEARLS REQUIRED, and PUT OUT THE CIGARETTE NOW, ASSHOLE. No light or sound came from within; steam quietly rose from the kitchen vent, like breath from a tomb. The city stank from fifteen mountains of garbage uncollected during the garbagemen's strike. But the stench emanating from the building overpowered all else.

Fleisher knocked on the green door of the dilapidated building at Twenty-third and South.

The door cracked open, and a young blond woman let him in. She was tall and buxom in a white T-shirt and shorts that disclosed elegant long legs. Fleisher grinned; he was feeling better already. Behind her rose a vast, hidden warehouse studio with a concrete floor and no windows, its bulk concealed from the street. In the high-ceilinged gloom, broken only by light filtering through a row of skylights, were crude wooden shelves lined with sculpted human heads. But next to them was a lovely walnut museum case with a bronze handgun shaped like a penis. The plaque read, THE SEX PISTOL THAT WON THE WEST.

He chuckled. "The sex pistol? At his age, I thought Frank would shoot blanks."

"He's been up all night," she said coolly, leading him through a steel door into the studio. "When he gets going, there's no stopping him." The studio was cluttered with nudes of young women, ladders and piles of bricks, erotic Parisian postcards. On the shelves were heads cracked by tire irons; mouths twisted in lipsticked horror; the bald head and psychopathic eyes of a man who had killed his entire family; a Negro slave whose bones had been dug from the grave. It was a gallery of murderers and victims of murder without equal and a somber mood came over him.

An abominable smell floated from the makeshift kitchen in the rear. Frank Bender, shirtless and barefoot on the cement floor, was stirring a huge steel pot. From the pot rack hung ladles, spoons, and a pair of steel handcuffs. A Norman Rockwell calendar looked down on a 1950s aluminum kitchen table.

"Bill!" he cried in the luminous voice of a man high on life. His eyes were unusually bright, like a cloudless sky. More female voices sounded from somewhere in the warehouse.

"What's cooking?" Fleisher walked over to the stove. The smell was awful.

"You don't want to know." Bender grinned and quickly put the lid on the big pot.

Fleisher recognized the smell. "That's it. You're not coming to the potluck."

Bender didn't like working with flesh-eating beetles. He boiled his rotting heads: fill water above the head, add half a cup of bleach and a dash of Borax, boil until done.

"I make a mean chicken in this pot," Bender said. Bender did most of the cooking, and most of it in the same pot. "Jan and Ella hate it when I use it to de-flesh the heads."

Fleisher rolled his eyes. "Why don't we go out for lunch."

CHAPTER 10

ON THE TRAIL OF THE ASSASSIN

The Day by Day Café was noisy and crowded with August light filtering through skyscrapers to find the corner plate-glass windows. Outside, winos and addicts slumbered in a church doorway; at a small table in back, Fleisher bent over a cheeseburger while Bender picked at a salad and ogled Wendy, a twentysomething waitress with pale skin and dark hair. Bender's eyes gleamed in his balding skull like azure marbles. He was trying to persuade her to sit nude for him. She had dropped by the studio for a glass of wine. But he hadn't yet convinced her to remove her clothes.

"She moves like sex personified," he said as he watched her walk away.

"Jesus, Frank, I don't know how you get away with it."

"Jan wants me to have a few girlfriends," he said, his tone completely earnest. "She doesn't like me hanging around the house all the time. She just likes to meet my girlfriends first. I never get involved with someone Jan doesn't like. Jan likes Ella. It's Ella who gets jealous of the other girlfriends."

Fleisher shook his head. "I can't keep it all straight." Fleisher had been married to Michelle for thirty years, and his passions were conventional: Besides nineteenth-century detective stories, they included gourmet dining, travel with Michelle, and spoiling the grandchildren. He teased and joked with Michelle as mercilessly as the day he started courting her; in many ways, he had never stopped courting her.

Bender never stopped loving his wife, either. He spoke of her with great fondness. He'd stopped sleeping around with strangers, he said. All his girlfriends were close, intimate friends.

"Let me get this straight," Fleisher smirked. "In other words, you're not sowing wild oats anymore. It's all about relationships now."

"Right."

Fleisher laughed out loud. "Frank, if you were in my family I'd chase you with a rifle like your father-in-law did. But on a murder case, you're the best."

At this, Bender leaned forward, lowering his voice confidentially. "Bill, listen, I'm working on this case that's really worrying me," said Bender. "The marshals are tracking down a fugitive killer, a legendary hit man, and they asked me to be the 'eyes' of the task force. They say I have an ability to see faces none of the others have."

"Congratulations. It sounds like a fantastic opportunity."

Bender frowned. "I'm supposed to do sketches and a bust showing 'age progression' so they know what they're looking for. The marshal deputized me and I'm carrying a gun. They were very upfront about the danger."

Fleisher's eyes widened.

"I know, I haven't seen his face up close, but the guy looks just like me. He's the same size, same age, same body type. He's also an artist. It's spooky. I feel like he's my doppelganger, an evil twin."

Fleisher scowled. Bender took a sip of coffee. "I'm not afraid of anybody," he said. "But I saw him once through a telephoto lens and his eyes were so cold. He knows who I am and the threat I represent to him. I can feel it—he wants me dead.

"His name is Hans Vorhauer," Bender continued. "He's a German American like me, but killing is in his blood. His father was a Nazi S.S. officer. And he's a genius—he has the highest IQ tested in the history of the Pennsylvania prison system."

Fleisher practically lunged out of his chair. "Hans Vorhauer! I can tell you all about Hans Vorhauer. I chased him all over the East Coast in the 1970s for the murder of a federal witness friend."

Vorhauer was one of the most wanted and dangerous fugitives at large in the United States. Accused by federal agents in a rare interrogation of killing seventeen people as a hired assassin, Vorhauer openly mocked them. "No," he smirked, with the arrogance of a man who had never been charged with any of them, "it's thirty-three." Vorhauer was a brilliant tactician of murder, a master of disguise, black-market gunsmith, drug dealer, armed robber, and the uber–hit man for East Coast gangsters, elusive as a ghost. A self-taught chemist, he operated one of the largest methamphetamine laboratories on the East Coast until he was finally arrested and convicted of meth possession and armed robbery charges in the late 1970s. Vorhauer was sentenced to twenty years in Graterford Prison outside Philadelphia, the state's largest maximum-security lockup. A model prisoner, he worked his way into the position of head of the prison shop.

On November 17, 1983, Vorhauer staged a spectacular escape from Graterford that the headlines called THE BREAKFRONT BREAK-OUT, escaping in the hollow compartment of an armoire he had made in the shop for sale and delivery outside. Crouched with him in the pine armoire—stained to resemble oak to better explain its great weight as it was wheeled outside to a waiting pickup truck—was convicted killer Robert Thomas Nauss, the sadistic leader of the Warlocks biker gang, who had strangled and carved up his beauty-queen girlfriend. An unknown couple driving the pickup truck drove away with the armoire, and the killers were never seen again. It was believed they had separated, but they were considered highly dangerous, and profilers thought it inevitable that they would kill again. The marshals had no higher priority than getting Vorhauer and Nauss off the streets—and they'd recently had a break in the long-dormant case. An old neighbor of Vorhauer's thought she saw him in Philadelphia, where his wife lived, but she wasn't sure; she hadn't seen him in fifteen years. The marshals weren't sure, either; the problem was photographs of him were seventeen years out of date, and nobody knew what the fugitive looked like—or was even sure he was in Philadelphia until Bender spotted him on a stakeout. Bender's job was to produce sketches and a bust showing how Vorhauer looked today, and he was stumped. It was his first federal case, his first case of national importance. His future forensic career—and perhaps his life—depended on it. He was stumped.

"I saw him at a distance, it was way too fuzzy a view," Bender said glumly. "There's something I'm missing about him. I need to know more about him, something that will help me capture his look and his personality in my art."

Fleisher's big face was flushed. The memory of the hit man had haunted him for over a decade.

"I'd do anything to help you get that bastard. He has the coldest eyes I've ever seen."

CHAPTER 11

DEATH OF A B-GIRL

Fleisher knocked on the boxer's door in Queens and stood to the side with the other special agents. The old boxer was saving for his retirement with a part-time job doing Mafia hijackings.

He answered the door in his underwear. His wife was cooking in the kitchen. The feds said they wanted to talk to him about the murder of a federal informant—one of Fleisher's informants, the dumbest ever, had *told* the mob he was talking to the FBI.

"Can I put some pants on?" the boxer asked.

"Sure," the feds said.

"I'll go with him," Fleisher said.

In the bedroom the boxer reached for his pants, an arm's length from a rifle against the wall. Fleisher put his hand over his service .38—worn gunslinger style over the groin, with the attitude *I'm small and I'm Jewish, make my day*—and said, "I hear on the street you're trying to whack me. Get the rifle and let's get this over with, *mano a mano.*"

The mobster backed down politely: "No, Mr. Fleisher, I'd never do such a thing."

Fleisher was soft like the Italians were soft—emotional, wild, a little crazy. The Italians and the street people liked him, a reputation that had led his supervisor, Jim Scanlon, to call him into his office one morning in 1971 at the FBI headquarters in Boston.

As he sat down, Scanlon said, "I want you to look into the murder of a B-girl in the Combat Zone."

Fleisher's sources included hookers, bouncers, and bar girls. "They all love me there," he famously bragged to the older agents, leading to the inevitable question, "What do they charge for that?" Yet in fact the special agent could wheedle information from any-body. He didn't spend a dime of the thousands of dollars in tax-payer money available to buy off informants. With the sweet smile of a Boy Scout and the street smarts of a bookie, Fleisher got people to open up, then he picked them clean.

"Her name was Vicki Harbin. She was fiftyish, a dancer work-ing at the 222 Club," Scanlon said. "They found her in her room at the Avery Hotel. She was lying on the floor near the door, stabbed to death."

Fleisher's eyes narrowed. "An over-the-hill B-girl, still dancing around a pole, hustling drinks, living the life in the Avery." He shook his head sadly. The Avery was a narrow, ten-story landmark gone to seed, a respectable turn-of-the-century hotel turned hooker Hilton. In the 1940s and '50s, Tommy Carr and his orchestra played "Good-bye to Paris" in the Cameo Bar, and vaudevillians Jackie Gleason and Art Carney and actor Jason Robards camped in the hotel's mod-est rooms, cheapest in the theater district. Filled with touring young performers, even then the Avery smelled of sex. The line was, "At two in the morning in the Avery a bell rang, and everyone went back to their own rooms." By the spring of 1971, the Combat Zone's doz-ens of adult bookstores, girlie shows, and massage parlors stretched outside the door. "The Avery had the saggy, tattered quality of a locale in a Raymond Chandler novel," a journalist wrote.

"A bad john?"

"No, she wasn't a prostitute. She was a dancer. You know— the body's gone, but she's in it for life. They found her lying on two dollars, the tip she always gave the bellhop for bringing her a bucket of ice at the end of the night."

Fleisher's brown eyes softened. "Everyone dreams of some-thing."

"Vicki Harbin was stabbed in the heart. It was a professional hit."

"It's terrible, but so what?" Fleisher shot back. "Is it a white-slavery case? Otherwise, it's a Boston homicide, a police case."

Scanlon frowned. "Until a black man by the name of Orange Harbin—"

"Orange?"

"The same. Mr. Orange Harbin, Vicki's husband and by all accounts a fine gentleman, walks into the Boston PD last week and tells the desk sergeant his wife was killed on orders of the Baltimore gangster Bernie Brown."

Fleisher's eyebrows went up. "Wild Bernie Brown?"

Scanlon nodded.

"He's quite a package," said Fleisher. "Murder. Extortion. The rackets. Wild Bernie is about as mobbed-up as you can get without being Italian. He's not a made guy, but he's kicking money upstairs to someone, paying the street tax. I think he might be Jewish."

"Whatever. Baltimore says Vicki was testifying against Brown before a federal grand jury," Scanlon said.

Fleisher whistled. "The murder of a federal witness. He thought of a very effective way to shut her up. I guess Bernie's still not going to choir practice on Sunday. He's not flossing before he brushes."

Scanlon was stone-faced. One of Fleisher's weaknesses was he thought he was funny. It was part of his charm with informants. A bad joke or pun made them even more comfortable than a good one.

"They're bringing in a lot of witnesses to the grand jury, putting the squeeze on him," Scanlon said. "Bernie's the king of the bust-out bars. The bar girl hangs on you all night selling a fantasy, but you never go home with her. She just busts out your wallet for watered-down gin. So the grand jury is after the bust-out bar empire, and Wild Bernie is busy knocking off witnesses."

"More than one?"

"Talk to Baltimore. Before Harbin, they put a contract out on another witness down there, some guy involved in the bars. They put a bomb under the seat of his car, enough to obliterate him and a Buick. They didn't want to kill his wife, so they figured this guy works at night, he'd turn the lights on and—*boom*—he's in the next zip code. What they didn't figure on was the wife, who's a night person, too, sets the alarm, gets up early the next morning, and takes the car in for inspection. The mechanic checks the lights and *boom*—"

"They killed the mechanic?"

"No, only the blasting cap went off. Moisture might have got in it. It sounded like a cherry bomb, ripped up the seat, burned the guy's ass, and scared the hell out of him. He was lucky."

"So Vicki Harbin saw the handwriting on the wall and ran up to Boston and a new life in the Avery Hotel?"

"Right. The question is, what crawled out from under a rock and followed her? It's the $64,000 question."

"Nah," Fleisher said. "It won't cost that much." He said he'd work his sources. "I bullshit with them all the time. They like me. Everybody likes me." He grinned. "I don't pay for it in the Combat Zone."

Fleisher drove to the Bradford Hotel on Tremont Street. A Boston landmark built in the 1920s, the redbrick neoclassical hotel that was once "In the Heart of the City." In the 1940s, big bands played on the rooftop and in Boston's largest ballroom. Now the Bradford was a hooker hotel in the heart of a living hell.

Fleisher had learned from FBI agents in Baltimore that Brown had sent his enforcer, Jack Sugarman, up to Boston to find Harbin. Sugarman was a World War II Marine hero from Delaware County, Pennsylvania, who came back from the war and ended up a gangster's right-hand man. According to informants, Sugarman was the finger man—he went to Boston to find the dancer and point her out to the hit man. The hit man was Hans Vorhauer, whom Fleisher had never heard of. Baltimore said he was the best in the business. When the fax came in from the Baltimore office, Fleisher was chilled by the killer's eyes in facsimile.

The Bradford was a sad twin sister to the nearby Avery. He figured it was the most likely place Sugarman would have stayed—if indeed the enforcer had come to Boston.

He would never stay in the Avery with the victim, and the Bradford is in the area of the Combat Zone, he thought to himself. *A lot of hookers, pimps, and miscreants stay here.*

"Hey, Bill, what do you want?" Paul, the hotel manager, a tall, balding man with stooped shoulders, stopped him near the elevators.

"I need to see the records." Fleisher shook hands with the manager.

"More hookers?"

He nodded, but the manager had already turned around and was briskly leading him downstairs into a gloomy hallway. The hotel manager was a friend.

He'd helped Fleisher make his name working white-slavery cases. The White Slavery Act made transporting women across state lines for prostitution an interstate, or federal, crime. Along with tax violations, it was a favorite federal tool for tripping up gangsters; Lucky Luciano and Al Capone were arrested on white-slavery charges.

On one case, Fleisher had approached Paul with photographs, saying, "Have you seen these two women? I have a lead they're hookers in town from Minneapolis." To prevent the cops from zeroing in on them in their home cities, white slaves followed a circuit like a troupe—Chicago, Minneapolis, New York, Boston, Baltimore, New Orleans.

"They're here right now, come with me!" the manager had cried. He took the elevator to the fifth floor, then walked down the long hallway. Reaching their room, the manager had started banging on the door screaming, "Get out of my hotel, you whores!"

Now Paul led him to a small, dusty room and put three long cardboard banker's boxes on a table in front of him. The boxes were stuffed with the hotel's three-by-five registration cards, stacked and bundled with rubber bands. Fleisher riffled through three stacks of the cards for the previous month with great impatience, working rapidly.

Three weeks before the murder there was a chicken-scrawl signature reserving three nights: *Jack Sugarman.*

Two weeks before the murder, another three nights: *Jack Sugarman.*

The week of the murder, just one night: *Jack Sugarman.*

Bingo, he thought. *I've got Sugarman in town. The first time he comes up from Baltimore to stake Vicki out, see what she's doing. The second time, he works on her schedule, gets her hours and habits down. The third visit is brief—he points her out to Vorhauer.* It would be trickier proving Vorhauer's whereabouts. Vorhauer was a wanted fugitive and master of disguise; he would never have used his real name.

That evening Fleisher went to the dim, smoky cave of the Caribe Lounge, the best known of the Combat Zone's nude bars. A young redhead was dancing on a small stage circled with men watching through clouds of cigarette smoke. The redhead would occasionally flash her G-string and pasties—total nudity was banned in Boston—but not with a cop in the room. George Tecci, the owner-manager, stopped him cold near the door.

"What do you want?" Tecci asked, his lip curled in distaste.

Fleisher took out his wallet and showed his badge. "FBI, I'm looking for Cinderella."

"What about?"

"I want to talk to her about the murder of Vicki Harbin, who danced at 222." He showed Tecci a portrait photograph of the dancer, a brunette with a round, aging face. As the manager led him downstairs to the dressing rooms, a tall woman in her twenties, at least six feet in heels, blond and buxom, came walking toward them with a leonine grace that took his breath away. She was the sexiest woman Fleisher had ever seen, and when he studied her face, one of the prettiest.

"Cinderella, this fellow wants to talk to you," Tecci said. She smiled—she had high and delicate cheekbones, and her smile was dazzling. The eyes were big and blue and brittle. Fleisher took the portrait out of his folder.

"I understand you were a friend of Vicki Harbin's?" Cinderella's smile disappeared as she led him to her dressing room.

"I don't know anything."

They sat in the mirror lights, so close Fleisher breathed her scent, and he gave her his warmest, most sympathetic smile. She was a knockout and she was sweet and she liked him; he could feel it behind the hard eyes. Their legs were almost touching. She had incredible legs. He looked closer in the hazy light and focus returned like a blow to the head—*Her Adam's apple is the size of Johnny Appleseed's,* he thought. *Her hands are as big as Sonny Liston's.* A fantasy about a he-she, he thought, could wake you up like twenty-four ounces of cold coffee.

When had she last seen Harbin?

Her eyes were dead. "I don't know anything."

Was Harbin afraid of Bernie Brown?

"I don't know anything."

Had she seen these two men? He took out the faxed photos of Sugarman and Vorhauer.

"I don't know anything." It sounded like a mantra to an empty universe.

Fleisher knew it would be difficult. According to his sources, Cinderella's husband was Bobby Urbin, a doorman for Bernie Brown. He watched the gangster's door in Baltimore and "ran a card game for some wise guys in Boston," Fleisher said. He and Cinderella traveled the circuit together.

"You don't know anything, but now you know this. Let me show you what they did to your friend Vicki."

He reached into the folder for the close-up of Harbin with the knife wounds in her heart.

Cinderella let out a small gasp and put a hand over her mouth; the big blue eyes were moist.

"I'm trying to find out who killed Vicki. Here's my name and number. Call me if you want to help." She said nothing as he gave her his card and left.

It was time, he thought as he got in his car, to put pressure on Cinderella and her husband.

At ten that night, he drove to the 222 Club. The bouncer—a squat, heavyset man, five foot three inches tall and nearly as wide—stopped him at the door. He wore thick glasses on a pudgy round face, had hair dyed a shade too dark, a cigarette hung on fleshy lips, and had a blackjack in his back pocket. One of his brown eyes wandered in the socket like a satellite to the moon face.

"Cockeyed Benny," Fleisher said in greeting. They shook hands warmly. "I'm looking into the murder of Vicki Harbin, and I'm looking for these guys." He held up photos of Sugarman and Vorhauer.

Cockeyed Benny nodded at the picture of Sugarman. "He was here." Sugarman left the 222 with a hooker, Benny said; he'd watched them walk out. He took her back to the Bradford, and "he paid her with a check that bounced."

"Do you know Bobby Urbin?"

Cockeyed Benny grunted. "Sure. He's always in here." Fleisher had never met Cinderella's husband and didn't have a photograph of him. He and Cockeyed Benny worked out a signal that evening. Fleisher would sit at a table with a drink, Benny would stand at the bar; when Bobby Urbin walked by, the bouncer would light a cigarette. Just as Urbin strolled by, Benny lit up, but at that moment some guy at the bar passed out, and a crowd formed. Cockeyed Benny waded into the crowd with Fleisher and tapped Urbin on the shoulder; Fleisher said, "FBI. I want to ask you some questions," and hustled him out of the 222 and into a car. Fleisher sat in the back pumping Urbin with questions, while the street hustler put his hand inside Fleisher's thigh.

I'll let him do it to get the story, he thought, amused. *He likes me, too. They all like me.* But Urbin refused to talk about the Harbin murder. He had to let him go.

Frustrated, Fleisher went back to FBI headquarters and called Frank Mulvee, the Boston police detective assigned to the case, and told him Urbin had knowledge of the murder and marijuana in his apartment, a tip he had gleaned on the street.

The next morning, the police raided Urbin's apartment; Urbin and Cinderella were both at home, and Mulvee called the FBI agent. Fleisher went to the apartment and tried to get Urbin to cooperate in the Harbin murder. "You don't know anything," Fleisher said. "I don't believe you, and neither do the police. Why don't you just take a polygraph?"

"Oh, Bobby, take the test," Cinderella chimed in. Boston police took him to a private examiner; the polygraphist attached the blood-pressure cuff, the pneumograph tubes across the chest and abdomen, the electric sensor plates on the fingertips. Urbin answered a few questions, then ripped off all the instruments and ran out of the office. They had only one chart on him, but it showed clear deception.

Fleisher's head was spinning. He had placed Sugarman, the finger man, in town, but nobody had seen the hit man Vorhauer; Vorhauer was a ghost. Brown's people were scurrying like rats from a ship. The police couldn't find Urbin. He had failed to get Harbin's friends to talk. Finally he got the name of a dancer who knew Vicki intimately—Terri Emanuel, a gorgeous copper-toned young woman, half Filipino, half Cajun American, half man, half woman until recently; now Terri was as pretty as Cinderella. He put her at the top of his interview list.

That night he was at a bar with two friends, deputy agent in charge U.S. Marshal Mike Assad, and his brother Eddie, a Boston cop, when an extremely shapely woman walked by their table. The three bachelors whistled as they watched her go, then sucked in their breath for a moment of silent contemplation.

"You think she's endowed," Fleisher said, "you should have seen the knockout I interviewed at the Caribe the other night, Cinderella."

"Cinderella, pretty name," Mike said.

"She makes this one look like a schoolteacher, and she's a guy."

Mike and Eddie groaned.

"That's strange," Eddie said. "We had a job this morning, before dawn, a mysterious death of a woman and she was a he-she, too."

"What was her name?"

"Terri Emanuel."

"Jesus Christ!" Fleisher cried. "I'm supposed to interview her."

After pressing Eddie for details, Fleisher left the table and called Mulvee from a pay phone. He agreed to meet the Boston detective at police headquarters. At two in the morning, the police report gave them the address where Emanuel's body was found. She lived in an apartment with some guy named Art Nettles.

At three in the morning, they knocked on the door and Nettles cheerfully let them in. Art was a brunette, "half man, half woman, not finished with the operation," Fleisher said. "She had boobs but didn't have her winky removed yet." Terri roomed with Art and slept on the sofa. Now Art sat on the sofa in a bathrobe left open to show off the new breasts and was glad to talk about Terri's death.

Art and Terri had been frightened at an after-hours club by two very tough-looking Italian guys who wanted to take them home. They were relieved to get away from the men and back to their apartment. In the middle of the night they were awakened by the buzzer, and Art let the caller in. Through the crack in the door she saw the two Italian guys, who pushed their way in. One of them punched Art in the jaw; the other grabbed Terri, who always slept in the nude on the sofa, rolled her in a blanket, and ran out. Art had the presence of mind to yank the fire alarm. As the alarm sounded, the two goons dropped Terri and ran away. Terri and Art went back to sleep, adventure over. In the late morning, a dancer friend from Chicago called and asked Art, "How's Terri? I had a dream about her and I smelled flowers. Is she all right?" Art went out to the sofa to wake Terri. She was dead. The ME had no idea what killed her.

The ME was a piece of shit, Mulvee said.

"Jesus," Fleisher said. He had a feeling Bernie Brown was

trying to erase all his witnesses. But he had nothing close to proof. He'd hit another wall.

That night, Cinderella called him. She wanted to talk. Yes, she confirmed, Vicki Harbin knew her life was in danger and was afraid; she was looking over her shoulder constantly. The week before she was killed, Harbin had an experience on the stage that terrified her. While dancing, she looked out and saw the big, ugly, scarred face of Jack Sugarman. Sugarman, who won the Navy Cross in World War II for killing 132 Japanese soldiers in one night on Guadalcanal, and whose face had been since rearranged by a baseball bat, was sitting in the pit watching her with a leering smile on his face. Seated next to Sugarman was Bernie Brown's ace hit man, Hans Vorhauer. She knew them both. Vorhauer was expressionless. His wolf eyes stared through her as if she wasn't there.

Scanlon thought Fleisher was "really shaking up the bushes," but he didn't feel he had a case until Cinderella cooperated.

Then, that summer of 1971, the FBI transferred Fleisher to Detroit; he was off the case.

Bender looked up from his coffee. "Man, that's frustrating. Wow, I would have loved to have met Cinderella. Did you ever get Vorhauer?"

Fleisher scowled. "No. We trailed him all over Boston. He was in a lot of bars, but nothing we could nail down. Then in Detroit I got a call from an agent I'd been working with in Baltimore. He says, 'Guess what? We got Vorhauer.'"

The FBI had received a tip that Vorhauer, a Most Wanted fugitive, was hiding out in Sugarman's house in suburban Baltimore. Half a dozen FBI agents and police officers went to the house, heavily armed. Sugarman answered the door and let them in. A middle-aged man with red hair was sitting at the kitchen table, an arm's length from a brown leather briefcase. None of the agents recognized him; they demanded identification. The man's driver's license and Social Security number said Joe Smith; his credit cards and club membership said Joe Smith. The last piece of paper in his wallet was a folded-up Western Union receipt documenting money wired to his mother, Barbara Vorhauer, in Hanau, Germany. Vorhauer's disguise had fooled all of them. Agents arrested the hit man, and brought Sugarman to Boston for questioning. Sugarman flipped immediately to avoid charges of harboring a fugitive.

Bernie Brown paid Vorhauer $5,000 to kill Harbin, Sugarman said. Vorhauer scouted the dancer's movements and knocked on her door in the evening after a show, the finger man said. She must have thought it was the bellhop with her bucket of ice; Vorhauer pushed his way in. He told Sugarman he stabbed Harbin three times in the heart.

The agents were lucky to arrest the hit man before he reached his brown briefcase. A .22-caliber silencer fired out of the side; there was a ring trigger on the handle. Vorhauer had taken Sugarman into a Baltimore grocery store, said, "Watch this," and walked down the aisle shooting up the cereal boxes—*pfff, pfff, pfff*—with the briefcase and walked out calm as a banker on lunch hour. Nobody heard a thing. Vorhauer was a genius, Sugarman said, who created black-market weapons unequaled in the world.

"Vorhauer is a beast," Bender said. He glanced over his shoulder as if he expected the hit man to be standing there. "That's what I thought. He's brilliant and he's a psychopath. This will really help the bust." He shifted uneasily in his seat.

Fleisher shook his head sadly. "We never did get him. Murder charges were never filed against Vorhauer. There wasn't enough corroboration, and they let him go. We all have cases we wish we could go back in time and fix. That's one of mine."

They were quiet for a moment, and Fleisher said, "One more thing. It's strange, but we followed Vorhauer for months, and this is the oddest thing about him. He liked to hang out in gay and transvestite bars."

Bender's face lit up.

"He wasn't gay," Fleisher said. "He recruited disaffected homosexuals as enforcers. Some of them enjoyed hurting heterosexuals."

Bender grinned like he wasn't listening; his eyes were suddenly somewhere else. It was like making eye contact with the Milky Way.

"Earth to Frank."

Wendy had sailed back into the room.

The ASAC grinned and shook his head once in a swift jerking motion, like he was shrugging off a fly. He often wondered what it felt like to be Frank Bender. Was it like being a bloodhound obsessed with sex and death; did ideas come like radio signals to the teeth?

Wendy came with the check, and Bender chatted her up, his voice as smooth and warm as grade-A honey, all anxiety gone. The ASAC finished his coffee and laughed.

"Frank, you're a hit man yourself."

Bender smiled to himself. His mind was wandering in familiar territory. He was thinking about brunettes—brunettes and blondes.

CHAPTER 12

THE VISUAL DETECTIVE

The studio was very still. Far off he heard a sound like the sea breaking, but it was only the ceaseless pounding of cars on the expressway. Above in the dimness, filthy skylights held the dawn. Vorhauer's face snarled from the shadows, hideous in the slanting red light of the morning star. The face was half-formed, twisted, and grotesque, as if the lump of clay experienced the pain of being pinioned on the steel armature. It reminded Bender of Michelangelo's slave trapped in rock, mightily struggling to emerge. He looked down at his coffee and back at the face.

"Aw, hell," he cursed. He slapped the side of the clay and felt like throwing it. What was missing?

Bender had made fifteen drawings of Vorhauer in addition to the half-done sculpture. He had obsessively researched the hit man, as he did all his subjects. He'd studied police files, the newspaper, the morgue, the thirteen-year-old photo. He'd annoyed the marshals with endless questions. The official view was one-dimensional—the hit man was as elusive and as pure a distillation of evil as they had ever pursued, end of story. It wasn't enough to mold into the three dimensions of life. Somehow, he'd failed to capture the essence of the master of disguise.

Bender had confronted Vorhauer himself on a stakeout and come away shaken in a way secondhand sources couldn't convey.

Vorhauer was "cold as ice, cold, cold, cold," he said. "I could feel clearly from his eyes that he wanted me dead." Still Bender searched for a missing ingredient, a clue to Vorhauer's soul, if he had one. The marshals couldn't catch what they couldn't see. Maybe he needed to think like a hit man. He was sipping the cold coffee in front of the head, trying to see the world through the eyes of a cold-blooded assassin, when the doorbell rang.

A heavyset man of medium height, unkempt gray hair falling over a round face, sized up Bender with a cocksure grin. It was Paul Schneider, a Delaware County detective deputized as a U.S. Marshal. Schneider was one of the best detectives Bender had ever worked with—tough, smart, relentless. "If these TV series wanted a real investigator, it wouldn't be the good-looking people they always have," Bender said. "It would be a guy with a gut like Paul Schneider." Schneider wasn't just any deputy; he was in charge of the marshals' Vorhauer task force.

Schneider's grin flickered in the gloom. "I saw him, plain as day. I saw Vorhauer."

"You're kidding!" Bender's face flushed; his eyes flared with excitement. After nine months of futilely chasing the phantom assassin, they finally had a break.

Schneider gave a short jerk of his head. "He was on Wellington Street an hour ago, a block from the wife's house. He was getting into a car with another man."

Bender's eyes went inward, a dreamy look, as if the machine inside were suddenly unplugged. Thousands of cops and informants and the nation's top bounty hunters were on alert in the hunt for Vorhauer. But no one had seen him except Bender. Bender saw him the first time as he stood on a crowded sidewalk outside a pharmacy. Vorhauer wore a baseball cap, sunglasses, and a cigarette on thin lips. Somehow he intuited Bender's presence raising a camera in a parked car a block away. Vorhauer glared into the telephoto lens for an instant; the hard, mocking face cracked into a smirk and vanished. The film barely registered him, a fuzzy image impossible to sketch, a residue of light and shadow. It felt like ghost hunting, or waiting for a saint's statue to weep blood.

Bender's second sighting was truly frightening. He and Schneider posed as garbagemen to collect Barbara Vorhauer's trash on Wellington Street. Vorhauer was believed to be hiding out with his wife, a Philadelphia nurse. Bender was extremely cautious; Vorhauer would shoot anybody who threatened him. Dressed in the uniform of a municipal worker, he sat in the passenger seat of the city garbage truck with a loaded shotgun under the floor mat as Schneider steered behind the house. Bender kept his head down so he wouldn't arouse suspicion as he threw the garbage bags into the compacter. Quickly he pulled a camera from his coveralls and snapped pictures of the back of the house, zooming in on each of the windows in turn. As he focused on a darkened second-story window, he broke out in a cold sweat. The blinds were bent as if someone was peering down at them. Suddenly he felt utterly naked, completely exposed, flushed with terror. His heart accelerated as he waited for the rifle explosion and the darkness at the end of the world. The moment passed. But later when he thought about it his guts seized anew when he realized he had lived, he remained alive, on a killer's whim.

Or maybe it was just a suspicious nurse peering out her back window. Vorhauer seemed as real as death, as unreal as a ghost.

Bender snapped back to the world around him and picked up his pastels. He walked to his easel and said, "Let's get this down in detail so the task force knows exactly what he looks like. I want to nail the guy."

Schneider nodded, and stood behind Bender at the sketch board. The artist's hand moved rapidly across the white sketch paper, creating a narrow street and a car almost as rapidly as Schneider described the scene. "We were doing surveillance of the wife, waiting for her to come out of the house," the deputy said. "I saw him on the street getting into a parked car on the right side of the street—"

"What'd he look like?" Bender's pulse raced. He felt they were finally zeroing in on their quarry.

"He looked nasty," Schneider said.

Bender nodded impatiently. "I could just see the side of the driver's face, his ear, as I drove by them," the marshal continued. "I had an angle on Vorhauer sitting in the passenger seat. Hard, lean, pockmarked face, reddish-brown hair. He was wearing a baseball cap."

"What color?"

"Blue."

The sketch quickly filled in to match Schneider's description.

Bender turned and looked at Schneider. "Did he know you were around?"

"No way, partner." The deputy's eyes narrowed, as if he had been insulted. "We've done this once or twice."

Bender lowered his heavy brow until his light blue eyes reduced to slivers of ice. His voice was measured and cool, as if some internal fan had slowed everything down. Bender knew Vorhauer was reputed to have the highest IQ of anybody in the history of the Pennsylvania penal system.

"He's extremely street smart. A guy like Vorhauer can sense when he's being watched—that's good enough for him."

Schneider shrugged. "Not a chance."

"What did you do?" asked Bender, his face flushing with adrenaline.

Schneider grimaced. "Nothing."

"What do you mean 'nothing'?" The artist's head turned the color of a ripening plum.

"We couldn't do anything," Schneider said, eyes downcast. "He'd think nothing of shooting at me. We've got to pick our time and place."

Bender's arm sagged over the easel. Schneider and the others always described Vorhauer in terms of awe. "This is a very formidable individual," Schneider kept saying. "Very formidable." Schneider couldn't get over the fact that after the genius hit man and finish carpenter engineered his prison escape, he attended college to study chemistry and constructed an autonomous meth lab that allowed him to manufacture the drug without being in the lab to risk arrest or potential explosions. Even the cops were afraid of Vorhauer, who was extremely violent and had shot his way out of stakeouts in the past.

"Cheer up. We can't lose with the Visual Detective on our side," said Schneider, referring to the nickname he had hung on Bender.

Bender grinned good-naturedly, but his eyes were again far away. He was hearing the voice he trusted most, "something from inside of myself." Others called it intuition, but to Bender the voice spoke with utter certainty, and gave him evidence that couldn't be stored in a police locker, or confined to court documents. The voice supplied now three fresh insights he decided were absolute fact, and worth a trip, late that night after Schneider left, back to the drawing board. First, Vorhauer knew he had been seen up close by a U.S. Marshal. Second, as a defensive maneuver the master of disguise would dramatically change his looks again.

Third, he would become a blond.

"A *blond*?" Tom Rappone, the head of the U.S. Marshals Service in Philadelphia, looked quizzically at Bender when he handed him the final sketch of Vorhauer that afternoon. It was a black-and-white sketch; there was no time to blend pastel colors, Bender explained. Still, the charcoal shading indicated light blond hair.

"This is what Vorhauer looks like," Bender said defensively. "If you catch him within two weeks, he's going to be bleached blond."

"Blond." Rappone flashed a humorless smile beneath dark, probing eyes. The deputies were constantly amused by Bender's off-the-wall ideas and visions, but this was a topper. A mob hit man disguised as the Breck girl.

"He's Aryan and proud of his Germanic heritage," Bender said. "The skin coloring is right," he insisted. "He's also an artist, very creative."

Rappone waited as if there must be more. Bender's face reddened. He didn't get timid when his psychic visions were questioned; he got mad, and sometimes he got even.

"I learned from Fleisher that when he was with the FBI in Boston they tailed Vorhauer to a lot of gay and transsexual bars," he said. "Vorhauer wasn't gay, he was recruiting enforcers. But he looks way too straight. Going blond would allow him to pass in tranny bars. Tom, I'm telling you, he's going to bleach his hair."

Rappone shrugged and made copies of the blond hit man for his agents. When Schneider saw the sketch, he sported a wide grin. "We believe in you, Frank, but an assistant DA says this is a joke, and a lot of the guys think you're nuts."

Bender smiled with his sheepish look that swayed moral women of all ages.

Bender was still struggling to perfect the Vorhauer bust a week later when the phone rang in the vast warehouse studio. It was Rappone, with the news that the task force's long surveillance of Barbara Vorhauer had borne fruit. She had led the marshals right to her husband.

"You're kidding me! What happened?" The artist's voice, childlike in its enthusiasms, rang across the line.

A night-shift nurse at Osteopathic Hospital, Barbara had gotten off work early in the morning as usual. But instead of taking her routine route home, she'd raced along a twisting, helter-skelter path designed to shake surveillance. Trained by Hans, Barbara had proven remarkably adept at avoiding the marshals for months.

But this time they kept pace with hairpin turns and U-turns, up blind alleys, and into the parking lot of the Penrose Diner. Barbara got out of her car and entered the diner. When she came out, she left her car in the parking lot and walked across the street to the Quality Inn, a twelve-story cylindrical edifice. Hans Vorhauer had picked the round hotel with views in all directions for a tryst with his wife.

Rappone posted a nondescript surveillance van in the hotel

parking lot intending to wait out Vorhauer. The day wore on, and inside the van, four heavily armed U.S. Marshals kept a relentless eye on the hotel entrance, unable to leave the van even to use the bathroom. Any unusual movement would spook Vorhauer into fleeing. The surveillance continued all night long. By morning, Rappone had called for backup.

At 10 A.M., Vorhauer and his wife walked out of the hotel and were immediately surrounded by U.S. Marshals. The hit man raised his hands in surrender. He was wearing a light jacket, a hat, and sunglasses, and when he removed the hat his hairstyle was dramatically different: It was cut short and bleached blond.

"Good work, Visual Detective. I don't know how you do it," said a still-stunned Schneider, who had dropped by the studio to congratulate his artist partner. "A lot of people owe you an apology."

"Good work yourself," Bender said. "You're the best detective I've ever worked with."

"Want to go get a beer?"

"Nah, I've got to paint this head."

Schneider looked at the bust of a dead man with a familiar face. "The Man in the Cornfield," Bender called the unidentified white male in his twenties whose corpse had been found by a farmer plowing his fields in Lancaster County, Pennsylvania. Over the weeks they had worked together on the Vorhauer case, Schneider had watched him transform the skull of the Man in the Cornfield into a clay mold and finally a plaster cast. The white plaster bust had a heroic profile, a handsome long-haired young man with a strong jaw and a noble nose. The Man in the Cornfield looked like Theseus about to face the Minotaur. "Now that you've found Vorhauer"—Bender nodded toward the head—"maybe you can find out who this guy is."

Schneider smirked. "You know nothing about him, right?"

"Nope, nothing."

Lines of discontent etched the sides of the detective's mouth. "Yeah, right. Tens of thousands of missing people in this country, and you want me to pull him out of a hat. I'm no magician. You think you are?"

The artist's eyes glittered. "No, it's a team effort."

On his way home from Bender's Philadelphia studio, Schneider stopped at the Upper Darby Police Department to get his mail. He hadn't been to the station in weeks. When he wasn't on loan to the U.S. Marshals Service, Schneider worked as a township detective, and because of his years investigating the Warlocks—and Vorhauer's fellow escapee Nauss—Schneider was chosen as a key member of the Vorhauer and Nauss fugitive task forces. He was known in the department as an expert on biker gangs. As soon as he walked in the door, an officer hailed him to look at a photograph in a missing-person flyer. The officer said he'd just learned from an informant that the missing person in the flyer was a man named Edward Meyers, who had been killed by a biker gang and buried in the Pennsylvania hills.

"This is the guy. Do you know him?"

Schneider's face opened in surprise. Staring out at him from the photograph was the Man in the Cornfield. "No, I don't know him, but I saw him not fifteen minutes ago in Frank Bender's studio."

Oblivious to his colleague's smirks and wisecracks, Schneider returned to the studio, and he and Bender held the flyer photograph alongside the bust. The Man in the Cornfield was a double for Edward Meyers. Police would match Meyers's dental records to the skull and confirm it.

"We're on a roll, Visual Detective," Schneider said. He had been a step behind Nauss for many frustrating years during the biker's reign of terror on his home turf. He saw this as his big chance. "Now we've got to find Nauss."

"Piece of cake, partner." Bender beamed in pride, his silver incisor winking in his own skull.

Bender and Schneider were secretly excited about their chances of finally nabbing Vorhauer's partner, the convicted killer Robert Thomas Nauss. Their enthusiasm was not dampened by the fact that the cunning Nauss had been on the lam for years after the prison break without once being seen by law enforcement, or that there was no reliable new information about his whereabouts or appearance. Nothing.

Success was all but assured, though it wasn't something they could discuss with most cops. It had been foretold by a psychic.

The psychic was Penny Wright, a nearly blind woman who had helped Schneider on several cases. The marshal had taken Bender to meet her several weeks earlier, and she had predicted that they would capture their next fugitive in a building with a large column. After the Vorhauer arrest at the Quality Inn, Schneider and Bender realized the hotel's unusual architecture was itself a large column. With new significance, they recalled Wright's other prediction that after the column arrest the next fugitive they would catch would be a man with a bad stomach. Schneider was fired with excitement. "Nauss was shot in the stomach by a fellow Warlock gang member when he was younger," he said. "I bet his stomach is giving him trouble."

Bender agreed. Schneider looked at his Visual Detective partner with a widening sense of possibilities. He'd been chasing fugitives for a decade, to country safe houses and urban hideaways, against impossible odds. But now it seemed that even the Most Wanted criminals were merely hiding in folds and twists in time, their movements apparent to the strangely light-colored eyes of Frank Bender.

"Mr. Nauss," Schneider said, "must be the Man with the Bad Stomach."

Bender grinned.

"No doubt."

CHAPTER 13

THE MAN WITH THE BAD STOMACH

After midnight, Bender took Ella to the white underground room. They danced and drank vodka in clear glasses. Outside the wind wailed over the dark shuttered row houses and dying river. They watched David Lynch's *Blue Velvet*. Bender was reminded of Lynch's dark but lovely Philadelphia vision and felt it "downloading" into him. "Philadelphia [is] . . . fantastically beautiful," the filmmaker wrote. "Factories, smoke, railroads, diners, the strangest characters, the darkest night . . . so much fear and crime that just for a moment there was an opening to another world . . . I just have to think of Philadelphia now, and . . . I hear the wind, and I'm off into the darkness somewhere." It was a blast of energy, but nothing helped.

In the middle of the night Ella returned home to her husband and two children in New Jersey. Bender crawled into bed with Jan for a brief, tortured rest. The sun rose pale and fractured by the dirt-streaked skylights. It was July, the steaming summer of 1987, and nothing could possibly help. His muse was gone.

"The Harmony of Form" was the name he gave his muse. Harmony was the blissful grace that allowed him to feel the inevitable shape of a dead man's mouth based on the eyes and nose. He entered a trancelike state of creation that others mistook for God-like arrogance. In fact, in these moments Bender felt the lowest humility and love for the implicit order of things. "There's a harmony flowing through everything: art, music, shape. Sometimes you can just feel the way things are and ought to be," he said. Sometimes not. And then he was like a junkie standing before the last clinic cut from the budget.

Without his muse, the half-formed head of the sadistic killer Robert Thomas Nauss was a stubborn scornful lump of undead clay, a brown-mud Beelzebub. The reborn killer, of Bender's own creation, seemed to be hiding from his true form, mocking him in a battle of wills. He felt like he lived with the spirit of his subjects, and Nauss was proving even trickier and nastier than Vorhauer. He was staring at the Warlock's merciless clay eyes when the telephone scattered the cats in the shadows of the warehouse.

"Frank Bender." His voice was clear and strong, an inverse of the chaos around him. The man on the phone introduced himself as Bob Leschorn, chief inspector of the U.S. Marshals Service at headquarters in McLean, Virginia. He sounded smooth and businesslike, with that commanding charm that's a half size too small to cover the blunt impatience of power.

"I've heard about your work on Vorhauer and Nauss, Frank. We need your help on a very important and sensitive case. I'm calling to see if you'll consider doing it."

"Sure, great! I'll do anything I can to help." Bender's breath came a little faster. His commercial photography was inconsistent and money was tight; he needed the work badly. Jan would be thrilled with another federal case—this time from the very top of the pyramid.

"Good. But let's take it one step at a time. We can't talk about this on the phone. We have to be very covert about this. It's an extremely dangerous fugitive, Ten Most Wanted. My assistants will bring you to me. Meanwhile, Frank, I don't want you to mention this to anyone. Not to friends in the police department, the FBI, even marshals not working on the case."

"That won't be a problem."

"We don't want anyone to know, not even your wife."

Jan wasn't interested in the details of his work, and Bender was uncomfortable sharing case information with anyone, even with Ella. He'd just have to be careful to cover or hide the new bust when anyone visited the studio.

"OK," he replied.

Three mornings later, marshals Tom Conti and Steve Quinn picked him up in a dark sedan with tinted windows. As they hurtled south on I-95, the deputies said they were driving him to the Philadelphia airport, and the chief inspector was flying up from Virginia to meet him. The only flight information the chief supplied was "afternoon." As the marshals scurried around the airport trying to find his flight, Bender sensed the chief was testing him and his men, as well as taking security precautions. They waited two hours for the flight to arrive.

Leschorn was in his fifties, tall and graying, a spit-and-polish lawman in an expensive suit and tie. He took them into an airport restaurant and chose a table in a back corner. After the waitress disappeared with their order, he leaned toward Bender and lowered his voice to describe the case while the deputies kept a watchful eye on the door. Leschorn said they were looking for Alphonse "Allie Boy" Persico, the underboss of the Colombo crime family in New York City. Persico, fifty-seven, had been groomed to be the godfather of one of the five major American crime families, along with his even more notorious brother, Carmine "The Snake" Persico. The Persico brothers had come up through the ranks as feared enforcers for the Colombo family. The titular heirs to the late, legendary godfather Joseph Colombo, the Persico boys had trouble staying out of jail. Allie Boy had served sixteen years for murder in Sing Sing, the maximum-security prison in Ossining, New York—allegedly taking the rap for his brother. After his conviction in 1980 for extortion and loan sharking, he jumped a $250,000 bail and went into hiding rather than face twenty more years in jail. He'd been on the lam for seven years.

The high-profile Persico had been so elusive a fugitive the FBI decided to wash its hands of the case and had recently pushed it over to the marshals. After spending a fortune on a worldwide manhunt following a trail of fake identifications and aliases, the bureau didn't even know if the mafioso was still alive. "The last seven years basically we have been getting anonymous tips," a federal spokesman said. "They were taking us all over the world— tips that he was in Honolulu, Japan, Miami, South America. They were numerous but they never panned out."

Leschorn emphasized the need for secrecy and speed. Even among the marshals, Persico had attained the status of He Who Must Not Be Named. Deputies could refer to him only by a code name.

"This is a top priority for the service," he said. "We're putting a lot of resources into this."

Bender smiled to himself. He knew the marshals liked to show up the FBI on big cases to affirm their reputation as the world's best bounty hunters. They saw themselves as the true hard-nosed federal lawmen, little known compared to their more glamorous, pretentious federal brethren.

Leschorn pushed two small prison photographs of Persico across the table to Bender. The three-by-five head shots showed the mobster in profile and also looking straight out of the photograph. They were nearly twelve years old. Like for Vorhauer and Nauss, current photographic evidence was nonexistent.

"What happened to his face?" Bender asked. The whole left side of his face below the eye looked like he'd slept on a pillow of pebbles and nails, leaving permanent scars. Trailing the swath of scars, part of his lower lip was dark blue.

"He got in a fight in Sing Sing and someone threw acid in his face," Leschorn said.

Whether he'd had plastic surgery since then nobody knew.

"This isn't much," Bender said.

"Are you willing to do it?" Leschorn wanted a finished bust in ten days.

Bender would need the same unlikely combination of art, science, and divination known as "age progression" that had nabbed Vorhauer and was stymieing him with Nauss.

"Absolutely." He grinned, with the shiny, drunken look he had when reality exceeded his need for stimulation. He wasn't happy unless the impossible odds against him held a tiny chance he could be a hero. "I need to find out everything I can about him."

The feds knew little. In the twelve-year-old photos, Persico was a lean, forty-five-year-old man who fancied himself a playboy, dark-haired and olive-complected with a dark mustache. He was a heavy smoker and drinker, and preferred Scotch. He was married, but had many other women.

His longtime girlfriend was Mary Bari, a stunning five-foot-two brunette he met when she was fifteen and he was pushing forty. In the glamorous heyday of the New York mob, he showered her with diamonds, furs, trips to Vegas, nights on the town in the white Rolls-Royce with pistol-packing bodyguard. In 1984, while away from her in hiding, he arranged for her to work as a cocktail waitress at the wiseguys' Wimpy Boys Social Club in Brooklyn so she could make a little money and hang out with the family.

She arrived at the club for the interview dressed like a gangland knockout in pearls, tank top, high heels, and a snakeskin belt, and was warmly embraced by longtime pal Greg Scarpa Jr., son of the capo. Scarpa held her tight as his father, Greg "The Grim Reaper" Scarpa Sr., came up for a kiss. Instead he pulled a gun and put three bullets in her head. They dumped Mary on the street two blocks away. She had been rumored to be talking to the FBI about Persico's hideout.

"Jesus," Bender said later when he heard the story. "This guy makes Vorhauer look like a gentleman."

The marshals believed Persico was alive and living in Florida or Connecticut, popular mob hideouts.

As Bender worked on the bust, the marshals shuttled him between Philadelphia and New York, the base of the Persico operation, on a plane with the tightest security. Deputies prevented security or even the pilot from inspecting the fiberglass box seat-belted next to Bender. Bender finished in ten days, depicting the aging mafioso with a shrunken face beneath dyed dark hair and mustache. An ex-mobster in the witness protection program who'd seen Persico in recent years previewed the bust for the marshals. The head looked good.

Four months later, around five o'clock on the afternoon of Monday, November 9, 1987, a marshal spoke to the landlady at a garden apartment building in West Hartford, Connecticut. It was one of 150 addresses they had to run down—150 Connecticut men, culled from a database of thousands, whose driver's license listed a similar height, weight, and birth date to Persico's, and whose surname ended in a vowel. A caravan of seven more marshals parked on the street, loaded with firepower.

The marshal showed the landlady the twelve-year-old photographs of Persico. She shook her head. "I don't know who that is." He showed her the recent photograph of Bender's bust. "Oh, that guy lives right upstairs. John Longo. He just called me to come up and look at his stove. He's making sauce and the stove went out. He's not too happy about it."

The marshal smiled. "Don't worry, we'll fix his stove." The phalanx of federal agents approached the door. Persico was known to be armed and extremely dangerous, and traveled with armed bodyguards. But now he answered the door himself. The underboss was alone, fretting over his spaghetti sauce.

The deputy flashed his badge. The aging mafioso's withered, scarred face darkened. But he gave up without a struggle. Deputies found $7,300 in cash in the apartment, which was rented by a woman not his wife. The underboss was receiving money from the mob in New York and preparing to help lead the Colombo family out of a dark hour.

Allie Boy had eluded marshals for seven years by living a drab existence. After being nearly caught at a California track, he sentenced himself to padding around his Connecticut apartment in slippers, cooking, watching TV soaps, and reading newspapers.

The flashy underboss would have been "taken down a lot earlier" if he'd continued to indulge his weaknesses for the horses, straight whiskey, and "lots of broads," a New York marshal said. Instead, said the marshal, "From what we've pieced together, he lived moderately and read a lot of newspapers. It does sound like jail."

The year before, his brother had been sentenced to a hundred years in prison on racketeering charges in a massive federal case that put away eight men who ruled the American Mafia through "The Commission." Thanks to Bender, Allie Boy would soon join them behind bars.

The sculptor was feted with international publicity. The deputies marveled that Persico's thin face, dyed dark hair, and mustache were the living image of the bust. "This case drove us crazy," the top Brooklyn marshal, Michael Pizzi, told United Press International. "But the bust turned out to be accurate." Said another marshal spokesman, "We hit pay dirt."

PERSICO RAN OUT OF THYME, quipped the New York *Daily News*.

Bill Fleisher's beard expanded around the oval of his mouth.

"Allie Boy Persico? I can tell you all about Allie Boy Persico!"

Bender had been prohibited from discussing the case with his friend until it was wrapped up, but now, three weeks later, he was celebrating at his regular luncheon with Fleisher. Bender was in a jovial mood. Once again he'd predicted the unpredictable path of time across a killer's face. The head he dubbed "Scarface" had been one of his most satisfying cases.

Fleisher wagged his big head. He felt that he and Bender were connected by whatever invisible strings the universe was pulling. "When I was with the FBI, I was assigned to the Colombo family squad in New York, and we were always chasing Allie Boy. We went to his farm in upstate New York and arrested him on an Alcohol, Tobacco, Firearms, and Explosives charge—he had an illegal rifle. It was early morning, and he smelled terrible. I don't think he brushed his teeth. And he looked like he hadn't slept. I interviewed him in the New York State Police barracks near his farm. He was a typical wiseguy of that era from Brooklyn, kind of gruff but charming. I can't say he wasn't a gentleman, except he'd kill you if you looked at him the wrong way."

Bender laughed. The luncheon marked a major triumph of his new life in forensic art.

Fleisher raised an iced-tea toast. "I don't know how you do it, Frank. You're a major asset to law enforcement in this country. Allie Boy was a big fish. I remember he had a bad stomach. Lots of ulcers."

"Allie Boy?" Bender leaned forward abruptly.

"Yeah."

Bender's mouth unhinged. His light hazel eyes got a shade lighter. He recalled one of the few things the marshals told him about Persico—the underboss had stomach problems. Allie Boy could eat only certain foods.

"My God, Penny Wright was on the money."

Bender told Fleisher about the psychic whom Paul Schneider took him to and her prediction that the next fugitive the marshals caught after Vorhauer would have stomach troubles. Schneider had prayed it would be Nauss, whom he believed had stomach troubles from an old .22 wound in the gut.

"It's Allie Boy," Bender said with a far-off look, turning the words over like golden coins of prophecy. "Allie Boy Persico is the man with the bad stomach."

Now they'd have to catch Nauss without unseen help.

CHAPTER 14

ON THE TRAIL OF THE WARLOCK

Before he escaped from prison in a pine armoire like Odysseus breaching the walls of Troy in a wooden horse, Robert Thomas Nauss had more in common with the monsters of antiquity than its heroes. He was a lean young man with a bearded face like a portrait of Jesus and soft brown eyes that blazed like a biker from hell. Men in Delaware County, Pennsylvania, quaked when Bobby Nauss strode into a bar with his Warlock gang members, bristling with black leather, chains, and threat. His soulless eyes were the last mortal sight of several pretty young women who vanished into the Tinicum marshes, police believed. Nauss was convicted of one murder and suspected of two others, in addition to his convictions for rape, robbery, and drug trafficking.

On the evening of December 11, 1971, the Warlock leader went on a date with his petite blond girlfriend, Elizabeth Landy, a twenty-one-year-old Philadelphia beauty queen. At the home of a fellow biker, they got into an argument and he tried to choke her, but Elizabeth hid in a locked bathroom. Later they made up and went to bed—where he bludgeoned her to death with a baseball bat. He strung her corpse up in a garage to show off to his biker buddies, and boasted, "She won't bother me anymore." Nauss cut off her hands and feet and covered her with lime to hasten decomposition and buried her in a shallow grave near the New

Jersey Pine Barrens. Nauss was the first man in Pennsylvania history, convicted of first-degree murder without a body. Landy has never been found. Nauss, too, had disappeared since his escape from Graterford with Vorhauer three years before.

Bender stood back and looked at his bust of Nauss, or what he thought time and trouble had done to Nauss's boyish face. It was less than a month after Vorhauer's arrest, and the U.S. Marshals were waiting for Bender's age-progression bust to jump-start another investigation, to reveal their quarry. Equally important, his wife, Jan, was expecting him to perform a second miracle to keep alive his string of big federal cases and its promise of bigger money. He had almost nothing to go on, less even than he had known about Vorhauer. At least there had been recent sightings of Vorhauer in the Philadelphia area, raw material for his sketches. There had been no sightings or leads in the Nauss case. The last photographs of Nauss were nearly a decade old, his 1977 intake pictures from the prison. In those photos Nauss was five foot nine, a lean, muscular, 190 pounds, bearded. His powerful arms were tattooed with a blue parrot, a skull and dagger, a swastika, and the legend "Born to Lose."

Bender studied the prison photograph of the menacing biker, then looked back at the bust. The bust depicted a conservative, thirty-five-year-old man in a button-down shirt collar. The new Nauss was clean-shaven, with short, neat, dark hair trimmed over the ears. The killer resembled a young Clark Kent. No matter how hard he tried to depict the biker as a burly thug in middle age, his fingers sculpted an all-American suburban family man.

Bender nervously ran his teeth over his lower lip. His muse was directing him; the harmony in nature and proportion that just felt right when he achieved it. But he could hear the marshals guffawing once more.

The mob hit man was a blond, and now the killer biker was Mr. Main Street, clean-cut Rotarian, straight as a banker's son-in-law?

He saw their faces twisted with skepticism. *Where we gonna arrest him, at the chamber of commerce breakfast? The country club?*

Bender's gut told him he was right once again. As a rule, he didn't doubt himself any more than the moon questioned its pale light or the river its banks. He was the natural. He was the artist who saw dead people. Still, he possessed the humility of a perfectionist, the pride of a craftsman. He liked to check and recheck his assumptions. He was always eager to learn more.

After ten in the morning, he left the clean-cut killer's head and walked back to his living area to clean up and put on a fresh shirt. He'd been up half the night, stripped to the waist like a rough tattooed John the Baptist with his hands on the head of a sadistic killer, mixing water and clay in a purification rite for a murdered girl. He needed some air. The city was filled with beautiful women and opportunity, he thought.

He combed his thinning blond hair in the mirror by the Fertility Godhead he had sculpted. Before noon, he threw on his coat and walked out into a bright fall morning, trailing his compact shadow along the broken sidewalk.

Eighteen blocks later, he went through a wide door into a great Egyptian-style lobby with sand-colored columns on all four sides supporting a balcony, and a chandelier that had dazzled presidents since Calvin Coolidge. The old Benjamin Franklin Hotel, affectionately dubbed "The Ben," as it stooped over the years like a favorite tattered old uncle, had been the scene of a few crimes since 1925. But it had never seen anything like the hundreds of private eyes, blood-spatter experts, medical examiners, and even a few hypnotists who crowded the hotel that morning. The prestigious American Academy of Forensic Sciences convention was in town.

As Bender crossed the lobby, he hardly had time to recall his simmering resentment of the AAFS—he could speak before them but not join without a college degree—when a sturdy woman with strong hands flashed a friendly smile and a broad Oklahoma hello. Big, round horn-rimmed glasses magnified soft eyes that Hollywood would have picked to serve homemade pie. The look was deceiving. Betty Pat Gatliff was the grande dame of forensic artists. She'd helped pioneer the profession worldwide. She'd done a facial reconstruction of King Tut published in *Life* magazine. Working with her forensic teammate, legendary anthropologist Clyde Snow, she'd rebuilt the skulls of seven of the unidentified victims of serial killer John Wayne Gacy.

Bender and Gatliff had met through the "Bone Detective" Wilton Krogman, who had worked with Eliot Ness and mentored the leading figures in what was once called "Skeletal ID." Many years after his work on the Boy in the Box case, Krogman had introduced Bender to the facial skin thickness charts that had been developed since the nineteenth century. He had inscribed his classic book, *The Human Skeleton in Forensic Medicine,* to Frank Bender, "A fellow seeker in the vineyard of the forensic sciences."

The bone cobblers exchanged a friendly hug, then went off to sit in the coffee shop alone, de rigueur for their grisly exclusive club.

Bender described the Nauss case and turned his palms up. "Betty, I need help," he said. "I don't have enough information about the subject." Gatliff was talking about the challenge of rebuilding a Florida murder victim's skull, missing the entire maxilla, for goodness sakes, when a tall, gaunt man in a blue suit appeared at the table and exclaimed, through a wisp of menthol smoke, "Betty!"

"Richard!" Gatliff said warmly. She gestured to her fellow artist. "Frank Bender, let me introduce you to my good friend Richard Walter. Richard is a forensic psychologist and criminal profiler."

Bender gawked at the thin man's long, withered face. He had the formal manners of a Victorian gentleman, but his small blue eyes glittered with irony. He hadn't seen such a strange man since he caught *The Fall of the House of Usher* on cable.

Walter's cold eyes appraised the small, muscular artist with his tight black T-shirt and cocksure grin—a face like James Dean on laughing gas. The forensic psychologist pushed his large round black spectacles down on his nose and said sardonically, "Oh, my dear boy, I see we're overdressed."

Bender howled with laughter. A guy who put himself out there like that, he thought, had to be a genius to back it up. Bender's laughter came from deep in his gut, a bold, infectious sound.

"Why don't you join us?" the artist said with his natural eagerness, as effusive as a twelve-year-old boy. "We're talking about cases."

Walter smirked and further lowered the black spectacles on his aquiline nose. "I hope your talent exceeds your couture," he said.

Bender laughed again even louder, ringing notes of pure joy. Gatliff grinned. Heads turned in the coffee shop.

Walter flushed to the flinty edge of his chin. It was terrible, he thought, the unwanted attention that TV crime shows had drawn to classic forensic science. He wanted to talk to Betty, not this straggler, clearly not a member of the academy. "Typical R. Walter, I became covertly hostile and sarcastic," he recalled. "But Frank stuck like glue. I couldn't get rid of the guy, and he laughed at my jokes. How can you hate anybody who laughs at your jokes?"

"What are you working on, Rich?" Walter bristled as he sat down. No one called him Rich.

"A few of us have been asked to do a profile of Jack the Ripper on the one hundredth anniversary of the murders, using modern profiling techniques," Walter said. He lit a cigarette, shook the match out with two fingers, and leaned back to take a smoke.

"We'll be presenting at the Home Office in London," he said, going on, raising an eyebrow with good humor. "I had never looked at the case before, but it's really quite obvious who the Ripper was. They got it right in the beginning but didn't know why."

Bender ogled the thin man. He had never met anyone like him. Lowering his head in his earnest fashion, Bender described his struggles doing the Nauss bust for the U.S. Marshals.

"I don't know enough about the killer to be sure," he said.

"Tell me about the murder," Walter said.

Nauss, Bender said, had rejected his middle-class childhood to become a leader of the violent Warlock motorcycle gang. He described Nauss's murder of Landy in detail.

"The problem is I don't know enough about him to depict how he looks. The photographs are a decade old, and I don't know his personality or habits. Is he married or single? Still slim or spreading with middle age? How does he eat? Does he exercise?"

Walter raised his eyebrow, signaling his interest. "I can tell you a bit about him. I've seen hundreds of cases like this, many involving bikers. He's tremendously macho, aggressive, with an exaggerated sense of importance. He's very concerned about image. He dispatched the body brutally, like tossing away trash, and simply for reasons of power, not sex or fantasy or Satanism or any other such nonsense. He's just tired of her and wants to move on."

Bender's eyes gleamed like go lights. "Rich, maybe you and I could work on this case together."

Walter frowned at Bender and leaned back, eyeballing him as if from a safe distance. He took a draw on his Kool and let the silence develop.

Bender leaned forward into the vacuum, speaking faster and with great enthusiasm.

"Rich, why don't you come talk to the marshals tonight? I can set it up."

"I'm afraid not, dear boy. It's well known I won't have my libations at the hotel bar interrupted."

Bender laughed again. Walter took a long draw on a cigarette and turned inward. *Bender is a very intense character, very intense, bright but off the wall,* he thought. *What the hell is he all about? Oh, well, I'll never see him again.*

At six the next morning, Walter shot out of a deep sleep in his hotel room. The telephone was ringing.

"Hi, Rich!" Bender sounded like he'd had five cups of coffee.

Oh, God, Walter thought. *What have I gotten myself into now?* He sat on the edge of the bed and reached for a Kool.

"The marshals want to meet with you today!"

Walter went to breakfast at the Downhome Diner with Bender and Tom Rappone, head of the U.S. Marshals Service fugitive task force in Philadelphia, to discuss the Nauss case. Bender played a trick on the somber psychologist. "You've got to try scrapple, Rich. It's a classic Pennsylvania delicacy. You'll love it."

"What is it?"

"Meat." The artist grinned.

Walter looked down at the odiferous brown extrusion of last-chance pork parts, snarled, and pushed his plate a foot away as Bender exploded in schoolyard laughter. Walter quietly took in black coffee and a cigarette, turning a hard flat gaze on the boisterous clown who seemed to be forcing his way into his life. "I was not pleased."

At four that afternoon, the thin man sat in a conference room at the marshals' office at Sixth and Market streets with Bender. With them at the table were Rappone and two other deputies.

"Listen up," Rappone said.

Walter looked down at a yellow pad filled with scribbled notes, and cleared his throat.

"I've conducted a brief crime assessment of the Nauss murder," he said. "Nauss was a closet case in the motorcycle gang in that he was very high up, but he also wanted to be in the mob, a promotion as it were. He had a middle-class background, and he's going to be a little brighter than your average semi-organized PA killer and he's going to be clever. He's going to clean himself up a little bit, be not as scruffy; he'll have more options available to him."

Walter looked down at his pad. "Frank Bender is right. He'll be clean-cut and living in the suburbs. He'll be married to a compliant woman who has no idea about his past, and present a wholesome image to the community."

Bender beamed like the father of a newborn son. "I agree with Rich. I think Nauss will be clean-shaven, short-haired, and living in suburbia," he said. "He's come from a good family and I think he'll go back to what he's known."

The marshals exchanged doubtful looks across the table. One deputy pointed out that their few leads were consistent with a biker lifestyle. The marshals had set up a cabin in the Poconos for several weeks following a tip that the biker was hiding out in the

Pennsylvania mountains. They followed another tip to a Western state, and set up surveillance across from a motorcycle parts distributor, with no luck.

Dennis Matulewicz, one of the lead agents, frowned. "I don't know about this. A biker is a biker is a biker."

Walter cleared his throat. "Not only is Frank right that Nauss is hiding in the suburbs, I have some idea what suburbs."

Rappone leaned forward, his voice nearly caught in his throat. "How do you know that?"

Walter that morning had called the Southern Michigan Prison at Jackson, with 5,600 inmates, the world's largest penal institution. The massive 1934-era prison complex, known as "Jacktown," was one of the most notorious and feared of American prisons. Riots in the 1950s and 1970s had killed a guard and injured dozens of guards and inmates. Walter had recently started working there as a prison psychologist, counseling and evaluating the most depraved criminals in the state.

He had spoken on the telephone that morning with an inmate who had been a member of Nauss's Pennsylvania motorcycle gang.

A heavy silence came over the table.

"Those guys never talk," a deputy said.

Walter nodded. "Quite true. It is a fact that a gang member, a criminal biker, is a very rigid, power-based personality. As such he is extremely loyal and pathological in how he counts on the group. He has rigid standards and principles." Walter paused and raised his eyebrow for dramatic effect. "But one can use that rigidity against him." The marshals fell silent, waiting.

"I made the point that Nauss had shot somebody," Walter said. "OK, fine, a real man can shoot someone. But he had shot and killed them in front of their child. It's not macho to kill people in front of their children. It's not a good thing; he'd broken a rule. And I used that to break apart the biker's loyalties. Nauss was not living up to biker standards, Nauss was a bad guy, he'd done bad things, he'd not lived by the code a man must live by. I undermined Nauss's masculinity to get the guy to talk."

Walter smiled coldly. "I will sometimes sleep with the devil to get what I want. As it happens, Nauss is living somewhere in Michigan."

Walter picked up several photographs of Nauss. He noted that the biker always wore a shirt that was patterned on one side and not the other. "It's part of the personality type. He's a black and white guy; there are no grays. I'll tell you that when you find him in Michigan, Nauss will be driving a black Cadillac."

Rappone's brow crinkled in puzzlement. "How do you know that?"

"Ah," Walter said. "Fair enough. We know he liked Cadillacs in the past. Cadillacs are prestige cars and he is a power guy who wants prestige and is cleaning up. Particularly rigid types like dark cars. Given his killer instincts it'd be either white or black, and he'd go for black. It's declarative, pureness and evil at the same time."

The faces around the table fell open with something like awe.

Bender's grin grew wider. The marshals planned to present his finished bust of Nauss to *America's Most Wanted,* the Fox TV show. Bender could see that a man like Walter could be of great use in the future.

"It's not wizardry," Walter said later as they left the federal building. "It's all a matter of probabilities. I've been around the block a few times."

"Rich," Bender said, "you can read criminals' minds the way I read women."

Walter's face darkened around a scowl as Bender's laugh rang down the gray canyon of Market Street.

In February 1988, *America's Most Wanted* broadcast Bender's bust of Nauss. The sculpted face of the biker appeared dark-haired and clean-cut. Dozens of calls came in to the show's tip line with sightings of Nauss from the East to the Midwest, but none amounted to anything.

Assuming he was still alive, the escaped prisoner and convicted killer remained at large.

CHAPTER 15

THE RELUCTANT KNIGHT-ERRANT

Richard Walter was sitting in his small, classical white house in Lansing, Michigan, sipping wine and listening to opera in the civilizing presence of his antiques. The scowling, life-size samurai warrior, sword raised to attack, was a particular favorite. He was recalling his chat that day with a serial killer when the telephone rang, and he frowned.

Walter had been promoted to the largest walled prison in the world, the Southern Michigan Prison at Jackson, from the desolate castle prison on Lake Superior. The high-tech prison gave him remarkable power over the inmates. He could turn off their hot showers by a remote switch, or put them on a diet of "Prison Loaf"—all their meals blended and baked into a hard, tasteless brick. "You will learn to control yourself or I will control you," he told them. Control gave him satisfaction, victory over chaos, and thus he found the voice on the telephone disconcerting. It blasted through the line, as loud and excited as a television car pitchman.

"Rich!"

He rolled his eyes. No one else called him that. Although Walter liked the forensic artist, he didn't enjoy being "shaped" by anyone. Furthermore, he didn't feel the need for human contact at that moment. He would dispatch of Bender quickly.

"Rich, a producer at *America's Most Wanted* called me, and

they want me to do a facial age progression of John List—the most wanted mass murderer in America."

"That's wonderful, Frank. I hope it works out for you."

"He's the bank vice president who killed his whole family in New Jersey. He's been on the lam for eighteen years!"

"Yes."

"He's committed the most notorious crime in New Jersey since the Lindbergh baby was kidnapped in 1922."

"It was 1932, Frank."

"Right."

Walter said nothing, creating a vacuum in the conversation. It was like a drawbridge pulling up.

Bender waded into the moat. "Rich, I thought maybe you'd want to help me. You could do the profile. I told *AMW* about you and they're all for it."

Walter said nothing. He looked around the room. His music, books, the classical lines of the library—for years these had been his constant companions. Home alone with a bottle of wine, he gazed fondly at his antiques and felt the powerful presence of the men and women who had lived with them; he imagined these spirits as friends and family. He was quite happy living alone. "In point of fact," he said, "I care not a whit for the general run of humanity."

Although he was compulsively charming and social, and regaled perfect strangers in bars with true-life Gothic horrors like a slumming Poe, there were few people in the world he could really talk to, even in law enforcement. He had married his profession, driven to be "one of the five best in the world," and accepted the sacrifices. He was obsessed with things that decent people were happiest not knowing about. His was a dark vision, the same one that made Machiavelli and Dostoevsky embittered men and geniuses for the ages.

Now Bender was pushing him toward a partner's intimacy of the kind one saw in cop buddy movies and read about in storybooks. Instinctively he shrank from Bender's salesman's affect. "I quite like Frank," he said to himself. But bamboozling excitement was something normal people didn't use unless they were selling something shiny and hollow. In his long experience with the criminal and the craven, it was the tool of a seducer and user.

"Rich, why don't you come to Philadelphia? It's spring, the weather's nicer here. *AMW* will put you up in a bed-and-breakfast near my studio."

"We'll see what happens," Walter said stiffly.

"I really want to catch this guy. The FBI hasn't had a clue for decades, and now they're using computer-drawn facial reconstructions. They don't believe in what I'm doing—the old human way, the real artist way, looking for the unique human characteristics. I want to know what List was thinking when he killed his family, what he's like now. I want to get into his head."

Silence on the other end of the line.

"This will really show up the FBI when we nail him together."

Walter laughed. "Now you're talking."

The darkness of the studio surrounded the halo of light on the makeshift kitchen table.

On the table was a stack of newspaper clippings as yellow and wrinkled as the gaunt face studying them through owlish black glasses. *The New York Times, The Star-Ledger, Philadelphia Inquirer,* and most every newspaper and TV station in America had broadcast the horror story as chilling as a Stephen King serial.

On November 9, 1971, John Emil List, a former bank vice president and Sunday school teacher in prosperous Westfield, New Jersey, had killed his wife, three young children, and elderly mother. The fastidious killer had left the lights blazing in his great house, Breezy Knoll, along with a polite note apologizing to his mother-in-law, a thoughtful list of sales prospects for his boss at the insurance company, another note instructing his pastor to remove him from the congregation rolls. Fretting over the noise of his car, he'd steered the old Impala and its coughing muffler into a quiet pre-dawn November rain and disappeared.

Walter lit a Kool and leaned back with his right hand bringing the cigarette to his lips. His left hand crossed over to grip his right bicep and he took a draw and lowered his head to think. He had been reading for an hour. As soon as Walter arrived in Philadelphia on an early flight from Lansing, Michigan, Bender had attempted a hearty hug or slap on the back, but Walter had successfully pushed him off with a firm handshake.

Walter had Spartan needs on a case. An ashtray was essential, and black coffee. Bender offered to make coffee, but Walter snarled, "Not from *that* stove, my dear boy." Bender got him takeout, handed him the file of newspaper stories, and went off gallivanting.

It took a few minutes before the psychologist recovered from the decrepit atmosphere of the art studio. It seemed to him that Bender fancied himself a male version of Circe, a sorcerer who turned his visitors into supplicant females and shrunken heads.

Now Walter blocked out the background noise and odors and concentrated on the five murders. He envisioned each in its turn, until the monstrosity was reduced in his mind to cold-blooded calculation. Eighteen years before, List had made his move. Walter saw the slaughter as theatrically staged, an intricately planned performance designed to hide List's true motive in plain sight and cover his tracks. Now it was Walter's turn—his chance to unmask the deceit and expose the fugitive's hiding place. It was just the two of them in a deadly chess game, a battle of mind and will with no boundaries of time or space.

Killers always make mistakes. What mistakes had List made?

The cops always miss something. What had the FBI and the police missed?

Walter had been moonlighting as a consulting detective on the most challenging and depraved murder cases in the world for more than a decade. It was what he did in his "spare hours" while working full-time for the Michigan Department of Corrections.

CHAPTER 16

THE PERFECT MASS MURDER

Early on that November morning, John List stood at his office window on the first floor of Breezy Knoll and watched the milk truck drive away. As usual Herbert Arbast, the milkman, had entered the unlocked back door to the nineteen-room, three-story Victorian and entered the butler's pantry where Helen taped her handwritten order on the refrigerator: six quarts of milk, butter, and eggs, twice a week. That morning instead was posted a curt note from John instructing the milkman to stop deliveries "until further notice." The family was going on vacation, the neat, careful handwriting explained. List and his wife, Helen; Patty, the oldest, blond and leggy like her mother and a budding actress; the two young boys, Fred and John Jr.; and John's eighty-five-year-old mother, Alma, would be gone "for a while."

At forty-six years of age, John List stood a gangly six foot one, gaunt-faced and straight-backed, with receding dark hair and a long, bony jaw. An accountant, former bank vice president, and Sunday school teacher in the Lutheran Church, he was an exceptionally bright and meticulous man. On his desk lay two beautifully kept handguns, gleaming with oil—a small, .22-caliber automatic Colt that had belonged to his father, and a classic Steyr 1912 automatic John had brought back from World War II. The Steyr was a World War I gun that had been retooled by the Nazis to carry a special nine-millimeter cartridge. Each pistol was loaded with eight rounds.

As the milkman left, empty bottles rattling in his carrier, List stood listening for the routine noises of morning. He heard Helen's soft footsteps coming downstairs to the kitchen. With the gentle sounds of the flame firing under the kettle as it jangled onto the stove, he waited a few minutes, then picked up the Steyr. His wife was sitting at the breakfast table over toast and coffee, her morning wake-up ritual. She wore a bathrobe and red satin teddy, and looked out the window. She was dreaming her thoughts into the bleak gray sky, and heard nothing until she sensed a shadow two feet behind her and half-turned to look. She never saw her husband or the bullet he fired into the left side of her head from eighteen inches away. The shot knocked Helen to the linoleum floor, a bite of toast jammed into the back of her throat. Walter noted that List fired several aimless shots at the wall, one pinging a radiator, but the children were at school and heard nothing. If any noises escaped the foot-thick walls of Breezy Knoll, they were carried away on the cold November breeze. What police had called for decades the perfectly planned murders had begun to move like clockwork. As his wife lay dying on the kitchen floor, List headed up the back stairs.

His mother's cozy apartment, where he read the Bible with her most evenings, was on the third floor. Alma, tall and gray-haired, was standing in the small kitchen holding a plate with butter, waiting for the toast to pop, as he opened the door without knocking. "What was that noise downstairs?" she asked. Without a word, List raised the Steyr and shot his mother above the left eye from point-blank range. She died as she hit the tile floor. Walter noted, with one eyebrow arching above the old newspaper account, what List had done next. He shoved her body into a narrow hall space with a force that shattered her knees, and threw a carpet runner on top of her. He covered his dead mother's face with a dish towel.

Heading back downstairs, he dragged his wife's body through the center hall to the ballroom, and laid her facedown on a sleeping bag under the Tiffany dome skylight. He placed two other open sleeping bags perpendicular to Helen's, whose body formed the top of a T, and covered Helen's body with a bath towel. He covered his wife's head with a dish towel.

Next he went upstairs to his wife's bedroom, smeared his bloody hands all over the sheets until he vomited, then showered and shaved. Wearing a fresh suit and necktie, his hair combed and fingernails cleaned, he walked crisply downstairs as if to start an ordinary business day. There was much to do.

He called the office of State Mutual Life, where he sold insurance, and left a message on the machine canceling his ten o'clock appointment. He said he was taking the family to North Carolina to be with his wife's mother, who was seriously ill. Then he wrote school notes for his children—Patricia, sixteen, at the high school; and John Jr. and Frederick, fifteen and thirteen, at the junior high—explaining their absence for several days because of the emergency family trip. He went outside to rake leaves while waiting for the kids to come home from school. It was cloudy and nearly freezing, a record low for November 9, and a neighbor woman was surprised to see List in his dark overcoat and tie meticulously raking the yard. After working up a sweat, he fixed himself a sandwich and ate lunch at the table where he had killed his wife over breakfast.

Walter noted the steady, implacable routine. Mr. List was being productive and efficient. He was having a good day.

Shortly after noon, List picked up his daughter, Patty, at school. She was sick and had asked to come home, and didn't feel well enough to work her after-school job at the insurance office. As she gathered her books in the backseat, he walked quickly into the house before her, and was hiding behind the door when she entered the kitchen. List shot her in the head from behind. Dragging her body through the house, he made a forty-foot track of blood parallel to his wife's blood, and laid her on one of the open sleeping bags. He covered his daughter's face with a rag.

At one o'clock, List, cleaned up and, wearing fresh business attire, went into town to do errands. He put a thirty-day stop on the mail. At Suburban Trust bank, he cashed out more than $2,000 in U.S. savings bonds, the last of his mother's savings. She died unaware he'd already gone through all of the $200,000 her husband had left her. He mailed a special delivery letter to himself at Hillside Avenue with a key wrapped in a folded blank sheet of paper.

At approximately three o'clock, young Fred, his thirteen-year-old son, called from the insurance office where he, too, had an after-school job, wondering, "What happened to Patty?" He wanted to come home. List picked him up at the insurance office, drove home, and hurried into the house to retrieve the gun he'd left behind the kitchen door. He shot Fred in the back of the head before he got his coat off. His father pulled the boy's small body onto the sleeping bag beside Patty. He covered Freddie's face with a small rag.

At four o'clock, John Jr., his husky fifteen-year-old, came home early from soccer practice, and sprang away from his father hiding behind the door with a gun. He grabbed his father's hand as bullets blasted a kitchen cabinet, a dining room window frame, the ceiling. As List stalked his son through the house, a pistol in each hand, bullets caught the boy in the back, behind the neck, in the head, and he fell, breaking his jaw. Walter knew that a fifteen-year-old male had a narcissistic selfishness, a will to survive, unmatched at any other age, and John Jr. wouldn't quit. He crawled desperately away from his father in the parlor. List stood over him and pumped eight bullets into his oldest son. A ninth into the eye and a tenth through the heart were required before the boy would lie still.

List moved his wife's arm to rest on Freddie's shoulder, and as the fading light of late afternoon filtered through the stained-glass dome in a thousand colors, he knelt by his family and prayed for their souls. "Almighty, everlasting, and most merciful God, Thou who dost summon and take us out of this sinful and corrupt world to Thyself through death that we may not perish by continual sinning, but pass through death to life eternal, help us, we beseech Thee. . . ."

Walter studied the grainy newspaper photo of the ballroom crypt. "The accountant in him lined up the children by age," he said to himself.

It was a busy evening for List, making phone calls and methodically checking off items on his planner.

At seven o'clock, he phoned his Lutheran pastor and good friend Eugene Rehwinkel, apologizing because he would be unable to teach Sunday school class for at least a week. He explained to the director of the high school drama club that unfortunately Patty would have to miss rehearsals for a while, and so would be unable to continue as understudy in *A Streetcar Named Desire*. On stationery from a failed business enterprise, John E. List, Career Builder, he wrote to Eva Morris, his ailing mother-in-law whom the family was supposedly visiting in North Carolina:

> *Mrs. Morris,*
>
> *By now you no doubt know what has happened to Helen and the children. I'm very sorry that it had to happen. But because of a number of reasons, I couldn't see any other solution.*
>
> *I just couldn't support them anymore and I didn't want them to go into poverty. Also, at this time I know that they were all Christians. I couldn't be sure of that in the future as the children grow up.*
>
> *Pastor Rehwinkel may add a few more thoughts.*
>
> *With my sincere sympathy,*
>
> *John E. List*

Walter scowled at the faded words in the newspaper column. List wrote similar letters to his sister-in-law and to his mother's sister. *By now you know what has happened to Mother and the rest of the family. . . . Please accept my sincere condolences. John.* List spent the rest of the evening explaining his logic for killing his family in a blizzard of letters to family and his pastor, but he had outlined his reasons for the murders in the first note to his mother-in-law. He had lost his job at the bank and, consumed by failure, spent his days at the library when he said he was looking for work. Despite his recent efforts as an insurance salesman, the family was in dire straits. The fear of going bankrupt, moving, and putting the children on welfare weighed heavily on him. But his greater burden was the fear his children would go to hell. Helen refused to attend church, and the children were growing cynical about God. Patty's passion for acting indicated an immoral existence incompatible with a good Christian life. "So that is the sum of it," he wrote to his pastor. "If any one of these had been the condition we might have pulled through, but this was just too much. At least I'm certain that all have gone to heaven now. If things had gone on, who knows if that would be the case.

"I know that what I have done is wrong . . . but you are the one person that I know that, while not condoning this, will at least partially understand why I felt that I had to do this."

It was important to kill his mother, too, he added as an afterthought. "Knowing that she is also a Christian, I felt it best that she be relieved of the troubles of this world that would have hit her . . . to save Mother untold anguish over that result I felt it best that she be relieved from this vale of tears. . . . Originally I had planned this for Nov. 1—All Saints Day. But travel arrangements were delayed. I thought it would be an appropriate day for them to get to heaven."

List added one more thing for his pastor. "It may seem cowardly to have always shot from behind, but I didn't want any of them to know even at the last second that I had to do this to them. John got hurt more because he seemed to struggle longer. . . . Please remember me in your prayers. I will need them whether or not the government does its duty as it sees it. I'm only concerned with making my peace with God and of this I am assured because of Christ dying even for me. P.S. Mother is in the hallway in the attic—3rd floor. She was too heavy to move. John."

He wrote to Burton Goldstein at State Mutual Life thanking him for his support, and listing the four "best prospects for a quick sale . . . maybe Paul Greenberg can follow up on some." All the letters, the two guns, an envelope with the unused bullet, went into the filing cabinet into locked drawers labeled TO PASTOR REHWINKEL, BURTON GOLDSTEIN AND ADMINISTRATORS and GUNS & AMMO. He taped a note to the top of his desk:

> *To the Finder:*
> *1) Please contact the proper authorities.*
> *2) The key to this desk is in an envelope addressed to myself.*
> *3) The keys to the files are in the desk.*

Walter reviewed List's extensive documentation of the reasons that led to the massacre. It was an extraordinary record to be left by a killer. *And it's all bullshit,* he thought to himself.

Walter felt he knew the killer better than the murderer knew himself. That evening List quickly grew tired. He'd had a long day. He made a light dinner and once again ate at the table where he'd murdered his wife that morning, then washed the dishes and put them in the drainboard. He slept in the billiard room in the basement, beneath his murdered family. Though there was no information on it, Walter wagered that he'd slept very soundly. He said that for List, "It had been a wonderful day."

In the morning List packed his suitcase with two days' worth of clothes and a briefcase with an assortment of motor club maps, and tidied the house as if preparing for vacation. He turned the thermostat down to fifty degrees and put three supermarket bags stuffed with bloodied papers and cloths neatly by the back door. He switched the lights on in every room except for one, the ballroom crypt. Finally he turned the radio to the only station he had allowed the children to listen to. Classical music, good for the soul, filled the house as he drove away.

Ten days after the murders, a policeman writing parking tickets at JFK airport found List's old Impala, but the abandoned car raised no red flags. List had planned the murders so meticulously that nobody realized something was wrong at Breezy Knoll until police discovered the five bodies on December 7, almost a month later. The headlines trumpeted THE CRIME OF THE CENTURY. Overnight, List entered the upper echelons of twentieth-century mass killers that the media tracked like a home run contest.

Walter took a sip of cold black coffee and rubbed his eyes to focus. The newspapers described a massive, international manhunt for List that became an embarrassment to law enforcement.

No wonder they couldn't find him, Walter thought. *They didn't know what they were looking for.*

The FBI spent more than $1 million pursuing reported sightings of List across all fifty states, Europe, and South America. New Jersey police and prosecutors interviewed dozens of potential witnesses. The police catalogued more than 150 pieces of evidence. But the investigation went nowhere. Detectives resorted to black humor to overcome the shame. Vacationing police sent postcards to the department from Florida, Barbados, and elsewhere: *Wish you were here. Your good pal, John Emil List. Having a ball. Nice to finally have a vacation without the kids! John E. List.* The trail had long gone cold. The last significant evidence was the car discovered at the airport eighteen years before. In the police evidence room, mold grew on the dried blood on the victims' clothes, and the garments were discarded.

Walter looked up from the yellowed newspapers, his concentration broken. He heard Bender's voice and the voices of two women. It had only been an hour, but it felt like days had passed since he'd immersed himself in the case.

"How's it going?" Bender appeared at the kitchen table.

"Quite well."

The sculptor's eyes gleamed. "What else do you need?"

There was a lot of digging Walter could do. He could talk to the police and FBI investigators who spent years on the case. He could study the police file, read the mountain of interviews, look over the hundreds of photographs and pieces of evidence, review the psychological evaluations of List. He could reinterview potential witnesses, praying their memories hadn't evaporated.

Walter met Bender's eyes and said he needed nothing else. The yellowing newspaper accounts were sufficient. The grainy old newspaper photographs of the murder scene were particularly helpful. He didn't wish to read anything or talk to anybody. The killer had directly communicated to Walter all he needed to know.

"The profile is done," he said. "He thinks he's the smartest man in the world, and he pulled off the perfect crime, he's fooled everyone," Walter said. "But in point of fact he's not difficult to read."

List's extraordinary confessions, thousands of words of admitted guilt, were elaborate, carefully constructed deceptions, he said. "List spouts ink like a squid, to obscure himself from his pursuers." But unknowingly, he had left indelible documentation of the truth in a special language.

List had written out his motive and his fate in blood and bullets in the stone-walled rooms of Breezy Knoll.

CHAPTER 17

THE MASK OF THE INVISIBLE MAN

Sunlight and traffic noise flooded the dim studio, startling the gallery of grinning, frontal-nude blondes and somber heads of the dead. "Rich, let's go for a long walk! It's a beautiful day." Bender stood in the open door, a hazy dark shape within the blinding halo of light.

"My dear boy, my exercise is inhaling. Do I look like a sophomore on the cross-country team?" Walter chuckled from his chair, quite pleased with himself. The flexible lines of his mouth tugged downward around the cigarette-like tent stakes.

"C'mon, Rich!"

The thin man rose slowly. "Well, then. I suppose one could."

They walked down South Street. They were an odd pair, the short, loud, muscular, tattooed man firing questions at the tall, blue-suited, balding gentleman with stiff Victorian airs.

Bender wanted Walter's insights into List's character— character that would have helped shape the contours of the killer's face all these years later.

"I need to know what John List was like," Bender said. "How would John List stand on this corner? What would be the expression on his face?" As if on command, the tall man in the suit stood rigidly and tipped his long jaw into a double chin, like a game of charades in reverse.

"Here, let me show you which facial muscles stay tight and which lengthen." The thin man pushed his owlish black glasses back on his nose and appeared sterner than usual.

Bender's voice rose a pitch. "Rich, what would his face look like? I mean, he's sixty-four years old now. In his early forties, he had dark hair with a widow's peak of M-pattern baldness. I see him almost completely bald now, with tufts of gray hair on the side."

Walter nodded agreement. "Yes. And what little hair he has left will be carefully trimmed, very neat. He is still an accountant and careful about his appearance in a professional way."

"We know he has a scar behind his ear from mastoid surgery," Bender said. The artist had interviewed craniofacial surgeons at the University of Pennsylvania Medical School to document the aging process in the facial tissue, brow, eyelids, bone. Bender had also spent a few days in Westfield, watching the men of List's generation on the streets, and in church. He studied the faces, eyes, and mouths, their paunches and how they treated their wives. He had already made a rough clay head of List and sent a photograph of it to Westfield police for comment.

Bender had learned from the Philadelphia surgeons that the mastoid scar, though softened with age, would still show unless List had plastic surgery.

"I figure he wouldn't be the type to have plastic surgery," Bender said. "Or the type to go to the gym and work out."

"Exactly," Walter said. "He was a meat-and-potatoes man and would remain one. He's not from the jogging generation. He's a very rigid personality. It's the extreme rigidity, at a pathological level, that enables him to kill his family."

"So he'll have jowls now, a slackened jaw, and look much older."

"Quite."

They sat in a riverfront park crowded with its Saturday morning population of Frisbees, romping and sniffing dogs, young professionals, and homeless men. Walter lit a cigarette. Bender's eyes wandered to a tall blond woman chasing a black Labrador, and came back into focus.

"Do you think he's very religious? How will that alter how he looks or behaves?"

Walter frowned. "This has nothing to do with religion. Many terrible things are done in the name of God. It's just a cover. Behind his Caspar Milquetoast churchgoing façade, he was a pure psychopath all about power. He was fed up with his dominating wife and mother, the little brats who wouldn't listen to him, and he wasn't going to take it anymore. He wanted a new life and he wanted it on his terms."

The thin man's eyes shone with excitement. "This is the typical personality type of a man who destroys his family. It's a man who chooses a stronger, older woman who criticizes him so he will never have to take responsibility for himself. They can become quite pathological about it."

"So he's crazy."

"Oh, no, not at all. He's *extremely* rational. He's something of a snob, feels quite superior to other people. He lives beyond his means, the world starts to collapse on him. His first move is to plunder his mother's money, for years. No conscience. He deserves it, after all."

Bender took a deep breath. "So what pushed him over the edge?"

Walter gave a dark smile. "It's typical to have a strong matriarchal figure, like his mother, a wife who is aggressive and pushy and also status-seeking. Controlled, structured men who feel they are being pushed too far can seethe. That turns into anger and righteous indignation. He doesn't face challenges and own up to his failures like a man; all his failures are because of 'that bitch wife.' He's losing power, control, becoming more isolated. The threat increases when his daughter enters puberty. He is able to justify the killings in his own mind. He felt his family was demanding too much."

The thin man removed an old newspaper story, yellow and

creased into a permanent fold, from his suit pocket. "Notice the corpses of his wife, mother, and three children. He covers all their faces with rags or rugs or towels. I've seen this many times. The killer can't let the victim's eyes reproach him, and he can't let the victim's eyes see egress. It's the final trump card of rage and power. All the drama and the over-killing—he pumps ten bullets into his oldest son, shoots his mother and then breaks her kneecaps—is how he sates the rage that drove him to kill in the first place. When the rage is satiated, he feels an instant wash of relief and triumph."

"So is there anger in his face? Have anger and guilt worn him down over the years?"

Walter laughed out loud. "Guilt? Are you kidding me? He doesn't know what the word means. He doesn't feel anything at all, except for relief and triumph. He was thrilled with what he did! Thus he could coolly sit and call his pastor and his daughter's drama coach, eat lunch and dinner in the kitchen where he killed his wife over breakfast. The lack of guilt would allow him to disappear and adjust to a new life without any awkwardness. The following day to him was just that, the next day, except it's a great relief."

"You want to talk about guilt?" Walter continued. "List stalked his victims. It's very typical with this type. Note his conversation at the dinner table the week before, quizzing his children on how they would like to die."

Bender nodded.

Walter arched his left eyebrow. "May I be bold and make some predictions?"

"Sure."

"List would have settled into a reasonably comfortable life much like the one he left after a period of reinvention," Walter said. "At first, he would have moved a great distance from the crime to gain a sense of freedom. His first job would probably be a night clerk in a motel—a logical occupation for a bright but underachieving man, good with figures, who wanted a job where he would not be seen and recognized.

"As he grew comfortable, however, List would move up in the

accounting profession," Walter said. "He would rejoin the Lutheran Church, remarry, and eventually move back to within three hundred miles of the murder scene. He would not be able to tolerate the differences of another region that was alien to him. Familiar turf would give him a sense of control. Beneath the veneer of respectability, trouble would still be simmering. He'll still be living beyond his means. He'll still have financial problems."

List would fit in easily in a conventional suburban community, a steady churchgoing man of high intelligence with a serious look, the profiler said. "He'll be wearing a suit and tie. Given his history and rigidity, I figured the most modern he'd get would be to wear a striped suit. He'd always wear the white shirt and plain tie, probably striped. He'd also wear dark shoes and dark argyle socks. He'll be wearing thick, black glasses—not wire rims. It will give him an aura of intelligence and authority. He'll be remarried to a subservient woman who has no clue about his past. He's just good ol' John."

"Rich, this is great."

"Just so. You're asking brilliant questions. In the information game, the most important part of the equation is the question, not the answer."

That evening, Bender put the finishing touches on List. His age-progression bust had a broad, bald pate, deep wrinkles, sunken cheeks, and a stern, unforgiving mouth; the bust included the neck and shoulder line of a dark suit and white oxford collar. He found a pair of old tortoiseshell eyeglasses with a thick rim at an antiques store in the neighborhood, and put them on List.

They looked right.

On Sunday, May 21, 1989, *America's Most Wanted* aired the story of fugitive mass murderer John Emil List. Host John Walsh introduced the segment as New Jersey's most famous unsolved murder case. More than twenty million viewers tuned in.

That night in Denver, Colorado, Wanda Flannery thought the bust of John List looked like her former neighbor Bob Clark, who had moved to Virginia. Bob Clark, like John List, was an accountant from Michigan, had a scar behind his right ear from a mastoidectomy, had chronic money problems and trouble holding jobs. Wanda was worried about Delores, Bob's wife, a shy, pretty woman fifteen years his junior. She was worried her friend's life might be in danger. She called in a tip, one of more than three hundred that flooded into the show's hotline from around the country.

Eleven days later, FBI agents followed Flannery's tip to a ranch house in Midlothian, Virginia, outside Richmond. Delores Clark was vacuuming the living room carpet. Bob wasn't home, she said. He was at work at the Richmond accounting firm of Maddrea, Joyner, Kirkham & Woody. Delores looked at the photo of the bust of mass murderer John List, and reacted with disbelief. Trembling and weeping, she said, "This looks like it could be my husband. But it *can't* be my husband. He's the nicest man in the world." He was a good husband and neighbor, she said, a member of the Lutheran Church. She went into shock.

Agents arrested Bob Clark at his accounting firm that afternoon. The tall Clark, wearing a bow tie and large glasses, was walking down an aisle with a Xerox, and didn't resist being led out in handcuffs. He vociferously denied he was John List, but fingerprints confirmed a match. The eighteen-year search for the killer of Alma, Helen, Patty, John Jr., and Freddie List was over.

The next day, Bender and Walter's brilliant work was national news. *The New York Times* hailed the dramatic arrest of "one of the nation's most wanted fugitives" with a front-page story. On page one was also a photograph of the suspect John List and Bender's eerily matching bust. The List case launched Bender as an internationally known figure in forensics. *AMW* host Walsh said Bender's detective work was the most brilliant he'd encountered in his career.

Bender was ecstatic. He called Walter in Michigan to celebrate their triumph.

"Rich, your profile was right on!" As List's story emerged in court and in the press, the mass murderer's life read as if Walter had written it. List told of fleeing the crime for the distant haven of Colorado, where he took the name Bob Clark and found a job as a night clerk in a motel. In Denver, he slowly rebuilt his life, finding a job in accounting and marrying Delores, who never questioned his story that his first wife had died of cancer. He rejoined the Lutheran Church in Denver and taught Sunday school. Those who knew "Bob Clark" described him as a friendly, if taciturn, man who always wore a suit and tie, dark shoes and argyle socks, and thick-rimmed glasses. He had recently landed the job in Virginia, so he could be back on the East Coast. His home in Midlothian, Virginia, was 240 miles from his former home in Westfield, New Jersey.

Walter was cautiously pleased with all the attention. "It's nice but it's kind of scary," he told the press. "The issue then becomes 'How did you do it?' It's hard to explain the synergy. It's both powerful and empowering, but with it come expectations for consistency, so the standard always gets higher."

On April 12, 1990, about a year after Bender and Walter had helped bring him to justice, List was convicted of five counts of first-degree murder. Though there was no capital punishment in New Jersey at the time, he was sentenced to five consecutive life terms, ensuring he would never make parole. Superior Court judge William Wertheimer said the case reminded society it must defend its bedrock values. "The name of John Emil List will be eternally synonymous with concepts of selfishness, horror, and evil," he wrote. "He is without remorse and without honor. After eighteen years, five months, and twenty-two days, it is now time for the voices of Helen, Alma, Patricia, Frederick, and John F. List to rise from the grave." While Bender and Walter were both gratified, Walter said, "Unfortunately he was spared the death sentence he had issued to his family."

It was a spring of justice and redemption, of joy and celebration for Bender and Walter. They were suddenly an artist-psychologist detective team with few peers, as well as fast friends, bonded brothers, drinking buddies who'd just as soon close down a bar together as open up a cold case. But there came too intimations of a false spring. They fought like brothers, too, and over time, the voice of Bender rose in sharp complaint that Walter was stealing credit for the List case, while Walter, in stunned defense, accused Bender of slandering him and going off the deep end.

Bender and Walter were arguably the most talented detective duo on the planet, it was said in forensic circles—if they could be content with outsmarting psychopaths, redeeming victims, defeating evil, and generally destroying the lives of criminals, rather than each other.

CHAPTER 18

THE RETURN OF VIDOCQ

On President's Day, 1990, the city was dark and icy and the sky spanned the rivers like an arch of gray stone, but the small yellow café was awash in light. Fleisher pushed through the glass door on the corner of Twenty-first and Sansom, rubbing his hands from the cold. The small tables were crowded and noisy, the warm air smelled of soups and coffee. It was a federal holiday, and Bender had invited him to meet his partner Richard Walter, the forensic psychologist. Walter was in town from Michigan to work with Bender on tracking escaped killer Robert Thomas Nauss.

Fleisher was eager to meet the famous Walter and be cheered by Bender's energy.

The news in the *Philadelphia Inquirer* over breakfast had disturbed him. Even the small print told of absurd and tragic things happening in the city, with a frequency that numbed the soul. James Wayock, husband, father of four, was selling cable-TV hookups when he was shot and killed by Benjamin Frazier, forty-one, with a stolen .38, for fun. Frazier said he just wanted to kill someone. Linda Garcia, sixteen, was shot in the neck by strangers and killed coming out of a movie theater; her fatal mistake was shouting at the car that had swerved and almost hit her. A fireball of gasoline-soaked rags was thrown into the mausoleum of the Victorian industrialist family of the Champion Blower &

Forge Company, and a 125-year-old corpse attacked with a hammer. Finding a black candle at the scene, police said the attack had "Satanic overtones."

The big man saw Bender's face, beaming like a second sun. Then he saw the tall, balding, sallow-faced gentleman sitting with him, a thin line of darkness in a formal blue suit. *Richard Walter.* He had the strange and instant impression that the two men belonged to the same firmament, like the sun and the moon. Yet he'd never seen two more mismatched human beings.

Bender had said, "You've got to meet my friend Richard Walter, the profiler. He has the coldest eye for evil you'll ever see."

The thin man was wan and withered as an English butler, but Fleisher was surprised as his handshake crushed like iron tongs. Walter's booming tubercular laugh filled the coffee shop. Above his starched Oxford collar, his words flowed as arch and cultivated as Winston Churchill's; beneath it the blue suit was polyester and stank of a thousand cigarettes.

Wearing his trademark black T-shirt and jeans, Bender sat between the two veteran forensic detectives grinning like a boy who'd happened upon a candy-truck accident or a stack of *Playboy*s in his father's closet.

He'd picked the Day by Day Café to introduce them. It was loud and bustling with news and gossip that morning—the 76ers were winning in Philadelphia and the Communists were losing everywhere—perfect cover to discuss murder and other gruesome subjects. If lunch was disappointing, he could still advance his seduction of his favorite waitress. It was a win–win.

"Richard is the best profiler I've ever worked with," Bender said eagerly.

Walter winced. "Quite true. There are only five of us in the world who know what we're doing. Frank doesn't know any of the others, I'm afraid."

Fleisher laughed heartily, enjoying himself more than he had in a while. He was especially intrigued to see the wan psychologist and manic artist together for the first time. He had been stunned like every other cop in America by the duo's prophetic work on the John List case, and now he wasn't disappointed. He considered Frank a genius, and, he later noted, "It didn't take long to see that Richard had an unsurpassed knowledge of the criminal mind." Walter was equally impressed with Fleisher. "The Customs chief was quite affable and extremely bright. He had a remarkable memory for every case he ever worked."

Wendy came to the table. Bender began to sketch her face on a napkin, demonstrating a technique to her. "A cheeseburger," Fleisher said. "No fries." The waitress wrote down his order. Fleisher was grinning. "Atkins is going to save my life."

Walter ordered a cup of coffee, black.

Bender ordered a teriyaki salad, coffee, and cherry pie.

"You have quite an appetite today," Fleisher deadpanned.

Bender watched the brunette's hourglass figure return to the kitchen. "Look at that," he whispered. Fleisher chuckled.

Walter stared into the gray afternoon as if he'd rather have been watching iron oxidize than Bender's libido on exhibit.

Before the food came, the three men fell into an easy camaraderie talking murder and mayhem, including the case that connected them. They'd all worked on the U.S. Marshals' pursuit of the fugitive killers Hans Vorhauer and Robert Thomas Nauss. "It's because of Bill sharing his investigation with the FBI that I got a breakthrough that helped lead to Vorhauer's capture," Bender said. "And Richard helped me with a profile of Nauss. I still think we'll get him one of these days."

Bender's face reddened in sudden anger. "That's how it *should* work. But when I went to Washington to see the FBI about the List case, they were practically hostile to me. They wouldn't give me anything. I think they had a profile of List they wouldn't share."

Fleisher and Walter nodded in agreement. "I've seen victims victimized by the justice system for thirty years," Fleisher said sadly. His brown eyes had a faraway look.

"But why is solving a murder so hard?" Bender went on. As

an artist relatively new to forensics, he was frustrated by the rigid thinking of most policemen. "They never think out of the box!"

"Police are very procedural," Walter said, frowning. "It's the foundation of investigative procedure, to build a case on what's there. But sometimes what's not there is even more important." He smiled wickedly. "For instance"—he chuckled—"if I were sitting here naked, what was missing would become very relevant, as old and ugly as I am!"

Walter well knew the virtues of sharing information. He told them of the infamous Case of the Underwear Killer. He had just finished speaking about murder personality subtypes at a forensic conference in Atlanta when Georgia police approached him for help on the baffling case. Three women's slips had been found strewn across the bushes of a park. The slips were bloodied and appeared to have been slashed down the middle with a knife. The garments had the letter "J" sewn into them. But there was no body. No sign of a struggle. What did it all mean?

"The police looked at it and said, 'What happened here?'" Walter said mockingly. "Well, what the fuck do you mean what happened here? Anyone with half a brain can see a murder happened here. But often one doesn't have to have half a brain to be in law enforcement." Cutting and slicing were evidence of picquerism, Walter told them, the pleasure of causing pain through puncturing or slashing. It was the grave sign of a sadistic serial killer on a learning curve, like Ted Bundy, who evolved into even worse behavior, such as murder for the pleasures of necrophilia or cannibalism.

Fleisher looked up from his cheeseburger. "Thanks for mentioning it."

"Not at all. The point is that some weeks later I was at a forensic conference in St. Louis listening to Roy Hazelwood, the FBI agent, describe a murder. It was a mysterious case of women's corpses in Ohio. The torsos had been slashed open, and the slips were missing."

Walter arched his eyebrow. "As it happens, Roy and I have known each other since Christ wore tennis shoes. After the speech, I said, 'Roy, I have a question for you—what does a "J" sewn in slashed women's underwear mean to you?' His mouth fell open. It was the first initial of one of the victims, says he." The two profilers pieced together the case of a serial murderer, a long-distance trucker who was convicted of killing his victims in Ohio and scattering their slips in Georgia.

Wendy came and took plates away, pouring coffee with a free hand. Walter grinned. "So there's a certain inherent value in sharing information. We can put two and two together, make connections that others don't see."

Bender's voice rose in excitement. "Exactly! Bill and I have always said we ought to form a group of forensic experts who share information and cut through all the red tape and bullshit. We could work around law enforcement, and really get things done."

Fleisher chuckled. "They already have people doing that, Frank. Their names are Batman and Robin. We can't skirt around law enforcement like vigilantes. We need their cooperation and information."

He turned to Walter. "We've talked about getting together talking over cases like we're doing now."

Walter sniffed in disapproval. "I'm not much of a joiner."

Fleisher burned to join the battle of good and evil where it counted, in the suffering of individuals crying for help. If their private club of detectives didn't take on the mantle of crusaders, it could at least be a social club, old cops hashing over cases together in their golden years.

But their dream was missing something. The ASAC wielded tremendous power but sat dreaming with it like an aging king reluctant to rise and draw his sword. The humdrum routine of life enveloped him, sealed with an ineffable sadness he couldn't identify.

The café emptied, Wendy came with pie and more coffee, the long shadows of skyscrapers striped the street. As night closed in on the café, the figures of homeless men passed like forgotten ghosts. The three talked about the serial killers who stalked Philadelphia, and the unprecedented levels of anxiety and fear they saw in the faces of ordinary Philadelphians. "I'm seeing criminals who are much more vicious, violent, and depraved than in the previous generation," Walter said. "People who kill for the fun of it." The enormity of their battle settled over them with the dusk, challenging their easy bravado.

A sharp, excited voice broke the quiet. "What are we going to call our club?" Bender asked. "The Sherlock Holmes Society?"

Fleisher grinned. His irrepressible friend was never down for long. "That's the right idea, but too obvious. I have a better name in mind. Let's call it the Vidocq Society." To puzzled looks, he told them that Eugène François Vidocq of nineteenth-century Paris was the greatest detective who ever lived. "And he's my hero."

Fleisher had rediscovered Vidocq as a young man in the FBI Academy while studying the history of criminology. The Frenchman was legitimately the father of modern criminology. In 1811, Vidocq founded a plainclothes detective unit, comprised mostly of ex-cons like himself, which Napoleon Bonaparte signed into law as a state investigative agency, *Brigade de la Sûreté*, the forerunner of the FBI and Scotland Yard. Vidocq invented criminal record-keeping, ballistics, plaster foot casts, and invisible inks, experimented with fingerprinting, and was a master of disguise. Accused of staging crimes to solve them, he was ousted from *Sûreté,* and in 1833 founded the first private detective agency, *Le Bureau des Renseignements* (Office of Information), seventeen years before Allan Pinkerton formed the Pinkerton National Detective Agency in Chicago.

But it was Vidocq's remarkable story of redemption and his belief in the redemption of others that touched Fleisher most deeply. The chief cop of Paris was a great friend of the poor and said he would never arrest a man for stealing bread to feed his family. Vidocq was Hugo's model for Javert, the relentless detective in *Les Misérables,* as well as for Valjean, the ex-con who reforms and seeks redemption for his deeds.

Fleisher would write to law enforcement specialists around the world to recruit members to the Vidocq Society.

Bender's face pinked with excitement. "We really bonded," he told Fleisher on the way out. "We have a name, we're going to get this done!"

Walter did not share his comrades' excitement. As the fevered talk of forming societies and clubs and rooting out evil swirled around him, he grew quiet, and left the table early.

"I'm not much into groups," he said. "The Vidocq Society, some kind of Sherlock Holmes club? It was simply preposterous. I quite enjoyed Frank and Bill, had a nice time and humored them both. I was trying to be polite, OK. But frankly, I thought the whole idea was foolish."

PART THREE

·

THE VIDOCQ SOCIETY

CHAPTER 19

THE GATHERING OF DETECTIVES

At high noon in the Navy Officers' Club, Fleisher looked down a long table into the faces of the best and brightest federal agents and cops from New York, Philadelphia, Boston, and Washington. This was the core group Fleisher had handpicked to start the Vidocq Society, the most accomplished and colorful experts from his various tribes: federal agents, Philadelphia cops, polygraph experts, and Jewish lawmen. On either side of him sat Frank Bender and Richard Walter. Following his luncheon with them, Fleisher had written a letter to twenty-eight law enforcement colleagues around the country and world inviting them to join a private detective club dedicated to "cuisine and crime." Twenty-six of the twenty-eight replied with a swift and enthusiastic yes.

The air in the room was electric. Never had any of them seen so much detective talent at one table. They were a collective endowment with no obligation to any government or agency. Bender was "really excited."

Even Walter, ever the skeptic in his crisp blue suit, launched his left eyebrow into a reappraising point as he looked down the table of renowned investigators. *The big gun at Customs really did it,* he thought.

The charter members of the Vidocq Society had gathered to

take their collective measure, determine their purpose, vote on leadership, rules, and bylaws.

Most were men Fleisher knew like brothers. Some, like veteran Customs agent Joe O'Kane, had worked with him for years on major cases.

"Me and Bill [Fleisher] and the other guys have spent the equivalent of two lifetimes together," said O'Kane. "We live out of suitcases, sleep in cars eating burritos on surveillance, urinate in gas station men's rooms. 007 it ain't . . ." Others had worked with Fleisher with the FBI or the Philadelphia PD, men who'd lassoed murderers and mobsters and stood guard for everyone from the governor of Pennsylvania to the queen of England.

"Fleisher, this is the dumbest thing I've ever heard of. It'll never work," laughed U.S. Treasury Department special agent William Gill, the Treasury ASAC in Philadelphia, surveying the band of tough, independent-minded cops, all of them accustomed to bureaucratic jousting and rivalry and armed to the teeth. "But I love you and if it's a good lunch, I'm in. I'm one of Fleisher's disciples."

Gill was impressed with how Fleisher in the past had brought together all the ASACs who helped run federal law enforcement offices in Philadelphia—FBI, Marshals, Customs, DEA, Treasury, ATF, IRS, Secret Service—for a monthly luncheon. They got to know one another and worked together in new ways. "It was great to be able to call a guy and say, hey, Bob, I need some equipment, or I need some men."

One of Fleisher's ASAC lunches was aboard a cabin cruiser sailing on the Delaware, a DEA surveillance boat confiscated from drug smugglers and equipped with all the latest listening devices. "The DEA was showing off, and it worked. It impressed the shit out of everybody." Gill later borrowed the boat to put away a revenue agent who was taking huge payoffs to ignore corporate audits. The bribes were passed in clandestine meetings on a small boat in the Delaware, and it was easy for the cabin cruiser to listen in. The boat was skippered by DEA agent Steve Churchill, who would become a VSM.

"Bill's a genius at organization," Gill said, "at remembering everybody's name and bringing them together."

"You got that right," O'Kane said. "He talks to everybody, every agent, every cop, every snitch, every reporter, every hooker, everybody. He has lunch with everybody. He wanted to talk about this new society over lunch. I said, Bill, I can't do all the lunches you do, I can't eat like that. There's never been a networker like Bill Fleisher."

The federal agents at the table, Fleisher's peers, were a flashy group. The bounty hunter, intense U.S. Marshal Dennis Matulewicz, a St. Joseph's University graduate, liked to quote Hemingway: "There is nothing like the hunting of man, and those who have hunted armed men long enough and liked it, never care for anything else thereafter." Star Alcohol, Tobacco, Firearms, and Explosives agent Philip Schuyler Deming, chestnut-haired and movie-star handsome, wore the ring of Washington's officers, the Society of Cincinnati, handed down by his ancestor Alexander Hamilton. Edgar Adamson had once given his life to Christ in the seminary, but was now based in Washington, D.C., as deputy chief of Interpol.

"Deming was so blue-blooded, if you cut him he bled Main Line," said Customs agent O'Kane. "But he was a regular guy, not foppish. He wouldn't tell you his middle name unless you made him."

Treasury ASAC Gill sat with his former boss, Ben Redmond, reminiscing about the summer day in New York City in 1971 when their agents were scheduled to go undercover and receive a bribe in person from the godfather of the Colombo crime family himself, Joe Colombo Sr. It would have been a spectacular coup. But at Colombo's earlier appointment to speak at an Italian rally at Columbus Circle, a gunman shot him three times in the head, putting the godfather in a seven-year coma he never came out of. The infamous phrase of chief rival and suspect Joey Gallo was, "He was vegetabled," Gill said to laughter.

In comparison, the Customs tribe was a roughhouse gang. O'Kane, son of a Kensington millwright, didn't know what Customs agents were until half a dozen of them with sticks and guns jumped him when he was removing a repossessed car from

Customs bonded storage. The young loan officer hadn't filled out the proper forms, and Customs agents saw it as a theft. But agents Burke and Murphy liked the way the big Irishman handled himself in the fight. When they realized it was an innocent mistake and moreover the kid was Dutch O'Kane's son, "they clapped me on the back like I was the greatest guy in the world and told me to apply to Customs." Like another big Irishman, Frank Dufner, he caught on as a sky marshal. Dufner had been applying to be a letter carrier—his grandfather's trade for fifty years—when he saw President Richard Nixon on a poster recruiting armed undercover men to stop airplane hijackings. They loved the undercover work, sitting there in coach in a suit with a .38 jammed in their pants, "Just waiting, wanting, *wishing* something would happen," O'Kane said. It seldom did, except when Dufner had to tackle a man who was furiously pounding on the pilot's door. "It turns out he was a gay guy whose lover was pretending to have an affair in the men's room, and it was the only door he hadn't checked."

At Customs, both men trained under the "Forty Thieves," the hard-boiled inspectors who worked the night docks in Philadelphia with sticks they used to smash smuggled vodka bottles hidden under longshoremen's coats. "Those guys were two-fisted drinkers and I loved them," O'Kane said. "I mean they literally stood at the bar with two drinks, and they'd just as soon punch you in the mouth as say hello. They were hardball guys with hearts of gold—Irish mostly, some Italians, a smattering of German types, a few tough Jewish guys."

Fleisher was one of the tough Jewish guys, one of the polished, college-educated federal agents, even though he happened to have come up the hard way from Philadelphia's ethnic neighborhoods. But there was no caste system dividing the men at the table. Common achievement was the leveler. Masculine stoicism and modesty were the code in the room. "Guys don't talk about things," said O'Kane. "Gill was a hero on helicopter bombing missions in Vietnam, but I've never heard him talk about it. It gets mentioned in passing, and you know what a guy's got." They all had a lot.

Renowned attorney Kenneth Freeman, one of the tough Jewish guys, had walked the Philly police beat with him as a young
man; Freeman went off to law school and encouraged Fleisher to
attend the FBI Academy. Another tough Jewish guy, Customs special agent in charge Dave Warren, Fleisher's boss, had helped bring
him over from the FBI and its endless transfers so Fleisher could
settle in Philadelphia.

Farther down the table, and back in time, was Fleisher's Philadelphia tribe, the men he'd grown up with or served with at the
police department. Short, wisecracking medical examiner Halbert
Fillinger, who went to homicide scenes in his vintage fire department vehicles, had arrived in his red Thunderbird with the HOM-
HAL plates. There was city homicide captain Frank Friel, legendary
investigator of four thousand murders. "Frank's the best man on a
murder I've ever known," Fleisher said.

The Philly cop family was as tight as any mob.

Only Fleisher's cofounders, Walter and Bender, weren't part of
the family. Many of the Philadelphians had worked with Bender,
but all knew Walter only as a Midwest forensic psychologist whose
brilliance and temperamental nature seemed to match Bender's.
With their booming laughter and preternaturally gleaming eyes—
one lit with mania, the other darkly glittering with mockery—the
men flanking Fleisher seemed as ethereal as apparitions, shadowy
extensions of Fleisher. They were loud, outlandish; they broke the
code.

Yet Fleisher seemed to have an unspoken communion with
the strange men at his side. "I've always had a taste for characters
and eccentrics," he said. A taste that came from his father, who
enjoyed the company of gangsters, second-story men, showgirls,
and assorted figures on the borderlands of darkness.

Before lunch was served, Fleisher got down to the business of
creating the Vidocq Society. He introduced his cofounders, then
briefly described the swashbuckling Vidocq, the society's name-
sake, and his many accomplishments.

Special Agent Dufner, once Fleisher's partner in Customs,

chuckled. *So that's where he picked up that trick.* One winter day in 1980, they were investigating a major theft of TVs and microwaves from cargo containers when Fleisher found a footprint in the snow. He went to the store to buy plaster of paris and made an impression. "A lot of the guys in the office were laughing—you've gone too far, what's this, Perry Mason?" Dufner said. "But we made about twenty arrests, and one guy gave himself up because we had his Converse sneaker impression. Fleisher was one of those guys who knew everything. I thought, *FBI agent, Philly PD, I can learn a lot from this guy."*

Led by Fleisher, the men at the long table quickly hashed out the details of their new fellowship. They quickly chose a commissioner (Fleisher) to lead them, along with a deputy commissioner— an immodest organization model also used by the New York City Police Department, the Hong Kong Police, and the Metropolitan Police Service (Scotland Yard).

They would meet quarterly over a hot lunch at the Officers' Club to discuss cold murders. Nate Gordon, the esteemed polygraph operator, proposed that membership be restricted to eighty-two men and women in honor of Vidocq's life span of eighty-two years. (Born in rural Arras, France, July 23, 1775, a baker's third son, Vidocq died in Paris on May 11, 1857.) The proposal was quickly accepted. Membership would be a "rare privilege" extended to the top forensic specialists in the world, and endure for life. No one could apply; one had to be invited through sponsorship by an existing member, and approved by a vote of a board of directors that included the commissioner and deputy commissioner. A single blackball would sink a candidate. The eighty-two charter Vidocq Society Members would be formally known as VSMs.

Their meetings would exude the elegant, privileged, old-world atmosphere of a Victorian men's club. Coffee and iced tea would substitute for brandy, cigars were verboten, and talented women and men of all races would be enthusiastically welcomed as members; it was a different time. But they were not shy about making the club exclusive; one had to be a renowned crime-fighter to even be considered. It would be one of the most exclusive clubs in the world.

There was an air of whimsy about the Vidocq Society. Among the many previous dining-and-mystery societies that sprang up, mostly in New York or London, the most famous was the Baker Street Irregulars, founded in 1935. The Irregulars meet for dinner in New York City to discuss Sherlock Holmes in a jovial atmosphere where "it is always 1895." Notable members included Presidents Franklin D. Roosevelt and Harry Truman, science-fiction writers Isaac Asimov and later Neil Gaiman, and Rex Stout, creator of the Nero Wolfe novels.

Like the Baker Street Irregulars, the purpose of the Vidocq Society would be strictly fraternal, Fleisher said. Working or retired, detectives could catch up with old friends or make new ones and stretch their minds on fascinating unsolved cases. It would be a social club for detectives.

Fleisher was even happy to admit people who were not law enforcement professionals if they brought a unique talent to forensic inquiry.

Walter frowned at that. He wanted no part of amateurs.

CHAPTER 20

BUSTED

In the fall of 1990, as Bender and Walter hurtled over the dark Pacific on a flight from San Francisco to Australia, the artist couldn't remove his eyes from the stewardess. He'd never taken such a long flight and he was ebullient; his career was soaring. The John List case had propelled him to superstar status as an international forensic artist, hailed for works of genius on the front page of *The New York Times*. Now he'd been invited to give a week of forensic lectures in Adelaide and Sydney with Walter and FBI agent Robert Ressler. His first appearance before the international forensic community would be alongside two of the most renowned profilers in the world. Things couldn't be going better.

But it was a long flight, and Bender's mood rose and fell and finally went into a free fall at 30,000 feet. The truth was, he told Walter, that it was his first long trip away from his wife in their twenty years together, and he was filled with worry. He had called her from all their airport stops, Philadelphia, New York, and San Francisco, to tell her he loved her.

He was still finding it hard to believe, but his wife had recently informed him their marriage was officially on the rocks. Not with Wife No. 2, as some friends referred to Ella, but with Jan—the original pretty blonde, the rock of his life.

"Jan's talking to a lawyer about divorce," he said glumly, staring out over the black ocean.

"As your friend, I'm trying to act surprised," Walter said tartly.

"I know, I know. I never thought it'd come to this. Jan's the center of my life. I've always had affairs, but I made a mistake. I had the wrong kind of affair."

"Yes, of course," Walter said sarcastically. "I see."

Bender didn't seem to be listening. ". . . Jan thinks the celebrity stuff is going to my head. I can't help it if my work attracts attention."

In the modern media age, Bender was becoming better known in his time than Michelangelo was in his. *People* magazine asked him to sculpt the bust of one of the "25 Most Intriguing People" of 1991—Ötzi the Iceman, the 5,300-year-old hunter found in a glacier at 11,000 feet in the Italian Alps with a stone arrow in his back and a knife in his hand, on the losing end of the first known European murder. Ahead of the scientific proof, Bender gave the Iceman short hair because "it just felt right." The Sonnabend Gallery in New York City made him the featured artist in an exhibit with the work of Andy Warhol called "Monster," Ronald Jones's installation about crime. From photographs of a young Jewish girl killed by the Nazis, he sculpted an old woman, imagining that she had survived the death camps. "She had a beautiful singing voice," he told the Associated Press. "She sang for Mengele. Then he shot her. It was the most moving experience of all the work I've done." Now it wasn't just Philadelphia newspapers calling; it was *Time* and *Newsweek* and *Match* in Paris, movie producers, Hollywood agents, and celebrities on the phone, in addition to the coroners, city cops, grizzled private eyes, models, photographers, reporters, cranks, quacks, collection agencies, and jealous husbands who had long burned up the wires on South Street.

Jan wrote in her diary that her husband was no longer the young, humble, devil-may-care artist who talked about being a voice for the dead who had no one to speak for them. He was on the phone with journalists and Hollywood and TV people day and night. "He talks about himself all the time," she wrote.

Things came to a head after they'd been fighting for weeks and months, with long, bitter silences and the tension building. On top of everything else, Jan was tired of being broke and poor. The week that John List was captured, a *Time* magazine writer had said that Frank Bender was more famous than the president of the United States. Bender's nearly forty forensic sculptures, which occupied most of his time for more than a decade, had produced spectacular results—but each bust paid only about $1,000, sometimes more, sometimes much less. Sometimes nothing at all. Meanwhile, Frank's steady money from commercial photography withered. Jan took a job as a perfume tester at Strawbridge & Clothier department store, and a second job as a law-firm receptionist. Frank found part-time work repairing nicked and damaged tugboat blades, diving underwater in the polluted Delaware River—with his extraordinary hands, he was brilliant at feeling the flaws in total blackness. They sold their belongings, including Frank's last motorcycle and his van, to keep going.

The bottom fell out recently, Frank said, when he was lying in bed one morning and Jan started screaming.

"Are you fucking Laura Shaughnessy?" Her shouting echoed through the old meat market, reaching the ears of their daughter Vanessa.

Frank was fed up with Jan's cold, dismissive attitude. "Yes, I am," he said nonchalantly. "Now can I go back to sleep?"

"Might I suggest," Walter said dryly, "that that was the wrong thing to say?"

"No shit, Sherlock."

Walter glared at him.

"I've got to restore The Balance," Bender said quietly and with reverence, as if it were a lost artifact of The Knights Templar. "I violated The Balance."

Walter raised his eyebrows. "Your idea of balance is Karl

Wallenda's. I don't know anybody else outside Dubai who lives with so many women."

The fact was that Ella, Bender's No. 1 Girlfriend, wasn't the problem. Jan liked Ella. In return, Ella adored Jan and respected her unassailable status as The Wife.

Jan didn't even mind the rotating cast of young women—waitresses, artists, art photographers, single women, separated women, and other men's wives—who served as her husband's Girlfriends Nos. 2 through 5 depending on Bender's needs and the oscillations of the moon. And she recognized that the deeper he explored death in his art, the greater his lust for young and nubile life. Jan was the power behind the throne; none of it threatened her.

Bender was accustomed to raised eyebrows about his domestic arrangements, but he cared neither about what others did in their own lives nor what they thought of him. Frank and Jan sought marriage counseling several times over the years for financial and other problems, but Bender's girlfriends never came up in their sessions. Adultery wasn't an issue. "It works for me and it works for Jan. She needs her space and I need mine. I don't want some psychologist telling us how to live our lives. It's a whole bouillabaisse, a mix of everything that makes us what we are. I'm an artist, but the fact I went to art school is the least important part of me. A gift is a delicate thing and you don't want to throw it off."

But Laura Shaughnessy was different. They met through a woman sculptor friend with whom Bender had once shared studio space. He agreed to do promotional photographs for Laura and her handcrafted leather apparel, never expecting a lovely young woman with long, lustrous red hair and a musical laugh who returned his stares with compound interest. "Laura had the hots for me immediately," Bender said. As he tells it, it wasn't his idea. But a beautiful young woman throws herself at you, what are you going to do, say no?

She asked him on a date Bender couldn't refuse—a museum exhibition on Hollywood special effects, including classic Hitchcock horror artifacts that enchanted Bender: the miniature town from *The Birds* and the dead mother in the rocking chair from *Psycho*. Soon they were sleeping together, and Bender had a wonderful time. "Who wouldn't?" Laura took him to a beach house with friends on the Jersey Shore, then to a friend's cottage in Maine. They laughed over red wine and the taped-over bullet hole in the window of a South Philly restaurant famous for mob hits. He reveled like a Dionysian god at her family estate in New Jersey, the gated compound with mansion, Olympic-size pool with brick bathhouses for men and women, golf course, boat slip on the lake. "She had this fur coat, really nice expensive fur coat, and I made love to her in it in the living room of her parents' house one day. I love doing it anywhere, over the kitchen table, not just with her. I like spontaneous combustions."

Bender had a theory that the source of his creativity and happiness was following his heart's desires. Bender was convinced that once artists lost touch with their uninhibited lust for life, they fell out of step with the dance of the universe. He feared he would lose his ability to hear the dead, his intuitive mastery of forensic art. He had a finely tuned sense of The Balance.

"So let me get this straight," Walter said. "You can't be a great artist unless you can sleep with whomever you want."

"Well, The Balance is important to my work."

"Right."

But then Laura did something no other girlfriend of Bender's had ever done. She became extremely possessive of him. "She wanted me to leave Jan and Ella and drop any other girlfriends. Said she didn't like Jan and Ella." Ella didn't like Laura much at that point, either. Jan was furious; her husband had finally reeled in a woman who—God forbid—wanted Bender all to himself, and she was starting to think, *She can have him.* Bender was still enchanted with the affair, but his lovely young woman and his new stardom had tilted his world, and he felt like he was flying off into space.

Bender brooded across the Pacific about his imperiled marriage. But at Adelaide, the first stop, he began to feel better. He couldn't afford the hotel room Walter had booked for him, so the profiler agreed to share a room. It didn't bother him in the least that the room had no heat. Meanwhile, Walter was coming down with pneumonia, which made him more annoyed than usual with his traveling companion. *I'll never do this again,* he thought. *He's a pain in the ass. He thinks it's clever to be unreliable.*

In Sydney, Bender was again bursting with optimism. Even Jan had agreed the trip was a great career opportunity. After the List triumph, he'd been looking for bigger gigs with the feds, Interpol, and Scotland Yard, and now here he was lecturing on criminal personality profiles and crime scene assessment on a program with Ressler, whom he'd been eager to get to know. Bender spoke on the first day of the conference to the prestigious Association of Australasian and Pacific Area Police Medical Officers. He was a big hit and made a great impression on Ressler. Then he told Walter he was headed to Bondi Beach. Walter reminded him it was a four-day forensic conference. But Bender said he couldn't stand being around "a bunch of fuddy-duddies at a conference" when he could hang out at a famous topless beach.

Bender sat on the sands looking out at the dramatic sweep of the Sydney beach. He was in paradise: The sun was high, the bikinis cut low, and he had three whole days, all expenses paid, to work on his tan. He talked to everyone who went by—about the shark net, the killer riptide, the hermit in the rocky cave, the record number of bikinis. (Bondi Beach holds the Guinness World Record for the largest swimsuit photo shoot, of 1,010 bikini-clad women.) Soon he became known as "that famous American artist" and "the guy who caught John List." He met a lot of cute women. Things were looking up.

On the third day of the conference, he came back to the hotel to find a message from Philadelphia. "Your wife rang!!!" read the note at the front desk. "At 4:07 P.M. . . . the marshals' office rang her to let you know they have caught Nauss. He apparently was living in suburbia with a wife and children and they knew nothing about him."

Jubilant, Bender told Walter the exciting news. "Rich, they

caught him in Michigan, just like you said they would. And he was clean-shaven, just like I said."

"This is good," Walter said.

Bender said he needed to get back to the United States immediately. Walter said he understood, thinking to himself, *It's a good thing he's going, because I'm on the verge of killing him.*

America's Most Wanted had shown the Nauss episode twice in the past two years, and mentioned Nauss a couple more times, as did other TV shows, including *The Phil Donahue Show* in recent weeks. Marshals had traced down literally hundreds of dead-end tips in California, Montana, Washington State, Texas, Arizona, New Jersey, Delaware, and throughout Pennsylvania. But on November 2, out of the blue, a tipster called and said a man who resembled the Nauss bust on *AMW* lived in Michigan.

"I told them he was in Michigan years ago," Walter sniffed.

The tip led marshals to Luna Pier, a small town on Lake Erie an hour south of Detroit, and a man who went by the name Richard Ferrer. Nauss, thirty-eight, had taken the alias from the name of a cell mate back in Graterford. He was living a quiet life in Luna Pier with a new wife and three young sons in a ranch house with three picture windows overlooking Lake Erie.

Marshals had pieced together his trail of deception.

The year after his escape, a gentlemanly, charming, solidly built Nauss, then thirty-two, met and married Toni Ruark, thirty-seven, a single mother and government clerk in Detroit. "Rick" introduced himself as a lonely orphan, divorced, an investor, the owner of fourteen lucrative rental properties, who had "moved to Michigan to try to get his life together." When he told his life story—orphaned with five siblings after his father died in a car accident—his friends in Luna Pier said they felt so bad for him they didn't press him for details.

Having grown up in an upper-middle-class home in suburban Philadelphia, it was easy for Nauss to shave his heavy biker's beard, cut his hair short, and fit right into the middle-class town. "Rick Ferrer" was a devoted husband and father, and loved to take his buddies fishing on his twenty-seven-foot boat. The lonely town of 1,500 had only four police officers, who considered him an upstanding citizen.

"When she met him, she thought she'd died and gone to heaven he was so nice," Toni's father said. "I liked him, too."

Though he had no job in Michigan, Rick cultivated the image of an easygoing, successful tradesman around town. He wore his trademark baseball cap, chinos, and long-sleeve flannel shirts (always long-sleeve, no matter what the weather) as he drove his pickup truck with the toolbox he used for repairs on his properties. Occasionally he took trips out of town and came home with rent money of $2,000 or $3,000. He bought a beachfront camp up in Brimley, Michigan, on Lake Superior in the Upper Peninsula, for a vacation home, and started selling off the extra land in lots. Life was good.

At 8 P.M. Tuesday, Halloween Eve, Rick and Toni and the kids were driving home in the Chevy Suburban, still planning for the trick-or-treaters. Toni had fixed the kids' Teenage Mutant Ninja Turtle costumes, carved pumpkins for the yard, hung a paper ghost in the window, and strewn tiny lighted pumpkins in a tree by the front door. Until the moment carloads of U.S. Marshals, guns drawn, surrounded the Suburban, she had no idea who her husband was.

The marshals handcuffed the docile, solidly built Nauss in front of his children. Then they handcuffed Toni to keep her under control, though she would not be charged. As Toni stood in shock, a state police sergeant pulled down Nauss's plaid shirt. And there, extending almost from the shoulder to the elbow, was Nauss's trademark tattoo, an enormous parrot. The parrot was crucial to confirming his identity. "Some of his tattoos had been altered, but not this one," said Dennis Matulewicz of the U.S. Marshals' office in Philadelphia. "He had a special fondness for the parrot."

The parrot told a tale—of leading Pennsylvania's most violent motorcycle gang, rape, murder, dismemberment, and prison escape—that none of his new family or friends could believe.

Looking at his wife and children, Nauss said, "Sorry. This is it."

"He's a changed man," Toni Ferrer said as her life unraveled. "At least from what they tell me. He never beat me. He never beat the kids." There was no Richard Ferrer, no investment properties, no rents to collect. A marshal in Detroit said he was a "classic Jekyll and Hyde," a charmer who killed one woman and fooled another. Toni thought she'd found happiness only to find out she was a cover. "They just wonder when he's coming back," she said of her children. "I just told them the truth."

Large amounts of cash were found in Nauss's house, along with a number of false IDs. The marshals believed that Nauss had continued to work with his partner Vorhauer, probably in drug manufacture and distribution. The Detroit region was known for nearly two hundred biker gangs that would have helped the escaped fugitives resettle, they said, and surely it was more than coincidence that Luna Pier was only a hundred and ten miles south of Yale, Michigan, where Vorhauer had been operating a methamphetamine lab on a farm before his recapture four years earlier. Nauss was spotted by several witnesses riding a motorcycle near Vorhauer's farm when the meth lab was busted.

Clamped in leg irons, Nauss was flown to Philadelphia on a chartered marshals jet. Bender returned immediately to Philadelphia, where marshals supervisor Tom Rappone asked him to take the booking photograph, as he had with Vorhauer, who had refused to look at him.

Nauss was friendly, amiably putting his hand on Bender's shoulder. "Hey, you did that bust of me, right?"

"Yeah. How does it feel to be immortalized?" Bender felt completely at ease with the charming killer.

"I wish it was under better circumstances," Nauss laughed, adding, "Didn't you also play Vorhauer, my partner, on *AMW*?"

"You saw it?" *AMW* had asked Bender to play the hit man in a reconstruction of the case.

"Yes, but you're better-looking than him. He's ugly, isn't he?"
They both laughed.

Within two days, Nauss was back in maximum-security
Graterford Prison outside Philadelphia, the scene of his dramatic
escape, to continue serving his life sentence for the 1977 murder of
his girlfriend Elizabeth Ann Landy. A Montgomery County judge
gave him a light additional sentence of three and a half to seven
years for escape, crediting him with time off for good behavior
for his "rehabilitated life" in Michigan. Nauss was separated from
his partner, Vorhauer, who was locked up more than a hundred
miles away in Huntingdon State Prison in northern Pennsylvania,
serving a twenty-to-forty-year term for armed robbery, plus seven
years for escape.

Walter's profile was eerily on the mark.

Nauss had a second car parked in his driveway.

"You got it right, Rich," Bender said.

It was a Cadillac.

CHAPTER 21

THE DETECTIVE OF SOULS

I t was the second floor of the Customs House, one of those grand stone Depression-era buildings with a lighthouse motif borrowed from the Colossus of Rhodes. The heavy wood door was ajar, and the ASAC was talking about the goose-down jackets from China that came through Philadelphia International Airport. Murray had tipped them off to the scam—the "goose-down" parkas were stuffed with chicken feathers. They confiscated the contraband, made arrests, and locked up the case. Murray was their best informant.

"So I'm thanking him and he asks me, 'Bill, how much do you stop, really? Give it to me straight.' Murray was a good guy so I told him, 'Eh, two percent. Washington says it's ten percent, but it's not close.'"

It was June 1991. Out on the river low brown air shrouded the tankers, but above was a clear sky in the east with the feel of the sea in it.

"What's the moral of the story?" the ASAC said. "Six months later we stop a little gold Buddha statue at the airport. We drill a hole in it and heroin spills out—two million dollars' worth on the street. We work the case through informants in Asia and trace it back to the shipper—it's Murray. We arrest Murray."

Fleisher shrugged. "I guess he liked his odds at two percent."

The agents laughed. The agents were a proud, veteran crew, working big cases all over the world—Operation Steeltrap in San Francisco targeting Japanese steel industry corruption; Operation Florida on smugglers' money-laundering. They nailed mobster "Fat Vinnie" Teresa, who'd given up Meyer Lansky and went into federal witness protection, where he smuggled Komodo dragons until O'Kane went undercover as a gay entrepreneur dragon buyer and got sixty hours of tape. They raided a Brooklyn warehouse, busting two Colombians and $60 million in cocaine that came in on a Baltimore freighter hidden in the false sides of emollient barrels. "We used the old tire-kick test," Fleisher quipped to the press. "We got a dull thud instead of a ping." It was important, dangerous, all-consuming, thrilling work, and the only way to do it was to think that it made a difference. In other words, not to think about it.

"Eh, what are we doing this for, men?" Fleisher asked, waving his pinkie ring.

The ASAC had become a critic of the war in which he was a four-star general, what President George H. W. Bush called the war on drugs. "I'm tired of sending my men undercover—good men with families, friends of mine—wondering if they'll come home," he said. "For what? Prohibition didn't work, and it got more Customs agents killed than at any time in history.

"I'm honored to be in a long line of distinguished federal officers," he quipped, "such as George Armstrong Custer. This is my last stand."

The numbers were absurd. Customs had time to inspect only 3 percent of the three million containers arriving annually in the Philadelphia ports alone, and it took eight inspectors all day to open 1,500 boxes in a single container. With its large port and central location on the East Coast, the world's largest and deadliest Colombian drug cartel had chosen Philadelphia as the perfect hole to stuff crack cocaine through to feed a hungry America. The port was FedEx for smugglers.

Fleisher's nine drug smuggling agents were also expected to

cover a dozen Pittsburgh port terminals on the Ohio, Mononga-
hela, and Allegheny rivers, the ports of Erie, New Jersey, and Delaware, and the Pittsburgh, Harrisburg, Allentown, Wilkes-Barre,
Wilmington, and Atlantic City airports.

He oversaw his empire from a small rectangular office with
an old wood desk, credenza, two visitor's chairs, thin carpeting,
white walls—"standard government bureaucrat," he said. As if to
express his unease, the walls were conspicuously bare. Settling into
his crowning federal assignment, he'd hung none of the dozens of
awards and commendations from a brilliant career. "I'm not into
ego art anymore," he said with a shrug. Only two framed artifacts
hung on the wall—a letter of praise from FBI director William
Webster, and a portrait of a man with a wide head and brazenly
arrogant eyes, wearing a greatcoat and cravat of nineteenth-
century Paris.

When he wasn't high on the adrenaline of leading his men,
he took solace in a routine as predictable as the sun. Every day on
his way to lunch he took the stairs to appease his wife and doctor,
then drove the government Crown Vic the ten blocks to the oyster house he had patronized for fifty years. He ordered the traditional oyster stew with heavy cream, the same dish he had enjoyed
with his father and grandfather at the same table, served by the
same waitress he had flirted with when they both were young. The
ASAC was a very sentimental man.

The job took a toll on Fleisher. He could not tolerate failing;
the stakes were too high. One night, at home, he wrote a Declaration of Independence Against Drugs for children in Philadelphia. If
there was anyone worth fighting the drug war for, it was innocent
children. His men found the powerful ASAC pensive at his desk.
His ruminations turned bleak and philosophical. He had taken to
discussing the tender hopes of redemption linking Yahweh, Buddha, Muhammad, and Christ. A paperback copy of Victor Hugo's
Les Misérables had replaced his own book on interrogation techniques in his top drawer.

In a sentimental mood, he would open the well-thumbed

paperback of *Les Misérables* and discuss the classic nineteenth-century novel of the French Revolution in light of the ongoing debate on whether law enforcement should be punitive or redemptive.

"This is my favorite scene in all literature," he would say. It was the famous moment when Jean Valjean, the thief who steals to feed his family, is caught by the gendarme stealing a basket of silver from old Bishop Myriel, who had sheltered the ex-con for the night. Valjean is hauled before the bishop for punishment, but the bishop says there has been a mistake, he gave Valjean the basket of silver as a gift but the ex-con forgot the silver candlesticks, which the bishop now hands over to him. The thief is stunned by the force of forgiveness, and the bishop says, "Do not forget, never forget, that you have promised to use this money to become an honest man. Jean Valjean, my brother, you no longer belong to evil but to good. It is your soul that I buy from you; I withdraw it from black thoughts and the spirit of perdition, and I give it to God."

Fleisher could not read the passage without looking up, his eyes wet with tears.

"This is what I want to do with my life. I want to devote my life to what really counts, redeeming the suffering, fighting the battle of good and evil. I want to be a force for good. I want to buy souls."

CHAPTER 22

THE DEATH ARTIST

No woman was so young, blond, and lovely, no feeling so pure, no night so exciting as Tuesday: Polish vodka, pale Eastern European skin, dazzling white light that cleansed the darkness.

If it was Tuesday, it must be Ella.

It was Tuesday evening in the art studio and home of Frank Bender, the Casanova of the Caliper, the Da Vinci of the Dead, the greatest forensic artist who ever lived.

Bender was laughing with unadulterated, adulterous joy. His laughter rang from beneath the floor in the center of the warehouse, from the underground room, the pit. He was five foot eight, slim and muscular, an ex-boxer with a leprechaun's grin and light hazel eyes of manic intensity. MOM was tattooed on his arm from his days in the Navy, a scar sliced his lip from a beer-bottle fight, and just above his groin was a butterfly tattoo he had displayed in public, dropping his drawers for a comely barkeep.

Now in his fifties, Bender was making a living doing commissioned sculptures for clients around the world and diving into the Delaware River's polluted waters to repair damaged tugboat propellers. In the dark cold waters of the river he was like nobody else, feeling blindly the nicks on the blades with the gift of his hands. In his studio, laying hands on the bones of the murdered dead, he felt his psychic visions and molded clay busts of the decayed and unidentified dead, of fugitive killers. Seven Most Wanted killers were sitting in jail, and many more victims had been avenged, because of Bender's gift for seeing dead people. His forensic art had provided Bender with fans around the world. He was profiled on *60 Minutes; Esquire* named him "Man of the Month." Cops were awed and spooked by his wizardlike powers. The work occasionally involved opening graves and cutting off the heads of corpses like some Dracula avenger, being chased by gangsters, and checking through airports with a head in a suitcase. Bender needed, he said, to "download the horror."

He did that best on Tuesdays. Tuesdays were Ella days, and from evening through dawn Wednesday, Bender "downloaded the horror" with her. The pit was sacred space, blindingly white, perfect. They went together naked, hand in hand, down the white wooden stairs, past the white sign painted with black letters, WHITE HIGHWAY CAFÉ. It was white walls, a white bar, and white barstools with a red 1952 model Chevy, a car from his childhood, on a painted highway running down the bar. They sipped Polish vodka, listened to Brubeck, Johnny Rotten, blues, any damn thing. They drank, danced, and made love all night long. He was nearly sixty, and his all-night Bacchanalias gave him more energy than did a good night's sleep. "It's how I restore my innocence," he said. Meanwhile, his wife slept peacefully in their room next to the old meat locker.

Shortly before dawn, he climbed the white stairs into the dim studio gallery. It had been a flawless evening. In the gloom he went to the stove and put water on to boil for coffee. He lifted the lid on the big pot and gave a stir; the head was coming along fine. Ella wrapped her arms around him from behind. Bender lived life ordered purely by his own desires. He didn't own a watch, and the clocks in the place kept their own separate times. The Norman Rockwell calendar was fifty years behind. Friends had to tell him what day it was. Or he measured time, like Tuesday, by trysts. He floated in a timeless ether of his art, "the mistress I was born to serve," as one of his role models, Michelangelo Buonarroti, once wrote.

As they sat sipping coffee under the curling Rockwell, the phone rang.

The murky skylights were graying the studio with early light. He could dimly make out the rows of human heads; the women with smudges of red lipstick and rouge and pleading eyes that seemed alive; the wolflike faces and vacant, hollow eyes of sadists, hit men, mass murderers. The mute chorus of the doomed. Visitors were awed, or spooked, by his collection of skulls. It was a sensory overload of darkness. But this was only a museum. They should only see inside his head; that's where the action was, the active cases, the crowds. The dead appeared in his dreams with their ruined faces, crying for justice, mouthing the names of their killers.

He let the phone ring, running through the possibilities. The hit men who'd vowed to kill him seemed to be placated for now. No husbands were after him at the moment. His father-in-law wasn't chasing him with a rifle anymore. Things were relatively calm these days. Still, he had a bad feeling. It was nothing he could put a finger on.

His partners had warned him about the physical dangers of murder investigations. Stare into the abyss and it could darken your whole being. Turn away from the pain and suffering, if you were one of those called to it, and you lost your mind. He was the latter. The cops saw it in him. Fleisher said, "We're all driven to find justice, driven to a fault." He had been swallowed by it. He was a simple happy-go-lucky sex-loving artist and all-around charming manipulative lothario before he was recruited for something higher. Recruited by fate. He'd never noticed the news racks, the radio, the talk of the abduction and murder of innocents jamming the airwaves of his city, of every metropolis. The numbers meant nothing to him; it was the tortured eyes of the first murder victim that did it, that recruited him, snatched his soul.

The telephone testified to the change. His tape machine, once filled with girlfriends, was crammed with messages from cops, reporters, medical examiners, grieving families seeking help. And here was the rub: The calls wounded him. Injustice made him angry. It pissed him off. But it angered all of them. That's what kept him going. It angered all of them.

He knew as he listened to the phone ringing under the watchful gaze of the heads that morning that things would never be the same, no matter how many women he bedded. Until the world was a better place, until he did something to knock sense into it, he'd have that bad feeling.

Things were going good. It was just that bad feeling.

He picked up the phone and said, "It's five in the morning, asshole."

CHAPTER 23

DREAMS OF MORPHEUS

Richard Walter slept easily in his antique Chinese bed.

He'd retired with a head full of wine. As his head hit the pillow, he said aloud, "And now I enter the arms of Morpheus." In Greek mythology the three sons of Hypnos all produced dreams. But Phantasos generated tricky, unreal dreams and Phobetor fearsome nightmares.

Morpheus spun the clear-eyed dreams of heroes.

He cherished his solitude.

"I married once, too long ago to recall or discuss. I shan't make *that* mistake again. As it happens, I simply loathe cats, dogs, and children. A child should never be present to hear what I have to say." He had consciously sacrificed the pleasures of life "to be one of the five best in the world." He believed it was a profound sacrifice, his life a journey marked by loss. "But it is those scars that give us character, that make us who we are."

He made coffee in the darkness before dawn. The sky was still black when he called Philadelphia.

"Frank?"

"Richard!" came the manic shout.

"It's Wednesday morning, remember?"

"Right, Ella and I danced all night. Nineteen sixties rock and Polish vodka. We had an in*credible* time!"

"Frank, what the fuck are you thinking? Did you sleep at all? Are you alone?"

"Uh, well, no. Ella is leaving soon." He lowered his voice confidentially. "Christine's husband is driving her over this morning."

Walter frowned. "Frank, you've had quite enough sex for one twenty-four-hour period. Make a pot of coffee. And try not to let your little head do all the thinking until I get there."

Bender howled in delight. "Rich, man, you're just jealous!"

"I think not," Walter said. He hung up.

The sky was leaden and filled with snow. *It's dark, it's cold, I'm miserable, the weather is evil,* he thought as he swept acorns off the engine block where a squirrel was nesting for the winter. *It's not good.* As he drove to the airport and the cabin pleasingly filled with cigarette smoke, he started to feel better. In the cloud of smoke his small blue-white-red gold pin on the lapel of his suit, the badge of *les couleurs*, rooted in medieval heraldry, was scarcely visible. Each man had a purpose in life, Walter believed; his was to identify, torment, and defeat the most depraved psychopaths on Earth. To be good at it, to be one of the five best in the world, he had rid himself of distractions, had married his profession. Destroying evil gave him the greatest pleasure.

The sky was dreary and the colors of the chivalric code, glory and justice, gods and kings, glittered dully as the old Ford sped down the highway.

CHAPTER 24

A CASE THEY CAN'T LET GO

On the afternoon of Thursday, September 27, 1990, Joe O'Kane took a bite of chicken almondine and a sip of hot coffee, and looked down at three decaying corpses with their heads plunged into an overflowing tub.

"Nice lunch," O'Kane said, dabbing the corners of his mustache with a cloth napkin. He gingerly passed the photograph down the banquet table in the Navy Officers' Club. "I hope this club has a budget for Tums."

The big federal agent was dressed to kill. He was the picture of a brawny, dandified Irish cop in a custom-tailored, three-piece Italian suit and black alligator cowboy boots. Clipped to a wide, silver-buckled belt was a small Beretta pistol, his "Sunday going-to-church gun." His big silver beard was neatly trimmed—the final touch that made him Kenny Rogers's double. With the husky build of a former semi-pro football player and a sweet tenor voice, O'Kane sang at weddings and parties as the country crooner. Special Agent O'Kane was loquacious, brilliant, cocky, a self-described "two-fisted drinker." He'd signed up for the Vidocq Society for a few laughs. There were enough tears on the job.

O'Kane was in the prime of a major law enforcement career. He'd been a key man on covert operations all over the world. Despite his accomplishments, O'Kane never forgot that he was blue-collar Irish, son of a Kensington millwright, product of a high school education, and proud of it. He was one of Customs' "Mustangs," the Army term they borrowed for the Horatio Alger grunts who made it to the top on merit. "None of us waltzed into some fancy job out of college," he said. The Irishman had a wild, rebellious streak; he'd grown his beard just to piss off a supervisor who insisted he be clean-shaven, and it became a permanent part of him. He followed his own muse. The burly cop was a poetry lover who'd read thousands of novels and had written three thrillers for kicks. "Chesterfield put it best," he said. "The Irish are a merry race and surely they are mad, for all their wars are merry and all their songs are sad."

The last thing he needed was some uptight, buttoned-down agent trying to re-create the FBI over lunch. He wanted to have fun! He was the first man Fleisher approached about joining the society.

"Bill, that sounds great but I'm not a big joiner," he said. "I don't join the FOP [Fraternal Order of Police]. I don't join the Sons of Ireland. These people get carried away with themselves; everybody's got an agenda. I don't need any of that in my life. Tell me we'll have fun. If we can sit around and have lunches and have fun with the guys, I'll do it. If everybody takes themselves serious as a shoelace, I don't need that. I'm working twenty-three hours a day on major cases against the scum of the earth. I don't need that over lunch."

Fleisher promised a good time. "He said we'd sit in an elegant room over lunch and talk about Billy the Kid, hundred-year-old crimes, we'd bring in experts on Jesse James, even a session on Meriwether Lewis and Clark," O'Kane later recalled. "I said, 'OK, I'm in. Sign me up.'"

Now, at the Vidocq Society's second luncheon, the very first case they formally discussed was a triple murder in North Carolina as serious and senseless as *In Cold Blood*. In fact, the 1972 massacre of the wealthy Durham family in the western Blue Ridge Mountains reminded O'Kane of Truman Capote's description of the Clutter family slaughter in Garden City, Kansas. It was hardly his idea of a relaxing midday repast.

"What, do they expect me to solve this before dessert? This isn't fun."

"No, 'tis not any fun in this kind of case," Richard Walter sniffed. "Except, of course, for the killer. One can discern from this crime scene that for this kind of personality, it's the satisfaction of a mission accomplished, a job well done. Oftentimes, the uninitiated fail to grasp how much pleasure is involved for the killer."

Walter was standing at the head of the banquet table presenting the unsolved case to a couple dozen VSMs. The mass murder had baffled the police for eighteen years, and recently Walter had been hired by the North Carolina State Bureau of Investigation to review the cold case. "It's a wonderful case," he said as he passed around crime-scene photos and case documents. "There's all sorts of drama here." Fleisher thought it sufficiently cold and fascinating for the Vidocq Society to discuss.

Walter looked down at the case file while gathering his thoughts. "As it happens, the killer was rather obvious," he said. "This kind of killer always thinks he's smarter than he really is."

The Durhams were a quiet, respected, affluent family that, according to police, had no known enemies, Walter said. Bryce Durham, fifty-one, his wife, Virginia, forty-six, and son Bobby Joe, nineteen, had moved from Raleigh two years earlier to Boone (pop. 13,472), the Watauga County seat in the state's far western mountains, ninety miles northeast of Asheville. Bryce owned a local automobile dealership, Modern Buick-Pontiac. They were conservative, devout Christians.

On the evening of Thursday, February 3, 1972, Bryce left a 5:30 Rotary Club meeting and returned to the dealership to pick up his wife, a secretary at the family business, and son, a student at nearby Appalachian State University, for the ride home. After his last class, Bobby Joe had driven his Buick sedan to the dealership and left it there to join his parents in the GMC Jimmy. A major snowstorm had blown in, and they all climbed into the four-wheel-drive SUV.

Sometime between 8:30 and 9:00 that night, the Durhams reached home, the SUV slowly climbing the icy road to the large brick split-level atop a steep hill. The family settled down for a quiet Thursday evening of dinner and television. Outside, the house was nearly invisible in the blowing snow. It was a night to stay indoors. But the killer knew the local roads and mountains and the Durham house, Walter said, and proceeded through the storm.

That night, Troy Hall, the Durhams' son-in-law, and his wife were quietly watching TV in a trailer home four miles from the hilltop split-level. At 10:30, the phone rang, and Troy picked it up. On the other end was the barely audible voice of his mother-in-law, he told police. "Help," she begged, whispering as if afraid of being heard. Intruders were in the house, she said, and they "have got Bobby and Bryce." Then the phone went dead.

Hall told police he thought the call was a practical joke. He immediately called back, certain his in-laws were all fine, but he got only a busy signal. Growing concerned, he and his wife pulled on their coats and jumped in the car—but the car wouldn't start, so they asked a neighbor, private detective Cecil Small, to drive them through the storm. It took the three of them twenty minutes to reach the Durham house at the top of the hill. Hall told his wife to stay in the car while he and Small, his handgun drawn, checked out the house. At 10:50, the son-in-law and private eye discovered the bodies and called police.

The crime scene told the story of domestic tranquillity suddenly shattered. The house had been ransacked. In the living room stood three glasses of soda and a half-eaten plate of chicken on the coffee table in front of the sofa, next to Bobby Joe's solitaire cards. A large patch of blood stained the carpet. Virginia had died from strangulation, the coroner determined. A short piece of nylon cord still encircled her neck. Bryce and Bobby Joe had deep rope burns scarring their necks, a clear attempt to strangle them, but their cause of death was drowning. All their faces were badly bruised. The water was still running, overflowing the tub.

From the beginning, the police were confused. They launched a massive manhunt through the snow-covered mountains of western North Carolina. Within minutes, they found the Durhams'

GMC Jimmy, which the killer had stolen to make his escape. It was abandoned a mile away from the house on a snowy, deserted road known only to locals. The car's lights were on and the motor was running. On the backseat was a sack of silver plates stolen from the Durham residence.

The state police believed it was a robbery. But then why did the robber(s) abandon the silver plates? And why, Walter asked, were two bank-deposit bags, with cash inside, left on a dining room chair in the house? Police had no answers to that. The Watauga County sheriff surmised it was a grudge killing. But he knew of nobody with a mortal grudge against the Durhams.

The pressure to make an arrest was intense. Newspapers all across the mountains printed the horrors. North Carolina governor Bob Scott joined local business leaders in offering a reward for an arrest leading to conviction. United Press International broke the news that in her frantic last phone call to her son-in-law, Mrs. Durham had said, "We have three niggers here." The next day, the Watauga County sheriff told UPI, "We have some good clues and we hope to have early arrests. And we definitely are investigating blacks."

No black men were ever charged. A month later, the sheriff rounded up three Asheville men in their twenties who were part of a burglary ring. The trio was charged with first-degree murder in the commission of a robbery, but the three men were quickly released for lack of any evidence putting them at the crime scene.

"I would argue that the system worked," Walter said, to the extent that "innocent men were not prosecuted." Nobody was ever brought to trial for the murders.

As Walter concluded, Fleisher stood and opened the floor to questions.

Was robbery a motive for the murders? a federal agent asked.

"No," Walter said. "On the contrary, it was rather clumsily staged to look like a robbery. But it was a killing all about power and control."

What about the son-in-law? another VSM asked.

"It's interesting that all was not well in the marriage," Walter said. "The Durham family was pressuring their daughter to leave Hall." The couple eventually divorced after the murders.

"But police never considered him a major suspect," Walter said.

What about Cecil Small? someone asked. Wasn't it odd that a neighbor who just happened to be a private eye was the only witness to the crime scene outside of the family?

Walter raised his left eyebrow to a fine point. "I have my doubts about Small," he said. "There's reason to question his general credibility. For the last thirty years he's told anyone who listened that he knows who killed JFK, and it wasn't Oswald." Guffaws swept the table.

The story beggared belief, but Small had insisted so loudly that a Hispanic man had assassinated JFK that FBI agents finally interviewed him in 1967, Walter said.

Small said he and his wife were in their pickup truck in Dallas, Texas, on November 22, 1963, on their way home to their Georgia trailer from a western trip with their little dog. Suddenly they found themselves riding in JFK's motorcade. Small saw the first lady stand up and heard his dog bark the instant the president was shot (the dog always barked at gunfire). Then he saw a short Cuban or Mexican man cross in front of his truck, running away holding a rifle with a scope partially hidden in a bag. Minutes later, Small happened to give a pleasant young hitchhiker named Lee Harvey Oswald, whom Small believed couldn't have done it, a ride to the library from the Texas Book Depository.

According to FBI records, agents decided not to further investigate because Small's memory of Dallas streets and landmarks wasn't accurate.

"That's quite a witness," a federal agent said. "Maybe he knows where Elvis is living now."

So who killed the Durham family? a VSM asked.

Walter grimaced. "I have a theory. We'll see if the state police are savvy enough to go forward with it."

O'Kane was agitated. "It was a gruesome case," he recalled,

hardly appropriate for a social club. He and the other investigators were fundamentally men of action, not words; if you put an unsolved triple murder, a grave injustice, in front of them they naturally wanted to solve it. O'Kane was convinced Walter knew who the killer was, but there was nothing the vaunted members of the Vidocq Society could do about it unless they conducted their own private investigation.

As they left, Walter was disappointed that there had been so few questions from such an esteemed group of investigators. He attributed it to "natural caution. This is the first time we've done this, and they don't know much about it. The guys were pretty much just following along with what I told them."

William Gill, the decorated special agent in charge of Treasury agents in three states, sat silently through the presentation, stunned by Walter's knowledge. After a lifetime in the military and law enforcement, he realized with a start that "homicide investigation is a very specialized field"—one he knew nothing about. "In Treasury, I'm a white-collar guy—mostly bribery, extortion, white-collar crimes. We follow the money, just like the IRS special agents. I don't do homicides. I don't do blood splatter."

Gill dourly reflected on the irony that "Fleisher had gathered together these extremely talented people to examine murders and the majority of them are not homicide investigators." An irrepressible optimist, the Treasury ASAC was confident that he and the other federal agents would make significant contributions, drawing on their own expertise. He decided the league of extraordinarily diverse talents was, like most things new and unusual, hard to grasp because it was a product of pure inspiration, "the simple genius of Bill Fleisher."

Gill decided to test that genius at the very next meeting. At his request, the Vidocq Society examined the brutal execution of IRS agent Heidi A. Berg, shot to death six years earlier in suburban Virginia while jogging. Berg was a bright, athletic thirty-year-old woman from the Midwest who was slain in broad daylight. Her murder had never been solved. Virginia-based IRS special agent

James Rice, whom Gill had assigned to the case in 1984, came to Philadelphia to present it with his former boss.

"Everyone has a case they can't let go," Fleisher said to Gill. "This is yours."

Gill took the case personally. "A sadder thing I've never seen," he said. Gill was head of the IRS Internal Security Division for the Mid-Atlantic region of Pennsylvania, Delaware, Maryland, and Virginia. He was responsible for protecting IRS employees and investigating threats and assaults against them. When Berg's murder landed on his desk in Philadelphia, he felt his blood pressure spike.

Early on the morning of August 12, 1984, Berg was jogging through a park near her home in suburban Merrifield, Virginia, about ten miles west of Arlington. Berg, a dark-haired young woman wearing athletic shorts and a T-shirt, was a highly disciplined IRS agent and a habitual runner. She was a reserved woman from Wisconsin, a devout Christian, gave anonymously to charity, and dreamed of writing children's books. She hadn't an enemy in the world, police thought.

But at 6:30 that morning, just a few minutes into her jog, she was shot six times in the back with a handgun. She ran a few steps before collapsing and died where she fell, on the grass in front of an American Automobile Association building, where her body was discovered by a passing motorist. A single assassin apparently ambushed her, for reasons unknown. "She was executed by an excellent shot who emptied the gun on her," Gill told the VSMs. "Someone really wanted Heidi Berg dead."

He assigned Agent Rice and eight other veteran IRS agents in Virginia to the case. Rice became obsessed, spending parts of vacations working on the murder.

The crucial question hadn't changed in six years: Who wanted to kill Heidi Berg? Police had no idea. The murder made no sense. As Fairfax County prosecutor Robert F. Horan Jr. put it, "Of all the people who jog in Fairfax County, you wouldn't find many less likely to be the target of a homicide." They even suspected a professional assassin may have killed the wrong woman.

Gill didn't see it that way. "There were thousands of reasons someone would want to kill Heidi Berg," he said, "each one printed with George Washington's portrait."

Heidi Berg was an IRS revenue officer, a difficult, dangerous job, Gill said. She was essentially an unarmed, civilian bill collector for the IRS. "When people *really* don't pay their taxes and have had a lot of opportunities, letters, the revenue officers have to go out and knock on doors and do seizures," Gill said. "Everybody hates the IRS, and if you say 'bill collector for IRS' you're doubly hated. We had a high incidence of threats against revenue officers, and a few assaults.

"Naturally," Gill said, "we assumed the killing was tied to her work." In fact, Berg had recently been threatened in her job as a revenue officer based in Bailey's Crossroads, Virginia. The threats had seemed serious enough that she received a transfer to the Washington, D.C., office and a less contentious job as program analyst.

But it was a dead end. "We pretty much exhausted the idea that it was job-related. We were reasonably sure it wasn't anybody in her case files." Then they found entries in Berg's diary about a secret boyfriend, unknown to her friends or family. Her secret boyfriend was an FBI supervisor, a married man. Agents got excited when they learned the bullets that killed Berg were of "the same caliber issued by the FBI at the time," Gill said. "It looked very promising. We went down that alley aggressively."

FBI internal security gave the potential suspect a polygraph test, but it was inconclusive. Agents also gave polygraph tests to the man's wife and his son, who was off at college. "It ruined the guy's life for a while," Gill said. "Bad luck for him that she maintained a diary." The FBI supervisor was eliminated as a suspect. Another dead end.

"It's a very frustrating case," Gill said. "We had ten good agents in that office and a lot of money to spend. But we couldn't get anywhere."

So who killed Heidi Berg?

Richard Walter cleared his throat to speak, and Gill leaned

forward. "Everyone seems to think if she's pretty and young it was sexually driven," Walter said. "I don't see evidence for that. The killing is consistent with the angry taxpayer theory—Heidi is just disposed of, thrown away like trash, a killing all about power, which is what money represents. The gun is all power. But if everyone in her case files has been ruled out, the probability is she is a stranger to the killer. She was there and he had the needs and weapon and did her, a variant form of a drive-by shooting."

The group fell silent. But why kill her? Bender asked. Walter frowned. "He may have tried to put the make on her and she said no, and he didn't have the ability or testicles to take her down, so he satisfies himself with the gun. It's also possible that he's impotent or whatever else and that's the most he can do, he feels isolated and he wants to take somebody out, and she's a good-looking girl."

The thin man smiled coldly. "We don't like to imagine these fellows out there. They're the sharks in the harbor. That's why it's a high risk to go running alone, to be isolated at six o'clock in the morning in a park, on a pathway—particularly for an attractive girl."

Gill's face lost color. He didn't doubt Walter, but it seemed a tragic, absurd end to Heidi Berg. The questions from the VSMs had seemed relatively weak. Someone had actually asked Gill if he had checked Berg's phone records. "Of course," Gill had shot back. What were they accomplishing?

The next month was even more disappointing to Fleisher. On the morning of Tuesday, July 3, 1984, Donna Friedman, thirty-three years old and eight and a half months pregnant, left her two young children with a babysitter and went to her regular obstetrics appointment. Friedman, a doctor's wife, was due the second week in August. She received great news from her obstetrician, Dr. Robert S. Auerbach. The baby was a "perfectly formed, healthy baby boy," Dr. Auerbach said. "She was very happy and doing beautifully. She said that she didn't care whether it was a boy or a girl. She had only wanted it to be healthy. She lived for her other two children so completely."

Leaving the doctor's office, Friedman said she had some shopping to do. First Friedman, who was redecorating her suburban Philadelphia home, went to All-in-One Linens to inquire about bedroom curtains. Then it was on to Toys"R"Us to look for a stroller for her brother's newborn son, a gift for the child's bris. Unable to find the special stroller, she called her brother at about 1 P.M., and he suggested she go to Cramer's Juvenile Furniture on Frankford Avenue, which was advertising the stroller. She bought it with a credit card, and asked a clerk to help carry it to the trunk of her car. The store clerk watched her drive away at 3:30 P.M.

When she didn't return home by 4:15, her husband, hematologist Dr. Alan Friedman, was worried. Donna was always punctual and knew she had to be home to relieve the babysitter for Scott, eight, and Lee, four. The couple also planned to attend a 6 P.M. birthday party for Dr. Friedman's grandmother at a local restaurant. When his wife didn't show up for the party, Dr. Friedman called hospitals and the police.

Police began an urgent search for the missing woman. Dr. Friedman spent two days retracing his wife's steps. At 8:25 P.M., Thursday, police found the family's 1984 Oldsmobile Cutlass parked on Ogontz Avenue, a few blocks from the Cheltenham Square Mall. Blood was seeping out of the trunk. Friedman and her unborn child were both found dead in the trunk. The young mother had been bludgeoned to death with two blows to the skull, then shot twice in the back of the head, "for good measure," the police said.

Fleisher choked up listening to Philadelphia Police Department detective Frank Diegel describe the case. Fleisher had grown up not far from the Friedmans. At the funeral service for mother and unborn child, people wept and cried out in anguish. The rabbi had told the story of a man who cried over the death of a loved one.

"Why do you weep?" the man's friend asked. "Your tears will not bring back your loved one."

"That is why I weep," the man replied.

A week after the murders, the *Philadelphia Daily News* offered

$10,000 for information leading to the arrest and conviction "of the person or persons responsible for the murder of Donna Friedman and her unborn child." Family and friends of the Friedmans offered a separate $10,000 reward. Homicide detective Diegel had a primary suspect, but the police investigation foundered. The money was never collected. No one was ever arrested for the crime.

The Vidocq Society discussion was spirited. The society helped focus and reenergize Diegel on his primary suspect, whom VSMs were convinced had killed the pregnant woman. But in the weeks that followed, Fleisher was deeply frustrated. "We know who did it, but it was never pursued by the police. It was stonewalled, and we don't know why."

Fleisher said they were taking on a Sisyphean task if they tried to solve cold murders. Police often interviewed the killer within forty-eight hours of a murder, but if they didn't recognize him, the case dried up fast. Memories faded. Evidence disappeared. Other cases clamored for attention. Once a case officially went cold, the difficult turned nearly impossible. "There are good reasons a case doesn't get solved in the first place," Fleisher said. "You have to deal with those." It took a highly motivated DA and police department, and often a passionately involved family, to blast a case from the ice. On top of all that, the Vidocq Society lacked police power to arrest and subpoena. Their power was brainpower. "We almost always know who did it," Fleisher said. "But to find a solution, get an arrest and conviction, the stars would have to be aligned."

Gill, the high-ranking Treasury agent, left the Friedman case with a humbling lesson. While he was busy chasing Mafia kingpins, "A lot of people in this country get away with murder. A lot more than I thought." A restless mood seemed to grip the VSMs. Was the point of the exclusive club to expose difficult truths and break hearts? It wasn't at all what Fleisher intended.

CHAPTER 25

THE BUTCHER OF CLEVELAND

Yet to Fleisher's surprise, the Vidocq Society grew quickly and dramatically, and just as quickly gained a remarkable reputation in and out of law enforcement. By the fifth meeting, on April 18, 1991, the size of the society had more than doubled to sixty-two members. The buzz about the dining and detective club reached the media. A *New York Times* reporter had asked to attend the fifth ratiocinative luncheon. The Vidocq Society, he later wrote, "may be the only club in which real sleuths try to solve real crimes for recreation."

The new VSMs were, if anything, even more prominent. The director of *Brigade de la Sûreté*, the French equivalent of the FBI founded by Vidocq in 1811, signed on, making the trip to Philadelphia from Paris. So did FBI agent Daniel Reilly, an organized crime expert from Long Island. Agent Reilly wanted to relax from his job of tracking "really horrible, no, make that repugnant people."

New VSM Charles Rogovin, a Temple University law professor and criminologist, knew something about cold cases. He sat on the select congressional committees that investigated the assassinations of John F. Kennedy and Martin Luther King. Yet he was now eager to help the everyday cop "who's got a tough nut to crack. An old case is very tough to deal with." The virtue of the Vidocq Society, he believed, was that "if the assigned investigator is working as hard as he can and he runs out of trump, sometimes it takes an outside investigator to say, 'How about this?' "

Rogovin looked around the room proudly at the record turnout for the fifth meeting. "This is not a collection of English club members," he said. "You've got some seasoned people here."

Cuisine and crime that day would be served at the Dickens Inn, a small colonial tavern, built in 1788, facing the broad cobblestone boulevard of South Second Street. The society had left the Naval Officers' Club, finding it insufficiently atmospheric for their deliberations, in addition to which some VSMs voiced concern about privacy. The new digs were an intimate English pub named in homage to Charles Dickens, who actually visited Philadelphia. The *Times* reporter was taken by the irony of the setting, noting "waitresses dressed in eighteenth-century barmaid uniforms brushed past a detective who remarked, 'She was shot to death on a Sunday.' "

Fleisher was excited. The setting matched his vision for the Vidocq Society, and so did the case. He had finally scheduled a classic murder case that detectives could discuss and debate over a leisurely repast. It was the 1930s Butcher of Cleveland, who had committed the ghastliest series of murders in American history. The Butcher tortured, dismembered, decapitated, and drained the blood from more than thirty men and women from the 1920s through the Great Depression and beyond. Seventy years later, the murders, which had stumped hundreds of lawmen including Eliot Ness, remained unsolved.

Ness had been hired as Cleveland's safety director in 1935 with a shining reputation. In Chicago in 1931, the dashing young U.S. Treasury agent headed an elite unit of eight federal prohibition G-Men (Government Men) who raided Al Capone's speakeasies and helped bring down the gangster on tax evasion and liquor charges. Men of unassailable integrity, Ness and his Chicago feds could not be bought—thus they were "The Untouchables."

By all accounts, he made great strides cleaning up a corrupt city. He attacked gambling and the city's organized crime operations, going after crooked police and politicians who were in the mob's pocket. He dropped the crime rate 30 percent to make

Cleveland the nation's safest city. Ahead of his time, he reduced auto deaths by cracking down on speeders and drunk drivers. He even dropped juvenile crime two-thirds by starting citywide Boy Scout troops.

Then he encountered a new type of criminal. This was a supremely clever, Machiavellian type who could not be investigated or bullied like Al Capone by simply raiding a speakeasy. Sadistic serial killers, with IQs notably higher than other killers and the ability to imagine and fulfill the darkest, most complex criminal needs, were an increasing plague of the twentieth century. They didn't seek money or power or revenge. They tortured and killed strangers in a shadowy nightmare-world created and ruled by their own insatiable desires.

The first who gained infamy in the new century was New York City pedophile and cannibal Albert Fish, "The Brooklyn Vampire." In January 1936, as Ness took office in Cleveland, the pale, mustached, deranged house painter was electrocuted at Sing Sing for strangling, killing, and eating ten-year-old Grace Budd. Fish had tricked the girl's parents into thinking he was a kindly old farmer who promised the father a job, but first wanted to take the girl to a birthday party at his sister's house.

Unknown to Ness, the Fish case would provide rare insight into the mind of this penultimate category of killer. Trickery, the ruse, was essential to the sadist's excitement, as was the denouement, or "gotcha." Six years after Budd's kidnapping and murder, Fish sent a letter to her mother boasting of his crime: "On Sunday, June 3, 1928, I called on you. . . . Brought you pot cheese—strawberries. We had lunch. Grace sat in my lap and kissed me. I made up my mind to eat her. On the pretense of taking her to a party. You said yes she could go. I took her to an empty house in Westchester I had already picked out. . . . When she saw me all naked she began to cry . . . she said she would tell her mamma. First I stripped her naked. How she did kick—bite and scratch. I choked her to death, then cut her in small pieces so I could take my meat to my rooms. Cook and eat it. How sweet and tender her little ass was roasted in the oven. It took me nine days to eat her entire body. I did not fuck her tho I could of had I wished. She died a virgin."

As Fish, suspected of five murders, died in the electric chair, the Mad Butcher was already well on his way to being the most prolific serial killer of the twentieth century. He was on a pace to match Dr. H. H. Holmes, who admitted to at least twenty-seven killings and may have murdered dozens more in his gloomy "Castle" of death during the glittering Chicago World's Fair of 1893. Compelled by some of the same insatiable needs as Holmes, the Butcher seemed intent on re-creating a gruesome history, littering Cleveland's world's fair of 1936 with bodies.

The killer operated with strength and stealth, and a horrifying appetite to torture and degrade his victims. In September 1934, the grisly Lady of the Lake surfaced in Lake Erie—the torso of an unidentified woman in her thirties, beheaded and legs cut off at the knees. In September 1935, two nude male bodies—beheaded and castrated—were found in Kingsbury Run, a Depression tent city of hoboes in a gloomy downtown ravine cut by the Cuyahoga River and railroad tracks. The younger victim, Edward Andrassy, twenty-eight, a small-time hoodlum of profligate bisexual appetites, was cleaned and completely drained of blood. Both men were decapitated while alive. The fourth victim was a prostitute, Florence Polillo. One arm and both thighs were found in a bushel basket, wrapped like a ham.

The pattern was clear to police: decapitation, which was extremely difficult and rare in the history of murder, followed by dismemberment and sexual mutilation. The killer had to be a very strong man, the coroner said, and also must be a surgeon, given the skill and exactitude of the beheadings. A cop said it more bluntly: "A maniac with a lust to kill is on the loose."

The city was frightened. As headlines grew hysterical, the mayor and newspapers demanded the city's safety director stop the monster. Random beheadings in the shadow of its new skyscrapers were a public relations nightmare for Cleveland in 1936. The city that year drew three million visitors to the Great Lakes Exposition, a heroic attempt, supported by federal money, to boost its sagging fortunes. Architects had designed a gleaming modernist expo city on 135 acres on Lake Erie. Rivaling the Chicago World's Fair's White City, it was "a city of ivory, a new Baghdad risen in the desert," one writer said. Olympic swimmer Johnny Weissmuller, the future movie Tarzan, and Esther Williams performed on the Aquacade, a floating stage, while jazz from the Bob Crosby Orchestra floated out over the water. In June of that year, Cleveland also was preparing to take a second bow in the national spotlight, hosting the 1936 Republican National Convention, which would send shy Kansas governor Alf Landon to be crushed by FDR in the fall. Yet Ness, absorbed in fighting municipal corruption, showed little interest in the murders. The safety director was letting a serial killer terrorize the city.

But on June 5, as delegates poured into town for the GOP convention set to start in three days, a head detached from the body of a tattooed man was discovered by the train tracks in Kingsbury Run. In a brazen affront to Ness, the killer hid the body in bushes in full sight of a police station. On the Sunday afternoon in September when star Cleveland Indians pitcher Bob Feller struck out seventeen Philadelphia A's, more than five thousand people gathered around a sewage pit to watch a diver retrieve the arms and legs of the Butcher's eighth victim.

The mayor ordered Ness to act. The *Cleveland Press* demanded: "Unusual means must be taken to bring the detection of one of the most horrible killers in criminal history."

Ness responded by putting twenty detectives on the case, including undercover hoboes. He sought advice from the experts at Scotland Yard. He expanded the investigation to the largest in city history. Police brought in ten thousand possible suspects for interviews, focusing on physically strong men who were surgeons, medical personnel, male nurses, and animal butchers. Detective Pete Merylo paraded through shantytowns in his long johns under the moonlight to "bait" a killer he was convinced was homosexual. Nothing worked. By 1938, the Butcher of Cleveland had killed and dismembered twelve men and women.

Ness's dragnet finally turned up a prime suspect. Dr. Frank E.

Sweeney was a surgeon from a prominent family, the first cousin of a local Democratic Party boss. On the surface an impressive, articulate man, Dr. Sweeney was known to be an alcoholic, mentally unstable, and abusive; his wife had left him. Furthermore, he was physically huge, quite capable of all the cutting and moving about of human remains. His frequent disappearances from the hospital where he worked, timed to some of the killings, had aroused suspicion, and Ness himself had been frightened by the big man's anger when alone with him.

Ness's instincts were confirmed when another crime-fighting legend, Leonarde Keeler, inventor of the polygraph machine, came in from Chicago and administered several lie detection tests to Sweeney, who failed them all. The surgeon, the polygrapher told Ness, was "a classic psychopath." Sweeney was following in the footsteps of his father, an alcoholic, violent schizophrenic who was committed to mental hospitals at the end of his life. Keeler said, "You've got your man."

But Ness faced a quandary. He was reportedly convinced that Sweeney was the Butcher of Cleveland. Yet he didn't believe he'd ever win a conviction of the politically connected Sweeney. Two days later, in what some suspected was a deal Ness cut with the prominent family, Dr. Sweeney voluntarily committed himself, and never saw the outside of a mental hospital or hospital for the rest of his life. The Cleveland killings stopped, but the murderer moved on to other parts of Ohio and Pennsylvania. Meanwhile, it was too late for Ness. His reputation had already been damaged by allegations of heavy drinking and skirt-chasing that facilitated the breakup of his marriage. His long failure to stop the serial killer's reign of terror left him especially vulnerable to political enemies and the press. It was the makings of an American tragedy.

On an icy winter night in 1942, after he fled the scene of a car accident at 4:30 in the morning following a night of drinking and clubbing, Ness was forced to resign his post. His second wife, a young model and art student, left him soon after. The former crime-fighting wunderkind descended through a series of career and business failures in New York and Washington, D.C., to the remote mountain town of Coudersport, Pennsylvania, where he drank heavily with his third wife and continued to tell wild stories in the bars about Al Capone that few believed. An old friend, sportswriter Oscar Fraley, embellished those stories in his highly fictionalized account of Ness's life, *The Untouchables,* which made Ness an American legend. But Ness didn't live to see the book. In May 1957, he walked back to his small-town apartment from the liquor store with another whiskey bottle and died of a heart attack at the kitchen sink, at the age of fifty-four. It was said the Butcher had taken yet another victim.

The subject seemed "graphic" to the *Times* reporter. Philadelphia boasted "enough bizarre killings . . . to keep a full house at the morgue and make homicide detectives and medical examiners wish they could get away from it all," he said, marveling that "when some of them do take a break, they like to sit back and listen to the one about the Cleveland torso murders."

Adding to the sense of drama in the room, the case would be presented by two renowned investigators from sharply different traditions that were increasingly in conflict. Philadelphia homicide captain Frank Friel was an old-school, shoe-leather detective, rooted in the solid nineteenth-century procedure of building a case from fact-gathering at the crime scene. He would be followed by forensic psychologist Richard Walter, one of a small group of pioneers who read bloodstains and patterns at murder scenes like Rorschach tests. At their best, they seemed to be wizards capable of reading a killer's thoughts. It was a face-off between natural opponents—two proud, strong-willed figures who were oddly well matched, both tall, lean, and charismatic men who used wit to mask a fierce demeanor.

As lunch dishes were cleared, Friel opened the floor to questions. He challenged the Vidocqeans: Who was the Butcher of Cleveland? Fleisher was delighted. It was just the kind of forensic puzzle he had imagined. Could a college of top investigators surpass Eliot Ness? Could they solve the mystery of "The American Jack the Ripper"?

The question-and-answer period was brisk. Friel and others maintained that Ness correctly focused the investigation on cutting trades such as surgeons and butchers. "The principal characteristic of the assailant was that he decapitated the victims while they were still alive," Friel said.

Customs agent Frank Dufner saw it as the work of an angry medical student. "Did anyone flunk out of medical school?" he asked.

The fact that the bodies were drained, did anyone consider an undertaker? a police officer asked.

Yes, Friel said, medical students and undertakers had been questioned.

"Seven out of twelve of the heads were not found," Dufner continued. "Were they kept as trophies?" Friel couldn't say.

Fleisher had scribbled in a notebook: *undertaker, butcher, abattoir.* But by the end of the presentation, he was convinced the surgeon, Dr. Sweeney, was the killer. "If Leonarde Keeler says he was the guy, he was the guy. Keeler was one of the inventors of the polygraph, and a master at it."

While busboys removed the lunch plates, "the fact of the matter is, Eliot Ness did some good things, was a hero to an extent," Walter said, "but was out of his depth in this case because of his limited knowledge in the 1930s of serial killers."

Walter leaned in and said, sotto voce, "Of course, the FBI still doesn't understand much of this, so we shouldn't be so hard on Ness." Several VSMs chuckled along with him.

To start, Walter said, Ness was mistaken to narrow the investigation to large, strong men and professionals or tradesmen expert with a knife. "You don't have to be a butcher to carve someone into little pieces or an undertaker to drain them of blood. The fact of the matter is anyone can do it, and do it competently. You just have to want to." He smiled coldly, and went on. "In addition the killer doesn't have to be big or powerful. He can be a small man. All he has to be is clever. He gets them drunk, then he can do anything to them."

Second, Walter said, Dr. Sweeney, Ness's main suspect, "was a lousy choice to be the Butcher, for all the reasons that supposedly implicate him. He's violent, alcoholic, schizophrenic. That makes him an asshole, but it doesn't make him a sadist." It was clear from the corpses that the Butcher of Cleveland was a sadistic serial killer, and Sweeney didn't fit that profile.

"There's a big qualitative difference between a guy who is just unpredictably violent, like Sweeney, and a guy who had a system like the Butcher," Walter went on. "A sadist has a long complicated growth pattern to fulfill his darkest desires. He's organized, cunning, he plans, has the ability to change direction when things go awry."

Sweeney is also eliminated by the fact that the killings didn't stop, Walter said. "The police at the time couldn't understand it, but more than twenty other killings and dismemberments in eastern Ohio and even western Pennsylvania clearly bear the mark of the Butcher," Walter said. "I believe the killings stopped only when he died of natural causes, was killed, or committed suicide in 1950."

Given Ness's limited knowledge at the time, the Butcher was basically an unstoppable killing machine, he said. "The Butcher was smarter than Ness, and proved it." The Butcher gained sexual pleasure by creating dependency, dread, and degradation in his victims. It was the same desire that governed the behavior of modern serial killers like Ted Bundy and John Wayne Gacy. The sadist's pleasure is almost always sexual, and is insatiable.

Hoboes were an easy target. "The Butcher would lure them off into the woods with offers of booze, food, sex, whatever. That's the ruse. They go into the woods and they don't leave—that's an exciting story for him. It's not enough for the sadist to bash somebody in, he has to enjoy it, and part of that enjoyment is the ruse. Then he gets them into a situation they can't get out of, reveals himself as a monster. He creates situations where he can systematically triumph."

As dessert was served, Walter said, "Yes, he took the heads as trophies, like Bundy did." In his secret lair, Bundy masturbated over his female victims' decapitated heads. What the Butcher did with the heads will never be known. But the drained bodies are a profound clue to his perverted sexual pleasures.

When the waiters came around with fresh coffee, Walter urged the Vidocqeans to try to imagine the pleasure the killer experienced when he drained his victims of all their blood in water. "The water heightens the pleasure. Try squeezing a sponge under water at home. When you feel the water gently tickling the hairs on your arms, it's sensual. That's the kind of pleasure the Butcher experienced, an intense sexual pleasure."

Fleisher was beaming. The meeting was a success. He bragged to the *Times* reporter, "Sherlock Holmes was a great detective. But he was all imagination. We're the real thing." The Vidocq Society, he said, was "like a college of detectives. You couldn't get a more astute group of detectives." But the question was, would the society be a college that discussed murders as an academic exercise, or would the detectives come down from their ivory tower and try to solve crimes? The *Times* reporter asked Fleisher, "When are you going to actually solve a murder?"

Fleisher said the Butcher of Cleveland was probably past solving. He was confident after just a handful of meetings that "we will solve ninety percent of these cases that come before us. Everyone in the room knows who did it. But it's a lot more complicated bringing a cold killer to justice."

"We haven't solved one yet," Fleisher added. "But we're getting close."

When he saw his words conveyed around the world to millions of readers in the pages of *The New York Times,* Fleisher only wished it were true.

"Clearly this is not another show at the local mystery dinner theater," the *Times* concluded, "nor a meeting of Sherlock Holmes buffs."

"He did a grand job of saying who we aren't," Walter quipped. "But who the hell are we?"

CHAPTER 26

IMPLORING GOD

As the lights dimmed in the Texas ballroom, the faces of the dead appeared, larger than life yet so young and small, to soft music accompanied by a staccato of gasps and sobs from the audience. Each child's face brought another cry from a banquet table, another candle sizzling in the dark, until the great hall glimmered like a concert—a hushed and otherworldly concert where parents implored fate or God for an encore.

Retired Philadelphia police captain Frank Friel sat in the ballroom of the San Antonio Hilton, chain-smoking and haunted by his thoughts. In his suit pocket was his keynote speech; in his hands was the national convention's Book of the Dead. At his table were the conventioneers, their faces distorted with grief or anger or flooded with tears, like rain washing over stone. It was Thursday evening, August 11, 1991, and the fourth annual convention of the National Organization of Parents of Murdered Children (POMC) was a gathering unlike any Friel had ever seen.

As he stood to speak to the hall filled with mothers and fathers, uncles and grandparents, of murdered children and young adults, Friel prayed for guidance. The enormity of the suffering in the room weighed on him; he was struggling to keep down a bottomless grief, to stare into his own soul.

In thirty years on the Philadelphia police force, Friel had

thought he knew all there was to know about murder. He'd investigated thousands of them as a cop and homicide captain. He'd been codirector of the Philadelphia Police–FBI Organized Crime Task Force that virtually destroyed the Philadelphia Mafia in the 1980s. He'd fearlessly stood up to the murderous don, Nicodemo Scarfo, who identified Friel as his "chief nemesis." He'd personally investigated the bombing assassination of Philadelphia godfather Philip "Chicken Man" Testa on the Ides of March 1981, when Testa was blown through his front door as he put the key in the lock at 2117 Porter Street in South Philadelphia. In the nation's fourth-largest city, Friel was the best of the best. The former city police commissioner and mayor Frank Rizzo once said, "No detective in the history of the Philadelphia Police Department was better than Frank Friel."

Retired from the Philly PD for two years, he'd taken a job as the public safety director of Bensalem, Bucks County, and worked as a consultant to the FBI and Major League Baseball on organized crime. He toured the country assessing the professional standards of police departments for the National Commission on Accreditation. He taught criminology at Temple, St. Joseph's, and LaSalle universities. But the POMC was something new. The group had 100,000 members, with chapters in most states, and provided a full range of services to suffering families. The convention seemed surreal to him. In seminars and hallways, at meals and over drinks, they learned from experts and one another how to endure a murder in the family: inattentive, inept, or corrupt cops and prosecutors; an exploitive press; the court system with its noble constitutional safeguards for the rights of their sons' or daughters' killers and none for them or their son or daughter; friends, neighbors, and church folk who shunned them; the sidelong glances that said, *This doesn't happen to good girls and boys*; the psychologists who had no true explanation, and thus no true word of solace, for evil.

Friel thought he knew the awful secret of murder in America. The awful secret was that since 1960, when he joined the police department at age eighteen, more than 500,000 Americans had been murdered—approximately ten times the combat deaths in Vietnam, nearly as many American deaths as the Civil War and World War II combined. The combat in Americans' private lives was the nation's penultimate war, and the troops were sadly undermanned.

Big city police were overwhelmed by a flood of new murder cases each week. With no time to do the job properly, they focused on easy cases and let difficult ones slide. The typical PD was a tragically inefficient bureaucracy that half the time chained the detective to a desk, pushing needless paper, Friel said. "Disgraceful turf battles for individual glory" consumed cops at all levels and prevented city, state, and federal agents from working together. The result was that "the streets are less safe for our citizens than they should be, and crimes—often very serious crimes—that could be solved are not." The result was that as many as 30 percent of murders nationwide went unsolved. Put another way, more than 100,000 Americans in a generation had gotten away with murder.

Friel knew all that. Then he saw "The Murder Wall" in the main lobby of the hotel. It was a simple display, with home-made posters and photographs, telling the stories of 120 murder victims. His eyes scanned the faces of the dead: not drug dealers or gang members, or the front-page victims of the Los Angeles Night Stalker or Chicago's Killer Clown. A twenty-three-year-old Chicago medical student. A thirty-four-year-old Michigan lawyer. Two young Minnesota girls who went shopping for school and never came home. America's slaughtered boys and girls next door.

Friel saw parents quietly approach the wall, heads bowed. They left notes and flowers as if at a war memorial. They seemed broken, invisible men and women whom he'd heard say in the hallways and seminars, "Don't let the killer take another victim." It hit Friel then that nobody had put into numbers the larger tragedy of American murder, the uncounted hundreds of thousands of people struggling to find a healing they knew would never come, a rough closure.

How they hated that word, "closure," he noted. They knew it was not possible.

JUST ONE PERSON IS MISSING, James Charles Kaloger's parents wrote at the wall. BUT OUR WHOLE WORLD SEEMS SO EMPTY!

Friel scarcely remembered his keynote address that night. Returning to Philadelphia, he knew he had seen through a fissure in the surface of American crime to an underground, a place of routine tragedy and suffering that was unimaginable and therefore unimagined.

"This is a tragic situation in our country," Friel said to Fleisher and the others at a luncheon. "How can we see this level of suffering and do nothing? There are lots of people who need our help." The mission of the Vidocq Society was finally clear.

CHAPTER 27

THE END OF THE AFFAIR

Covered with dust from an all-nighter in the studio, Bender sighed deeply and picked up the telephone. Jan was still asleep, and Ella was cleaning up from helping him finish a head. He had greeted the dawn with exhilaration; at moments like these, he felt half his age, which was fifty-two. Then the sexual energy and hectoring presence of twentysomething Laura Shaughnessy buzzed through the line.

Laura was furious that he hadn't yet left his wife; Bender was trying to tell her without coming right out and saying that it was over between them. She was demanding he leave Jan and Ella and settle down. She was trying to make him monogamous. Bender was starting to call her "Sarge."

They still dated. He'd still have sex with her. "You don't want to cut it off completely," he reasoned. But he was saying things like, "I'm not sure this is working out." He was letting her down slowly. By autumn 1991, he felt strongly reconnected to Jan and Ella, and Laura was trying his patience.

"Laura was a lovely person. We had great times together. It was a fun affair. But I felt like I was losing my space, my freedom. I just couldn't deal with that." After a period of self-examination, he had concluded, "I wasn't about to leave Jan over her, and I wasn't about to leave Ella over her. They're the two women in my life who mean an awful lot to me. It's times like that when you're tested that you realize how much you really care for certain people."

Now he thought ruefully, "The greater the pleasure, the higher the price." His bill for the two-year affair was coming due.

Laura sounded like she'd been crying.

"Kenny is devastated," she said. "He went on and on about this girl Zoia, this Russian girl, and now she's disappeared. It's his fiancée, he really loves her. I feel terrible for him. He's a big teddy bear, and he's falling apart."

"Whoa!" Bender said. "Slow down and tell me what happened."

Laura said she'd just gotten a distressing phone call from one of her best friends since high school in New Jersey, a Florida ophthalmologist named Kenny Andronico. Kenny had said his fiancée, Zoia Assur, who was living with her sister in New Jersey before moving down to be with him, had disappeared.

Zoia hadn't been seen in two weeks. The cops were telling Kenny not to worry, people went missing and showed back up. But they'd been going steady for five years, and Kenny had given her a necklace and they had plans to marry. He knew something was wrong. He was scared that something bad had happened to her. He went to pieces on the phone.

"Frank, Zoia is missing and Kenny wants your help to find her—through your contacts at the Vidocq Society, *America's Most Wanted,* or *Unsolved Mysteries* or whatever."

Bender suddenly realized he'd met Kenny Andronico. Laura had introduced them at a New Jersey train station the previous summer. Bender and Laura had just arrived on a train from Philadelphia, heading to her family's estate for an amorous weekend, and there in the parking lot was this lumbering big guy with a mustache in a casual suit.

Laura was effusive introducing her lover to her old friend, but Kenny didn't pick up on the emotion, Bender recalled. "He shook my hand, but he barely grunted at me. He was clearly possessive of Laura. I sensed he didn't like me being with her."

Bender sighed. He wanted to help Laura. But he had sensed a dark and controlling spirit in Andronico. He was happy to get away from the guy. He also had the unsettling feeling that Laura was trying to manipulate him into getting involved as a ploy to prolong their relationship.

But as he heard her troubled voice pleading for help for her friend Kenny, his doubts washed away. He was touched. He liked the girl and decided to help. He felt he owed it to her, being as he was going to dump her and all.

"Sure, I'll do anything I can," Bender said. "Have Kenny call me." Laura was deeply grateful, and Dr. Andronico didn't waste any time. He called Bender that evening.

The voice on the line was bold and assertive.

"Hey, Frank, my good buddy," he said.

Bender stiffened. "I barely know the guy. Now I'm his good buddy?" All six of Bender's senses went on hyperalert.

"Frank, I need your help," Andronico pressed on, imploringly. "My fiancée disappeared, and the police have no idea what happened to her, and I'm scared to death. I know from Laura that you're the best forensic artist in the world, and work with the best detectives. Please help me."

Bender remained cool. "I'll do what I can, Kenny. Who would want to kill Zoia?"

"She was living with her sister, but there were serious conflicts in the home." He explained that Zoia's brother-in-law, a state police sergeant, was having sex with Zoia—sleeping with his wife's sister under the same roof. He was afraid the cop might have had something to do with Zoia's disappearance.

"What's the story with the cop?" Bender asked. "Has anybody investigated him? Has he taken a polygraph?"

Yes, the policeman took a polygraph, Kenny said, and he passed it.

"OK, I'll make a deal with you. You take a polygraph and you pass it and I'll help you."

"Wait a minute!" Kenny sounded furious. He was practically shouting. "I'm your good friend!"

"Kenny, you're not my good friend. You're a friend of Laura's, but I barely know you. You want me to help you—you have to pass a polygraph."

Andronico was quiet on the other end of the line.

"I work with two of the best polygraph examiners in the world—Bill Fleisher and Nate Gordon, both in Philadelphia. Both are members of the Vidocq Society, a group of detectives I belong to that looks at cold cases pro bono."

He gave him Fleisher's telephone number. "Call Bill and set it up. You'll have to pay for the polygraph yourself—four or five hundred dollars. I also want you to call my friend Richard Walter. He's a profiler; he can tell you more about what might have happened to Zoia than anyone I know." He gave him Walter's phone number.

Andronico grunted OK.

"Kenny, can you pass a polygraph?"

"I think I can."

Bender's anger flared. "You *think* you can? Jesus Christ, Kenny, if you pass the polygraph I'll be happy to help you. If you don't, and Bill tells me you're a flat-out liar, I'll hunt you down until the day I die."

On Thursday, November 28, 1991, Thanksgiving evening, Richard Walter, home for a spell after trips to Hong Kong and Sydney on murder investigations, was dressing to go to a friend's house for turkey and all the fixings. He was standing at the gilt Victorian hall mirror knotting his red tie on a white collar when the phone rang.

He stared at the bleating instrument thinking if it didn't stop soon, one of them would have to go. Walter's hypersensitive hearing was a gift on murder investigations, when he heard suspects whispering far out of normal earshot, and detected suprahuman signs of fear, such as sub-aural breathing increases, during interrogations. But the auditory assaults were getting worse with age. He couldn't tolerate the sound of someone chewing food on the telephone line. When he detected the wet smacking of gum or the dry crunching of crackers on the other end, he hung up immediately.

His condition was apparently caused by sensory overload, the trademark of a man who absorbed too much information simultaneously. The aging ear sometimes lost the ability to screen noises, his doctor said.

He had been looking forward to crowning a successful year with a bottle of Chardonnay with friends. What execrable human being was delaying his celebration and jackhammering his eardrums? He picked up the telephone.

"Who?" he exclaimed.

It sounded like a sales call. Walter prepared to hang up. He did not recognize the slippery, unctuous voice. Then he realized it was a stranger asking for a favor, and his ire rose along with his suspicion.

"Dr. who?"

"Frank told me if you want to solve this, and exonerate yourself, call Richard Walter," the voice insisted. "He said, 'He's one of the best profilers in the world. He'll give you good advice.'"

As the voice purred on, it came back to Walter: It was Dr. Kenneth Andronico, the ophthalmologist in Florida whose girlfriend, Zoia Assur, was missing in New Jersey. The police were getting nowhere; the doctor feared foul play and wanted help. Bender had told him to expect a call from "a good friend of one of my girlfriends." Kenny was a confused and grieving man, Bender said, and needed some guidance.

Frank!

"Do you have a moment to give me some advice?" Andronico pleaded.

Walter scowled into the telephone. He instinctively didn't like the oleaginous, manipulative voice. He checked his wristwatch: five minutes to seven. He would be late for Thanksgiving dinner.

"Oh, all right," he said.

As Andronico told his story, from Zoia going missing to his suspicions of her policeman brother-in-law and general police ineptitude, Walter's scowl deepened. The doctor didn't sound like a confused and grieving boyfriend. He'd contacted a former FBI agent in Florida for help, and now Bender and Walter and the Vidocq Society. *This isn't making sense,* Walter thought. *He's right in the midst of everything, and he's coming up with all kinds of cockamamie theories.*

After a few minutes, Walter cut him off sharply. He joined Bender in insisting that the doctor submit to a polygraph examination with Bill Fleisher, president of the Vidocq Society.

"Young man, you're looking under all sorts of beds and stirring up a lot of dust. But the fact of the matter is you are the primary suspect because you're not credible. I won't be looking forward to the case unless you are checked out." Walter hung up.

As he drove to Thanksgiving dinner, Walter couldn't decide who was more confused, the doctor he now suspected of murder or his licentious partner Bender. Bender took the concept of knight-errantry, the wandering warrior, to a different dimension.

Some men are a heartbeat away from the presidency, he thought. *Leave it to Frank to be a penis away from a murder.*

CHAPTER 28

CATCH ME IF YOU CAN

The big, mustached ophthalmologist Dr. Kenneth Andronico sat in a small windowless room melting like a candle, which was better than his fiancée, Zoia Assur, who had been found in a shallow grave in the New Jersey Pine Barrens. But he wasn't in great condition, either.

Dr. Andronico's powerful face, wide in the jaw, wore a slick yellow sheen under the hot lights. He refused to make eye contact; his pupils darted along the rims of his eyes, as if looking to escape his head. But there was no escape. The big man was strapped into the subject's chair with arm and finger cuffs. Rubber pneumograph tubes bound his chest and abdomen. He couldn't see an exit. He couldn't see much around the dominant, five-hundred-pound shadow formed by two very large men, renowned polygraph examiners Fleisher and Gordon. They leaned close with their cool voices and big, manicured hands.

Gordon tossed Andronico a softball question, a standard warm-up.

"How do you think you'll do on the lie-detection test?"

"This thing, I think I can beat it," Andronico said.

Gordon smiled to himself. *Where do we find these guys? Let the fun begin.*

The helicopters, dogs, and search squads had combed every inch of the Pine Barrens since August.

Four months later, the corpse was discovered in a place they'd already looked.

In December 1991, a hunter found Zoia Assur in a shallow grave in the piney woods, one of the largest remaining tracts of East Coast wilderness. Animals and the moist coastal sand had quickly reduced her to little more than a skeleton. Enough remained for the Ocean County medical examiner to determine the cause of death: Zoia had been shot three times in the chest. One of the bullets pierced her heart.

James Churchill, chief investigator for the Ocean County prosecutor's office, said Assur was taking medicine for depression, and had killed herself near the spot where her sister had fallen to her death in a horse-riding accident seven years earlier. Fleisher and Gordon thought the police inquiry was "a joke."

So they piled into a car with Joe O'Kane and Frank Bender, a team of four Philadelphia VSMs, and drove seventy-five miles east to the wooded area near Toms River, New Jersey, to see for themselves. Maybe an ex-Customs drug agent, FBI agent, black-belt polygraph examiner, and psychic artist could spot something the cops missed.

"It was unbelievable," Bender said. Although the body had been removed and the scene cleaned up, they found fragments of Zoia's clothes, even a piece of fingernail. Fleisher was more surprised by the mile they had to hike into the woods to find the place. And the style and location of the suicide weapon—a heavy, German-made Heckler & Koch P7, an eight-shot automatic found in a bag twenty-seven feet from the body.

"I get it," he said sarcastically. "This petite young woman who is weak and sickly fights her way almost a mile through thick brush carrying a gun she's incapable of firing. It takes twelve and a half pounds of pressure to fire the P7, and she's not going to be able to turn it around herself and find the force to pull the trigger at that angle." To test his theory, Fleisher asked Jan Bender, who was about the same size as Zoia, to try to shoot herself in the chest with the same gun, empty, at an indoor shooting range. Wearing a bulletproof vest, she awkwardly pointed the P7 automatic with both hands back at her chest, and pulled the trigger with all her strength for several minutes. She couldn't do it. When she finally succeeded, the gun was pointing over her shoulder.

Standing on the soft Pine Barrens sand, Fleisher continued his theory. "So now we're supposed to believe Zoia shoots herself once in the chest, has the strength to shoot herself twice more, once in the heart, then puts the gun in a bag and moves it nearly thirty feet away?"

The big man smiled. "Yeah, this was a suicide, and Gordon is Elvis Presley."

On the way back to Philadelphia, Fleisher drove them to a New Jersey psychic who claimed to have insights about the case. Standing in her kitchen, the psychic closed her eyes and whispered that the spirit of Zoia Assur was present, yet afraid to talk. Fleisher said tenderly, "It's OK, Zoia, you can trust us." He reached out into the air to gently touch her, making a gesture as if he was stroking her reassuringly on the arm or head.

They got no new information from the spirit world that evening.

As the car crossed the dark Jersey flatlands in the moonlight, Bender felt he'd never had more fun with the Vidcoq Society, all of them working together. O'Kane howled in laughter. "Bill, you will never live down the night you petted a ghost." O'Kane couldn't believe it. He kept saying it over and over. "He petted a ghost!"

O'Kane's booming laughter was joined by the artist's, the polygrapher's, and that of red-faced Fleisher himself. "Maybe Bill scared her away."

As Fleisher and Gordon prepared to run the test, Bender strolled into the outer office with Laura Shaughnessy, his girlfriend and

Andronico's old high school buddy. Laura was distraught. She had screamed at Bender in the car: "I should never have brought you in on this!" The relentless Bender and his Vidocq friends were trying to expose her good friend Kenny as a murderer, and Kenny couldn't have done it, she said. Bender was grinning now. Seeing that Fleisher and Gordon had matters well in hand, he left, saying, "Laura and I are going to go grab some lunch."

Fleisher laughed. "Leave it to Frank. We're trying to solve a murder and he runs off for a tryst."

Fleisher and Gordon turned to the interrogation of the man they suspected in the murder Bender's affair had brought to their door. Fleisher studied Dr. Andronico with hard eyes. *When he looks in a mirror,* Fleisher thought, *he finds his fiancée's killer.*

Wired to the machine, Andronico was supremely confident. He said he'd flown up to Philadelphia to take the test and rule himself out as a suspect—then maybe the Vidocq Society would help him find his fiancée's killer.

"He's agreeing to take the polygraph because he thinks he's smart enough to fool you and fool the machine," Walter told Fleisher before the test. Walter had completed his profile of Andronico after studying the crime scene. The shooting and disposal of Assur like rubbish confirmed his analysis of a power-driven killer of psychopathic arrogance.

Andronico had said he didn't believe Zoia killed herself, either. He suspected Zoia's brother-in-law, the state police sergeant who was having an affair with her. The P7 handgun found at the scene, which fired the bullets that killed Zoia, was the sergeant's service gun. But the police had ruled out the state trooper as a suspect, and the Vidocq Society believed he was innocent.

Walter scoffed at the doctor's story. "He had plenty of motives to kill Zoia. He's enraged to find out she's sleeping with a married man, and doubly enraged that it's her brother-in-law, under her sister's roof. The doctor is power-driven. You don't get rid of him. That's an intolerable insult. He gets rid of you."

The state police had also ruled out Andronico as a suspect. He was innocent in the eyes of the law. "So what's he doing here?" Walter asked. "Why fly fifteen hundred miles to pay for a polygraph to prove his innocence to a bunch of private cold-case detectives who may show that he's guilty? He thinks he is smarter than everyone, that's why, and it gives him a thrill to beat us. He relives the excitement and sense of control of the murder itself. He's playing that dangerous 'catch me if you can' game."

Andronico had even agreed to allow his polygraph to be filmed by the Vidocq Society for possible future use and shown on *48 Hours* with Dan Rather. The *48 Hours* crew was scheduled to film the upcoming Vidocq Society meeting, where the society would investigate whether Assur's death was suicide or murder and whether the doctor killed her.

Walter believed the doctor killed his fiancée, planted the gun to get rid of both betrayers, gulled the police, staged a murder, frame-up, and cover-up, and now would try to fool the Vidocq Society and CBS News in one nationally televised Machiavellian stroke.

Minutes into the test, Andronico's cool evaporated. His readings shot for the moon: flushed, rapid breathing, shifty eyes, jittery arms and legs. His big, eggplant-shaped face was sweating like it sat in a steam pot.

Fleisher and Gordon had seldom seen a man so clearly deceptive.

Dr. Andronico had a great memory for how he spent each hour of each day. "But asked to describe his whereabouts on the day his fiancée is missing," Gordon said, "he suddenly becomes very upset and no longer remembers clearly."

"When did you last speak with Zoia?"

The night before she died, Saturday night, August 10, Dr. Andronico said, he spoke with his fiancée on the telephone. "He told her he was coming up that Monday morning," Andronico's father, Carmen, told the *Atlantic City Press*. Now Dr. Andronico insisted he never made the trip to New Jersey.

Andronico stuck to his alibi. He was at his father's beach house in Florida more than a thousand miles from New Jersey on the Sunday Zoia disappeared. It was impossible for him to have committed the murder. His father corroborated his son's story.

But Fleisher wasn't convinced. Before the polygraph, he had checked airplane schedules between Florida and Philadelphia and the driving distance to the Jersey shore. He concluded there was plenty of time for Dr. Andronico to do the killing and return to Florida in one day. "That doesn't mean he did it," he said. "But it was possible." Fleisher pushed Dr. Andronico hard on the point, and the charts showed the doctor was being deceptive about his alibi. "Why would a man who was innocent lie about his alibi?" Fleisher asked.

Fleisher and Gordon conducted the polygraph examination three times that afternoon; each time, the doctor failed spectacularly. His answers about the murder and his alibi were overwhelmingly deceptive. The Vidocqeans also tested Dr. Andronico's father, who also registered as deceptive about his son's alibi.

"It was classic deception," Fleisher said. "I wish all charts were this easy to read."

Andronico was so flustered at one point he said, "I have to get my story straight."

But he did not confess to the crime.

In the topsy-turvy world of the psychopath, he must have been thrilled, Walter thought.

He was winning.

On May 17, 1992, *48 Hours* with Dan Rather aired its episode on the Vidocq Society in Philadelphia, "Murder on the Menu."

CBS correspondent Richard Schlesinger described the shooting death of twenty-seven-year-old Zoia Assur, a doctor's fiancée, and asked: "Was it suicide? Or was it murder?"

"The setting is colonial, but the subject is crime," he said. "Today, the eighty-two members will try to solve one before dessert."

As the VSMs nibbled on the entrée, members reached a consensus that Zoia's death was "definitely murder," but several members said there was no suspect yet, nor a motive. Walter, Bender, and Fleisher made their case for Andronico as the prime suspect, including the doctor's jittery, deceptive polygraph. Andronico had declined an invitation to the luncheon.

Schlesinger was shocked. "Why would a guy who killed his fiancée walk into a room with eighty-two experts in crime and say investigate this crime when it's already been ruled a suicide by local police? Why would anybody do that?"

Fleisher shrugged. "This is typical behavior of a psychopathic killer—to inject themselves into an investigation, to maintain some kind of control."

During dessert, Dan Rather said in a voice-over, "Did this man murder his own fiancée? We'll confront him with the conclusion of some master detectives, and give him a chance to respond."

The *48 Hours* team flew to Florida, and Schlesinger confronted Andronico in a room of his doctor's office with the camera rolling. Standing against a wall in a blue suit and yellow tie, Andronico said no one knew or loved Zoia "as much as I did," and he was suffering the greatest loss.

Schlesinger said that the Vidocq Society investigators believed he was a psychopathic killer; what did he say to that? Andronico calmly stuck to his alibi and said, "I have nothing to worry about."

"Did you kill her?" Schlesinger said.

Calmly, "No, I did not. No, I did not."

In February, Fleisher had sent a ninety-page letter to the Ocean County prosecutor summarizing the findings of the Vidocq Society investigation and urging him to reexamine Assur's death.

"We believe that there are enough inconsistencies regarding her death to cause a reasonable person to pause before declaring it a suicide, and that the case, therefore, should be revisited," Fleisher wrote in the *Vidocq Society Journal*.

The prosecutor never answered back.

By January 1993, almost a year after Fleisher's letter, nobody from the police or prosecutor or medical examiner's offices had shown any interest in looking at the Vidocq polygraph charts, reviewing the conflicting statements of alibi witnesses, watching the videotapes of Andronico and his father, or "for that matter, even listening to what we have to say," Fleisher said. The New Jersey case was closed: Assur had committed suicide. Andronico had never been considered a suspect. Therefore, Fleisher said, "The Vidocq Society is placing this case in a closed status."

He added, "There is much truth to the old saw 'You can lead a horse to water, but you can't make him drink.'"

CHAPTER 29

THE CASE OF THE SHOELESS CORPSE

In old Philadelphia, where horse-drawn hansoms rattled over cobblestones, stood an old brick tavern open for business on and off for two centuries, with the sign of the loaves and roasts creaking in the wind. The eighteenth-century edifice once commanded the New World harbor as "the most genteel tavern in North America," John Adams said. Washington, Jefferson, Franklin, Madison, and Adams dined and drank their way through the drafting of the Declaration of Independence and the U.S. Constitution there. Now it was an elegant neo-colonial restaurant and tourist watering hole that seemed lost in time. The mass of visitors walked by heading to Independence Hall as if the tavern at Second and Walnut was not visible.

During the great celebrations of independence two centuries ago, full-length portraits of Lafayette and General Washington were painted in the tavern windows, backlit by candlelight. On Thursday morning, April 30, 1992, the windows were marbled by more disturbing images. The corpse of a lovely young woman, blond and petite, filled the projection screen at the north end of the hall. Deborah Lynn Wilson, twenty years old, was lying on her back at the bottom of a stairwell on the campus of Drexel University in Philadelphia. The senior mathematics major, a former model, had been severely beaten and strangled to death.

Seven years later, no one had been arrested for the murder, and Vidocq Society Members had assembled from London, Paris, New York, and Virginia to examine their ninth murder case, the Death of Deborah Wilson.

Philadelphia police sergeant Robert Snyder, a homicide detective in his forties with sandy hair and intense blue eyes, took the podium. The highly respected detective had worked the case for much of seven years; Snyder worked headline cases. But this one stumped him. "You always feel bad about the cases you don't solve," he told the society. "Especially the ones involving the young, the innocent, and the aged. This is one of the innocents."

Walter, putting down his coffee, snapped to attention and looked up. He saw at once why no arrests had been made after seven years, and why police detectives and a private eye hired by the family were still confused. The murder scene contained no signs of the common motivations cops were trained to observe—no obvious clues implicating money or sex. No signs of robbery. Deborah's body was covered by the down-quilted gray overcoat she had donned that chilly morning of November 30, 1984, the week after Thanksgiving. Her winter gloves were still stuffed in the pockets of the overcoat. Her wristwatch was still on her wrist. Nor was there a recognizable sexual assault. Deborah Wilson died still fully clothed, in jeans and a blue, long-sleeve pullover blouse, except for her feet, which were bare. Only her white Reebok sneakers and socks were missing.

There was no rational reason Deborah Wilson had to die. The police would make no progress until they broke out of investigative routine and accepted the fact that the crime was beyond normal human comprehension and traditional standards of morality—or amorality, in fact.

This was no ordinary murder. It was a gruesome act of depravity. It was a New Age crime, a "Me Generation" murder. It wasn't one of those pre-1960s killings that cops now saw in a bizarre haze of near-nostalgia: A jealous man shoots his two-timing wife, a law partner gets snuffed for half the firm. Those old-time killers were almost understandable to average folks. The cops always knew where to look: the husband, the law partner, someone the dead man knew well.

But this kind of murder, a lovely, wholesome young woman killed for no reason at all—this was crazy time, cops figured. But it wasn't crazy; it was sane, methodical, cold, well-planned. Just another middle-class American exploiting the bounty of unprecedented affluence and freedom, steady employment, his own house and car, ample leisure time, a king's library of depraved instructional media images, a large supply of young, tolerant, fun-seeking acquaintances—all the resources, in other words, that only aristocrats like the Marquis de Sade once possessed to sample and deeply explore their hungers. Just an everyday late-twentieth-century American monster.

De Tocqueville warned of the dumbing-down of America, but he never imagined this. The elite forms of evil had gone mass-market.

Still looking up at the screen, Walter thought to himself, *Young man, I know what you're up to. One ought not to do such things. You can't hide from me.*

As Snyder began to describe the case, Walter sensed an air of excitement in the eighteenth-century hall. He detected a new seriousness, an intense focus from his peers. Fleisher had said the eyes of the world were on them now. Adding to the anticipation, another prominent journalist guest, Lewis Beale, a writer on assignment for the *Los Angeles Times,* was sitting at Fleisher's table, scribbling notes. Beale specialized in cop stories. He had interviewed the L.A. cops who advised *Hill Street Blues* director Barry Levinson about his TV series *Homicide* and Sidney Lumet, director of *Serpico.* When he described the Vidocq Society, it sounded like a '50s film noir band of forensic brothers "who pool their experience and intellect attempting to solve the unsolvable."

Fleisher, Walter, and Bender were astonished. The Vidocq Society had become the media flavor of the moment. A noted film agent who sold the classic mob pic *Goodfellas* wanted to represent them. A month earlier, the Sunday *Philadelphia Inquirer* had touted the colorful club as avengers of "unsolvable crimes." A week after that, the Sunday *Miami Herald* published the same story under the headline, THIS CLUB'S WHODUNITS ARE REAL. Suddenly there was pressure to solve crimes, not just discuss them. The Sunday *New York Times,* the previous spring, had captured the society's fanciful Sherlock Holmes style with its dispatch, FIRST THEY DINE, THEN TALK TURNS TO MURDER.

While opportunities were nice, Walter kept them focused on reality. "Point A: We didn't start this for recognition. Point B: We haven't done anything to deserve recognition. Point C: Journalists are romanticizing us, turning us into heroes, to sell newspapers. Point D: They wouldn't be able to do this unless there was a real need. It doesn't matter how they portray us. The fact of the matter is crime is out of control in our society. People need our help."

The publicity had brought requests flooding into the Vidocq Society's P.O. box in Philadelphia—in letters, packages, court files, pleas for help, songs of woe. A Los Angeles man wanted the society to investigate his father's murder, which had occured thirty years earlier. A United States congressman needed confidential assistance to solve a friend's murder.

The desire to help was animating the whole society. Friel's return from Texas and the National Organization of Parents of Murdered Children had lit a fire. Fleisher boasted in the *Times* that the society was a "college of detectives" without equal in the world. Now they had a chance to prove it.

Friel backed his Texas conversion with more than words. It was Friel who persuaded Sergeant Snyder to present Wilson's murder before the group for a "fresh set of eyes." Friel had worked with Snyder in the homicide division in 1984, when Deborah Wilson was killed, and although he didn't work the case, he and Snyder talked about it often over the years; the college student's murder still bothered him.

Friel knew what Snyder was feeling, especially toward the end of his career when he was running out of chances. "Bob Snyder is truly a legend in homicide, the consummate homicide detective," Friel said. "But there are cases you can't let go of."

Walter was impressed as he appraised Snyder at the podium. It was an important step that one of the city's finest detectives had asked for their help. When mobster Frankie Flowers was killed in the Mafia wars, Snyder was the shoe leather the department sent out to find the killer.

Walter felt bad for the hardworking cops, and also for Deborah. He knew how they stewed in a hard boil of grief and rage, haunted by an unanswerable question: Why? There was no rational reason; closure was impossible.

It's time to out the bastard, he thought. *That much I can do.*

As Snyder discussed the crime scene, Walter sipped his black coffee and listened.

On the evening of Friday, November 30, 1984, Deborah was working late on a computer project in Randell Hall, a landmark campus building, the detective said. The ornate stone edifice, built in 1901, was a huge labyrinth of classrooms and offices famously difficult to navigate.

At 11 P.M., Deborah called her parents' home across the river in New Jersey from a computer lab. She said she had to keep working to finish the assignment due the next morning. Gifted at mathematics, her major, Deborah struggled with other courses, including computer science. But she was a disciplined student who put in the long hours needed to excel. She didn't have a boyfriend, though young men were interested in her, and didn't smoke or drink. She had modeled and played clarinet in high school but focused on academics in college. Living at home with her parents and commuting to Drexel, she kept her eyes on the future. "She wanted to be an engineer," her sister Suzanne Leis had said. "She was determined she could do it." A photograph of a new Mercedes-Benz sedan hung on her bedroom wall as incentive.

Her parents often fretted about their open, trusting, somewhat naïve young daughter working late in the crime-ridden West Philadelphia neighborhood. But Deborah assured them the engineering building was safe, and when she was done she would get a security escort to her car.

Two and a half hours later, at 1:30 in the morning, Deborah called home again and told her parents she still needed another hour to complete the project, but they shouldn't worry. Her ex-boyfriend, Kurt Rahner, was there with her in the computer room. He'd wait and walk her to her car.

But Rahner didn't wait. He left the computer room shortly afterward. On his way home, he asked a campus security guard to make sure Deborah got safely to her car, and the guard passed word to campus guard David Dickson. Dickson patrolled the campus on the midnight-to-8 A.M. shift, and was responsible for the computer room.

A few minutes after 1:30 in the morning, Deborah was alone in the lab, working on the computer, when she was attacked. At 1:38 in the morning, computer records show, she made her "last transaction" on the computer. It seemed hurried as if "she was interrupted," said Drexel computer administrator John J. Gould Jr. "It looked like she stopped in the middle of what she was doing." Snyder had reconstructed the likely events. Her attacker apparently surprised her and beat her into submission, Snyder said. Then he strangled her to death with an electric extension cord; the cord was discarded near the computer, its grooves matching the marks on Deborah's neck.

At three in the morning, when her parents hadn't heard from her, they reassured themselves she was sleeping in the computer room while pulling an all-nighter. In fact, by three in the morning, according to the coroner, she was already dead. In the huge, dark, empty building, her killer carried or dragged her body through the maze of halls and through a door that led to a protected concrete stairwell on the outside of the building. At the bottom of the cold, quiet stairwell on the bitter winter night, he continued to savagely beat her corpse with two bricks, a yard-long piece of lumber, and a strip of metal. The three makeshift weapons were found lying near her body, smeared with her blood.

At nine that morning, two passing students found Wilson's body in the stairwell, on a landing eleven steps below street level.

As Snyder spoke, Fleisher passed around additional pictures of Wilson's body, a bloodstain found in the computer room and the type of computer she was working on when she died, and the type of sneakers she was wearing. White Reeboks. White socks.

Fleisher joined Snyder at the podium and opened the floor to questions.

"What about the security guard?" Fleisher himself started it off.

"Dickson was an immediate suspect," Snyder said. He was the obvious choice. In police interviews, he was shaky about his whereabouts during the course of the evening. But he had an alibi: He told the other guard on duty he'd been talking on the phone with his girlfriend and forgot to escort Wilson to her car. He failed part of a polygraph test, but polygraphs are inadmissible in court. "We never had enough to arrest him," Snyder said.

The questions came in a torrent.

"Was there a janitor on duty at the time?"

No, Snyder said.

"Were there any arrests for burglary made on campus that night?"

No.

"Have you tried DNA testing?" Heads turned to Halbert Fillinger, the veteran Philadelphia medical examiner. "There may be traces of the killer's skin nuclei on the cord he used to strangle her if he gripped it tightly enough," he said. "That residue could be tested for the killer's DNA."

Puzzled looks went around the room. DNA testing had not been available when Wilson was killed in 1984; nor was it a well-known technology eight years later. "It's a long shot," the *Los Angeles Times* reporter concluded. "But right now Snyder is willing to clutch on to any suggestion. He's frustrated by his inability to move the case forward."

After half an hour, Snyder slumped at the podium. The

question-and-answer session was winding down, and he'd gotten little more than free lunch, moral support, and a few interesting ideas.

Suddenly Walter, whose habit, like the anchorman of a relay, was to take the baton at the end, spoke up. He frowned and adjusted his owlish black glasses on his aquiline nose.

"If I might offer an opinion," he began crisply, "the key to the case is the absence of the victim's shoes and socks."

Snyder nodded. "We know the missing footwear was significant. We just didn't know how."

Walter nodded. "There is no robbery, yet her white Reeboks and white athletic socks are missing. Why?" he asked rhetorically. Not waiting for an answer, he raised more questions:

"The crucial question is, what is the value of the killing? What did he propose to get? Since he didn't sexually assault her, what value was it? He tells us by the absence of the shoes and socks. He doesn't want money. She's still wearing her wristwatch. He doesn't want a fuck. He wants the shoes. He's a foot fetishist."

Murmurs swept the room.

"Do foot fetishists kill for it?" a police officer asked.

"No, not often," Walter acknowledged. "A foot fetish is a paraphilia, a sexual deviance. Afraid to engage a living and breathing sex partner, the fetishist uses the shoe as a stand-in for anyone his imagination can conjure. He gains a secondary or tertiary level of sexual satisfaction through sniffing and feeling and touching and rubbing the shoe, and maybe masturbating with it on him."

To titters of amusement, Walter said, "Foot fetishes may be bizarrely amusing, but they can be very powerful and damaging. This is why the Chinese bound their women's feet into a shape they could slip their dick into, and there was so much resistance to change. The whole culture was bound by the power and fantasy of this fetish."

Walter quickly sketched his view of the crime. The killer is obsessed with women's shoes; he collects them, masturbates over them. In all likelihood, he probably can't even sustain an erection around a real woman. "It's the representation, not the reality, he craves." He has noticed Wilson before and her white Reeboks. He's probably never killed anyone before, but his fantasy is escalating from merely stealing someone's shoes to confronting the wearer.

Lost in his fantasy, somewhat akin to the Gentleman Rapist, he believes himself irresistible to women. Once he reveals his charms she's going to say, "Where have you been all my life." A large, powerful man, he intimidates Wilson when he enters the computer room, finding her alone. "He tries to chat her up for sex, or to go somewhere with him, form some sort of relationship, and she refuses. Possibly he threatens her, things like, she's a whore being there alone and this or that, he verbally assaults her to scare her. It doesn't matter to him. Either way it's just a vehicle to get what he wants. He may tell himself he wants sex, a conquest, but we fool ourselves. Really he knows the bottom line is the shoes and socks."

Wilson, like many victims in this situation, tells him no, timidly or forcefully, maybe she tells him to go to hell. It doesn't much matter. The response is fury—the fury that sparks attack, murder, and postmortem attack. "Intellectually he knows she's not going to cooperate, but on the level of fantasy when she tells him to fuck off or whatever he has an explosive reaction to the indignity. He's had a power loss, not the power gain he dreamed of, and he goes ballistic. This is the energy that fuels the crime."

The killer assaults her in the computer room, beating her face and head with his fists and possibly weapons, causing her mortal agony and terror. "She's screaming, pleading, and he has to shut her up so he strangles her." He drags her corpse to the bottom of the stairwell, now his dark, private lair. "This is very sexual," the forensic psychologist said, giving voice to his earlier thoughts. "In Freudian terms, it's the vagina and you're going down into it. It's a sensuality independent of the fuck. He doesn't want the fuck, he wants the shoes. He'll sniff them up at home. The stairwell is a foreplay kind of entrée; it helps set the sexual context later. He took what he wanted for that. He didn't want her tingly parts. He continues to beat her out of the anger of rejection of his fantasy, but really he wants the shoes. Basically, he needs to neutralize her so he can harvest from her what he wants. He does it and leaves."

Leaving with the shoes and socks, the killer is flooded with a powerful feeling of success. The power-reassurance killer, seeking reassurance of his power, had repaired the assault to his pride and dignity and won. "He already got what he wanted, the shoes, so he triumphs."

Walter turned and looked at Sergeant Snyder. "That murder scene also indicates a bit of a power-assertive guy who likes to dominate and control. A guy who lifts weights, exhibits macho power and strength with guns, hobbies such as karate."

Walter realized the fellowship of detectives was having an impact on him he hadn't expected. He thought the federal agents who lacked murder investigation experience were "quite brilliant in the questions they ask to keep me on beam." He told the *Los Angeles Times* reporter, "Our value isn't that we're a bunch of fucking geniuses. It's that we can call on each other." As usual, Walter's remarks required editing for the newspaper. They weren't "super-geniuses," he said, but they worked as a team.

Snyder was pleased with the session. "The profile fits my guy to a T," he said. His guy was Dickson.

Walter smiled. "Check Dickson's Army records, go back and interview his girlfriends, ex-wives, see if there were any problems with shoes."

CHAPTER 30

THE CASE OF THE PRODIGAL SON

Fleisher was sitting at his desk in the Customs House, watching sailboats dodge oil tankers on the river. It was a lovely May morning, women were out in spring finery, and the boiled brown water in the blue paper cup emblazoned with the Parthenon almost tasted like coffee. The mood in the office was light, as it was when the ASAC interspersed fighting the war on drugs with practicing his standup:

Why do Jewish men die before their wives? They want to.

I'm making a Jewish porn movie. It's 10 percent sex, 90 percent guilt.

Someone stole my wife's credit card, but I don't want him found. He's spending less than she was.

"Bill," his secretary called, "we got another one who saw you on *48 Hours*. Says he's been looking all over the city trying to find the guy who looks like Raymond Burr."

Fleisher chuckled. "I'm not that fat yet. Maybe by autumn."

The soft Texas accent on the phone belonged to Jim Dunn, CEO of a marketing company in Bucks County.

"Mr. Fleisher, my son Scott disappeared in Texas. He was murdered, and I've been investigating myself for a year, trying to help the police, getting nowhere. When I saw *48 Hours,* we were in New Mexico following a lead at the end of our rope and I said to my wife, the Vidocq Society is back home, in Philadelphia. I thought I'd see if it was at all possible for me to talk to these experts on homicide."

Fleisher was impressed with Jim Dunn. He sounded like a gentleman, highly intelligent, and a brokenhearted father.

"I went to the City Tavern three times asking about the Vidocq Society and the bearded fellow who looked like Raymond Burr. Finally a bartender said, 'Oh, yeah, he's a boss in charge over at Customs.'"

Fleisher's voice turned serious. "Jim, tell me what happened to your son."

"That's what I'm trying to find out. Scott and I were very close; we talked on the phone every Sunday. I hadn't heard from him one Sunday last May when a woman I'd never heard of called me at home very late and asked me if I was Scott Dunn's father. She said she was Scott's girlfriend, his live-in girlfriend, and she was worried because he was missing. Their bedroom had been emptied out—no mattress, none of Scott's clothes, nothing."

"That's certainly suspicious."

"There was blood all over the bedroom, Scott's blood. I won't give up until I find out what happened to my son. I was calling to see if the Vidocq Society might help me."

"I understand. It's a murder, obviously. What do the police think?"

"It's the Lubbock PD, and it started out as a missing persons case, but now they're investigating it as a murder. But they haven't arrested anybody, and the district attorney said we don't have a case because there's no body, no weapon. In Texas you can't have a murder without a body. I've been on the DA's case for a year."

"So the case is only a year old," Fleisher mused aloud, "and there's no body." He paused to take a breath. This was never easy. "I'm sorry to say this, Mr. Dunn, but this doesn't sound like a Vidocq Society case." He sensed the vacuum of quiet disappointment on the line.

"Number one, this case is just too fresh for us. Cases have to be cold for at least two years. You just haven't given the police enough time to do their job. If we come in they'll be saying, 'Whoaah, what are you doing on our case?' We provide advice and counsel to police departments when they ask for it. We don't steal anybody's thunder. We don't harpoon cases."

"I understand," Dunn said evenly.

"Number two, you don't even have a body. Technically, it's still a missing person case. We see those all the time. Some people just disappear, they want to drop out. He could come back. He could be a suicide. We just don't know."

"My son didn't commit suicide. He was murdered."

"OK, you're probably right. But number three, even if it's a murder it's almost impossible to get a murder conviction without a body. It's one of the classic standards of homicide investigation in our legal system. You need the corpus delicti. And it doesn't help that you've pissed off the district attorney, ultimately the only man who can seek justice for your son.

"I'm sorry to say we can't help."

Dunn didn't pause: "Mr. Fleisher, could I just meet with you? Maybe someone in the organization might have some ideas how we could proceed, just some advice. We live right here in the area and I will meet you anywhere."

"OK, then, why don't you send me some materials and I'll look them over."

"I'm sorry, I can't do that," Dunn said firmly. "I'm going back to Texas next week to keep looking for my son, and I want my materials with me—it's all I have left of Scott." There was a long silence, and then he said, "Mr. Fleisher, I believe you are the only chance I have."

Something clicked in that moment for Fleisher. "I knew then that Jim Dunn was a good man. He'd do anything to find his son." Fleisher knew all about the difficult bonds of fathers and sons, the longings that survived death.

His father had taught him to keep his mind and heart open, to always be willing to listen to a good man. He often thought about how his father had learned that lesson himself, when Temple University wouldn't let him in to take his final exam required to graduate from dental school during the Great Depression. He'd passed all the graduate school classes, but he was too poor to make his last tuition payment or even pay for his diploma. As the exam was being given, he went to see the university president, Charles

E. Beury. Beury's secretary said the president was going to a meeting and couldn't see him. Herbert Fleisher said, "Tell him it's a
matter of life and death." The president invited him in. Beury,
a tall Princeton grad, class of 1903, looked at his watch and said,
"You have five minutes, son. What's the problem?"

Fleisher's father began, with tears in his eyes, telling the president about his financial problems and that they would not let him
take his dental final.

A half hour later, Beury looked at his watch and said, "You
have five minutes left."

When the time was up, the president took out a piece of paper
and wrote a note to the dean of the dental school to let Herbert
Fleisher take the test. But when he got there the test was over. The
dental dean instead made him take an oral final exam, which was
very tough. "My father passed and became an excellent dentist."
Years later Beury was quoted in the newspaper saying, "A university
should teach not only the rudiments of education, but it should set
standards whereby young men and women may learn to recognize a
good man when they see one."

Jim Dunn was a good man. *I'm going to try to find a way to help
him,* Fleisher thought.

Fleisher spoke rapidly with the no-nonsense tone he used when
he wasn't cracking jokes.

"OK, Jim. We get hundreds of requests, and most people we
can't help. But we'll try to give you some advice and guidance. I'll
call Frank Friel, who is the police chief in Bensalem, near you in
Bucks County, and we'll both meet with you at his office." Dunn
said he would come with his wife, Barbara. The meeting was set
for eight the next morning.

Dunn was speechless. "Mr. Fleisher, I don't know what to say."

"Frank was a legendary police captain with the city of Philadelphia," Fleisher continued. "He's a Vidocq Society Member and
one of the most astute men I know on homicide cases. I don't
know if we'll be able to help beyond this. But if anyone can give
you guidance, it's Frank."

CHAPTER 31

THE SAGE OF SCOTLAND YARD

The night flight from London landed in Philadelphia in the rain. The thin man in coach was not pleased. "It's ugly, I'm exhausted, I'm miserable, it's not good," Walter mumbled. "And I'm out of my last goddamn cigarette." He was disgusted by the sallow faces in the gloomy concourse, and got in the taxi thinking, *I've got to get away from stupid people.* The other passengers gave the gaunt, stiff-backed gentleman with the shining aluminum attaché a wide berth. This pleased him. "It reduces the time I must spend with the dull and ignorant." The last thing he needed was someone to start asking him who killed JonBenet Ramsey, or who Jack the Ripper really was.

Walter was physically spent. On the road he lived on cigarettes, Chardonnay, cheeseburgers, and sedatives for long flights. Sleeping little, he often fell ill during trips, and depended on the kindness of strangers—pathologists in London to prescribe medicine, a boy in Istanbul to follow the frail American around with a chair, kindly folks everywhere to help him find his way. He was always getting lost. To restore his self, he told the cabbie, he needed to find the essentials: cigarettes, diet soda, laxatives, and a drink.

"The cigarettes must be Kool Menthol Kings. The diet soda must be red. The laxative must work." Then he'd collapse in his hotel bed.

The trip to Scotland Yard had nearly done him in. He had

been woozy with lack of sleep when he lectured to three hundred of the brightest minds in the Home Office on murder. Walter had consulted with London's Metropolitan Police, also known as Scotland Yard, for years on major cases. He would later help them catch the serial killer of homosexuals who terrorized London, explaining that the slayer threw his victims out high windows because this variety of killer was enchanted by nasty sarcastic puns, in this case "Fairies can't fly!"

At Scotland Yard, "they consider me a guru—the guru of all perversity," he said with humor and no small pride—meaning sadism, Munchausen syndrome, Munchausen syndrome by proxy, and the other "isms" he seemed to grasp as if he'd created them. But the Brits were damned tired of hearing how smart the Americans were on the most difficult murder cases.

Looking out across the sea of faces, he saw the narrowed eyes of "the enemies of my ideas"—the Old Guard, old men trapped in the orthodox nineteenth-century procedural method of murder investigation. Walter was a heretic. The depth of the psychology of the murdering mind, its artistic, symbolic expressions in the positioning of the body just so, the hidden meaning of the knife in the chest (six inches long, the average penis length; look for a perp, like most sex criminals filling the prisons in seething rage, who couldn't get it up). They were horrified by him. He was peddling "a cross between New Age folderol and witchcraft." His challenge was to convince them his work was empirical, "not just bad gas from a good meal."

He started by trying to amuse them with his "tale of woe." After working a full day at the prison in Lansing, Michigan, he'd driven to Detroit, flown all night to London without sleeping a wink. He'd landed and "fumbled around like I do, getting lost in the airport and train system," losing more time. He'd arrived at the London office at 11:30 A.M., eager to rest for the speech the next day. "Oh, no," they said. "The speech is today. It's right now!" He was standing before them now nearly cataleptic with fatigue, and hoped for their forbearance.

It was true, but they were not amused. "They didn't seem to care I hadn't slept in thirty hours." Instead, sensing his weakness, they attacked. Even one of his friends set him up, put him on the spot.

Now he had his Philadelphia cab driver stop at an all-night drugstore. Walter found the essentials and put them on the counter. The young clerk asked for ID to buy the cigarettes. He glared at her in disbelief.

"Madam, you're carding me! I'm sixty goddamn years old! Look at this face!" Sweeping out the door, he muttered, "I'll go somewhere where they require an IQ above seventy."

Later in his Center City hotel room, overlooking Broad Street, he calmed down with a cigarette. His temper had come from addiction. "My exercise is inhaling," he'd joke, or, "My exercise is coughing after smoking." He was not proud of it, it was simply a fact. "During nicotine withdrawal, I become like a hawk eyeing a mouse. I simply cannot tolerate human frailty."

He did not apologize for it. It was the cost of being R. Walter, bane to psychopaths on four continents. "With psychopaths I am far more predatory and in control, using a surgeon's knife, in the superior position rather than being vulnerable to the biological charms of addiction," he said. "And I am *always* in the superior position."

Walter had many friends and more than a few enemies. Some forensic scientists refused to sit next to him at the American Academy of Forensic Sciences convention because he verbally destroyed presenters every year. Friends described him as a shining blade, too sharp for everyday use. Walter saw life, as Teddy Roosevelt once did, as a test of manhood. "One of the final tests as a man matures," he said, "is to identify those things one loves enough to protect." He'd risk his life to protect or avenge man, woman, or child. Like Roland and Siegfried in the old and forgotten stories, he would go alone into the cave in the dark with the sword when it counted. A week after Walter's trip to Scotland Yard, FBI agent Robert Ressler had signed a copy of his new book, *Whoever Fights*

Monsters: My Twenty Years Tracking Serial Killers for the FBI, "To Richard Walter, My good friend and fellow monster slayer."

The red light was blinking on the telephone in his hotel room. *A goddamn red light,* he thought. *Who the hell wants me now?* He was planning to go to the bar. He wanted to hear only five words the rest of the night: "What will it be, sir?"

Reluctantly he picked up the phone. There were two messages. The first was from Bill Fleisher welcoming him to Philadelphia—and asking a favor.

"Richard, would you call Jim Dunn? He's a bereaved father from Bucks County whose son disappeared a year ago in west Texas, a murder; the cops haven't a clue. The case has got your name on it. Jim's a good guy, and I felt sorry for him. Maybe you can find a way to help him when you're in town." Scowling, Walter wrote down the number.

The second message was from Dr. Richard Shepherd, forensic pathologist at Guy's Hospital, London, internationally known consultant to Scotland Yard, the queen's coroner. Shepherd, a good friend, had introduced Walter to the Scotland Yard audience. Shepherd was tall, commanding, a wicked wit, a pilot (bored with an AAFS convention in Chicago, he rented a small plane and flew over Lake Michigan), and a pathologist of "unsurpassed brilliance." Walter hoped he was calling to apologize. By the end of his speech Walter felt he'd done passably well, parried with the critics, held his own. Then Shepherd pulled the doozy.

With a twinkle in his eye, Shepherd flashed a photograph of a murder scene on the screen. Lying on his back in the middle of a tidy, middle-class parlor was the corpse of a man who appeared to be in his sixties, prosperous, with short-cropped salt-and-pepper hair. He was wearing a wool shirt and casual, around-the-house gabardine trousers.

At first glance it looked like a heart attack or a stroke. But on closer inspection it was evident the trousers were unzipped at the fly. The man's penis had been cut off. There was very little blood, considering. There was no knife or other weapon in the picture—and no penis. The penis was missing.

Walter had never seen the photo before. He didn't know the case.

"Let's see what the profiler can really do when he's got nothing to go on but the crime scene," Shepherd said. "Richard, the question is, what happened here? What does the photograph tell you? Who killed this man? And why?"

Walter's eyes gleamed with the challenge.

Walter quickly sized up the victim by his age and condition and asked himself: *How many circumstances can you think of where somebody's going to lose their dick?*

Then: *This dick was punished for doing something. What did it do?*

Walter ran through the possibilities.

He was murdered by a jilted lover or a vengeful husband. But the body said otherwise. "If it were a jilted lover, I would expect to see additional trauma on the body, hitting in the face and head, the sating of that anger. This was just cold and calculated, in and out."

He was murdered by a jilted homosexual lover. The missing penis put him in mind of a homosexual murder in California in which the jilted queen murdered his lover, "who had a big dick, and he chopped it off, put it in the freezer, and was suspected of continuing to use it." *But if it were gay lovers you'd also see the highly emotional hitting and striking to try to achieve catharsis through all that anger and pain. The killer in this case made it clear the penis wasn't important to him. He just wanted to deprive the guy of his penis. He may have thrown it in the sewer or whatever. It had no intrinsic value. He wasn't a pervert putting it in the freezer and sucking on it as a lollypop.*

He was murdered by a random sex killer acting out dark fantasies on a stranger. *But if it were a sex killer, I would see more ritualistic things done to the body, such as excessive deep stabbings, leaving the body in a contorted, symbolic pose, the taking of souvenir body parts.*

Having ruled out sadism and fantasy as motives, Walter was left with power or anger. The anger-driven killer over-killed from fury and inevitably covered the victim's eyes, or threw him in a closet, as a final, "Take that, bitch!" This victim's eyes were staring straight up, uncovered. The body was lying just as it had fallen, and was otherwise unmarked. *One must always study the absence of evidence as well as the presence, and in this case the absence is important.* There was no sign of over-killing from profound anger.

The killer had one purpose only. He did what he had to do and got out. There's anger, but it's no longer hot—it's cold, controlled, organized.

The cold, efficient nature of the crime was the essence of it. The power-driven killer reacts to the sense of being wronged from a challenge to power rather than anger. Now the cold efficiency of the crime made sense.

It's a power crush for the perp.

Walter sensed the crowd waiting. *Given what we have here and what we don't have, what are the remaining possibilities of an errant dick?*

He was killed for making an unwanted homosexual advance on another man. *But if the guy tried to suck his dick or feel him up or whatever else, he would have coldcocked him and knocked him in ninety-three different directions. The parlor would be a mess. Nothing in the parlor seems disturbed.*

So what trouble is left for a dick to get into, particularly a man in his sixties? The probability is, you can pretty well surmise if he made sexual advances to an adult you'd have a very different reaction, so therefore what about a child? The answer is the victim had abused a child.

Self, quickly now, did the victim abuse a girl or a boy?

If it were a girl the father would have seen it as a deflowering and felt it as a father, but as a man he would have felt he failed to protect his child. In that case I suspect the father might not have cut off his dick, but may have just stabbed him violently, perhaps cut out his heart. It would have been a more hostile action, with more anger, more emotion. My intuitive answer is the father identified with the son and was able to symbolize it, incorporate it, see it as part of himself, see the harm of it as the deviant exploitation of manliness. The commonality of manliness with his son allowed him to narrow his anger to a very cold, focused thing—to send the guy to his grave without a dick like a piece of shit.

A couple of minutes had passed when Walter spoke aloud: "I believe the victim was a pedophile rapist who was murdered by the father in vengeance for the crime he committed against his son. In a nasty little work of symbolism, the father cut off the pedophile's dick. He bled to death."

Shepherd slowly grinned and said, "That's right." The murder victim had forced a twelve-year-old boy to have oral sex, he explained. The killer was the boy's father, who had avenged his son. In the audience, jaws went slack. The American was precisely right.

Now, in his hotel room, Walter allowed himself to reflect on the victory. *I earned my respect.*

He looked at the clock, after ten, not too late. With a groan, he picked up the phone number Fleisher had given him and dialed. *My sense of duty is inviolable. It's damn annoying at times.*

Duty also told him now to let it ring five times, no more. On the third ring, Jim Dunn picked up.

Walter introduced himself. "I'm a psychologist, Mr. Dunn, whose basic expertise lies in profiling serial killers. From the little Bill Fleisher has told me, I suspect my skills might be of some use to you."

The man on the other end of the telephone sounded stunned, then guarded—as if he hadn't grasped the fact that his son had been murdered in cold blood.

· CHAPTER 32 ·

THINK THEREFORE ON REVENGE

At eight o'clock in the morning, Richard Walter and Jim Dunn sat in Walter's room on the seventh floor of the Hershey Hotel, enveloped in brown gloom and cigarette smoke. Broad Street lay below in the bright spring sunshine of May 1992, but Walter had pulled the drapes to screen the bothersome light and noise. The profiler sat erect in a Queen Anne chair, a picture of stillness with his eyes closed. Dunn, a tall, silver-haired man with a craggy face and nervous blue eyes, faced him in a matching Queen Anne. On the table between them, Dunn had piled the notebooks, tapes, and newspaper clippings that chronicled his son's murder. There was a pot of room service coffee, two cups, and an ashtray with a Kool sending a lazy plume to the gathering cloud on the ceiling.

Walter opened his eyes and arched his brow. "It sounds like you're hurting, Jim," he said. "How may I help you? Tell me what you have. Tell me about the case."

Walter had spotted Dunn in the lobby at twenty paces. The deduction was instantaneous. The man's elegant suit, shiny wingtips, and silver hair bespoke the mature, prosperous gentleman of the telephone call the night before. The craggy, Scots-Irish face was open and bright-eyed in a manner unusual in the Eastern cities, more likely in a self-made man of southern mountains or western prairie. The suit and tie were too elegant by half, clearly the best suit and tie the man owned—the armor of a man girded for battle and feeling overwhelmed. Yet it was the eyes that neatly summed up the rest of the fellow and indicated it could be none other than Jim Dunn. "I have seen often in the parents of murdered children the eyes of a medical dog sniffing for cancer patients," Walter said. "He had expectant and engaging eyes that held the lightly masked sadness of loss. There is an ethereal sadness that underpins such a man," he said. "A sadness of the universal concept, not just feeling sad but a condition in which loneliness, mystery, and all the major universals seep into the bones. They often smile and whatever else but they rarely if ever belly laugh." He'd seen parents destroyed by that burden. Walter took special note that the man's briefcase (overstuffed, overburdened, like the man himself) was brown rather than black. The more pliant color was a hopeful sign, suggesting emotional vulnerability and capability of wisdom and growth (rather than unyielding rigidity). Flexibility would be the most important trait of all if it was genuine, the undoing of the whole affair if it disguised weakness.

Walter had suggested they "go up to the room for a cup of coffee, a smoke, and a little chitchat." As Walter studied Dunn's gaunt face and hollow eyes in the yellow lamplight, he recalled his misgivings of the night before. A man weakened by grief and self-pity could not bring his son's murderer to account. Walter smiled to himself as Henry VI came back to him: "Oft have I heard that grief softens the mind, And makes it fearful and degenerate; Think therefore on revenge and cease to weep."

A man's grief could not be denied but it must be "set apart. The pain had to come out first." Walter tented his fingers beneath his gaunt face. As Dunn spoke, Walter's small blue eyes varied from steely interest to the softness of utmost patience. The angel of vengeance took many forms; in such a conference, it began with Walter as the ferryman poling parents of murdered children through blood tides of woe.

Dunn had been working late on that Sunday evening in his Bucks County, Pennsylvania, home office when the phone rang.

He thought, *It must be Scott.* The Sunday calls from his twenty-four-year-old son, who had moved to Lubbock, Texas, to make a new life for himself, were a father's joy. Dunn had urged the move; Lubbock was his beloved childhood home, a friendlier, more wholesome place than the East Coast, a place for Scott to start over. Scott had struggled in school in the East. He tried the U.S. Air Force, then tried community college in Texas and dropped out, but after that things started to come together for him. He had a good job, a job he loved and excelled at. Scott had always shown a mechanical gift. Even as a boy he could take apart anything and put it back together. Now in Lubbock, he got a job in an electronics store installing stereos—and became a star at it. He was a West Texas stereo cowboy. The region had rodeo-style competitions in which the "cowboys" vied for prizes, money, and prestige for the fastest installations and highest quality sound. Scott dominated the competitions. He'd found a way to maintain sound quality at unheard-of volumes by stacking ice on the system. His trophies filled the store. An athletic six foot two, 195 pounds with blond good looks, "The Iceman" also starred in the store's TV commercials. Women came into the shop to meet him. He'd loaded his own car—an '87 Camaro he called "Yellow Thunder"—with the finest stereo equipment, and took it booming down the prairie highways. He'd recently told his father he was bringing home for Thanksgiving a young woman named Jessica, a bright, lovely Mississippi State University student—his soon-to-be fiancée.

But the flat, cold voice on the line was someone he'd never heard of.

Her name was Leisha Hamilton.

"Are you Scott Dunn's father?" she asked.

She was Scott's live-in girlfriend, she said. She'd found Dunn's name on a telephone bill. Scott had been missing for four days and she was concerned.

Dunn was confused. "The only girl Scott ever told me about was Jessica."

Scott had moved out completely, Hamilton said. He'd taken all his clothes and just left. Even the bed they shared was gone. The only thing he'd left behind was his car, still parked at the office. When Dunn heard that he felt a chill. "I knew then something was really wrong," Dunn said. "Scott would never go anywhere without his car. It was his baby."

Hamilton called again, and Dunn recorded her call. Now Walter asked to hear the tape. "She sounds so cold," Dunn said, as the atonal voice filled the room. "I've never heard anything like it." Walter raised an eyebrow, but said nothing.

The police regarded Scott's disappearance as a missing person case, but when his son hadn't returned two weeks later, Dunn flew to Lubbock to push the investigation. Walter listened to Dunn describe his torment when he realized his son had been murdered.

Police ran a luminol test in Scott and Leisha's emptied bedroom to detect any blood that might have been cleaned off the whitewashed walls. Luminol detects traces of blood as diluted as one part per million. When sprayed on the walls in darkness, even blood that had been cleaned up would interact with the chemical and glow with a blue luminescence for thirty seconds.

The walls glowed as if they had been painted blue. Huge waves and spikes of blood splashed halfway up the wall. There were blood splatters on the door, blood splatters almost to the ceiling. The room was a chamber of horrors. A blood bath had occurred there. DNA tests showed it was Scott's blood.

Jim's voice broke as he showed Walter the luminol test photos. Scott had died in that room, Jim was now convinced.

Police, too, were convinced they had a murder on their hands. But if Scott had been killed, they couldn't find his body.

They'd combed the prairie with cadaver dogs and helicopters, turned over half the city dump, even brought in psychics, to no avail. "In Texas, the state can't bring murder charges without a weapon, body, or body part," the DA told Dunn. "You don't have a case."

With no body, police flailed trying to find suspects. They'd interviewed everyone Scott knew, including his colleagues at the car-stereo installation shop, but nobody stood out. Leisha was being very cooperative with the police. She didn't know why Scott had up and gone, although she speculated that he may have run off with another woman—women adored Scott. She had no idea how her bedroom had become soaked with Scott's blood.

The police thought she wasn't being completely forthcoming, but they figured she was scared and they hoped to coax her into greater trust. They didn't want to frighten her into not cooperating. There was no way the helpful, petite, twenty-eight-year-old woman committed murder.

Dizzy with grief, Dunn had pressed every power from the FBI in Washington to the governor of Texas, George Bush, to take an interest in the case, to no avail. He stalked the West Texas prairie looking for the body himself, and spent hours talking to psychics in Baltimore and Philadelphia.

Dunn went to Texas and took Hamilton out to dinner to form an alliance with her in his cause. After that, Leisha kept calling, but her phone calls grew darker. One day she'd say she loved Scott and was doing all she could to find him; in warm tones, she expressed deep sympathy for Jim. The next day, she'd sound vague and distant, hinting that she might know where Scott's body was, but Jim would never find him. Growing suspicious of Hamilton and frustrated by the police, Dunn did his own sleuthing. He traveled to New Mexico to investigate reports that Leisha had once been jailed for passing bad checks. But he was always eager to hear from her. Of everyone in the West Texas world where Dunn had sent his son, she seemed to know Scott best. Since she was the closest to Scott, Hamilton said, she thought it was only fair that she get his car. She kept pressing Dunn to give her the keys.

The thin man sitting in the Queen Anne chair had said nothing for almost three hours.

Dunn's voice cracked. "Well, Mr. Walter, what do you think I should do? Is there a case here?"

Walter stubbed out his cigarette and stared hard at Dunn.

"Jim, aren't you tired of being the grieving father?"

Dunn's mouth fell open. "I . . . I thought that was what I was supposed to be."

Walter shook his head. His jaw was clenched.

"No! You're supposed to be goddamn mad! That bitch murdered your son! Let's go get her!"

Dunn sat stunned as the profiler stared at him, awaiting a response.

Slowly, Dunn's gaunt face creased in a big, toothy smile.

"I'm in," he said.

But Walter still had concerns about Dunn's emotional frailty, and he addressed them immediately.

"First we must encapsulate the difference between your emotional issues and the things we need to do with solving the case," he said. "As for your love or anger or hatred or whatever else, you must express these things in terms of your son, but not let it bleed over into the case because it dilutes it and you start to misplace emotion into the structural issues and you don't know where you're at. I certainly don't have a problem chatting with you about internal things, things that are important, but we need to do business on a different plane. We need a cold, businesslike approach."

Dunn quietly nodded his understanding.

Second, he told Dunn, there would be no more phone calls to or from Leisha Hamilton.

"Jim, don't you see what she's doing to you?" Walter's voice was filled with urgency. "Leisha is running a number on you! She's trying to make you her next victim. She not only killed your son, she's bragging about it, and killing you, too."

Dunn's eyes widened.

"She's pulling your strings like a marionette," Walter went on. "One minute she's telling you she loved Scott, too, and the next she's squeezing you about the car. And you, the devoted father, are too close to see the pattern. You don't know how to deal with her because you don't know what she is. What she is is a psychopath, and a good one at that," he said. "And this is the biggest scheme she has ever played out. She is trying to shape you. She knew you would want to know where your son was, so she is laying the framework in hopes of deflecting your suspicion away from her."

As Dunn sat quietly, in a well of contemplation, Walter shot him a look.

"Don't you hate her—even a little bit?"

Dunn's face flared in rage. The emotion exploded from him. "Hell, yes! I hate everything about her! But I keep thinking that as long as I can keep her talking, I may learn something about what happened to Scott. Maybe she'll slip up."

Walter took off his glasses and gave Dunn a stony stare that caused the father to lower his gaze.

"She murdered your son," he said, his nose tipped in disdain as if she were not worthy of contempt. "You don't need to cut her any slack. She's not some sweet, innocent thing. We're going to make sure she comes to justice. It's all right to hate her. She's a vicious killer and none of her bullshit is going to change that."

Dunn reached for the newspaper clippings, as if he were eager to get to work.

"No," Walter said sharply, waving his cigarette in the air. "I don't need to see all these other bits and pieces right now. This is what happened: Leisha Hamilton is a psychopath. Your son was caught up in a web of sexual domination and manipulation by a very cold, powerful, controlling woman. She did him in."

Walter stood and walked to the balcony window and looked out between the curtains. Traffic was crawling up Broad Street under a hazy yellow sun.

"She's calling you and continuing to call you to shape you and control you, so what we want to do is take the power away from her and regain it ourselves. She's manipulating you to gain information because information is power and to a psychopath it's everything. The moral of the story is, limit your sympathy and chats with Leisha Hamilton because she's playing you like a violin and you can't afford it, nor can the case."

Dunn blinked and swallowed. "I didn't know what else to do—"

Walter cut him off. "Not a problem, Jim. You're a grieving father. It's not an issue of laying blame, it's an issue of trying to blunt her aggression. We need the control instead of giving it to her. And we are just signaling by our meeting that we are taking control."

Dunn nodded.

Walter saw a new color in Dunn's face, heard emotional depth in his voice. *He still seems downtrodden,* Walter thought. *He needs to feel empowered.* Walter feared police had been hard on Dunn about his son's lifestyle, which included dropping out of high school and minor drug possession. Dunn seemed to be struggling with shame.

"Jim, I know you've told me Scott had some issues, and had not yet lived the life you had dreamed for him," Walter said.

Dunn nodded gravely.

Walter waved his cigarette impatiently, as if Dunn wasn't getting the point.

"Look, Jim, Scott was in his early twenties, and sometimes kids do foolish things and get involved in issues that are high-risk. And sometimes those errors in judgment result in dastardly deeds. It would appear that Scott's worst crime, so to speak, was judging the wrong person, and sleeping with the wrong person, and forming an alliance with the wrong person."

"I know my son wasn't perfect, but I was proud of his progress," Dunn said in defense of his son.

"That's exactly my point, Jim. Many times what young people will do if they feel they have failed their own class or standards is they will regress back to a lower class or group because the pressure for performance isn't as great," the profiler continued. "Then across time those who have any substance in them at all will repair themselves, pull themselves back up to the expected standard, and join their own class. I know that sounds elitist but that's just the way it is."

The "living Sherlock Holmes": Richard Walter, forensic psychologist and criminal profiler

E.F. Vidocq's inheritor: Bill Fleisher, federal agent turned private eye, at the Vidocq Society headquarters

Forensic artist Frank Bender with his reconstructions of three murder victims including Anna Mary Duval (right), his first case. Bender's bust led to her identification and the conviction of a mob hit man.

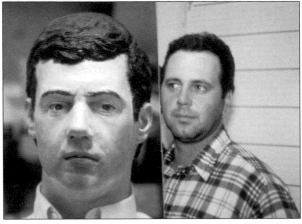

Frank Bender's bust of escaped murderer Robert Thomas Nauss, who Bender predicted would change his look from bearded biker to clean-cut family man. Clean-cut Nauss upon arrest.

Scarface: Bender's "age progression" bust of fugitive mafia kingpin Alfonse (Allie Boy) Persico bore a telltale acid scar from a prison fight.

Frank Bender

Carmine Donofrio, New York Daily News

Frank Bender

Bender's sketch of fugitive hit man Hans Vorhauer, showing what he would look like thirteen years after this mug shot was taken, led to his capture.

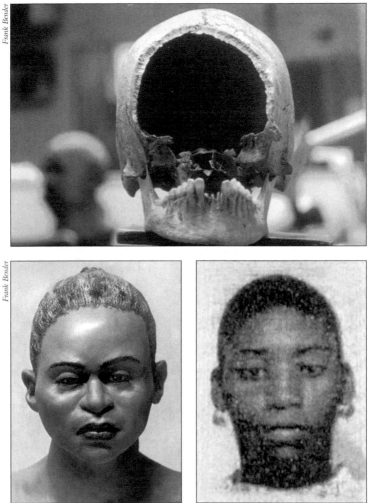

Frank Bender followed his intuition to sculpt a face for the unknown murder victim in "The Case of the Missing Face." Anthropologists had said it was impossible to reconstruct the face of the victim when unearthed after more than a decade in Manlius, New York. Some accused Bender of playing God when he created the face of slain prostitute Lorean Quincy Weaver from nothing—and her mother recognized her.

Frank Bender sculpted fugitive mass murderer John List for the most brilliant *America's Most Wanted* capture ever, TV host John Walsh said.

Frank Bender's uncanny bust of how fugitive mass murderer John List would look after eighteen years made the front page of *The New York Times* and vaulted the artist to international renown.

Next page: The poster of the "Boy in the Box" that haunted young Bill Fleisher in the winter of 1957, when police circulated hundreds of thousands of posters

POLICE DEPARTMENT, PHILADELPHIA, PA.
INFORMATION WANTED

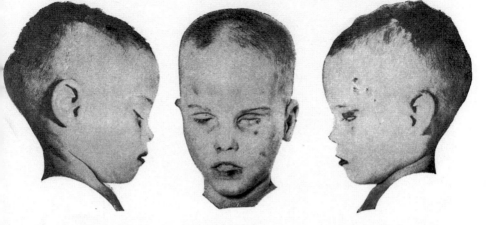

Photographs depict unidentified boy, whose nude body was found in a carboard carton, in a thicket, near Susquehanna and Verree Roads, Fox Chase, Philadelphia, 3:45 p.m., Monday, February 25, 1957. Death caused by head injuries. Multiple bruises over entire body. Death estimated to have occurred from three days to two weeks prior to discovery. No clothing found. Body covered by blanket. Man's cloth cap found adjacent to body.

Description of Boy: 4 to 5 years, height 40½", weight 30 lbs., blue eyes, fair complexion; medium to light brown hair, crudely cut; full set baby teeth; no deformities; "L"-shaped scar under chin; no vaccination scar; tonsils not removed; no bone fractures; finger and toe nails neatly clipped; clothing size probably 4; shoe size, 8-D.

Blanket made of cheap cotton flannel, patterned with diamonds and blocks in green, rust and white, colors faded. Overall size 64" x 76" with section 31" x 26" missing. Clean, apparently washed recently. Mended with poor-grade cotton thread on home-type sewing machine.

Man's cap, size 7⅛, leather strap in back, royal blue corduroy material. In excellent condition, with large roll of paper tissue in sweatband. Manufacturer's stamp in lining of crown, Robbins Bald Eagle Cap, 2603 South 7th St., Philadelphia, Pa.

Carton, size 15" x 19" x 35". Originally contained white bassinet, price $7.50, sold at J. C. Penney store, 69th and Chestnut Sts., Upper Darby, Pa., between December 3, 1956 and February 16, 1957.

It is requested that citizens and law enforcement, welfare, and child caring agencies supply information concerning boys of this age and description, known to be in the custody of persons who would abuse them; also, the disappearance or absence of any child answering this description. Newpaper, radio, and television publicity requested.

NOTIFY HOMICIDE UNIT, DETECTIVE HEADQUARTERS, CITY HALL, PHILADELPHIA, at any time, day or night, in person or telephone, MUnicipal 6-9700, or submit information through your local Police Department.

March 8, 1957

THOMAS J. GIBBONS
Commissioner

Prepared by The Philadelphia Inquirer as a public service.

VSM investigator Richard Walter (standing) devoted six years of pro bono work helping marketing executive Jim Dunn find and convict the killer of his young son, Scott.

Michael Bryant/The Philadelphia Inquirer

Scott Dunn

Lubbock, Texas police thought a helpful young woman like Leisha Hamilton (*above*) could not have committed a vicious torture murder. VSM Richard Walter entered the mind of the killer to put the "clever psychopath" behind bars.

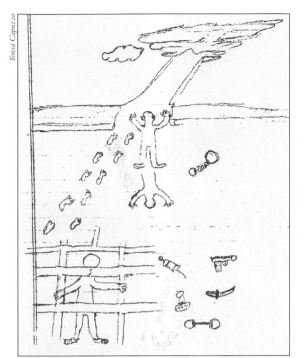

The Killing Room:
The private sketch Leisha
Hamilton made to memo-
rialize her torture killing of
her boyfriend Scott Dunn,
analyzed by psychologist
Richard Walter.

Jan and Frank Bender in their studio home, November 2009

Cuisine and crime: Vidocq Society founders Bill Fleisher, Richard Walter, and Frank Bender with VSMs after an investigative luncheon in the "murder room" in Philadelphia.

"I was excited for Scott because he was really turning things around," said Dunn.

Walter nodded. "He's staying away from drugs, doing well on his job. And while he's screwing his brains out with Leisha Hamilton, as twentysomethings are wont to do, he's found a better thing, the real thing, in Jessica. He's working his way back to legitimate society. Then of course Leisha finds out she was going to be dumped and you don't dump Leisha Hamilton, she dumps you. He had the bad fortune of forming an alliance with a violent psychopath. He's not the first. They don't call it 'psychopathic charm' for nothing."

Dunn sighed.

"Jim, we're not just solving a murder. Scott was cut short of his ability to rehabilitate himself and be honorable and productive. What we're doing—part of the ethic of being a father—is to take up that challenge for him and make a strike for decency."

"What do we do next?" Dunn's eyes were fastened on the thin man.

"The Lubbock Police Department must call me and request my help. The Vidocq Society does not become involved in a case unless it is invited in with full cooperation by the police department. Until that happens, all we've done is have a conversation."

"I'll call them right away. They'll understand," Dunn said passionately. "They'll have to."

"Then it's up to the police to call me," Walter said, "or we have wasted our time. And another thing."

Dunn appeared dazed. He was feeling relieved, emboldened, optimistic, and overwhelmed all at once.

The thin man's face sharpened in the sallow light of the room.

"The Vidocq Society will help you as best we can. As for myself, I'm not going to let that bitch get away with murder."

CHAPTER 33

MURDER IN THE CATHEDRAL

The week before Christmas a little blond girl, dead for thirty years, materialized on a screen in the City Tavern. The tiny figure, bruised and beaten, ashen face drained of life, shimmered in the midday sunlight in the front of the room. Fleisher started trembling. He looked like he'd seen a ghost.

That morning in the Strawbridge & Clothier department store, he'd seen Ebenezer Scrooge quaver before the Ghost of Christmas Past in the store's annual portrayal of Charles Dickens's *A Christmas Carol*. But the slain little girl before him now, nine-year-old Carol Ann Dougherty, was not a figment of anyone's imagination, and Fleisher was not trembling in fear. He was shaking in fury.

Dougherty's murder was one of the saddest and most disturbing images of his childhood. Carol Ann had been found raped and murdered in St. Mark's Church in Bristol, Pennsylvania, a Philadelphia suburb not far from Fleisher's house, in October 1962. A fifth-grader at the parish school, she had been killed in an era when police and the public were not fully aware of the perverse sexual needs of many priests, or the long practice in the Roman Catholic Church of allowing pedophile priests, cloaked wolves, to prey on victims, simply transferring them from flock to vulnerable flock. Carol's killer had never been brought to justice.

Now on the morning of December 17, 1992, as the Vidocq

Society began its examination of the Choir Loft Murder, Fleisher converted his anger into a desire to fix the past. Thirty years, one month, and twenty-five days after the murder, Bristol police chief Frank Peranteau and detective Randy Moore stood before the society to present the case. Peranteau had said, "We need all the help we can get." A series of articles in the Bucks County *Courier Times* by reporter J. D. Mullane had recently reawakened interest in the county's coldest case. The county district attorney had impaneled a grand jury to investigate it. Chief Peranteau had inherited the case from Chief Vincent Faragalli, retired now for thirteen years, who had obsessed over it. Faragalli kept Carol's picture in his wallet.

The case was always "just out of reach," investigators said.

Now the screen in the Long Room showed Dougherty lying on her back in the choir loft the day she was raped and murdered. It was one of those cases where the waiters and waitresses looked away as they carried silver cloches in and out of the Murder Room.

Light from a stained-glass window revealed her blond hair mussed and untied. The red plastic barrette that had held it in a ponytail was lying nearby on the landing. One of her feet was bare. The shoe was tossed to the side; the sock was stuffed in her mouth, gagging her. Carol's small right arm was wrenched behind her back. Her left hand was straight out, clutching three dark hairs, a man's pubic hairs, which she had grabbed during her fatal struggle. She had been forcibly raped; semen was found at the scene. The grooves on her neck, from the rope that strangled her to death, appeared to match the pattern of a cincture, the long, ropelike cord tied around the waist of a priest's alb, the full-length Roman tunic. To Roman Catholics, the cincture was a symbol of the priest's chastity and purity.

One of the few surviving original investigators had told the *Courier Times* that it broke his heart. "I really took that case to heart because I had a daughter the same age, nine years old. You saw that little girl laying in that choir loft, and you just wanted to cry."

Fleisher felt a chill displace his holiday cheer. As he walked the city garlanded in holiday lights that morning, Fleisher had allowed himself a moment of pride in the Vidocq Society. Vidocq agents were working for justice wherever need took them. Richard Walter was in West Texas that morning, consulting with police on the Dunn case. Fleisher smiled, imagining their sardonic dark knight flashing his rapier wit at the suspected killers of Scott Dunn, the police—whoever got in his way. U.S. Customs special agent Joe O'Kane, the Vidocq case manager, was fielding heaps of letters signed by grieving and aggrieved men and women across America. Word was out that a band of pro bono detectives in the City of Brotherly Love was standing for truth in cold murders beyond the grasp of police.

But now he noted that a quiet pall had fallen over his fellow Vidocqeans. "Everyone was deeply disturbed," he recalled. Though Fleisher knew that one of the most notorious murders of his childhood was on the menu, he had not expected to be so deeply affected. Looking around at his seasoned investigators, he was confident they could help.

On Monday, October 22, 1962, President John F. Kennedy went on national TV to announce that the Soviet Union had installed nuclear missile sites in Cuba, ninety miles from Florida. That afternoon after school, Carol rode her bicycle to the library to take back a book and meet two girlfriends. Police never learned why she stopped at the old stone church on the riverfront, but the nuns often said that if you were passing the church you should stop and say your prayers. Witnesses saw Carol enter the church at 4 P.M.

At five o'clock, when she didn't return home for dinner, her parents went looking for her. Frank Dougherty, a newspaper printer, found his daughter's bicycle on the steps of St. Mark's, and went into the church looking for her. When he found his daughter's body in the choir loft he ran out into the twilight screaming for help. As word spread, a thousand people gathered behind rope barricades outside the church, a fixture in the community since the nineteenth century. As the night went on and police and the coroner came and went through the arched entrance, they shouted and wept, stood numb and whispered, "A girl killed in a church!" and did not move, as if they would stand there until the world was made right again. After seven hours, Chief Vincent Faragalli told them to go home. "As of right now, we are without any leads."

Faragalli learned that the parish housekeeper had seen someone kneeling in a pew a few minutes before Carol entered the church. He was eager to learn the identity of this "mystery witness," but his attempts to extensively interview church staff were quashed by Monsignor Paul Baird, the leading cleric at St. Mark's, who refused to let police interview the reverends Joseph Sabadish or Michael Carroll.

But police had already interviewed Father Sabadish once before. Monsignor Baird withdrew cooperation, and now they began to focus the investigation on Sabadish. Sabadish had been extremely nervous and evasive during the interview. He gave an alibi that police easily discredited. The priest said he had been a few blocks from the church on West Circle, making his rounds on the annual parish visitation, during the time of the murder. But the surviving investigator interviewed by reporter Mullane said that Sabadish had lied.

"He left a note at one of the houses that showed he was on West Circle a couple of hours before the murder," the investigator said.

In 1962, a clerk at a Bristol shoe store told the police that Sabadish came into the shop shortly before 4:30 that afternoon— when Carol was apparently already dead—acting strangely. Nervous and distracted, he asked the clerk for the time, and also asked a bizarre question in a shoe store, "Do you sell underwear?" The clerk noted that Sabadish was wearing a wristwatch and knew the time. Police believed Sabadish was trying to create an alibi for himself. And they became increasingly suspicious of the priest's possible sexual perversions when they obtained receipts for purchases he had made at an upscale ladies' lingerie shop.

They were still looking at other possible suspects. But the night before Halloween, a week into the investigation, Chief Faragalli received disturbing information that made Sabadish the primary suspect. A married woman in nearby Fairless Hills told police that Sabadish had threatened to rape her three or four weeks before Dougherty's murder. She knew Sabadish from years earlier when she lived at a home for unwed mothers where he was the chaplain. Now on the telephone he had made sexual advances, including a threat that he wanted to rape her. Sabadish said she needn't worry about becoming pregnant because he was "sterile."

Furious, the woman's husband called Sabadish and confronted him, while taping the phone call. Sabadish admitted making the obscene telephone calls and sexual threats. He apologized and promised not to do it again. Chief Faragalli had obtained the tape.

When Sabadish was making his rounds on parish visitation, the chief and a detective picked him up in an unmarked car and took him to the Bucks County Courthouse in Doylestown, where a county detective gave him a lie detector test. The priest passed the polygraph.

After that, police turned to other suspects they considered equally compelling. A town drunk admitted he killed Carol. Later, it was discovered that the man was mentally ill, and furthermore a Bristol cop had coerced his confession. A local convicted child molester rose to the top of the list, but he proved he was in another state at the time of the murder.

At the Vidocq luncheon, the police said that Frank Dougherty could not forget how the church had shunned him and his wife after Carol's murder. Father Sabadish refused to make eye contact with him. Neither Sabadish, Reverend Carroll, nor Monsignor Baird called on the family to comfort them. When Dougherty asked Sabadish in the church confessional, "Father, am I wrong in assuming a priest could have killed my daughter?" the priest stood up and left the confessional.

Police never questioned Sabadish again. "We had no concrete

evidence to tie Sabadish to the murder, except that he was very evasive during the interrogation," said the surviving investigator.

Shortly after the polygraph, Sabadish was quietly transferred from St. Mark's with no explanation to parishioners. He returned months later, again without explanation from the monsignor. Five years later, he was transferred to St. William Parish in Philadelphia. Then followed more than a dozen transfers in eighteen years within the archdiocese in eastern Pennsylvania. In recent weeks, Mullane, the reporter, had tracked down Father Sabadish, now in his seventies and still employed by the Archdiocese of Philadelphia as a chaplain at a Montgomery County Catholic hospital. Mullane asked the aging priest if he killed Carol Ann Dougherty. Sabadish vehemently denied it, calling it "an absolute, positive lie." He denied that he had made obscene phone calls to a Fairless Hills woman, saying, "That's news to me," and called police detectives "crazy." After the newspaper stories were published he called Mullane, furious, and called him "anti-Catholic."

Now the Bristol police were seriously considering other suspects as they reopened the investigation. The Vidocq Society urged police to test the semen, pubic hairs, and a badly smudged fingerprint left on Carol's plastic hair band, presumably the killer's.

After the luncheon, Fleisher left the City Tavern determined to solve the case. "It was the priest," Fleisher said. "We all knew it was the priest."

Within days, the Vidocq Society had formed a task force to bring the killer of Carol Ann Dougherty to justice.

CHAPTER 34

What I Want to Hear Are Handcuffs

The light in the room was storm cloud gray, and ice glistened on the sidewalks below the municipal building. A bitter north wind beat the windows of the detective division of the Lubbock Police Department. The man from Philadelphia had not enjoyed his week on the high plains of West Texas. He had sat in the police car grimly staring at cotton fields rolling under black judgment-day skies. Goose hunting country, they said. *It's a fucking wasteland is what it is,* he thought. *You can see a pimple on a cat's ass.* He detested the bone-chilling cold but was warmed by a *Lubbock Avalanche-Journal* story open on the desk:

SUPER SLEUTH CALLED TO SHED LIGHT ON BIZARRE DISAP-PEARANCE.

It was the front-page story that touted his arrival, followed by a second front-page story in the *Avalanche-Journal* that had made him something of the talk of the town.

INVESTIGATOR EXPECTS TO CRACK DUNN CASE.

Walter had confidently declared that Lubbock police would soon solve the case of Dunn's disappearance. After spending one day studying the case, interviewing suspects, and talking to police, Walter promised that the "nasty and clever" killers' eighteen months of gloating would soon come to an end. His analysis of the murder indicated that the killers were "smart" but made "mistakes." They unknowingly revealed their patterns to him, leaving "trails, bits and pieces" that would be their undoing.

"Success will be based on two things," he said. "A) The case merits success, and B) I don't like losing a case. I have a bulldog mentality, and what I want to hear are handcuffs, and I want to do it right. . . . If I were the suspect, I wouldn't feel comfortable. I wouldn't buy any green bananas."

Now at eight o'clock that morning in December 1992, Walter sat down with a police corporal, sergeant, and detective to discuss the Dunn case. The thin man looked fresh and energized in his blue suit, his blue eyes shining above the French tricolor pin on his lapel. Tal English, the tall, twenty-seven-year-old detective, had an aw-shucks manner that matched his sandy hair and cowboy boots; he and Walter had bonded working the case for months over the telephone. The older man had croaked, "Young man, we're going to go into the jaws of hell and bring this case back out." Corporal George White, distinguished-looking with gray in his dark hair, and Sergeant Randy McGuire, large and bald, sat stoically appraising the profiler. They all got along in an atmosphere of mutual respect, but the two veteran cops had not seen eye to eye with the "super sleuth" from the Vidocq Society in their previous meeting.

After the cops' courteous Texas welcome, which Walter always appreciated, he got right to his point: They should immediately take the case to District Attorney Travis Ware and press for murder charges. Walter wanted the charges filed against Leisha Hamilton and her neighbor and lover Tim Smith, fiercely jealous of Scott, whom he believed was an accomplice.

Corporal White and Sergeant McGuire took a long look at the man from Philadelphia. The case had been a top priority for a year. Jim Dunn was a hometown boy, a hall-of-fame alumnus of local Texas Tech; his best friend was still his old college roommate W. R. Collier, president of the largest locally owned bank in Lubbock. There was great public interest in the gruesome disappearance of a prodigal son in a cloud of sex, blood, and duct tape, and the police had invested thousands of man-hours. Murders were relatively rare in the Texas city of 186,000 people, but they were reading about this one over coffee from Plainview to Dallas to Jacksonville, Florida. The police wanted nothing more than to solve it. They liked Walter, and he them—"they were all great guys"—but they just couldn't see how a petite, charming twenty-eight-year-old woman had orchestrated a vast conspiracy of lies and cold-blooded murder.

Walter tried to convince them.

"This case is like shaking hands with smoke," he said. "It's a matter of you can see it, you can smell it and taste it, but it's difficult to get your hands around it."

Walter urged them to look at the crime scene, the killing room with blood halfway up the walls and splattered on the ceiling. They all agreed Scott Dunn had no doubt died in that room. The point of departure was that with no body and no weapon there was no case, according to the police. Without that foundation of physical evidence, it wasn't possible to bring murder charges under Texas law, as the DA never tired of reminding them.

Walter saw it differently. "I say, OK, we don't have a body. Its absence is a clue. Let's use that to move forward."

The problem, as he privately saw it, was that "cops are concrete. They think in structure. The whole investigative process is structural, and wisely so. Traditionally, you work from the inside out on a case. You work from the evidence forward. Here you don't have a body, you don't have the primary evidence; that's it, end of story. So in this case one must work from the outside, the pathology, back to the crime scene." He smiled to himself at the small irony that it was eccentric Eugène François Vidocq, in nineteenth-century Paris, who first had the gall to reveal broader and deeper patterns to the straight-thinking gendarmes.

"The police are correct in that what we have at the crime scene is vital," he said to himself. "One must always remain rooted in the facts of the case, but one must think differentially, not just linearly. Unfortunately, there are not many people who are capable of it."

He took a sip of his coffee, which was already cold. "Sometimes, gentlemen," he said, "what's missing is more important than what's present." He held up the photograph of the blood-soaked room revealed by the luminol. "What's here and what's not here?" he asked. "A minimalist version of the crime is left, but the essence remains.

"Something dire happened in this room," he continued. "It was a bloodbath, and the careful cleanup speaks to a very careful, elaborate plot. The murder is very purposeful, not recreational." At the word "recreational" eyebrows rose, and he explained: "A Bundy type who chose a random victim and killed for sadistic pleasure would have left a far messier, more symbolic crime scene. So the killers knew Scott." He let that sink in a moment.

"As it happens, the carefully organized crime, cleanup, and the brutal destruction and disposal of the body point to a power-assertive, or PA, killer," he went on. "It's a recognizable type I've dealt with many, many times. The killing is all about power—not the acquisition of power through fantasy but a John Wayne–type power, the macho direct assault—simple, in-your-face, incapacitate, restrain, torture, kill, throw away. 'I win, you lose' kind of power." A cold smile crossed Walter's face. "The whole thing just reeks of PA at all levels."

He asked them to examine Scott and Leisha's relationship. Scott was twenty-four, a ladies' man, handsome, bright, cocky. He would have seen Leisha as a stimulating challenge. She was an older woman, also very bright, sexy, flippant, and "fun in the sack, without giving much thought to her essential character as a manipulative, Mata Hari figure.

"Leisha had a long litany of situation lovers, husbands, one-night stands, wanted and unwanted children," he continued. "She had six children without knowing who was the father of several of them." His voice took on a sarcastic edge. "She told police she only loved the ones conceived in love." He paused to let that take root.

"Leisha would have seen Scott also as a challenging conquest, and a link to money, his father's wealth. But like a lot of twenty-four-year-old men, Scott had found someone to take to bed, not home to meet Mom and Dad. Scott was rebuilding his life, and when he found a 'decent' girl, the real thing, it was time to dump Leisha Hamilton."

The day Scott's would-be fiancée called and Leisha answered the phone sealed his fate. "Nobody dumps Leisha Hamilton. Oh, no."

Walter's complexion took on a grave cast. "When we look at Leisha's history, we recognize that she absolutely cannot stand rejection, that loss of control. She has a series of short-term relationships which are not monogamous because she needs not so much to conquer men as emasculate them. Scott is a relatively strong-willed man himself. He sees this rather malevolent, vixenish woman whom one wouldn't mind having an affair with, but he wouldn't want to introduce her to his parents. Now he has Jessica and he's gathering strength. He doesn't need Leisha anymore. If anything is going to get you killed, it's to reject the psychopath and say, 'I'm better than you are.'"

His voice turned dour. "All her behavior points to a psychopath. She's just a power-hungry witch who chooses men younger than herself and tries to seduce and control through sex and intimidation. She found one that didn't play, or played for a while, but it was his game not hers, and she simply wasn't going to tolerate the insult and the challenge to power."

Walter believed Leisha had ensnared some of Scott's coworkers, who were caught in her web of intimidation, in a conspiracy to murder him. There was powerful resentment of Scott at his job, "a lot of competitiveness, rivalries, and jealousies with coworkers." Not only was Scott the star "stereo cowboy" and the handsome face on the shop's TV commercials, he was cocky and brash. "He rubbed it in, got in their faces about it without realizing the risky game he was playing," Walter said. Walter speculated that the shop was stealing and reselling its stereos, a common racket. "Scott would have gotten in their faces about that, too. One more thing to trump them with." The week before he disappeared, Walter reminded them, "He and his boss had a fistfight out behind the shop."

The police were tracking down Leisha's numerous ex-boyfriends, but Walter believed the suspect list was short. "Few people had access to Scott." The sequence of events leading to Scott's murder began with a party at his boss's house. Leisha was at the party, but Scott arrived with a tall, gorgeous blonde. Walter believed the blonde performed oral sex on the other men. "When I asked them they all denied it, but a lot of eyes hit the floor," he said. At the end of the evening, he believed that Scott had trumped them all. "You think you guys are so smart, that was a transvestite! Needless to say, they were not pleased." The revelation of that indiscretion would have ruined the life of at least one of the men at the shop. "Thus a crime already planned became a crime of improvisation and opportunity," the profiler said.

Scott became seriously ill with the flu at the party, too sick to stand, Leisha said. Walter saw it differently; the murder conspiracy was already in motion. "I believe he was poisoned, organophosphates, something from under the sink. His extreme sensitivity to light and noise is telling." Scott slept on the sofa at the party house, and the next afternoon, Leisha showed up and brought him home. A neighbor saw Leisha supporting the weak, stumbling young man as she led him into the apartment. It was the last he was seen by anyone other than Leisha or a coworker. Leisha said she went out to get soup and a thermometer to nurse Scott that night and the next day. When a coworker came by in the morning to pick him up for work he was still too ill. It was the last time anyone saw him alive.

It was a simple enough matter for Leisha to call on neighbor Tim Smith, a young, submissive evangelical Christian, to help with the murder. Smith had flooded her with a series of fawning love letters that included, "If only Scott wasn't around, we could be together." Duct tape from a roll in Smith's apartment was used to patch the blood-soaked carpet that had been cut away and replaced in the killing room.

"This is a classic setup for a PA killer," he said. "Just classic. A female PA relies on sexual performance and seduction, but if her power base is threatened, she will resort to violence. She'll typically enlist trickery to disable a stronger male and/or acquire a sympathetic and weak accomplice. Leisha did both. And the PA killer classically needs to brag or flaunt the killing to claim credit, and inserts him- or herself into the investigation to exert control and power and prolong the fantasy of the murder."

Calling attention to herself was Leisha's big mistake, Walter said.

"How do we find out about the crime? We find out when Leisha calls Jim Dunn. She's laying the framework, not only shaping the investigation—she knows ultimately Jim's going to look for Scott—but she's also exhibiting her own insatiable greed for power. She's already done in the son; now she wants to do in the father, too. Then she tried to be coquettish with the detectives, casting herself as the wronged woman, calling them all the time with new information, pretending to be afraid of Tim Smith. She moved in with Smith so she could continue to set up her dupe to take the fall. This need for stimulation is quite insatiable for a psychopath, the ego gratification to prove they're smarter than anyone, the gotcha."

In the *Avalanche-Journal* story on Walter's arrival in town, Leisha was quoted as saying Smith was a "suspect" in Scott's disappearance, and had been "fiercely jealous of her relationship with Scott."

Smith was absent from work the day of the murder, Walter said, and Hamilton can't account for her activities that day, although her memory is extraordinary for the days around it.

The murder itself was a monstrous affair, Walter said. Scott was incapacitated with poisons, imprisoned and restrained and tortured for two days before his death, Walter believed. "This kind of killer typically uses a gun to restrain or intimidate, but close-up weapons, the kind that caused all this splattering and gives the killer emotional satisfaction, to pummel, cut, utterly destroy the victim until the killer's fear of vulnerability is sated, and power restored. There would have been a lot of 'You think you're leaving me now, bitch, try this.' What the absence and presence of evidence at the crime scene tells us is Scott intolerably challenged somebody's power base, and paid with his life."

After the murder, Walter said, Leisha and Tim had sex together that night in the apartment. "A little thank-you from Leisha," Walter said. "But only after they had removed the body and cleaned up." He smiled wickedly. "Even they have standards."

Detective English shook his head sadly, acknowledging the depth of evil, and sat back with an audible sigh. He was persuaded by Walter's profile of Leisha Hamilton as a psychopath—he saw why Jim Dunn had termed Walter's insights "miraculous." But the young detective didn't buy the wide conspiracy, and the others weren't nearly as impressed. All the cops knew Hamilton was withholding information; all of them considered Smith a suspect. "They were Texas polite," Walter said. "But the whole thing was too ethereal for them." None of it would matter, anyway, the cops said, to the DA, Travis Ware. As Sergeant McGuire told Dunn, "I have seen Ware cut people right off at the knees when he feels they don't have a strong case. Believe me, you don't want to talk to Travis Ware."

Walter wasn't listening. He was ready to see the DA. "Let's do it," he said. "I don't like to fuck around." Reluctantly, the cops led him to the office of the top lawman in Lubbock County, Texas.

The district attorney's office was large and redolent of masculine power. Travis Ware, six feet tall, dark-haired, and impeccably attired, rose from his high-backed leather chair behind a huge polished wooden desk. In a remarkable display of dominance, he hitched one expensive black leather shoe up on the desk, towering over them with the flamboyance, Walter thought, of a matador. *Leisha's not the only PA in the room,* the profiler thought, amused. *Let's see who gets gored.*

Walter, Detective English, Sergeant McGuire, Lieutenant Dean Summerlin, and Captain Frank Wiley, head of Crimes Against Persons, sat in five small chairs positioned around the district attorney's huge wooden desk like pawns around a king. In a glance Walter evaluated Ware—fortyish, reasonably good-looking, expensive gold watch peeking from under the cuff. *Ah, narcissism,* he thought—*a weakness.*

For twenty minutes, the DA talked about himself. As if to match Walter's experience with Scotland Yard, Walter thought, he discussed his education abroad in England and the many brilliant murder prosecutions that "attested to his greatness." Appealing to the DA's sense of vanity, the profiler offered, "Yes, there are indeed many connections to England in this room," and casually mentioned a "quite brilliant friend," Dr. Richard Shepherd of London, who had helped him with the case.

Ware said brusquely, from his elevated pose: "Well, you've asked for this meeting. What do you want?"

Walter snapped back, "We want charges filed against Leisha Hamilton and Tim Smith in the murder of Scott Dunn."

The DA scoffed. His voice filled with condescension, he said, "You don't have a murder charge. All you have is a missing person. You don't even have a body. Without a body you don't have a murder. Come back to me when you have a body."

In a second interview, the profiler removed his horn-rims and glared. "If you want a goddamned body, I'll give you one. It's right here, in Dr. Shepherd's report." His face flushed with color, Walter stood and dropped on the desk a slim blue-bound report titled "Forensic Pathology and Analysis of the Crime Scene in the Murder of Roger Scott Dunn."

"What the hell are you talking about?"

"It's right here," Walter said. "Dr. Shepherd's report proves conclusively that Scott Dunn died in that room, and was murdered."

Walter had asked Detective English to have a forensic pathologist examine the crime scene to determine if enough blood had been spilled to indisputably have caused the death of a six-foot-two, 170-pound man. Dr. Sparks Veasey, the Lubbock County pathologist, had refused the job, saying there wasn't enough information to reach a conclusion. At Walter's direction English had mailed a large package with copies of the entire case file, photographs, and bloody carpet samples to Walter's friend Dr. Richard Shepherd, forensic pathologist at Guy's Hospital, London, England, internationally known consultant to Scotland Yard. "Dick's brilliance is unsurpassed," Walter said. "And he owes me a favor."

After studying the sprayed blood on the south and east walls, ceiling and doorknob of the bedroom, Dr. Shepherd wrote that the "by far most likely cause" of the blood spatter was "repeated blunt trauma." Furthermore, "The distribution of the spraying of blood is entirely consistent with the victim lying on the floor while the blows that resulted in this spraying were struck." Although the amount of blood lost was impossible to calculate, the blood spatter indicated Scott Dunn was forcefully and repeatedly bludgeoned about the head and such blows to the brain were "the prime cause of death in such cases."

As DNA testing indicated the bloodstains were 958,680 times more likely to originate from the offspring of James Dunn than from anyone else on Earth, Dr. Shepherd concluded that bloodstains in the room:

"(1) have not resulted from a natural disease process; (2) are entirely consistent with the infliction of multiple blows from a blunt instrument or instruments; (3) are entirely consistent with those blows being delivered with a force of sufficient strength to cause death; (4) that a child of James Dunn has suffered severe multiple blunt trauma injuries while in the corner of the south and east aspects of this room, and these injuries resulted in the death of that individual."

The report was signed: "Richard Thorley Shepherd, B.S.C., M.B., B.S., M.R.C.C. PATH, D.M.J., senior lecturer and honorary consultant in forensic medicine. United Medical Schools of Guy's and St. Thomas's, Guy's Hospital, London."

The DA looked up from the report, his chin set in defiance. There still was no body in the case, he said. "I'm not sure what Texas law would say about this."

"I just happen to have that section of Texas law with me," Walter said, grinning.

Ware issued a wan smile. "I thought you might."

Walter opened a statute book and read, interpreting as he went. "In essence, Texas law says we have to have A) a body, B) part of a body, or C) a confession with corroborative evidence. We have B. We have blood; blood is connective tissue; ergo, we have part of a body."

Ware leaned back in his chair, tenting his fingers. He stared at the profiler.

"All right," he said. "You've got a murder."

For an instant the thin man's smile flashed triumphantly, but his voice was soft.

"As it happens, I agree."

CHAPTER 35

THE CONSULTING DETECTIVES

The three men huddled in the smoky light of a Philadelphia pub, discussing their coldest cases.

Bender said he had been asked to do a facial reconstruction of John Wilkes Booth. It could help solve mysteries surrounding President Lincoln's assassination in 1865.

Walter was chosen as the profiler on an eight-person forensic all-star squad, including Los Angeles coroner Dr. Thomas Noguchi, investigating Jack the Ripper on the one hundredth anniversary of the murders. "It was quite easy. The murders show a clear learning curve not understood in 1888, and only Montague Druitt was capable of it.

"The Old Guard begged me not to make a fuss about it." He smiled. "Kill the mystery, and there goes all that tourism."

"Good work, men. Maybe you two can figure out who killed King Tut," Fleisher cracked, holding up a *Philadelphia Daily News.* "Meanwhile, check out the twentieth century." The June 9, 1993, headline in the tabloid newspaper said: FETISH MURDER? KILLED BY FOOT FETISHIST? DREXEL STUDENT WAS SLAIN IN '84.

Walter picked up the story: "A twenty-year-old Drexel University student, strangled more than eight years ago, was killed for her white sneakers," he read.

"No kidding," Bender deadpanned. "That sounds like an interesting case."

"Good for them," Walter said. "Justice is done."

The day before, Philadelphia police homicide detectives had arrested David Dickson Jr., a thirty-three-year-old U.S. Army sergeant and former Drexel University security guard, at the Army office where he now worked as a recruiter. Police charged him with "murdering Drexel University student Deborah Lynn Wilson in November 1984 because of his fetish for women's white sneakers."

Walter raised an eyebrow and read on.

Wilson may have been murdered after she dozed off in front of the computer in Rendell Hall—and caught the guard trying to remove her Reebok sneakers.

"Law enforcement sources" said Dickson was believed to have a "foot fetish" and "gets enjoyment from smelling women's sneakers and socks."

"Clever of them," Fleisher said. Walter smiled.

According to accounts in the *Daily News* and the *Philadelphia Inquirer,* Dickson had been a suspect all along, but police never had enough evidence to arrest him. They decided to take a fresh look at the cold case but weren't getting far until "investigators learned of his alleged foot fetish and linked it to the fact that Wilson's sneakers and socks were missing." For eight years, investigators thought the missing footwear was important, "but they didn't know why. Then, in 1993, police said they found a clue in the files of the U.S. Army."

Dickson had been arrested and court-martialed for the theft of women's sneakers on an Army base in Korea in 1979. Army Sergeant Gwendolyn Garrett-Jackson, who now lives in Birmingham, Alabama, was prepared to testify that Dickson broke into her quarters on the Korean base and stole her white sneakers, video camera, and other belongings. Based on the Army court-martial, police obtained warrants to search Dickson's apartment on City Avenue and his storage bin at the Philadelphia Navy base.

In both locations, police seized more than a hundred pairs of women's white sneakers, all used, and confiscated seventy-seven videotapes of women wearing white sneakers. The tapes were pornographic, including sex scenes of women in white sneakers, and women fondling other women's feet. There were shots of Dickson's Florida vacation to Disney World, with the camera trained on his female partner's feet, and a scene in a fast-food restaurant where the camera was focused on women wearing white sneakers. There was a home-shopping commercial for a cross-country ski machine showing a woman on the machine wearing white sneakers, and a naked store mannequin wearing white Keds.

Dickson's foot fetish was not a harmless fetish, the prosecution said, but a sexual deviancy that led him to psychopathic behavior. Three years after Wilson's murder, police said, Dickson was fired from a maintenance job at the SmithKline Beecham pharmaceutical company after admitting he had written a love letter to a female chemist, asking her to leave him her sneakers. Three other women were prepared to testify they believed Dickson had broken into their apartments to steal their white sneakers.

Dickson's ex-wife told police Dickson "was obsessed by, and drew sexual satisfaction from, women's feet, sneakers, and socks . . . when she came home from work, tired and wearing sweaty sneakers, her husband removed her shoes and rubbed, kissed, and fondled her feet and toes." She saw him masturbate in their home while watching aerobics tapes of attractive young women exercising in white socks and sneakers. When she found other women's sneakers in her closets on several occasions, her husband said "he was giving them to Goodwill."

Police had shattered Dickson's alibi for the murder. He claimed he'd been talking to his girlfriend on the telephone at the time of the murder and "forgot" to check on Wilson and take her to her car. Yet the woman, now his estranged wife, testified that Dickson phoned her only once that evening, for fifteen minutes between midnight and one in the morning, when Wilson was alive. She also testified that she received a frantic phone call from Dickson saying, "Felicia, you've got to help me. You're my alibi. You've got to help me."

Reached at her home in Woodbury, New Jersey, Dorothy Wilson, Deborah's mother, said the family felt "very, very thankful . . . it's been eight and a half years. . . . We just can't say enough for the Philadelphia Police Department and district attorney."

A Drexel spokesman said the university was "gratified" by the "break in the long-standing Deborah Wilson case." Police credited a grand jury for recommending Dickson's arrest on murder charges after an eighteen-month investigation. The police homicide special investigations unit and the district attorney's office investigated the case extensively. Chief of Detectives Richard Zappile said he "feels very sorry for the family of the victim and we are glad that this case has finally been resolved."

The *Daily News* said "it was not clear why the old murder case was reopened, although the special homicide investigations unit periodically goes back to take a fresh look at unsolved slayings." The Wilson family hired a private detective to work on the case, police said.

The Vidocq Society was not mentioned in any of the stories. Nor was the investigative luncheon at the Downtown Club, or any individual VSM.

"Let's remember we're consulting detectives," Walter said, "not crime-solvers. That's what the police do. We've done our job."

"It's just like *The Adventure of the Naval Treaty*," Fleisher said. Walter glowered at him.

Fleisher ignored him. Sherlock Holmes, he said, was accused by the police of stealing credit for solving the theft of an important naval treaty from the Foreign Office.

"His reply is a classic. 'On the contrary, out of my last fifty-three cases my name has only appeared in four, and the police have had all the credit in forty-nine.'"

"That's us," Bender said.

"I don't have any problem with it," Fleisher said. "We're

territorial and tribal animals. It's a very, very natural phenomenon. I saw it in the government all the time, squads competing for cases like children with sibling rivalries, agents competing with each other. It's prize envy."

"The fact is, we can't work for the approval of others," Walter said.

"There's a better way to say this," Bender said, raising a shot glass of vodka.

"Virtue is its own reward." Fleisher had a lopsided grin.

"Stoli is its own reward." The sculptor threw back the shot and smacked the empty glass on the bar.

Two years later, in December 1995, David Dickson Jr., thirty-five, would be convicted of the second-degree murder of Deborah Lynn Wilson, the twenty-year-old math major at Drexel University, so he could steal and sniff her white Reeboks and socks.

A jailhouse snitch told the court that Dickson had confessed "the whole story" of the murder to him in prison, where Dickson was known as "Dr. Scholl." Inmate Jay Wolchansky, serving thirty to sixty years for a string of burglaries, said that Dickson told him he had asked Wilson for a date, but the student rejected him. During his late-night rounds on November 30, 1984, Dickson, a martial arts expert, attacked her in a basement classroom by grabbing her hair and hitting her on the head.

As she fell to the ground, Dickson, who once boasted of his ability in ligature strangulation, told Wolchansky that he choked her with one hand. She fell unconscious and he removed her sneakers and socks, smelled the sneakers and rubbed her feet. When she groaned awake, Wilson choked her to death. Then he "had his way" with her feet, rubbing them against his face.

Dickson had said he killed Wilson because she "deserved it, and he had a fetish for white tennis shoes." He told Wolchansky that he kept the sneakers for about a year "and would masturbate with them from time to time." A psychiatrist testified that Dickson kept women's white sneakers in plastic bags to preserve the smell for his fantasies.

Wolchansky, thirty-three, denied he was in line to receive any reduction in his term for his testimony. "It bugs me that people do that [sniff sneakers]. I'm not a violent man. . . . To know how that lady was killed, Miss Wilson, disturbs me. I pray for her every night."

The testimony perfectly matched Walter's profile of a power-reassurance killer, a Gentleman Rapist type lost in a dark fantasy world, an illusionist who explodes in rage when his fairy tale shatters. He's imagining that the victim will fall in love with him at his approach but "he knows goddamn well in reality the chances of that, the chances of him ever even getting a hard-on, are very slim." Wilson was "just shoes and socks to him." When she fought back, it was a power loss. "He took what he wanted and got power reassurance. In his mind, he triumphed."

Dickson said he was innocent. He told the court he enjoyed sniffing women's feet but said he never used violence to enjoy his fetish.

Common Pleas judge Juanita Kidd Stout sentenced Dickson to a mandatory life sentence.

Deborah's parents, Dorothy and Joseph Wilson, said they went to their daughter's grave and told her the news. "The wound has been closed," said Dorothy Wilson. "It's settled. Maybe she can rest now."

PART FOUR

·

BATTLING MONSTERS

CHAPTER 36

TAKE ME TO THE PSYCHOPATH

Lubbock police detective Tal English drove the unmarked car through the breezy Texas spring morning, with Richard Walter smoking in the passenger seat. They pulled into the parking lot of the Copper Kettle, a popular lunch spot. They were thinking takeout.

One Leisha Hamilton, to go.

The tall, dark-haired waitress saw them across the restaurant and scowled. English said, "Leisha, let's go outside and avoid a scene." She nodded and quietly followed them out to the car. They put her in the backseat, and Walter turned around to face her.

"It's time for a little chat," he said. He didn't smile.

Four months after meeting the DA, Walter was frustrated by the case's lack of progress. In April 1993 he returned to Lubbock, determined to "stop fucking around" and "explain the case to them." He tried to sell the detectives once more on his idea that Leisha Hamilton was a psychopath and the primary suspect, but it was an old idea and nobody was buying. He muttered under his breath, "Gentlemen, you have no idea what you're dealing with," then turned to Detective English: "Young man, take me to the psychopath." It was time to take the fight to Hamilton.

They all exchanged small talk as Hamilton got in the backseat. The death stare she'd leveled at them in the restaurant was gone.

She was smiling, chatty, flipped her dark hair back off her forehead. She'd recovered composure remarkably fast.

Walter could sense the sex in the air, the flirty gestures and smiles she routinely used to entrap young men, the fluffy illusion concealing the hard, calculating mind beneath. He glared at her. *With a psychopath, go straight for the kill. Don't mess around.*

"This is not a social visit, Leisha. I wish you would explain something to me. I don't know anybody else in America who does a murder and then cleans up the crime scene afterward. That is, unless it is done in their own home. And in this case, you're the only one who had access to that house. And you don't have an alibi for the murder."

"But I do have an alibi," she protested.

"You mean you know when he died? Only the killer knows when he died."

"I know when I found out he was missing—"

"Scott Dunn is not missing," Walter sharply interrupted. "I don't want to hear this charade about him being missing. It offends my sense of propriety. Scott Dunn was murdered. We've got that established and you're a suspect."

The eyes and voice now went flat as prairie and held there, unshakable. "Then I guess I don't have an alibi."

Walter appeared to be lost in contemplation, then stared balefully over his horn-rims.

"Leisha, I've noticed you seem to have a great ability to attract men, especially younger men. Now, granted I'm old, I'm ugly, I'm tired. But for the life of me I can't figure out what they see in you. Can you explain it for me?"

A startled silence filled the car. She smiled awkwardly. "Well, I don't know."

"Is it because of all the sexual tricks you'll perform for them? Because you are a sexual Disneyland?"

"I guess so." She nodded sharply. "I've got to get back to work." She opened the door, and she was gone.

English sat stunned. "Richard," he said. "Am I mistaken, or did you just call her a dog?"

Walter grinned conspiratorially. "I thought I did."

"But why?"

"I wanted to see how she reacted to unexpected situations, to see how quick she was in her thinking and what her game was all about. And it worked. It's plain that her game is all about power—power and control. She's a good little psychopath, so information is crucial to her power. I planted seeds of doubt, as well as direct information I wanted her to know, such as she is a suspect. I wanted to create some anxiety and I succeeded."

Walter lit a Kool. "Leisha thinks she is smart enough to outwit everybody and can play a cat-and-mouse game with the police. What we must do is make her feel insignificant—unimportant. This will drive her crazy and she may well make a mistake."

The detective nodded.

"But it won't be easy. It'll take time and patience. She's very strong, very powerful. I looked in her eyes and saw she was having fun. It was a game and she was in control. I knew then without a doubt that the bitch killed him."

Shortly after he returned to Michigan, Walter opened a package from Detective English. Out fell a single piece of white paper on which was drawn "quite intriguing original art."

It was Hamilton's pencil sketch of the murder scene—a crude, childlike drawing that documented the prolonged torture of Scott Dunn.

The drawing showed an empty bedroom with a wooden pallet in one corner to which was chained a stick-figure man, labeled "S." At the bottom of the drawing was a legend or key depicting handcuffs, a needle, a knife, a gun, and a sketch of a penis and scrotum.

The middle of the drawing showed the "S" man running across the room toward an open door, with the sun shining outside promising freedom. But the "S" figure collapses before the door and dies; a ghost of "S" leaves the body.

Studying the sketch, Walter thought, *Scott suffered worse than I imagined.* The gun was clearly used by Leisha and perhaps a confederate to subdue the bigger, stronger Scott with the handcuffs and tie him to the pallet; the needle would have been employed to keep him doped up for forty-eight hours of torture with a knife, fists, and a blunt instrument that delivered the fatal blows to the head. The "companion ghost" next to the fallen "S" figure indicated Scott had died trying to escape, Walter said. "Furthermore, the future, through the door, is clean and unused."

The drawing of "detached genitalia" indicates Scott suffered "sexual abuse with a dildo, or, more than likely, it was representative of emasculation," the forensic psychologist wrote in a formal report for the police. Walter believed Scott had been cut in pieces and disposed of in a way that he would never be found.

"Where'd you get it?" he asked Detective English.

"An ex-boyfriend she took up with after Scott by the name of Karl Young. He gave it to me in a coffee shop, looking nervously over his shoulder the whole time. She scared the shit out of him. He thought she'd killed Scott and had Tim Smith clean up."

"Of course he's afraid," Walter said. "This is an extremely powerful woman. She gets what she wants when she wants it, and God forbid if you get in her way."

The drawing indicated that Hamilton had chained Scott to a pallet right where their bed had once been located. A coroner and blood-spatter expert determined, by the angle of three drops of blood on a far wall, that Scott had died from three lethal blows to the head.

It was Hamilton's "pictorial of the murder scene, a keepsake," Walter said.

"This is a classic," he added. "It's her personal pictorial diary of the murder. Rule number one is the murder isn't over until the murderer says it is, until he or she stops deriving pleasure from it. Scott Dunn is dead, but for Leisha Hamilton, it isn't over yet. She drew this to memorialize her achievement. She gains fresh pleasure each time she looks at it."

The drawing confirmed his profile of Hamilton as a power-assertive killer, a woman who was "a user and all about power," he said. "She has to be the top dog, the alpha dog, the bitch if you will. You don't break up with or dismiss Leisha Hamilton. She dismisses you. I see lots of anger, rage, domination. 'You're going to leave me, are you? Now try and leave me, bitch.' That sort of thing."

Torture was a favorite method of power-assertive killers. In this case the pictured implements of torture were all "masculine symbols" employed in the PA's goal of total physical dominance. Simply shooting Scott wouldn't provide the necessary pleasures. "Her real payoff was the close-up use of fists and knives and whatever inflicted terrible pain. Her goal was to crush, destroy, extinguish her betrayer."

Hamilton had made dramatic changes in her life that also were classic post-murder behavior. Few cops understood how killers used murder to stimulate personal growth. It was a very dark self-help movement—"I'm OK, You're Dead."

"Murder helps the killer grow, or enjoy the illusion of growth," Walter said. "It's the culmination or resolution of a long series of internal issues, and they use it as a springboard to change. That's why killers often make dramatic post-crime life changes. They find God or new love, move far away, get in shape, and so on."

Since murdering Scott, Hamilton had dropped Tim Smith, whom Walter believed she had seduced into helping with the crime, and took up with Young, a local restaurant cook, with whom she had a child. Meanwhile, she attended nursing school, while continuing to work as a waitress, and graduated at the top of her class. She was living the American Dream. Leisha Hamilton was going places.

"Her success doesn't surprise me," Walter told English. "I always said she was extremely intelligent—psychopathically bright and charming. But the nursing school is really quite rich. If you're accused of being a murderess, draped in the black robes of torture, how do you ritually cleanse yourself of all suspicion? You enrobe yourself in white and become a healer."

Walter saw Hamilton as a brilliant and cunning adversary, "a highly skilled psychopath." She had gotten away with murder for years. She had brazenly killed Scott Dunn, toyed with his father, manipulated lawyers, cops, and the justice system as easily as she had a parade of lovers. She had seduced and bullied a whole circle of men, through raw sexual power and intimidation, to assist her in murder. The waitress had destroyed her betrayer in the very bedroom where he had deceived her—a waitress rising to the role of a vengeful queen.

She was a poor woman's Clytemnestra, the queen who slew King Agamemnon for his affair with the prophetess Cassandra, striking him in their royal bed with a "threefold hammer blow."

Curious, Walter found his old college copy of *Agamemnon* by Aeschylus, "The Father of Tragedy," and thumbed through the ancient Greek classic to the murder scene. It caused him to raise an eyebrow:

> *She goes down, and the life is bursting out of him—*
> *Great sprays of blood, and the murderous shower*
> *Wounds me, dyes me black and I, I revel*
> *Like the Earth when the spring rains come down,*
> *The blessed gifts of god, and the new green spear,*
> *Splits the sheath and rips to birth in glory!*

It was murder as self-improvement seven centuries ago. Clytemnestra, like Leisha, had blossomed *". . . from that drenching marriage-rite the woods, the spring burst forth in bloom. And I, I cause it all."*

The profiler judged the drawing worth adding to his collection of original murderers' art, which came in handy as a teaching tool. It included a watercolor by an Australian male nurse-turned-serial killer and a classic portrait of Pogo the Clown by John Wayne Gacy, the Chicago contractor, Democratic ward heeler, and clown-for-hire at children's parties convicted in 1980 of murdering thirty-three men and boys and burying most of them under the floorboards of his house.

Jim Dunn was devastated by the documentation of his son's torture and the idea that the perpetrator of torture not only got away with murder but was using it to inspire personal achievement and growth. It gave him the defeated feeling that "Leisha wins in the end."

"Not at all," Walter said. "By attempting to reinvent herself and escape her past, she only further identifies herself as the murderer. Leisha is a drama queen, a remarkable woman, in an evil way, for a trailer-trash waitress. But she's not especially well-educated, and she doesn't seem to realize that dramas end in tragedy."

It deeply offended Walter that "a bunch of psychopaths were getting away with murder. They were trying to pass over the ruse on society that Scott Dunn had just disappeared as if he had never existed. There are standards to uphold in civilization. This kind of thing cannot be allowed to stand." The police weren't buying his conspiracy theory, but Walter was convinced Mike Roberts, a muscular six-foot-four young man who worked with Scott, knew something about the murder.

Roberts had quit the Lubbock stereo shop shortly after Scott's disappearance and moved to Tacoma, Washington—classic post-crime behavior. While on business in Seattle, Walter made a side trip. He asked the police to pull Roberts out of his workplace onto the sidewalk, then sent the cop to get some coffee.

"It's time for us to have a man-to-boy chat," Walter said, leaning close to the muscular young man. One of Roberts's shirt buttons had come undone, and Walter observed his heart thumping wildly against his chest.

Roberts jumped back. "I remember you—the Englishman. I'm scared of you. Should I get myself a lawyer?"

Walter noted Roberts was "a fine liar, never losing eye contact," but the tall man's jumpy Adam's apple gave him away as well, slithering up and down "with great rapidity."

"Young man." He glared. "If you have not been involved in murder, you needn't call a lawyer. If you have been involved in murder, however, I daresay a lawyer won't help. I'll chew your dick down so far you won't have enough left to fuck roadkill!"

CHAPTER 37

THE STRANGER IN BIDDLE HOUSE

The mansion in the remote Pennsylvania Appalachians was filled with the gloaming of twilight, except for the lamp in the parlor where the thin man lounged on an eighteenth-century Italian divan, a king Kool perched in two fingers haughtily aloft. "Oh, it's a *wonderful* case," Richard Walter said, as he glanced at a photograph of the lawyer who had been shot through the heart by his best friend, a doctor, some twenty years earlier. "A man desires another man's wife and simply takes her. It's quite common. It happens to be the plot of the novel *The Talented Mr. Ripley,* as well as, I might add, *Hamlet.*"

"I see retirement hasn't affected your confidence," snickered state trooper Steve Stoud, a dark-haired, broad-shouldered man in his thirties sitting in a wing chair opposite Walter. Corporal Stoud's brilliant cold-case work had recently put the murderous doctor behind bars, and earned him membership as one of the young lions of an aging Vidocq Society.

Walter laughed—laughter that dissolved into a hacking cough that left him bent over red-faced like he was expelling a lung. His smoker's cough was getting worse.

Night fell with the utter darkness of the country and the hush of the surrounding ridge-and-valley Appalachians. The parlor was the largest of twenty-two rooms in the Greek Revival mansion. There were seven bedrooms and seven fireplaces, rumors of ghosts and the Underground Railroad. A grand stairway soared for the needs of society; back stairs shuttled servants from sight. It was Biddle House, a country retreat built in the 1830s by the illustrious Biddles of Philadelphia, including Nicholas Biddle, the disgraced president of the Second Bank of the United States, his bank and his career destroyed by President Andrew Jackson. Walter lived in the house alone.

"Didn't a doctor just tell you to quit?" Stoud teased.

"Yes." Walter frowned. "I told him, 'My dear boy, I am quite obviously aware of the risks and pleasures of smoking, and you see I have made a bargain with which I am quite pleased—I had a choice of being a thin man and enjoying life or being too fat to fit into my coffin. So let nature do what she will, I will have the last word—with sodium pentothal one can lie down to quite pleasant dreams. . . .'"

Stoud shook his head. "Jesus, Richard."

"I explained that I am a Scorpio, one who would rather destroy himself than lose control, and one who thrills to attack."

As he composed himself and took a sip of Chardonnay, Stoud, big hand around a can of beer, said in a teasing voice, "Richard, speaking of suicide, I've found a note. . . ."

"Oh." The thin man leaned forward expectantly, his left eyebrow arched in a fine point. The two men collected suicide notes. It was a friendly competition.

"A guy in Georgia shot himself in the head, left a note, 'Some say death is the end of life. Some say life is part of death.' I say, 'Let's put the fun back in funeral!'"

Walter's eyes shone with merriment. "Oh, that's wonderful," he enthused. "The best yet. I quite like it." It illustrated the kind of point the police had such trouble accepting: At the dark edges of human behavior, the cruel and the tortured did not think or feel like the rest of us. Murder could be fun! Suicide could be a joke!

"Consistency," Walter said, "is the hobgoblin of little minds."

Walter was instructing Stoud in a course on murder, with particular attention to the most depraved serial killers and other sex murderers. Stoud was a plainclothes detective with the elite

Criminal Investigation Assessment Unit (CIAU) of the Pennsylvania State Police, which boasted more criminal profilers than any police agency in the world, including the FBI and NYPD. He roamed 2,500 square rural miles in the northeast corner of the state investigating serial killings and other "behavioral" crimes. The state trooper was near the top of his profession; but the only way for an ambitious young detective to further his education in the criminal mind was to apprentice to a master.

"Richard is one of the few who have ideas about killers that really work for the detective in the field," said Stoud.

For years he had longed to find a protégé to pass on his knowledge. He was conscious that he was running out of time.

"I'm one who believes when you're dead, you're dead. If I am to live on, it will be through my ideas. I believe we have an obligation to pass our knowledge on to the next generation."

Walter, now in his fifties, had recently retired from the Michigan Department of Corrections, and sold his house in Lansing. With no family but two sisters on the West Coast, he moved east to Montrose, Pennsylvania (pop. 1,596), a small Victorian town forty-six miles north of Scranton coal country at the lonely "Top of the Endless Mountains."

The remote location had numerous advantages. He was relieved to be on the East Coast, "where my acerbic wit is better appreciated." It was only 170 miles, a two-hour drive, south to Philadelphia; he would no longer have to get on a plane for the monthly meetings of the Vidocq Society. The Biddle House was "quite grand," with room for his grand piano and antiques to at last stretch their arms and legs. After a lifetime immersed in cities and murder, he planned to enjoy the leisurely life of a country gentleman. He would go skeet shooting and antiquing, sip wine with long views of the mountains, host "little soirees" for the local cognoscenti and friends from the city.

Steven and Susan Stoud, their children and dogs, lived in a farmhouse over the hills, seven miles east of town. The Stouds fussed over him like a lost uncle, fixing his car and computer and sewing his curtains, for Richard Walter was one of those towering intellects who could not "tie his own shoes." Thus the course in murder could continue over lunch, dinner, and drinks, in the parlor ringed by cigarette smoke, opera music, debate, and ribald laughter.

Walter hung out his shingle as the proprietor of the Omega Crime Assessment Group, offering the rarest expertise in "Munchausen syndrome, sadism, and serial murder." He would restrict his investigative efforts to "select fascinating cases." But it was not lifestyle or friendship that originally brought him to the remote hills. It was the scent of an old murder, a tale of lust and betrayal he called "quite worthy of the Greeks," that drew him six hundred miles east, like an aging bloodhound.

On June 2, 1976, prominent Montrose physician Dr. Stephen Scher and his close friend lawyer Martin Dillon, were skeet shooting on the Dillon family preserve, "Gunsmoke," when Dillon died from a sixteen-gauge, pump-action shotgun blast. Dr. Scher tearfully explained to the police that his friend accidentally tripped on untied shoelaces and fell while chasing a porcupine, discharging the gun. The doctor could do nothing to save him; Dillon, shot through the heart, died instantly. Dillon was thirty-six years old and left behind his wife, Patricia, a nurse, and two young children. That the mortal shot came from Dr. Scher's rifle, and the bullet was a hunting round, not the less powerful round used on clay pigeons, raised eyebrows, as did rumors that Dr. Scher had been having a torrid affair with his friend's wife. But Dr. Scher tearfully denied the rumors and deeply mourned his friend while offering stout moral support to the widow and children. All involved had suffered a tragedy; the coroner ruled the shooting an accident.

Yet two years later, when Dr. Scher married Patricia Dillon and the couple happily moved to New Mexico and later North Carolina, where they raised Martin Dillon's children and adopted their own, Dillon's father, Larry, redoubled his claim that his son had been murdered. It took twenty years before the state attorney general's office charged Dr. Scher with murder, based partly on new facts unearthed by Corporal Stoud. The attorney general hired Walter to testify for the prosecution as an expert on murderer personality types.

"It wasn't much of a mystery," Walter said, lighting another menthol Kool. "Beneath his impressive sheen of physician's respectability, prestige, caring, and what have you, the good doctor was a fucking psychopath. He took what he wanted when he wanted it, and he wanted Patricia Dillon."

The small Susquehanna County courthouse was crowded with national TV journalists covering the rural county seat's "Crime of the Century." Celebrity pathologists Dr. Cyril Wecht and Dr. Michael Baden, a witness in the O. J. Simpson trial, testified for the defense. Walter, frustrated as legal maneuvering prevented him from being called to the stand for the prosecution, then utterly bored with the proceedings, left the courthouse and strolled the same charming but small Victorian main street for two days until he walked into a carpet shop and demanded, "Where can you get a drink in this goddamn town before noon?" Grinning, the rug merchant produced a bottle of bourbon and two glasses from beneath the counter, and the fast friends drank until, as Walter later put it, "I said to myself, 'Self, this isn't such a bad town after all.'" That afternoon, Walter strolled by the magnificent Biddle House with a "For Sale" sign in the front yard. He decided the asking price of under $200,000 was a "grand bargain" for a retirement abode, and made an offer.

After a four-day trial, on October 22, 1997, Dr. Scher was convicted of the first-degree murder of Martin Dillon. Stoud's investigation had helped destroy the doctor's alibi. Scher claimed he was a hundred yards away from Dillon when the shotgun went off, but FBI lab work revealed he stood six to nine feet away—close enough that Scher's boots were splattered with Dillon's blood, and a tiny piece of the victim's flesh was found on Scher's pant leg. Dillon's body was exhumed to measure his arms, and it was proven they were too short to have held Scher's shotgun in a position to create the gaping wound. Confronted with the new evidence, Scher admitted on the stand that he had concocted the "porcupine story." Yes, he admitted, he'd been having an affair with Patricia Dillon. Now he claimed he and Dillon were struggling with the shotgun during a "conversation that led to an argument" about Patricia when the gun accidentally went off. However, Dillon was wearing earplugs when his body was found, and couldn't have heard Scher talking to him.

As Dr. Scher was taken to a state prison outside Pittsburgh to serve a life sentence, Richard Walter moved into the grand home at 78 Church Street. Across from the old stone Episcopalian church, Walter would lead Stoud to the lowest region of hell.

Walter's previous attempts to find a worthy protégé had failed miserably. He'd agreed to train three different young men, including a forensic psychologist who interviewed killers all day long and a homicide detective with twenty-five murder investigations under his belt. He'd warned them, "Someday you'll have to interview a sixty-five-year-old man who enjoys destroying children by cutting them into little pieces. You can listen to me tell it to you now, but to be with him alone, to confront this reality, can be something else again if you are not highly structured and sound in your knowledge and belief system, if you are not of the right age or understanding to deal with it. Ideas can be very dangerous if you're not ready for them."

All three protégés dropped out. They couldn't take it. The veteran homicide detective said, "I have a wife and a child. I want a sense of normality, a sense of innocence about life. You're destroying that for me. I just can't do it." Walter was deeply disappointed. Reluctantly, he resigned himself to the fact that, unlike FBI agent Robert Ressler and other profiler friends, he would never have a protégé; his lifework would die with him.

"What I do is too eccentric for a healthy, normal person," he told himself.

He discouraged the young people who approached him at parties or forensic conferences, as *CSI* became an international TV hit, looking for advice on how to become a "profiler." "Young man," he'd say, "while I understand your enthusiasm, you seem quite too normal. You look like a fine fellow who'd like to marry, have children, have a happy life, not devote yourself to something that can destroy your marriage and, ultimately, your soul. This is not for the faint of heart. There are few of us who are cut out for it."

Few cops wanted to explore the netherworld of the criminal mind, or could do so with the scientific training of a psychologist. On the other hand, few psychologists had or wished to have experience at crime scenes. Since Freud, leading psychologists had focused on everyday behavior and its disorders with a single-minded determination not to make old-fashioned moral judgments. Murder, evil, they left to the burly, often uneducated police officer or constable.

Walter was astonished, while lecturing to prominent European psychologists on the personality subtypes of murderers, that "none of them had any idea what I was talking about. They could look at John Wayne Gacy and see schizophrenia, but they had no training in sadism. There is no psychology of evil." Walter was a man without a country.

Then, in 1995, he was listening to Ann Rule, the bestselling true-crime author, lecture on psychopaths at the American Academy of Forensic Sciences convention in Seattle. Walter was a distinguished fellow and frequent lecturer at the conference with FBI agent Bob Ressler and others. Now he scowled in disgust. There was absolutely nothing a popular writer like Rule could teach him about psychopaths, even if she had been friends with Ted Bundy, the basis of her book *The Killer Beside Me*.

"Are you believing this bullshit?" Walter asked the large man sitting next to him.

"I'm good friends with Ann Rule," the big man barked, eyeing the wan, bespectacled figure beside him. "Who the hell are you?"

Thus began one of the most important friendships in the modern history of criminology.

The big man was Robert Keppel, renowned chief criminal investigator for the Washington state attorney general's office, nationally known for his decades-long pursuit of Ted Bundy and the Green River Killer. A criminology Ph.D. and ex-Seattle cop, the formidable

Keppel was known for a brilliant analytical mind, relentless bulldog attitude, and pioneering use of computers in criminal investigations.

Keppel quickly realized his remarkable bond with Walter. The Washington state detective and the Michigan psychologist had spent their careers like a right hand and a left hand that each didn't know what the other was doing, until now. While Keppel had spent two decades as a homicide detective arresting killers and investigating fifty serial murder cases, more than any living cop, Walter had interviewed thousands of incarcerated killers, descending deeper into the criminal mind than any scholar. Both men were mavericks and outspoken critics of the FBI's Behavioral Sciences Unit, the acknowledged leader of the science of criminal profiling. On their own, they had developed almost precisely the same theories—revolutionary ideas that would transform modern murder investigation.

"There's only one problem with what the FBI is doing," said Keppel, who like Walter had been a friend or rival of the leading FBI agents for years. "It's a lot of bunk." Star special agents John Douglas and Robert Ressler had traveled the country in the 1980s interviewing an incarcerated murderers' row of thirty-six famous serial killers and assassins to try to determine what made them tick. The list included Bundy, Charles Manson, David "Son of Sam" Berkowitz, John Wayne Gacy, Richard Speck, Edward Kemper, and last, James Earl Ray, Sirhan Sirhan, and Lynette Frome, respectively assassins of Martin Luther King and Robert F. Kennedy, and attempted assassin of President Gerald Ford. Douglas and Ressler's resulting book, *Sexual Homicide: Patterns and Motives,* coauthored with a psychologist, became the bible of the new criminal profiling, dividing sexual murderers into two broad personality categories based on the crime scene, organized or disorganized.

Unfortunately, Keppel said, "they made it up. There's no data at all. It wasn't created out of a data set or known empirical study, it's just there. As a result, FBI agents swoop into town, sit with the local cops, and begin their Kentucky windage estimate of what the offender was like. 'We know he's young and thin and a clothes-horse so I think he's attractive to women'—and so on. The agents are in a room talking, never at the murder scene, not a one of 'em. As my detective friend Frank Salerno says, you know they never smelled the blood."

Walter agreed, but was slightly more diplomatic. He saw the FBI as flawed and hidebound by bureaucracy, but deserving of credit for originating the systematic psychological study of killers. "I may disagree with the FBI or whatever, but we're all on the same Roman road, trying to understand murder, evil, for the betterment of mankind."

Walter had studied the history of murder back to the Greeks, but the modern road of criminal profiling began in November 1888, when Scotland Yard surgeon Thomas Bond attempted the first psychological profile of a killer after performing the autopsy of Mary Kelly, the fifth victim of Jack the Ripper. The Ripper, he wrote, would be physically strong, quiet, and harmless in appearance, possibly middle-aged, and neatly attired, probably wearing a cloak to hide the bloody effects of his attacks.

Both Walter and Keppel were aware of how little progress had been made in a century of trying to peer into the minds of killers. There were few highlights. In a 1943 profile of Adolf Hitler commissioned by American intelligence, New York psychiatrist Walter Langer correctly predicted that if the Third Reich collapsed the Führer would likely commit suicide. In 1957, the psychiatrist James Brussel, "The Sherlock Holmes of the Couch," successfully profiled the Mad Bomber who had terrorized New York City in the 1940s and '50s, injuring fifteen people with thirty-three bombs planted everywhere from phone booths to libraries, including Penn Station, the New York Public Library, and Radio City Music Hall. The Mad Bomber eluded cops for sixteen years until Brussel, after studying the bomber's many crimes and letters, successfully predicted down to the last detail that the killer would be a middle-aged, Catholic, Slavic ex–Commonwealth Edison employee living in Connecticut, who furthermore would be, as

George P. Metesky was when arrested at his sisters' house, wearing a double-breasted suit, buttoned. In the 1970s, Brussel helped the FBI create its Behavioral Sciences Unit, which developed the first "profiles" of suspects.

By the time Pennsylvania State Trooper Stoud attended a Vidocq Society luncheon in Philadelphia in 1995, as a guest of a senior state trooper who was a VSM, he had investigated more than a dozen murders and read everything he could get his hands on about murder and murder investigation, including all of Douglas's and Ressler's books, Truman Capote's *In Cold Blood,* and the biblical story of Cain and Abel. Yet he was deeply frustrated. In his thirties, he wanted to advance his career.

Walter had given a talk at the Vidocq luncheon about his murder subtypes. He discussed his method of solving the most notorious murder in modern Australian history—the brutal slaying of beauty queen and nurse Anita Cobby. Stoud was dazzled. He was desperate to become a profiler, but after reading all the books, there wasn't any more to learn.

Mindful that "you had to find a profiler to show you the road so you can walk it yourself," he approached Walter after the luncheon and asked if he could study with him, and was swiftly rejected. Late that night, he called Walter at home in Michigan, repeating his request to "be a learner." Walter snapped at him, "I said no, did you hear me? I'm not interested. You're too normal, a family and all the rest. I've tried this before, and it's never successful. It would be a waste of my time and yours." Half an hour later, Stoud called back and said, "I was just hung up on, but I won't take no for an answer." Walter cursed him out; Stoud said, "I'm going to keep calling." He called the next night, and the next. Gradually, the younger man and the older developed a dialogue. They discussed murder cases in the news, murder cases they were working, the nature of evil. Walter allowed himself to wonder if Stoud had the brains, the guts, the character, and moral fiber, to be his protégé. "You must learn to think horizontally as well as vertically," he said, "which very few of us in the world can do." Walter nurtured hopes the younger man could follow him, could stand witness to and stand against the worst evil human beings did to one another.

Walter drove over the icy hills in his aging Ford Crown Victoria to the Green Gables tavern. The car had 120,000 miles on it, and was always breaking down. Walter was always getting lost. Stoud pointed out he needed new shocks and brakes, and he snorted in reply, "You know I don't care about those things." The state trooper marveled at how little he knew about ordinary life—cars, computers, the World Series—for a genius. *I guess he's saving it all for sadism, necrophilia, and Munchausen syndrome,* Stoud thought.

Walter said that after a lifetime immersed in ghastly murders, he had decided to reinvent himself as a country gentleman. What was left of him, that is, after years of forays into the abyss and back again—little but the broad egg-shaped pate of his forehead, the consumptive cough, the withered frame hardened or wasted by unknown disciplines and battles with darkness. He wanted to pursue the good life.

Stoud smirked. "How many cars have you owned?"

"Seven."

"All black Crown Vics, like police cars?"

"Yes."

"And you ran them all into the ground."

"Yes."

"How many suits do you own?"

"One."

"Color?"

"Blue."

"And you wear it into the ground."

"Yes. Then I get another one. One does."

Stoud grinned. "If you're a country gentleman, I'm Earl Grey. You're a cop."

Walter laughed. "'Tis true."

CHAPTER 38

CITY OF BROTHERLY MAYHEM

Number 1704 Locust Street in Philadelphia was a dreary Victorian brownstone wedged among an imposing white-marble classical music school and the fashionable hotels and shops of Rittenhouse Square. An awkward wrought-iron staircase twisted sideways to a tall, forbidding black door with a tarnished knocker. The second-floor window was clumsily off center, like a misplaced proboscis. It appeared lost, an archaic, slightly seedy gent in a top-coat and homburg. A series of small and vaguely mysterious brass plaques on the brick wall to the left of the door got smaller as they descended, until the last one could be covered by a man's hand:

THE ACADEMY OF SCIENTIFIC
INVESTIGATIVE TRAINING
KEYSTONE INTELLIGENCE NETWORK
THE VIDOCQ SOCIETY

On the second floor, atop a white-marble nineteenth-century stair-case, were the new offices of the Keystone detective agency and its director, William L. Fleisher. Fleisher had retired from his federal career on December 31, 1995, and, true to his reputation as a workaholic, had taken all of two days off before starting his new career. On January 2, 1996, he partnered with VSM Nate Gordon to open the full-service private-eye shop under the slogan "the FBI for the other guy." On the same floor as the Keystone agency was the Academy of Scientific Investigative Training—their school for teaching the polygraph, with classes everywhere from down the hall to Dubai. The small warren of offices was also the first headquarters for the Vidocq Society, outside of home offices, trunks, and briefcases.

The agency door opened into a big room with a red Persian rug and Oriental prints on the walls. The secretary, Gloria Alvarado, sat next to a Victorian mantelpiece adorned with a bust of Vidocq, and a gray cadaver skull Fleisher's father had used in dental school in the 1930s. Down the hallway were the offices of Gordon; former Philadelphia police detective Ed Gaughan; and a couple retired FBI agents, all members of the Vidocq Society. Fleisher's office was a small, pie-shaped space with a leaded casement on a back alley. The shelves and walls were cluttered with awards and bric-a-brac, including a schooner in stormy seas painted by Michelle, a 1940s Psycho-truth-ometer, a picture of his father in Navy blue.

Gloria buzzed—Ron Avery, the *Philadelphia Daily News* columnist, was in the waiting room.

"Send him in."

The press loved the commissioner of the Vidocq Society, and Avery was an old friend. Now Fleisher sat back in his swiveling leather chair and listened as Avery said he was writing a book about historic Philadelphia crimes and looking for ideas. His thesis was that in 315 years it was tough to match the City of Brotherly Love for corruption and murder. *City of Brotherly Mayhem* was his title.

"My specialty." Fleisher grunted. "You need five books for this. What do you have so far?"

Avery had dug dirt as far back as founder William Penn's son, William Penn Jr., who was charged with assault during a drunken free-for-all in the early 1700s. The pastor at Christ Church—the church of George and Martha Washington—boasted of bedding the congregation's prettiest ladies, and fights and duels erupted. There was the nineteenth-century monster H. H. Holmes, America's first serial killer. Gary Heidnik, the cannibal minister of the 1980s, and his "House of Horrors," Ted Bundy's early years—he was leaving most of them out. It was an embarrassment of riches; there was too much. And there was one more.

"The Boy in the Box," Avery said.

The moniker sent Fleisher back in time. As Avery described the case, he saw himself as thirteen years old again, standing in front of the poster at the Penn Fruit Company market while his mother shopped. The hollow eyes in the sad pale face of death came back to him, his first brush with death.

The case, Avery said, had never been solved. The homicide bureau had taken a collection and paid for a monument, the only monument in Potter's Field, where the unnamed boy lay with rapists, murderers, body parts, and the indigent and forgotten. The detectives had the stone inscribed "God Bless This Unknown Boy." Remington Bristow, the medical examiner's investigator who had been assigned the case in 1957, had continued to investigate it in his retirement, keeping it in the news with his annual visits to the boy's grave. Bristow had died three years earlier, and with him a lot of the public interest in the case.

After Avery left, the resurrected image of the poster lingered in Fleisher's mind. As a boy he'd dreamed of solving the terrible crime, becoming a hero of the city. As an adult, he'd known many of the cops who became the boy's tireless champions.

He went home to Michelle and the kids and dinner, but it stayed with him. It bothered him that for four decades someone had got away with the coldest murder he'd ever known. It bothered him that nobody had come forward to say, "That's my child." It bothered him that the boy lay yet in Potter's Field, the graveyard for the forgotten and shamed purchased, in biblical tradition, using thirty silver pieces returned to the Jewish priests by a repentant Judas. "It's not right," he mumbled to himself at his desk in the pale lamplight, failing to concentrate on a corporate theft case. They were simple words that were the marching orders of his life. A sharp feeling came unbidden, but the large, bearded head wagged as if to shake it off. It was ancient history, a boy's dream. The man was too busy solving today's crimes.

He tossed and turned that night. He imagined the nameless boy all alone under the moonlight beneath the frozen crust of Potter's Field.

CHAPTER 39

WRATH SWEETER BY FAR
THAN THE HONEYCOMB

John Martini was a flashy Phoenix restaurateur, a high roller and a charmer filled with dark American dreams. He started as a mob hit man, worked his way up to FBI informant, and became one of the most brazen serial killers in modern times. By the time he reached death row, he was terrifying to look at, as if his body was indeed the smoky window of his soul—enormous, fat, balding, with huge hands and a broad, pockmarked face, loose fleshy lips, big hooked nose, glowering dark eyes. He was a pro who allegedly killed for New England gangster Raymond Patriarca. But he'd freelance killing friends and relatives if the money was good—including, police believed, his aunt and uncle.

He was a bad guy, in other words, for a woman to be introduced to by one of her best friends. That's what happened to Anna Mary Duval, a retired New Jersey office worker who'd moved to Arizona. Her new friend Martini persuaded her to put $25,000 in a hot real estate investment, and told her to meet him in Philadelphia in the fall of 1977 to complete the deal. Martini kept Duval's money and killed her, too—his version of a real estate closing.

Now, in 1997, twenty years later, Martini finally admitted to killing Duval and was convicted of her murder—brought to justice by the art and vision of Frank Bender.

"This guy Martini is the worst," Bender said, "except for maybe Vorhauer. He's too far out there even for the movies—sort of *Goodfellas* meets *Scarface*." Bender, Walter, and Fleisher were having lunch in a Center City diner.

"Richard, as a psychologist, how would you handle this type of criminal?" Fleisher asked.

Walter sneered in disgust. "Seven cents' worth of lead."

When Duval was introduced to the forty-four-year-old, Bronx-born Martini, the brother of one of her best friends, she was impressed. She was apparently unaware that he had served federal time for hijacking a truckload of women's underwear in New Jersey, or that the FBI considered him one of the "nastiest" criminals in America. She couldn't have known—not even the police did—that Martini also had been on the FBI payroll for more than a decade, tipping off the bureau about hijacked trucks in New York and New Jersey.

In October 1977, Duval flew through Chicago to Philadelphia, where Martini picked her up at the airport. He introduced her to another gentleman, an off-duty policeman, quietly sitting in the backseat behind her. Minutes later, the man in the backseat pulled out a handgun and pumped three bullets into the back of Duval's head, execution-style. The two men dumped the body near the airport. Martini later told police that the shooter was his apprentice. He was teaching the cop how to "work on a contract, you know, killing people."

The Duval murder sent Martini on a wild killing spree. He was the lead suspect in at least four murders for which he was never charged, including the shooting deaths of a cousin and his former son-in-law, and the shooting and stabbing of his aunt and uncle Catherine and Raymond Gebert in their Atlantic City home (Martini was awarded $175,000 as the benefactor of his aunt's estate).

By the fall of 1988, Martini was running from the law and desperate for cash. He was nursing a $500-a-day cocaine habit, being sued for divorce, and had recently lost his longtime employment with the FBI because of his "dishonesty with the bureau," according to court records. In October in Arizona he shot and killed his drug supplier and her companion. Three months later, with his girlfriend-accomplice Therese Afdahl, he kidnapped Secaucus, New Jersey, warehouse executive Irving Flax at gunpoint. Martini, cleverly eluding an FBI trap, extorted $25,000 from Flax's wife for his safe return, and put three bullets in Flax's head anyway. Finally arrested in a nearby hotel, Martini was convicted in 1990 for the kidnapping-murder. He was sentenced to New Jersey's death row, where he was also convicted of Duval's murder, and given a concurrent sentence of life in prison for killing her.

"Duval's family said in court they were happy about the conviction and sentence," Bender said. "They felt it showed their mother's life had worth."

"Frank, you are truly amazing," Fleisher said. "What you do for law enforcement can't be duplicated."

That spring of 1997 was a season of triumphs for the Vidocq Society. At the April 18 luncheon in the Downtown Club, a gruesome image appeared over the white tablecloths: The decayed corpse of a twenty-seven-year-old woman lay between hedgerows in a remote part of Delaware County, Pennsylvania, apparently strangled to death. The case had languished with the Pennsylvania State Police for six years. Walter and other VSMs picked a prime suspect before dessert. "It is not, in this case, rocket science," Walter said.

The victim's twenty-four-year-old live-in boyfriend was a pizza deliveryman with no criminal record. But he had abused and threatened the victim, and drew additional attention to himself with his unusual nickname, "Ted Bundy." It was one of many truth-too-strange-for-Hollywood moments in the Murder Room, and as it happened, a herd of Hollywood types was at the round tables listening.

They later were escorted to Frank Bender's studio, where they ogled the artist's unique collection of the living and the dead. The producers took the Vidocq founders to Le Bec-Fin, the renowned

French restaurant where dinner for two can cost $700, and wooed them for their life story rights. Walter, who hated to be sold anything, found the process disconcerting.

"Kevin Spacey will play you," a producer told him as a limousine whisked them through the Philadelphia night. "He'll make a great, great American detective."

Walter blinked in astonishment. "That's wonderful! That's truly grand! Who's Kevin Spacey?"

"You . . . you don't go to the movies?"

"Oh, no, my dear boy. I can't stand the sound of popcorn being chewed."

Four days later, Fleisher, Bender, and Walter celebrated as Jersey Films, owned by Danny DeVito, offered $1.3 million for the society's movie rights. Before long, DeVito was inviting Bender to Hollywood for a party, and Robert De Niro, it was reported, was an unabashed Bender fan. The artist's friends shuddered imagining the possibilities of Bender's social life in Hollywood.

By May, retired FBI agent Robert Ressler, VSM, was touring to promote his new bestselling book, *I Have Lived in the Monster,* including his exclusive interview with "the Monster of Milwaukee" Jeffrey Dahmer, the worst serial killer he had ever encountered.

Ressler had spent two days interviewing the gay cannibal convicted of murdering seventeen men and boys and eating from their remains. He was sickened by Dahmer's Milwaukee apartment. Three heads in a freezer, one in the refrigerator, hands in a cooking pot. No food in the apartment—just a chain saw for butchering, vials to drink blood. Dahmer had drugged and tortured his victims and told them, "I'm going to eat your heart," drilled holes in their skulls, and poured in battery acid to make them sex-slave zombies.

Yet Ressler surprisingly came away from his meeting with the killer feeling "only empathy for the tormented and twisted person who sat before me" who said he killed and ate his visitors to overcome loneliness. Dahmer was insane, Ressler said, and deserved life in a mental hospital, not his prison sentence of nearly a thousand years. He testified in Dahmer's defense.

Walter was horrified by his friend's view. Walter insisted that Dahmer was a sane, cold psychopath who must be held accountable. In all but a very few criminal cases, Walter said, "People make choices. If you deny them that ability, you take away their humanity and that of everyone around them, including the victim."

Ressler had grown up in the same Chicago neighborhood as John Wayne Gacy. When Ressler refused to attend the serial killer's execution, Gacy cursed him, saying he would haunt the FBI agent from the grave. Though Walter was skeptical of Ressler's account, there were few people not moved by Ressler's story that he had fallen asleep in a hotel room in Houston when he was awakened by an immensely powerful unseen force that was holding him down so he couldn't move or breathe. As he broke free with a desperate strength, he heard the TV on in the background—CNN reporting that John Wayne Gacy had just been executed.

"How does one avoid becoming the victim of a serial killer?" Fleisher asked in a rave review of the book in the *Vidocq Society Journal,* now published quarterly. "The conclusion I drew from Ressler's book is not to talk to, or get into a car, with strangers, to stay away from 'gay' S&M bars, and not to join a cult. Follow those rules and you can reduce your risk of being murdered by a monster to near zero. Simplistic? Maybe, but it couldn't hurt and it has worked so far for me."

Fleisher was proudest of Vidocq Society Members' work on major murder cases. Renowned forensic dentist and VSM Haskell Askin made headlines by providing the crucial testimony that led to the conviction of repeat violent sexual predator Jesse Timmendequas in the brutal sex murder of seven-year-old Megan Kanka in Hamilton, New Jersey, on July 29, 1994. Kanka's death inspired the creation of Megan's Law, a varied network of community laws requiring police to provide information about neighborhood sexual predators. In testimony on May 17, 1997, Askin matched bite marks on the defendant's palm to the young girl's teeth, evidence that so excited one juror he "punched the air with his fist and loudly clicked his tongue," a reporter said. The juror was relieved of his duty, but Timmendequas was convicted and sentenced to death.

VSM Barbara Cohan-Saavedra, an assistant U.S. attorney, successfully prosecuted Soviet spy Robert Lipka, a U.S. National Security Agency employee in the 1960s who pled guilty to photographing top-secret documents with miniature cameras and stuffing others in his pants and under his hat to sell to KGB agents for $27,000. Lipka was sentenced to eighteen years in jail.

The multitalented Cohan-Saavedra, a jewelry artist and pastry chef, helped persuade Fleisher to add another annual dinner celebration to the Vidocq Society calendar—July 14, Bastille Day. Fleisher thought it a splendid idea. "Vidocq's spirit of redemption lives in the Vidocq Society," he said. "How better than to celebrate that famous day in 1789 when the Bastille was stormed and the prison doors thrown open."

Fleisher had recently helped exonerate a man falsely accused of murder in Little Rock, Arkansas. After Fleisher appeared on *48 Hours,* he received a remarkable phone call from Little Rock schoolteacher Teresa Cox Baus, whose brother, restaurant manager William Cox, had been murdered in March 1991. Baus wanted the Vidocq Society to help exonerate a black dishwasher she believed was falsely accused of killing her brother. The schoolteacher had stopped working for the prosecution of her brother's alleged murderer—and was now helping the public defender. "I can't stand to see an innocent person convicted," she said. "I grew up in Little Rock, and I don't want to say this, but they're charging a black guy with a white guy's murder, and it's very hard for them to see it any other way."

Fleisher asked two renowned VSM profilers to examine the case file—Walter and FBI special agent Gregg McCrary, who had handled many major cases, including the Sri Lankan massacre of thirty-three Buddhist monks in 1987. After the profilers confirmed

Fleisher's suspicions of the dishwasher's innocence, the lawyers for the accused won an acquittal in forty-five minutes. "Teresa Baus is an American hero," Fleisher said. "That's how justice is supposed to work."

But the Vidocq Society's greatest victory in a springtime of good news was its least known.

On Friday, May 16, as Haskell Askin prepared to testify in the Megan Kanka trial in New Jersey, Richard Walter sat in the Lubbock County Courthouse in Lubbock, Texas, anxiously waiting with Jim and Barbara Dunn, waiting for justice to be served, at last, to Alicia "Leisha" Hamilton for the torture-murder of Scott Dunn. Minutes earlier, a cheer had erupted from the jury room and spilled through the thrown-open door and down the hallway; deadlocked for four hours, the jurors had reached a decision.

Hamilton stood erect and proud in the center of the courtroom, wearing a conservative blue dress that complemented her long, dark hair. Judge William R. Shaver, his square jaw and silver hair set off smartly by his black robes, had asked her to stand to receive the verdict. Now the judge frowned as loud murmurs raced through the overflow crowd.

Hamilton appeared confident and at ease as she had been throughout the four-day trial. That morning she had laughed and joked with her parents and attorney, and tossed a big smile at the jurors, especially the handsome young man she'd been hitting on with her big green eyes for four days. According to testimony, she had told an ex-lover, "There's no way I can be convicted because there's not a body and there's not a weapon."

Judge Shaver pounded his gavel for quiet. "I don't want any of the spectators to forget that this is a court of law," he said sternly. "I want absolute silence in the courtroom." The courtroom fell hushed in the dull light of late afternoon slanting through tall drapes.

Richard Walter, in his crisp blue suit, leaned forward in anticipation. Jim Dunn wore his best dark suit and tie, with a pocket handkerchief that was more than decorative. Barbara wore a lovely matching dress, and clutched Jim's hand. It was almost six years to the day since Roger "Scott" Dunn had been last seen walking with Hamilton into their apartment and was never seen again. Walter believed in the notion of proper revenge, which had fallen out of favor but the Greeks knew was essential to a civilized life. This was their chance. Their long wrestling with angels and demons had distilled to a moment.

At the state's table, Rusty Ladd, the lanky assistant district attorney in cowboy boots, nervously leaned forward. The case had been a prosecutor's nightmare, with the years of delays allowing memories and evidence to go cold. The first grand jury hadn't found sufficient evidence to indict; the district attorney who brought the case was bounced out in an election; the new DA had a conflict of interest—his old law partner had once represented Hamilton's alleged collaborator Tim Smith. So the DA reached out to Ladd in another county to be special prosecutor. A new grand jury labored over the case, and Ladd wrestled for eight months to get it to trial with its epic limitations: For one of the few times, if not the first time, in history he believed the state was asking a Texas jury to convict for murder without a body or weapon. It had been a daunting challenge to meet the most basic standard that a crime had been committed, to prove corpus delicti ("body of the crime"). In an arson case corpus delicti usually meant producing a burned building; in a murder case, producing the body. The jury needed to accept the psychological nuances of Hamilton's Machiavellian revenge—and in a terrible blow to Ladd's case, Walter, the profiler who could explain Hamilton's psychopathic charm and murderous rage, had been unable to testify. Judge Shaver ruled that a "profile" of an accused murderer was speculative and not worthy of his court.

In the third row, Walter was still quietly fuming over the slight. His esteemed testimony had been accepted around the world. Who was this West Texas wig, this country gavel jockey, to stand in judgment of him, an international expert?

The judge was unfolding the piece of paper the jury fore-man handed to him. He held the paper in front of him, cleared his throat, and read, his voice booming through the courtroom: "We, the jury, find from the evidence, beyond a reasonable doubt, the defendant is guilty of the offense of murder as charged in the indictment."

Murmurs swept the length of the courtroom. Jim and Barbara Dunn turned and looked at each other for a long moment, hold-ing hands, then Jim threw his arms around Barbara and held on, tears streaming down his face. Walter was thrilled to see husband and wife, now his good friends, emerge into light with one swift embrace. But he couldn't take his eyes off Hamilton.

Hamilton's mouth fell open, uncomprehending, then she raised her chin defiantly and closed her eyes, before she bowed her head and began to cry. "I will never, never, never forget it," Walter said. "The good psychopath was absolutely convinced she was going to be found not guilty. She was standing proud when she stood up to hear the verdict, and her head just flipped up, instead of down in a submissive position, flipped up in contempt and disbelief. How could anybody ever do this to me? You can see the pathology continues—in her refusal to accept justice, boundaries, her con-tempt for anyone who would put restrictions on her."

Judge Shaver sent the jury back to deliberate on a sentence. Even with a murder conviction, they had wide latitude in punishment—they could send Hamilton away for life, or only five years. Two hours later, the jury came back with a sentence. Hamilton stood in front of the judge, head high and proud. He opened the paper and read it: The jury sentenced her to twenty years in prison. Again, Walter noted, Leisha's face collapsed, as if it were inconceivable she would be locked up.

Outside the courthouse, nine of the jurors, all women, approached Dunn and eagerly told him they'd desperately wanted to give her life. "Oh, God, they hated her," Walter said. "They didn't know the word 'psychopath' but they knew the type and they said they saw the evil in her. However, they had to compromise because of Billy Bob, Mr. Macho, who just couldn't believe that a woman could kill a man." Yet it was satisfying to Walter that his judgment matched that of the community.

The handsome young man Leisha had tried to influence with her big green eyes introduced himself to Dunn. He'd voted resolutely to convict. He told Dunn he was frightened by her charm, and he easily could have ended up like Scott; "There but for the grace of God go I." Walter, chopping the words with a cigarette on his lip, commented, "That's fitting. She'd gotten everything before by lying on her back. Not this time. It puts her where she belongs."

Walter sensed a great weight lifting from Dunn. He had grown red-faced with rage even being in the same courtroom as Hamilton. He'd stalked out of a room when Hamilton's relatives or supporters appeared. It was time, Walter felt, for him to bury some of his anger. Vengeance is normal, healthy, and sweet to contemplate, Walter counseled him. "In fact, you MUST feel the need for revenge, sweet revenge, deeply." The just society does not repress it. It's important to feel the fury of being wronged and the deep pleasure of imagined revenge, the "wrath," as Aristotle noted in *Rhetoric,* "sweeter by far than the honeycomb dripping with sweetness . . . [that] spreads through the hearts of men."

"Then let it go," Walter said. "The virtuous man feels the proper anger for the proper things for the proper amount of time. It's important that he controls himself, moderates it, listens to the law, friends, family, standards of decency." For Jim Dunn, the time was coming. The time to let go.

Yet the father was not satisfied. Before leaving Lubbock, he had erected a fresh granite tombstone, engraved with Scott's yellow Camaro, in the Dunn family plot. Bowing his head before the vacant grave, he vowed he would not rest until his son's body was found and properly buried. Walter was certain that the young man's body had been completely destroyed to cover up the crime. Scott would never be found. But he could not convince Dunn of the truth. Recognizing the father's powerful need, he suggested

Dunn bury a piece of blood-soaked carpet in the grave. "Remember what the courts decided, Jim. The blood is the body. His blood is Scott." Dunn agreed.

That evening, the Dunns and Walter celebrated Hamilton's sentencing at a local restaurant. Wine and satisfied smiles ringed the table. Walter encouraged feelings of triumph; these were the sweet drafts of justice spiced with revenge. It was time to drink deeply.

The profiler was quite pleased with himself. "In the course of events, it's most satisfactory to vanquish a power-assertive personality, a killer who believes he can mow down anything in the way with raw power, even more than the other types," he said. Dunn asked him why. The profiler grinned conspiratorially. "Well, as it happens, I'm rather power-assertive myself." The two men laughed heartily.

But by the end of the evening, alcohol and euphoria began to ebb. Walter pointed out that Texas's lax parole laws would spring Hamilton long before her sentence was up. Walter saw Dunn still warring with the fates, still fumbling along between the rocks of retribution and forgiveness, trying to find the path of the virtuous man. He reached out and put his arm on his friend's shoulder and said they would press on together. They would do whatever it took, whatever could be done, whatever was just and right.

He looked in his friend's tragic face and hoped that would be enough.

CHAPTER 40

THE WORST MOTHER IN HISTORY

One evening in October 1997, William Fleisher stood in the formal, polished-wood elegance of the Mütter Museum in Philadelphia studying a gallery of horrors. In the brilliantly lit cases rested the conjoined liver of the world-famous Siamese twins Chang and Eng; the cancerous growth removed from President Grover Cleveland's throat; shriveled baby corpses; and the Soap Lady, whose fat mysteriously turned to soap lye in the grave in the 1830s. Dr. Thomas Dent Mütter, who founded the world-famous museum of medical oddities in 1858 to train physicians, had contributed a gangrenous hand and a woman's ribcage torturously compressed by tight lacing. Not far from Supreme Court justice John Marshall's gallstones was the skull of an ax murderer, an ancestor of the actor Jack Nicholson, who chopped up shop clerk Ellen Jones in 1863 in rural Pennsylvania.

Fleisher was waiting to hear forensic anthropologist Bill Bass discuss "Death's Acre," also known as "The Body Farm," his Tennessee laboratory for scientific study of decomposing bodies. Fleisher prided himself on his ability to spot a reporter crashing a roomful of cops—the longish hair, softer slacks and shoes, open collar, no tie—and saw one in the crowd. It was *Philadelphia* magazine writer Stephen Fried, who'd arranged to get into the speech through the good offices of a source, New Jersey pathologist Jim Lewis, to try to interest Hal Fillinger, the esteemed Philadelphia medical examiner and Vidocq Society member he knew as "Doc," in an ancient case he'd worked of a mass murderer Fried believed was still walking the streets. He hadn't expected to run into the president of the Vidocq Society, too.

"I want to talk to you and Doc about Marie Noe," Fried said to Fleisher. Fried, winner of national awards for investigative reporting, said he had been working on the long-dormant story of Marie Noe, the tragic Philadelphia woman who lost eight of her ten children, born between 1949 and 1968, to crib death. In 1963, *Life* magazine wrote a heartrending story of the deaths of Richard, Elizabeth, Jacqueline, Arthur Jr., Constance, Mary Lee, Cathy, and Little Artie, despite the couple's heroic attempts to make a family. Never in American history had such an awful fate befallen a mother. Fleisher knew all about sad Marie Noe; he waited for Fried to reach his point.

His point was that Marie Noe had murdered all her children.

That's what it looked like to Fried, who was inspired to dig into the case after reading *The Death of Innocents*, by Richard Firstman and Jamie Talan, the true story of a New York woman convicted in 1994 of murdering her five children decades earlier. The book explored new scientific research that indicated that many "crib deaths" were, in fact, murder.

Fried was looking for old police records on the case; the files had been lost or destroyed.

Fleisher shook his head. "I can't get you records, but I can get you help." Fleisher introduced Fried to Sergeant Laurence Nodiff, a Vidocq Society member who was Philadelphia PD's cold-case squad supervisor. "I made a *shidduch,* an arranged marriage, between Steve and Larry."

Surprised to have Fleisher's blessing, Fried also won the support of Doc Fillinger, who'd worked the Noe case with Dr. Marie Valdes-Dapena, now seventy-seven and the "grandmother of sudden infant death research." Dr. Valdes-Dapena, who had performed the autopsy on Constance, baby number five, in 1958, was already eager to review the case that had horrified her.

Fried later spent hours interviewing Marie and her husband, Artie, at the elderly couple's Kensington row house, turning over their scrapbooks. He also tracked down Joe McGillen, VSM, a retired medical examiner's investigator, a tough, diminutive Irishman who worked part-time as a "bird dog," or baseball scout, but spent most of his time trying to bring to justice the killers of nine children from the 1950s whose murders he had never stopped investigating—the Boy in the Box and the eight babies of Marie Noe. He'd waited for decades for somebody to ask him about his investigation of Marie Noe's babies, whom he always thought were murdered. He still had all the files—the only copies—a treasure trove of information.

The cold case was reuniting three graying forensic warriors, all stalwart figures from the renowned Philadelphia medical examiner's office of the 1960s. Dr. Fillinger had been treated for cancer; investigator McGillen recently had a quadruple bypass; Dr. Valdes-Dapena was becoming forgetful. Marie Noe's babies had been one of the first major cases of their careers; now it would be one of the last.

Dr. Fillinger had been long-frustrated by the case. "I remember telling a nun there were two ways of looking at this. 'If you give Marie Noe a baby, she'll either kill it quickly . . . or, if she had no hand in these deaths, nobody deserves a baby more than she does.'" He'd long-regarded the case as a "ditzel. A ditzel is a case that looks like a goodie but means nothing. It's a fairy tale you bought and you get it home and the last chapter is torn out. So there is no answer. . . . I wonder what happened to those little kids. But there are so many blind alleys. You think you've got something meaty, but it's like a papier-mâché pizza. You keep thinking, somebody must know something somewhere. But they don't, because, well, it's a ditzel."

McGillen brought his files to Fried's *Philadelphia* magazine offices for a meeting with Doc Fillinger, Dr. Valdes-Dapena, Sergeant Nodiff, and Fried. After reviewing McGillen's files, Fillinger changed "my whole concept of this case. This file really accuses them of murder. . . . I would have to go to the DA and say these people should be investigated." Dr. Valdes-Dapena said, "It just seems impossible that this woman is still walking around as free as a bird. . . . I'm ninety-nine percent sure that these deaths were not a natural happening."

Sergeant Nodiff was stunned by McGillen's old files and Fried's work—the reporter had conducted an investigation worthy of a top-flight detective—and decided after the meeting to reopen the long-cold case. One of his first steps was to take Marie and Artie's polygraph results to Fleisher and Gordon for a review. In the 1960s, both husband and wife had been judged to be truthful when they claimed to know nothing about how the babies died. If that was still the case in Fleisher's and Gordon's view, Nodiff was less likely to go interview the Noes. In the brownstone headquarters of the Vidocq Society, Fleisher and Gordon studied the charts. They shook their heads in bewilderment. "Marie's charts are clearly deceptive," they agreed. "Arthur's charts are inconclusive at best."

Fleisher registered it as Vidocq Society Case No. 55, The Babies Noe Case. It looked to him like Marie Noe, right in his hometown, had been the most prolific killer of her own children in modern history—and had gotten away with it.

· CHAPTER 41 ·

THE BOY WHO NEVER DIED

The child was dead, brutally murdered, and the cops were converging on the scene from across the region. But they were driving more slowly now, forty-one years later. Patrolman Sam Weinstein, who carried the boy for the trip to the morgue that distant morning, was seventy-one years old now, but still burly with a hard glint in his eye. Bill Kelly, the gentler-natured fingerprint man, in his late sixties with white hair framing his liquid blue eyes, doted on his six daughters—"Kelly's Angels"—and grandchildren. President Eisenhower, young pilot John Glenn setting a California-to-New York speed record, Hamilton's electric "watch of the future," the world they knew on February 25, 1957, was gone, but not forgotten. The cops were still working the case. From Ike to Clinton, through nine U.S. presidents, the Cold War, Korea, Vietnam, and the first terrorist bombing of the World Trade Center, they had never stopped.

Kelly, retired from the police department, still never passed a hospital without checking the footprints on file of newborns from the early 1950s; he'd studied 11,000 prints, but maybe the next one would identify the boy. Weinstein sorted through the case records, boxes stuffed with files, photographs, hundreds of tips and notes, looking for anything they may have overlooked. Remington Bristow, the medical examiner's investigator, had devoted thirty-seven years to the case, traveling everywhere with a death mask of the boy in his briefcase. When he touched the boy's death mask he grieved as if he had been touched by a spirit, and he urged others to touch it, too; some investigators believed he had gone around the bend on the case. When Bristow moved from Philadelphia to Arizona, where he died in 1993, his granddaughter drove him across the country, stopping so that her grandfather, sickly and half-blind, could check new leads all the way. "Rem was 'The Man,'" said Kelly, who had worked alongside him for years on the case. Rem's work went on.

The boy, who would have been nearly fifty years old now, still lay in Potter's Field, under the small monument the homicide bureau long ago purchased—the only monument in the field of body parts and the insane, criminals, and the forgotten. For four decades the detectives had visited with flowers in the spring, a yellow sand pail in summer, a newly oiled baseball glove for Christmas, as if he were growing up to be a fine young boy. Bristow had said that with his slender build the boy had the makings of a basketball player instead of football. The cold-case cops kept the boy alive with the heat of longing and memory. He was the boy who would never grow up, who would never die.

They prayed over the legend the homicide bureau once wrote:

"Heavenly Father, Bless This Unknown Child."

If devotion to solving a child's murder is a measure, the boy so little cared for in life had been more loved by two generations of police detectives than any child in Philadelphia history—loved when there was no hope.

Now there was hope. The Vidocq Society was on the case.

On Thursday, March 19, 1998, Weinstein and Kelly entered the old Public Ledger Building, across a side street from its twin, the Curtis Publishing Company building, where *The Saturday Evening Post* was once published, and took the elevator to the tenth floor, to the walnut-paneled Downtown Club. The former men's club was the new meeting place of the Vidocq Society; the white-linen-covered round tables overlooking Independence Hall were now the setting, on the third Thursday of each month, of the Murder Room.

Vidocq Society commissioner Fleisher greeted the retired cops warmly. Weinstein and Kelly, Fleisher's former police department colleagues, were now VSMs. Following an invocation by Kelly, the devout Catholic, and then lunch, Fleisher announced that the society was now investigating "one of the most amazing cases in Philadelphia history." Fleisher had put the full power of the Vidocq Society into finding the identity and the killer of the Boy in the Box.

The Murder Room was filled beyond capacity with more than eighty detectives and their guests. Some detectives were forced to sit on stools at the bar. The menu was chicken, steamed vegetables, and a corpse with a small and unforgettable face. After lunch, the beaten, bruised image of the boy floated on the screen at the front of the room, his sunken eyeballs painted in shadows. Kelly fought back tears, as if he was seeing the picture for the first time. Fillinger, the city coroner who'd worked on the dead boy forty-one years ago, was ready to reexamine the case.

Fleisher had made another *shidduch,* this one with homicide detective Tom Augustine of the Philadelphia Police Department, which had agreed to reopen the case and work with the Vidocq Society investigators on the case. Augustine brought forty-one years of case files to the society's brownstone headquarters on Locust Street. It was the sum total, from day one, of all "we've worked on day, night, and day year after year. Boxes and boxes, thousands of pages." In a private second-floor room, Weinstein, Kelly, and McGillen were in the process of going back through all the old records. The three VSMs had formed a Boy in the Box investigative team, headed by Weinstein.

Now, at the meeting, a radiant energy emanated from the table of the old cops, white-haired, stooped, and balding, men whom only a heart attack or cancer could stop from pursuing the next lead. The old Catholic and Jewish detectives saw the murder of innocence not as an end but the beginning of a soul's journey toward redemption. They were men who had a green thumb in the garden of death.

Fleisher introduced Ron Avery, the veteran *Philadelphia Daily News* columnist whose research for his new book, *City of Brotherly Mayhem,* had inspired the commissioner to revisit the case. Avery briefly reviewed the case he said was "indelibly emblazoned in our memory." He tantalized the detectives with the fact that the case had provided "loads of clues and loads of evidence . . . dozens, scores, hundreds of good leads."

Richard Walter was working on a profile of the killer based on the crime scene. Frank Bender, seated next to Walter, closely examined all the old photographs of the boy. Bender was doing an age-progression sculpture, but one even more challenging than John List's. Bender was sculpting the bust of what he felt the boy's father looked like, hoping someone would recognize the father and come forward with information on the case. With not an iota of knowledge of the boy's parents, he was flying purely on intuition. But Bender had performed a miracle with List, and *America's Most Wanted* had committed to airing a fall episode on the Boy in the Box featuring the bust. There was a sense of possibility in the air.

Weinstein stood, heavyset and balding, his face worn with the curse of a photographic memory. He was thirty years old again, passing through the tree line to the field off Susquehanna Road; he was kicking his rubber boots through the muck and wet underbrush. "I saw all this garbage," he said, "and a young white boy whose hair was chopped. It was a sad, heartbreaking thing to see. It was a dump. This was homicide."

Weinstein said the case had been taken away from him, a patrolman, and assigned to detectives forty years ago. He'd stubbornly conducted his own investigation, and through a confidential informant found a local man who had photos of himself with a young blond boy on his lap and "an Indian blanket spread out." He purchased the photos. He interviewed the man, who was "very cooperative" but "extremely nervous," in a restaurant. The man "started to get shaky." He had just agreed to go to the Homicide

Unit for questioning when a superior officer saw Weinstein in the restaurant and ordered him to leave, ending his role in the investigation. Weinstein said he welcomed a second chance he never thought he'd have.

Kelly dreamed of solving the case as the crowning moment of his career, and in many ways his life. McGillen's wife was proud of his efforts to help bring Marie Noe to justice and now perhaps helping to resolve the Boy in the Box murder. She was dying of cancer, and she prayed she would see him triumph in the cases.

Bender said he had a vision that the boy had been dressed as a girl. His caretakers had grown his hair out long and chopped it to conceal his identity just before killing him. Walter snorted and others laughed.

"Keep your day job, Frank," Walter reminded him, his favorite dismissal of his creative partner.

Fleisher longed to give the boy a decent burial. "This case is solvable," he said. Even if the killer or killers were dead, he said, their purpose would be to restore to the boy the dignity of his name, and avenge him with their only remaining weapon, the truth. They could bring the killer "to reckoning if not to justice."

"Bah!" Walter glared at Fleisher, a look he usually reserved for people who peddle Bibles door-to-door. The thin man had grown weary of the sentimentality in the air. He openly mocked the consensus that had initially started with Bristow that the boy had been accidentally killed by loving caretakers who fled with broken hearts, unable to afford a decent burial. In 1957, police had seen it as a murder, but over time, at Bristow's urging, they'd publicly said it was an accident.

The child, Walter thought, was sacrificed to the most malevolent murdering personality of all, and to preserve their own innocence the cops had made a fetish of his lost childhood, keeping him an eternal child as he moldered forty-one years in the grave. The killer represented a force so vile the cops couldn't face the truth. Without truth, how could they find the killer?

They had waited forty-one years for the truth, and in fact now seemed energetically devoted to the long martyrdom of failure; the mystery gave them such purpose, and the truth admitted none of the romance of beach toys and baseball gloves.

"It's hard to find something," Walter sniffed later, "when you don't know what you're looking for." The horror behind his cool, dry words seemed not to penetrate the others.

The fact was that after forty-one years of continuous investigation, thousands of police interviews across thirty states, and thousands of pages or pieces of so-called evidence, they still had nothing to go on. Never in American detective history, outside the Lindbergh kidnapping, had so much effort been expended on a child murder case to produce so little, he thought.

"We don't have much," Walter reasoned. "But I don't need much." The marks on the body told a plain and incontrovertible story, one the others were loath to hear.

CHAPTER 42

THE EIGHT BABIES CALLED "IT"

On a Wednesday evening in late March 1998, an unmarked black Ford Explorer carrying Philadelphia police sergeant Larry Nodiff and two of his detectives from the Special Investigations Unit parked on a narrow street in the old working-class river ward of Kensington. The murky industrial air along the river was gray with twilight. A crescent moon, nearly black, hung above the lane of small brick row houses.

Sergeant Nodiff knocked on the door of a row home that looked like all the others. Nodiff looked up at darkened windows. His partner Steve Vivarina chewed his coffee stirrer. The day before, Stephen Fried's investigative story on Marie Noe's long-forgotten tragedy, "Cradle to Grave," was published in *Philadelphia* magazine, and as the magazine hit the streets the city was abuzz with it. Sergeant Nodiff, who had read an advance copy, decided it was time to pay Marie and Arthur Noe a visit about the deaths of their eight babies. It was a historian's task as well as police work. The babies had died across nineteen years, from the Truman administration to LBJ. The police had not questioned the Noes about the deaths in thirty years. Now a few minutes passed.

Presently the thin, hard face of Arthur Noe, seventy-six years old, filled a crack in the door. Behind him loomed the larger frame of his wife, Marie, sixty-nine. Sergeant Nodiff showed his badge and asked if they would come to headquarters for questioning. The Noes had the right to refuse but they said yes, they'd just be a few minutes. They had just finished dinner, and needed to take care of their cats and dogs.

"Will you put Asshole downstairs?" Arthur called to his wife. Asshole, he explained to the cops, was one of their cats. Marie tended to the cat, then they put on light jackets and slowly climbed into the police van. They had been together most of their lives. Marie was diabetic, and not well. Arthur was trembling. Theirs was an unbreakable bond built, as many are, on things understood, things not said.

Marie and Arthur were taken to separate interrogation rooms in the Roundhouse, the cement police headquarters downtown. In Interrogation Room C, Arthur, a chain-smoker, was downcast and nervous. A sharp, quick-talking man, he had worked in Kensington's textile factories for years. He had served as a Democratic committeeman in the river ward and as an assistant to a city councilman. He hated to see Marie dragged through the tragedies again. Losing all those children between 1949 and 1968 had been like "taking away half her life." As he had told a reporter, "It may be news to you. It's suffering to us." Detective Jack McDermott quickly realized that Arthur had nothing new to tell them, and offered him a ride home. Arthur said he'd prefer to wait for his wife.

As night came, Arthur lit a cigarette and sat watching the television on the battered filing cabinets lining the homicide division. Marie was in Interrogation Room D with Sergeant Nodiff and Detective Vivarina. Arthur worried about his wife's health, looked at his watch, smoking all through the night. As the sky lightened, he was still waiting.

At five o'clock in the morning, Marie hobbled out of the interrogation room, her careworn face collapsed in fatigue and relief. It had been eleven hours with the detectives. Arthur came and touched her gently, his eyes lingering in concern. Marie held her husband's eyes and her secrets. Even when she'd tried to tell the

306 · THE MURDER ROOM

truth, Arthur always interrupted her. Among the couple's many unspoken routines during the past forty years together, this was the most important. It was as if he didn't want to know.

Sergeant Nodiff, the city's lead cold-case detective and a member of the Vidocq Society, was one of the department's sharpest interrogators. Detective Vivarina could amiably keep anybody talking. So they'd talked and talked with Marie all night. Then before dawn, Sergeant Nodiff confided years later to detectives at an out-of-town conference, one of the strangest things in his career happened to him. He blushed and said, "You just won't believe it," as he told it. Marie, sitting right next to the sergeant, reached out and put her wrinkled hand on the dark trousers covering his leg. Slowly, as she gently stroked the sergeant's inner thigh, the unspoken words of decades came tumbling out.

She confessed.

She had smothered her babies with a pillow, she said. She and Arthur had ten children. One was stillborn. Another died in the hospital six hours after birth. The remaining eight went home in excellent health. None of them lived longer than fifteen months. Marie admitted to killing them all. She waited until Arthur was out of the house, a pattern she repeated each time. She hid all the murders from her husband and relatives. Marie was alone with the babies in the house.

She could remember the deaths of only four of her children in detail. They were the first three and the fifth. The murders of Richard Allen Noe, 1949; Elizabeth Mary Noe, 1951; Jacqueline Noe, 1952; and Constance Noe, 1958, were etched in her mind. She remembered Richard, her firstborn, very clearly. He was born March 7, 1949, a healthy seven pounds, eleven ounces. "He was always crying. He couldn't tell me what was bothering him. He just kept crying. . . ."

"The day that he died," Marie said, she was getting Richard ready for bed. "I bathed him and put him in nightclothes and I was going to put him down for the night. I put him on his belly instead of his back in his bassinet, and there was a pillow under his face, he was lying facedown. Then I took my hand and pressed his face down into the pillow until he stopped moving." Richard Noe was thirty-one days old. His cause of death was listed as congestive heart failure, but no autopsy was performed. It was accepted medical wisdom in the 1950s that a mother would not kill her children.

Two years later, in 1951, alone in the house with Elizabeth Mary, Marie picked up and held her pink, squirming, squalling daughter, a healthy and vigorous five months old. She put Elizabeth Mary in the bassinet. "I put her on her back, and then I took a pillow from the bed and put the pillow over her face and suffocated her." Elizabeth was memorable because "she was fussing. Elizabeth was a lot stronger than Richard was, and she was fighting when the pillow was over her face. I held the pillow over her face until she stopped moving."

A year later, in 1952, Jacqueline Noe died in infancy. Marie admitted to killing her second daughter the same way she did her first son and daughter, but couldn't remember any details.

As she told the story, she called each baby "it." Detectives kept insisting she call the children by name.

Six years later, in 1958, Constance Noe was born at St. Luke's Hospital. Abraham Perlman, a pediatrician who treated the baby, was suspicious because Constance's four older siblings had all died. The pediatrician noticed a pattern to the deaths, he told police years later. Marie Noe was always home alone with the child. In each case, she took the infant to a hospital or called a neighbor to help her, saying, "Something's wrong with the baby." The children were all dead on arrival. Noe's explanation was always that the baby had been "gasping for breath and turning blue." It was medical orthodoxy then that children could suddenly stop breathing, and the fatal syndrome might be a defect that ran in families, so Dr. Perlman performed extensive tests on Constance to find any possible weakness. All the tests came back normal. Constance was a robustly healthy baby girl.

As mother and child left the hospital, Dr. Perlman told Marie that Constance was a beautiful child. Her mother replied, "She's not going to live . . . just like the others."

One month later, Constance, a healthy, thriving baby girl, was having difficulty sitting in a chair. "I was trying to train her on how to sit up in the chair," Marie said. "I don't know why, but then I took a pillow and laid her down on the chair, and I suffocated her."

The autopsy of Constance was performed by pathologist Marie Valdes-Dapena at the Philadelphia medical examiner's office. Dr. Valdes-Dapena, who would later become a recognized authority on sudden infant death syndrome (SIDS), was baffled. Pathologists were mystified by "crib death," she said. The scientific study of infant death was just beginning, and no one had coined the term "SIDS." Doctors had no idea why approximately 7,000 babies a year simply stopped breathing. Even years later, when doctors suspected many of those deaths to be infanticide, it was extraordinarily difficult for a pathologist to distinguish a baby who died of SIDS from one who was suffocated.

Marie Noe had discovered the perfect murder.

Marie did not cry during the confession. She said calmly that she killed baby Arthur Jr. in 1955, but couldn't remember how. Arthur Jr. was born nine months to the day after Marie said she was raped by a stranger and left bound with her husband's ties in the bedroom closet. Her last three children were featured in the *Life* story, a compassionate tale of the mother who lost all her babies—Mary Lee, born in 1962, Catherine Ellen in 1964, and the last born, Arthur Joseph. The ninth child, Catherine Ellen, lived the longest—one year, two months, and twenty-two days. She died on February 25, 1966, of undetermined cause. The last born, Arthur Joseph, died on January 2, 1968, at the age of five months. At the time, Marie told police that Arthur Joseph just turned blue and stopped breathing. An autopsy was performed, but no determination was made on the manner of death. Marie now confessed to killing all three babies born in the 1960s, but couldn't recall details.

As the sun came up, the confession was typed up. Marie read it over and signed it. She leaned back, her face flushed with relief. She told detectives she always hoped police would find out. "I knew what I was doing was very wrong," she said. She stood slowly to leave Interrogation Room D. Suddenly, she turned to face Nodiff and Vivarina. Her face was creased in concern, her voice a whisper: "Don't tell my husband what I told you."

Sergeant Nodiff and detective Vivarina looked at each other. An old lady who would barely walk without assistance had killed more people than David "Son of Sam" Berkowitz or the Boston Strangler. They had a detailed confession of eight murders— infanticide, perhaps the most taboo of human crimes. In God's name, why? And now what could they do with it?

Marie was weak; Arthur walked her slowly outside. They climbed in the police van for a quiet ride home.

Five months later, Marie Noe was arrested and charged with the suffocation murders of eight of her ten children. Noe's attorney denied the charges. Prosecutors said they would seek life imprisonment.

Her husband, Arthur, who was not charged, said he was standing by his wife.

"I've lived with this woman for fifty years," he said. "She was my life. That woman was not capable of doing such a thing. She wouldn't harm a fly."

CHAPTER 43

MURDER IN TRIPLICATE

She was murdered three times. That was the salient point of the horrific killing of Terri Lee Brooks, Richard Walter thought with grim satisfaction. He took a reluctant nibble of a thick-crust apple pie, a sip of black coffee—a Colombian blend, too weak—and stared at the corpse of the dark-haired young woman whose slaying had confused police for so many years.

Floating above the white tablecloths in the walnut-paneled club, the corpse lay in a large pool of her own blood, arms out in the shape of a cross. Her body was severely battered with cuts and bruises. A seven-inch butcher knife was sticking out of her throat, pinning her neck to the floor of the kitchen of the Roy Rogers restaurant on U.S. 1 in Bucks County. The knife had cut her throat and severed her spinal cord. Her head was wrapped in a clear plastic garbage bag. Her face was visible inside the bag behind a small cloud of condensation that itself had revealed a story of horror to the medical examiner. Paralyzed from the neck down, unable to move or speak, Brooks had still been breathing, watching her killer close in.

On the far wall the safe stood open—and emptied of its $2,579 in cash. The killer ransacked the safe and leaped out the drive-in window into the foggy predawn of February 3, 1984. He was careless, leaving fifteen fingerprints on the walls and floor. But the prints were all ruined in the thick restaurant grease. Police had never made an arrest in the robbery-murder in fourteen years.

A yellowed newspaper clipping from the *Philadelphia Inquirer,* published six months after the murder, still told the whole story: UNSOLVED KILLING STYMIES POLICE AND ANGUISHES FAMILY.

More than eighty detectives crowded into the Downtown Club in May 1998, an overflow drawn by a chance to reexamine one of the most highly publicized unsolved murder cases of recent years. VSM Lynn Abraham, the powerful Philadelphia district attorney, was among those once again forced to find a stool at the bar. After fourteen years of dead ends, the police of small Falls Township, Pennsylvania (pop. 34,000), twenty-six miles north of Philadelphia, had asked for help. Sergeant Wynne Cloud said he was grateful for the audience with the Vidocq Society, but had cautioned Brooks's long-suffering parents, Ed and Cindy Brooks, not to unrealistically get their hopes up. There wasn't much more that could be done.

"We investigated the murder quite strenuously over a two-year period," Sergeant Cloud of Falls Township told the gathering from the podium. The police had logged more than two hundred interviews, interrogated twelve suspects, and catalogued ninety pieces of evidence. "But after all that, we came up with absolutely nothing."

The restaurant safe was ransacked after the brutal murder, prompting the police to investigate the crime as a "robbery gone wrong" rather than a deliberate murder. They had never changed their focus.

Walter rolled his eyes. He had sipped enough coffee and heard quite enough from the police. But he kept his own counsel as he appraised the ferocious killing. *It's not a goddamn robbery,* he thought. *Any fool can see that. It was murder in triplicate. That was the point of the killing. But why? Who wanted to kill Terri Lee Brooks again and again and again?*

The robbery theory gained traction with the police because as far as they knew, the young woman had no enemies, or at least none with enough animus to kill her. A native of Bucks County, she had graduated from the University of Maryland planning to seek a career in human resources, but after waitressing during summers in college, she followed her heart home and into the restaurant business. Brooks had recently been promoted to assistant manager of the Bucks County restaurant, confirming her initial excitement at joining the restaurant chain that was owned by the Marriott Corporation, with plenty of opportunity to grow.

Brooks was alone in the restaurant long after closing on February 3, 1984, sitting in her back office, doing paperwork. She had just locked the outer glass door after letting out the two "closers"— teenagers who helped clean and prepare the restaurant for the next day; the inner glass door locked automatically behind her, offering double protection. It was after midnight, an unseasonably warm and foggy winter night.

The roar of traffic on U.S. 1 had quieted. The empty glass-walled restaurant glowed in the night, a cube of light in the misty darkness. Brooks often stayed late, focused on leaving the restaurant in perfect shape for day manager Joe Hampton.

Sometime after midnight, she heard knocking.

At about 6:15 in the morning, still dark in late winter, Hampton arrived to open up the restaurant. He was surprised to find the outer door unlocked. The inner door was locked as usual, and he turned the key and entered. Near the door was a pair of moccasin-style shoes he recognized as Terri Brooks's. Next to the shoes were her keys. He walked into the kitchen. Large swaths of blood were smeared on the floors and walls, mixed grotesquely with the kitchen grease. Terri was behind the counter lying on her back, brutally murdered. Police were admittedly stunned by the violence of the killing; indeed, Walter thought, they failed to understand it.

Vidocq Society Member Hal Fillinger, the noted medical examiner, had performed the autopsy in 1984, and recalled every gruesome detail. It appeared from the pattern of wounds that Brooks had been trying to leave, with her winter coat on, when a violent assault sent her purse, keys, and cigarettes flying. The killer repeatedly banged her head on the stone tile floor with tremendous force, immobilizing her. Then, sitting on top of her, he began to strangle her. He fractured her hyoid bone, a small U-shaped bone atop the Adam's apple that helps produce swallowing and speech and is often crushed during strangulation. But that didn't kill Terri Brooks. She struggled violently for her life, which prompted the killer to reach for the butcher knife. The cuts and slices on her hands indicated she had thrown her hands up in vain to stop the knife. It cut her throat and severed half of her spinal cord. A second knife thrust severed the spinal cord completely and with such force the knife blade stuck in the tile floor, pinning her throat to the ground.

Paralyzed but still alive, she must have heard the killer foraging in the restaurant supply area. He returned with the clear plastic trash bag, and wrapped it completely around her neck and head. It was Fillinger who noted the condensation inside the bag, indicating Brooks was still breathing and looking up at her attacker as he asphyxiated her.

As the corpse hovered above them in the gray light of afternoon, tall, broad-shouldered ex–major-crime homicide detective Ed Gaughan's lantern jaw flushed in contrast to his sandy hair, the only sign he gave that he wanted to take someone out. Gaughan was friends with Sergeant Cloud, who had shared his frustration with the Brooks case while the two were watching their sons play football for Pennsbury High School. Gaughan convinced Sergeant Cloud to bring the case before the Vidocq Society.

The Falls Township Police Department threw all its resources at the crime, Cloud said. The killing made headlines in the local newspapers, and the Marriott Corporation put up a $5,000 reward for the arrest and conviction of the killer or killers. It quickly became evident to police that it was a "robbery gone wrong"— terribly wrong. Brooks had interrupted the robbery in progress and tried to stop it, triggering her death.

Looking for the robber who, facing resistance, had become

a murderer, police interviewed fifty past and present restaurant employees. They zeroed in on an employee whom Brooks had discovered stealing from the cash drawer, and another employee at a Roy Rogers restaurant in Philadelphia who had threatened her. Both were cleared. They talked to an old boyfriend in California, and ruled him out.

They tried to link Brooks's killing to a spate of similarly violent fast-food robberies in the region and beyond. In April 1985 at a Philadelphia Roy Rogers only twenty miles away, fourteen months later, the day manager opened up to find the night manager stabbed to death, the safe empty. They contacted police in Massachusetts, Maryland, and California, where similar crimes had occurred, and interrogated suspects in all similar robberies they could find. On the tenth anniversary of the crime, a local television station crime watch program featured the case. The police received "lots of calls and our investigators ended up all over the place," to no avail.

Shortly after 1:30 in the afternoon, Sergeant Cloud concluded his presentation. "We appreciate your ears," he said. "We also appreciate your brains." The room seemed to exhale, gathering itself for the inquiry. The first suggestions from Vidocq members focused on DNA testing, a technology unknown in 1984. Could the killer's DNA be harvested from the victim's body and articles found at the scene, including the knife and hair follicles in her hand? Cloud would look into it.

Fleisher, Bender, Walter, Gaughan, and Fred Bornhofen whispered among themselves and called out their opinions almost as one. The consensus was the police department had botched the focus of the case from the beginning, fourteen years earlier.

"Initially the investigators seemed to have gone after robbers," Gaughan said. "Any time somebody was locked up who had committed a robbery like that, they were there interrogating the guy. They basically didn't focus the investigation properly. A robber wants money, to get in and get out; he'll kill if he has to but this was a more complex type of murder."

Bornhofen wrote later, "It's overkill and not the type of murder done by a robber. Even a rank amateur like me could see the case for what it was."

Gaughan, looking sympathetically at his friend Sergeant Cloud, said the police had to start over. They had to interview everyone again, as if Terri Brooks had just been killed. This time, the Vidocq Society would be there to help.

Walter stood. "My colleagues are quite right. Robbers don't swath the head of a victim in plastic. As it happens, this is the peculiar signature of a very complicated and dark personality subtype. It's not a robbery at all. It's a murder. The murderer staged the robbery to throw the police off. He succeeded, until now. We know quite a lot about the killer already."

Walter paused. "In the information game, answers are meaningless. You have to ask the right questions, and the question is: Who cared enough to kill her three times?"

His rakish smile pierced the gloom.

"For whom did Terri Brooks unlock the door?"

CHAPTER 44

FROM HEAVEN TO HELL

The sweet hymn to Jesus awakened Walter abruptly. He was snoozing in the parlor of his Greek Revival mansion when the glorious notes of "Lift High the Cross" floated in on the spring air. He put on his glasses and stood on the porch glaring at the offending Gothic tower of St. Paul's Episcopal Church, diagonally across the street. It was time to teach the Episcopalians a lesson.

Wearing jeans and a red sport shirt, he pulled the Briggs & Stratton mower out of the garage, filled it with gas, and mowed the front lawn—as he did every Sunday when the choir reached full song, whether the grass needed it or not. He was "quite pleased" as the rattling old mower drowned out the choir, and the clatter crossed the street to the opened stained-glass windows of the stone church. "The Episcopalians are perfectly loathsome neighbors," he later wrote to a friend. "When they get going on Sunday I must answer back with as loud a noise as I can muster."

"Have you finished being psychopathic yet?" Stoud grinned as he stepped on the porch, where the thin man was sitting, his face a sheen of sweat, sipping an iced tea in the sudden quiet of a late spring morning.

"It's terrible, isn't it, that people want to sing in church on Sunday morning?"

"Indeed." Walter laughed. "As you know, I don't make a very good victim. And I'm not feeling terribly charitable toward Christians at the moment."

Walter had just returned from Lubbock, Texas, where he'd watched Tim Smith, a devout Evangelical Christian, be tried for the murder of Scott Dunn as Leisha Hamilton's accomplice, a year after Hamilton was convicted of Dunn's murder and sentenced to twenty years in prison. Smith's attorney had portrayed the cold-blooded killer as a clean-cut, young, Christian family man, with a wife and three-year-old son, who had never done wrong until he met the conniving Hamilton. Members of Smith's church had mobbed the courthouse, calling for Christians all over the city to pray for him to be found innocent. "The nincompoops filled the courthouse wailing that the killer was an exemplary fellow in church," Walter said. "It had an effect on the trial. It wasn't good."

Smith, thirty-five years old, slim and blond, was a poetic, submissive young man who had been easily seduced by Hamilton, who "used men like you use a handkerchief," prosecutors said. He trailed Hamilton around like a lovesick sophomore, following her to the Copper Kettle just to look at her work as a waitress, and deluging her with love letters filled with jealousy of Scott. Smith believed if Scott Dunn "was out of the way everything would be bliss and happiness" with the woman he loved, according to the state.

Smith had been deeply involved in the murder for some forty-eight hours, prosecutors said. He cut away sections of blood-soaked carpet from the bedroom to hide evidence, helped wrap Scott's body in rolled-up carpet with duct tape, helped dispose of the body and clean up the crime scene. Fibers from the bloody carpet were found on a roll of duct tape in Smith's apartment.

According to Walter, Hamilton set Smith up to take the fall in an old-fashioned murderer's scam.

After the killing, while Leisha was toying with the cops, playing the role of a wronged but helpful young woman, she moved in with Tim Smith to finish setting up the dupe.

Smith, believing his romantic dreams had come true, had instead lived a nightmare, subjected to walking in on his girlfriend having sex with other men, and being beaten by her for questioning it. Acting ever eager to help find Scott's killer, Hamilton told police she was afraid of her new boyfriend. She showed them Tim Smith's love letters, addressed to "Dear Green Eyes" and signed, "Superman" or "The Flash," letters that called Scott a "snake" and an "asshole" and demanded she choose between them. "If only Scott wasn't around," Smith wrote, "we could be happy together." Hamilton confirmed to the *Lubbock Avalanche-Journal* that her boyfriend was a "suspect" in Scott's disappearance. He had been "fiercely jealous of her relationship with Scott." The police soon considered Smith a primary suspect.

Moving in on her prey was exciting for Hamilton. "This need for stimulation is quite insatiable for a psychopath, the ego gratification to prove they're smarter than anyone," Walter explained to Dunn. "The 'Gotcha!'"

Walter had rattled Smith in a private interview, squeezing him to reveal what had happened to Scott's body.

Smith had refused to say. He said he "couldn't turn on the others . . . it wouldn't be Christian."

"Is it Christian to commit murder?" Walter demanded. "Is it Christian to cover it up?"

Tim Smith didn't reply.

Walter watched the trial at the Lubbock County courthouse with Jim and Barbara Dunn, and the three of them exulted as Smith was convicted of the first-degree murder of Scott Dunn. After six years, justice was finally being served. Walter felt vindicated. Though he had once again been prevented from testifying as a profiler, Rusty Ladd, the prosecuting attorney, praised him for helping the state zero in on Smith as Hamilton's chief accomplice. Leisha would never have gone to jail, Tim Smith never would have been convicted, if it wasn't for Walter, the prosecutor said.

Smith was sentenced the next day. He faced ninety-nine years or life in prison for his involvement in Dunn's prolonged torture, murder, dismemberment, and disposal. Hamilton had received twenty years. Walter had hated to tell Dunn, but the truth was that Hamilton could be out in less than a decade for good behavior.

Now the jury deliberated for about an hour. Timothy James Smith received no jail time at all for first-degree murder.

He was sentenced to ten years' probation and a $10,000 fine.

Dunn was stunned. He couldn't conceive how "Tim Smith, convicted of murdering Scott, was free to walk the streets of Lubbock" and did not have to reveal the location of Scott's body.

Because Smith had no prior criminal record, the jury had the option of probation.

Walter was outraged.

"It would appear that the jury attempted to do God's work of forgiveness at the sentencing," he later wrote. "In these matters, it would seem the jury should leave God's work to God, and do the work of the State of Texas. Unfortunately, the jury allowed Timothy James Smith to benefit unfettered from the murder for which all life has been cheapened."

Walter was concerned about Jim Dunn.

Within days of the trial, the aggrieved father threw himself on Smith's mercy, now that the killer was "beyond harm," begging to Smith to reveal, even anonymously, the location of Scott's body. "Please . . . let him have the decency of a proper burial," he wrote. "Look at your son, who is alive, then contact me. In your heart you know the right thing to do. . . . I will be waiting for a message from you or your intermediary. Send it to Box 986, Morrisville, PA, 19067."

Dunn also returned to taking phone calls from Leisha Hamilton, hoping to learn where his son was buried. Hamilton kept calling the grieving father from her prison cell, toying with his emotions. Dunn was a wreck. Leisha had murdered the son; now she was destroying the father.

"Stop talking to her," Walter said, scolding him. "You're dealing with a classic psychopath. The murder is not over with the killing. The murder isn't over until the murderer says it is. The murder's not over for her. She's still enjoying it. Don't feel hate toward Leisha. It weakens you. The opposite of love is not hate. The opposite of love is neutrality, 'I don't care.' If you ignore her, she will lose her hold over you.

"Damn it, Jim, she got your son. Don't let the killer take another victim."

The quest to find his son's body to put under the stone was destroying him.

Dunn sat quiet while Walter lit a Kool, and watched the plume of smoke disintegrate over the porch.

"But it was quite fascinating," he said. "Here you have Leisha Hamilton, the dominating, power-driven killer, controlling and using submissive Tim Smith like a dog, seducing him into murder, setting him up to take the fall. The jury sees right through her, is repulsed by her, she goes to prison. Then you have Tim Smith, whose submissive nature makes him Hamilton's hapless victim, using that very quality to turn the tables on the jury. He's no less psychopathic, but he's dreamy, poetic, and the jury falls for his charming-nice-young-Christian-man act."

He stood and looked across the street at St. Paul's, rising quietly now from its grove of old trees.

"I'm probably more agnostic than I am an atheist, but in any event, even if one doesn't believe in God, in our line of work one must have substance, structure, strong faith, character." He snuffed out the cigarette. "It used to be that people had character; now houses have character and people have *personality*. That won't do. The eternal things, the good, the true, the beautiful, must be unbreakable."

"One must have standards," Stoud said, grinning.

"One must."

"One should."

"I do," Walter said, "and mine are quite *low*." They were laughing now.

Walter laughed himself into a coughing fit as he walked into the house.

CHAPTER 45

THE DESCENT

The thin man sat in a wing chair with his hard green pack of Kools, battered metal ashtray, and ceramic coffee cup resting on a walnut side table from nineteenth-century Lyon. The coffee cup, a gift from an admiring Midwestern homicide squad, was inscribed "When Your Life Ends, Our Work Begins." The parlor, dim at midday, was crowded with antiques; the front door was attended by the bust of a French knight, a chevalier of the last century, lit by an enormous red Chinese paper lantern.

The afternoon was quiet but for the ticking of the grandfather clock and Walter spinning the triple-digit combination on the steel-ribbed, aircraft-aluminum briefcase. It was the classic 1940s-style Zero Halliburton, the near-indestructible model that protects the U.S. president's nuclear codes and red button.

"This is strictly proprietary," Walter said as the double-bolt lock sprung and the case hissed open. "Not to be discussed outside this room."

"I saw that attaché on *Mission: Impossible*," Stoud teased. "I don't believe it's for country gentlemen." He knew the classic Zero was fashionable with spies, federal agents, and pretentious film noir directors—but that Walter, with justification, used it to guard information that had proved extremely dangerous in the wrong hands.

"Information can be harmful when you're not ready for it," Walter said. "Dostoevsky said there were some ideas you could eat, and some that ate you. These are devouring ideas."

Nested in the rich leather interior, protected from dust and moisture by the neoprene gasket-sealed case, was a stack of photographs of the corpse of Terri Lee Brooks with the knife sticking out of her throat. Under the stack were simple manila files.

Walter's subtypes.

He and Bob Keppel, the famous Washington State investigator, had spent years refining their grand theory of murder investigation. They would soon publish in the *International Journal of Offender Therapy and Comparative Criminology* a paper, "Profiling Killers: A Revised Classification Model for Understanding Sexual Murder," that would be internationally hailed as a landmark analysis and working system of murder investigation. Walter since the 1980s had been lecturing about murderer personality traits to detectives, prosecutors, and forensic specialists all around the world, from Hong Kong to London to Harrisburg, Pennsylvania.

It was a dream as old as the human condition, to understand the heart of darkness. To see the broader patterns. Walter hated to admit it, but his method was perfectly described in *Beeton's Christmas Annual* in London in 1887, in the first appearance of Sherlock Holmes, who explains to his roommate, Dr. John Watson, what a "consulting detective" does: ". . . we have lots of Government detectives and lots of private ones. When these fellows are at fault they come to me. . . . They lay all the evidence before me, and I am generally able . . . to set them straight. There is a strong family resemblance about misdeeds, and if you have all the details of a thousand at your finger ends, it is odd if you can't unravel the thousand and first."

In analyzing thousands of murders, Walter and Keppel discovered the most violent murders, sex murders, were invariably committed by one of four personality types. These distinct personalities inevitably expressed themselves, *could not help but express themselves,* their traits, desires, and learning curve in the murder itself. The crime scene was a vast canvas; the detective had merely to read the signature. Or, as G. K. Chesterton wrote in 1910, "The criminal is the creative artist, the detective only the critic."

The thin man returned from the kitchen with a fresh pot of coffee, and Walter and Stoud both lit fresh cigarettes. Shortly after noon, they began the descent.

The first personality type of murderers identified by Walter and Keppel was the most common, the power-assertive or PA killer. Walter nicknamed this type the John Wayne–style killer. He bristles with machismo, muscles, tattoos, guns, girlie magazines, a pickup truck. He preens over his automobile. Among his signatures, he strikes massively to the head to overwhelm his victim, much like the first big bite of the great white shark. He disposes of his victim like trash, his power needs fulfilled. This is a man of ironclad principles (no character, but firm principles). For instance, if he's raping and strangling a woman and she suddenly dies, he pulls out hurriedly because "he doesn't want cops to think he's a pervert," Walter said. "Only a pervert would fuck a corpse."

"Leisha Hamilton is a classic female PA," Walter continued. "Scott Dunn unwittingly involved himself in an intolerable insult to power, and the PA annihilated him and disposed of him to sate her power need."

Tim Smith, her collaborator in the murder, represented the seemingly gentler second type, the power-reassurance killer. He's the Caspar Milquetoast killer, Walter said, lost in his own imagination. Instead of a brute grab for power, the PR killer achieved power through fantasy. This was the high school geek who skittered along the sidewalk robed in black, and turned horror movies into reality. This was the Gentleman Rapist who fantasized a strange woman was smitten with him, assaulted her with the line "Here I am at last, baby, open your wings," Walter said, and flew into a murderous rage when "she let him know he wasn't the best thing since sliced bread." Unlike the John Wayne type, who scrupulously cleans the crime scene to avoid detection, this killer leaves a mess. Satiating the fantasy and rage is all that matters. James

Patterson employed this type in his thriller novels, featuring characters such as Casanova and the Gentleman Caller in *Kiss the Girls*. David Dickson, the shoe-fetishist, was a power-reassurance personality who thought himself irresistible to women. When his fantasy was shattered by Deborah Wilson's resistance to his charms, he murdered the Drexel student.

It was early evening, and Walter was sipping a glass of wine; Stoud's thick hand held a can of beer.

For half an hour repartee and ragged laughter had penetrated a blue haze of smoke that drifted toward the crown moldings, as *Rigoletto* echoed through the parlor. Now they grew quiet. The tragic figure of Terri Brooks, beaten, strangled, stabbed, and asphyxiated, looked up from the nineteenth-century cherry side table.

"It's an anger killing," Stoud said. "All the violence, the percussion."

"Indeed. This is darker, moving downward on the scale."

It was the third type, the anger-retaliatory or AR killer, the first personality type to begin to take pleasure in the killing beyond the simple satisfaction of power. Stalking the victim from a distance, like predator chasing prey, and covering the victim's face were two important AR signatures. Walter called the AR the O. J. Simpson–type killer.

"Although of course," Walter said that evening, "we know that O. J. is an innocent man." Stoud chuckled.

"This is classic AR, absolutely classic," Walter said, "followed by a clumsy attempt, after the murder was done, to stage the crime as a robbery."

The first sign of anger and passion was overkill, he said, as if Brooks had nine lives and the killer tried to extinguish them all. Next was the killer's choice of intimate, close-up weapons—a knife, a lead pipe, and as an asphyxiation device, his bare hands. "If you and I have a dispute over my salary, and I decide to kill you, I'll run and get my gun—it's a power dispute; the killing can be clean and more emotionally remote," Walter said. "But if it's an affair of the heart, a betrayal, the murderer needs percussion, the cutting, stabbing, and beating, to achieve gratification."

The AR killer's pièce de résistance is to conceal the victim's eyes. The killer of Terri Brooks did it with a plastic bag.

"In hundreds of cases I've looked at, an anger-retaliatory type will never allow the victim to view egress," Walter said. "It's a final expression of rage. A romantic relationship gone wrong is by far the most likely probability here. It's the most logical because the overwhelming feature of the crime is the specialized—if you please, identifiable passion—and when you generally have passion, you have to have a reason for that passion, and sex is probably the most common one."

Walter quickly developed a profile of the killer. "He's an underachiever, but not without charm she finds quite appealing. She's a nice strong woman, all the things he likes. He likes that tension back and forth, she allows him to be the immature little boy who never has to grow up. When she tires of his limits, in truth he's a user and a loser, she thinks she's ending her problem by getting rid of him, telling him to go peddle his papers, but now she inadvertently has signed her own death warrant because she's no longer going to be there for him to use."

He took a sip of wine. "Remember, with the AR the relationship isn't over until they say it's over. He's quite pathological about it. Whether she wants to break it off or not, she doesn't realize the fact of the matter is, he's going to continue. He's a parasite to her and has been all along, it just takes a more urgent, darker form. The coup de grace was 'I don't want you.' When she cuts him off, he can't stand it; that's the justification. He feels righteously indignant. She has done him harm, therefore he has a right to kill her, therefore he hasn't any guilt."

The killer, Walter predicted, would be a low achiever in his late thirties, unkempt, stuck in the old neighborhood, working at a menial job, living with his mother. Walter's profile explained why Terri Brooks let her killer in a locked door after 1:30 in the morning.

"She knew and trusted him," Walter said. "It was her boyfriend."

The fourth type of killer he was not prepared to discuss. "It's the most complex and diabolical, the most difficult type of killer to catch, the greatest of human nightmares. It's the black hole at the end of the continuum."

CHAPTER 46

IN THE WORLD WHICH
WILL BE RENEWED

Riding through the stone gate of Ivy Hill Cemetery in Philadelphia in his black sedan, Fleisher was happy the boy was moving up in the world. Around him were the immense tombs and obelisks of the great and notable: Charles Duryea, who invented the gasoline engine; gospel singer Marion Williams; Roaring Twenties tennis star Bill Tilden. The mausoleums of the wealthy towered over the simple stones and crosses of the masses. Through the good offices of undertaker Craig Mann, whose father buried the boy the first time, Fleisher and the Vidocq Society had secured from the Ivy Hill cemetery prime real estate near the gate for the boy, a place among the favored dead.

He should be here in hallowed ground, Fleisher thought, *with other children.*

It was November 11, 1998, Veterans Day. The morning sky was dark and brooding. It had rained all night on the hills of the nineteenth-century graveyard, darkening the stones and cenotaphs. The old detectives in dark coats and fedoras gathered around the fresh hole in the ground. Among them were Weinstein, Kelly, and McGillen; the young policemen of the winter of 1957 were disguised now as old men. A large black headstone, carved with a lamb symbolizing innocence, stood on the prominent new gravesite. The new burial plot and stone were donated, and the Vidocq Society paid for the reburial at Ivy Hill.

The small casket was a pearly white with a beveled lid. Weinstein, who carried the body to the police car long ago, now joined Fleisher in bearing the coffin from the hearse to the grave. A bagpipe wailed "Going Home," the old Negro spiritual:

> Goin' home, goin' home, I'm a goin' home . . .
> It's not far, jes' close by,
> Through an open door . . .
> Mother's there spectin' me,
> Father's waitin' too;
> Lots o' folks gather'd there,
> All the friends I knew.

Fleisher placed the casket on the hydraulic platform. Now the boy lay as close to the sun as he had been since 1957. His only family was two generations of cops.

The old stone, HEAVENLY FATHER, BLESS THIS UNKNOWN BOY, had been set in the foreground of the new one at Ivy Hill.

Fleisher wept.

The commissioner moved to a makeshift podium and tried to compose himself. More than a hundred people stood around the grave, including District Attorney Abraham and an executive from the National Center for Missing and Exploited Children from Washington, D.C. The media people stood at a distance across the road. In the crowd was a fifty-one-year-old woman nobody knew. She held a bouquet of blue carnations from the children who rode the schoolbus she drove. "I was ten when it happened, and I never forgot him," said Rita O'Vary. "The poor little guy. Somebody has to know who he is."

The old cops sat in folding chairs before the coffin. The clouds broke. Sun bathed the grove of rhododendrons and oak, and the cops said it was a good omen.

Fleisher reminded himself of the reasons to be hopeful. The

reburial was only part of their effort, only the beginning. Hundreds of new leads had poured in since *America's Most Wanted* aired the special show on the Boy in the Box. Host John Walsh had revealed Bender's speculative bust of what the boy's father might look like.

Eight days earlier, the Vidocq Society's lawyers obtained a court order to allow exhumation of the boy from his grave in Potter's Field near Mechanicsville and Dunks Ferry roads in northeast Philadelphia, and to move him ten miles to the historic Ivy Hill Cemetery. A backhoe had lumbered up to the grave in Potter's Field, and, after the stone was removed, opened the grave deep enough for the diggers with shovels, who scraped down to the lid of the coffin, then worked wide straps under the coffin. The backhoe lifted the boy's coffin out of the earth for the first time in forty-one years. The diggers cleared dirt from the coffin, and carried it into the back of a waiting ambulance. The FBI's evidence recovery team had done its work.

A woman from the neighborhood, in her fifties, had walked sadly away. She had come to watch, to let the boy know "we didn't forget." She was ten when the boy was found, and prayed for him her whole life. Like a lot of neighbors, she left flowers and toys. She thought of the boy as her little brother.

The ambulance drove to the morgue. The coffin was set on a worktable in the medical examiner's office. As Kelly watched the lid being pried off, he thought, *Rem Bristow should be here*. Kelly crossed himself when he saw, remarkably, the boy after forty years had not been reduced to dust. Such preservation was seen by ancient Christians as a sign of the Almighty. The boy was a small pile of bones within the rags of the suit a detective's son had long ago donated. A technician worked through the pile of dust and bones and found a tooth. It would be tested for DNA. With the boy's DNA soon in hand, if a suspect or family member emerged, they could learn, at last, the boy's name—and the name of his killer.

The new black stone said, AMERICA'S UNKNOWN CHILD.

Fleisher said the boy was "a symbol of our nation's abused children, missing children, and murdered children. We are validating this little boy's life. Our mission is to go forward from this day and put a name on that tombstone." A priest, a pastor, and a rabbi commended the boy's soul to God. Weinstein, seventy-two years old, stood and described finding the boy's body on February 25, 1957.

"I saw all his pain and his suffering and his anguish," he said. "It was as though he was speaking to me: 'What happened? Why?' And that was an answer I couldn't give." In a faltering voice, Weinstein said the Kaddish, the Jewish mourning prayer—"in the world which will be renewed . . . He will give life to the dead . . . and raise them to eternal life."

As the hydraulic groaned and the little coffin disappeared into the ground, Weinstein snapped to attention and gave the boy a military salute. Then he hugged a police sergeant, and then gripped Fleisher as if he would fall.

Kelly's prayer was simple: *Dear God, what more can I do? Tell me and I will do it.*

As the sun illuminated the little grove of fresh earth, Weinstein sat in a folding chair with his head in his hands, sobbing uncontrollably.

"C'mon, Sam," Fleisher whispered as they held on to each other. "We'll solve it."

Fleisher had told the stonecutter to leave room on the serpentine black surface for a name.

CHAPTER 47

"CONGRATULATIONS, YOU'VE FOUND YOUR KILLER"

As if the murder of Terri Brooks had happened only yester-day, Detective Sergeant Cloud started the case at the beginning, visiting her father and stepmother at their home in Warminster. George and Betty Brooks easily accepted the idea that the case was now newly open; for them it had never closed. The couple had been interviewed by the Falls Township police fourteen years ear-lier, but were pleased Sergeant Cloud wanted to talk to them.

Sergeant Cloud explained that he was new to the case and starting over. He had hundreds of pieces of old evidence, a thick case file, Walter's profile, and not much else.

George and Betty said they remained determined to find their daughter's killer.

"Hopefully, that son-of-a-gun is still out there walking around and something happens that will bring him out of his hole," Betty had recently told the *Trentonian* newspaper, when the reporter called to see what she thought of the Vidocq Society's involvement. The newspaper headline had read ROY'S RIDDLE: CAN GROUP CRACK CASE?

Betty reiterated her conviction that Terri had been killed by her boyfriend. "I thought it was the boyfriend all along."

Her husband, George, quickly disagreed. "They were engaged," he said, shaking his head. He just couldn't see it. But Betty said she'd had a funny feeling when the boyfriend showed up at their house to give them the terrible news that Terri had been murdered. He expressed his grief, but something was not right. They'd seen him only one more time in the ensuing fourteen years, and that incident still bothered her, too. Two weeks after Terri was buried, they ran into him on the street. "He made a point of letting us know he had a date," Betty said.

Sergeant Cloud held up his hand to clarify the point. He'd committed the case file to memory, all two hundred interviews, and the Brookses weren't making sense. The police had eliminated Terri's boyfriend as a suspect almost immediately fourteen years ago. Unable to pin it on him or any of Terri's coworkers, they quickly saw the crime as a robbery gone wrong.

"The boyfriend had an airtight alibi," Cloud said. "He was in California at the time."

Betty's eyebrows shot up. "Oh, no!" she exclaimed. "Not *that* boyfriend! There was another guy." Terri had already broken up with the guy who went to California. There was a new one."

"What was his name?" Cloud asked.

She shook her head. She couldn't remember. She'd barely gotten to know him during the eight months he was engaged to her daughter. "He was not the type that would come over to the house," she said. But a few minutes later, a surname came to her. "O'Keefe, I think." She couldn't recall a first name.

Thanking the couple for their time, Sergeant Cloud drove back to the Falls Township Police Department and asked around about O'Keefe. He got blank stares. He ran the name through the computer and came up empty. Frustrated, he called his friend Ed Gaughan, the private eye, at the Philadelphia brownstone head-quarters of the Vidocq Society, and asked him about "O'Keefe."

Gaughan had never heard the name, but he and Fleisher both searched for "O'Keefe" in their computers, using proprietary data-bases designed for lawyers, private eyes, and bail bondsmen to find anyone with an arrest record. Both men struck out on "O'Keefe."

Gaughan called Sergeant Cloud back. "Are you sure of the spelling?"

No, Cloud wasn't sure.

"Was he at the funeral?" Gaughan asked. "Check the guest book."

Sergeant Cloud had the large, leather-bound book right on his desk. He ran his fingers down the ruled pages where the mourners had signed in at Terri Brooks's funeral. There was no O'Keefe. But there was a different name: *Keefe*.

Alfred Scott Keefe. "Son of a gun," Cloud said.

Finding nothing on the police department computer, he called back Gaughan at the Vidocq Society. Gaughan and Fleisher ran the name "Alfred Scott Keefe" of Warminster, Pennsylvania, the town where Terri Brooks was living when she was killed.

"Alfred Scott Keefe" in Warminster was a hit. He was in his thirties, with a clean record except for a minor offense, driving under the influence.

Reading back through the case file, he found Keefe's name. The police had interviewed Terri's friends about Keefe fourteen years ago, and uncovered a story that made them suspicious. Terri Brooks and Alfred Scott Keefe were engaged to marry that summer. Two days before her death, Brooks and Keefe made a deposit on a honeymoon trip to Hawaii. Brooks was planning to buy a wedding dress in a few days. Yet even as they went through the motions, their relationship was tense, her friends said. Brooks was getting cold feet. Keefe was angry at her for leaving a better-paying job to seek advancement with the Marriott Corporation. He was obsessed with the fear that she was seeing someone else, and was threatening to break off their engagement. To the police at the time, a spurned lover had a passable motive, but they had no evidence implicating Keefe.

Sergeant Cloud learned that Keefe had stayed in the area. He had married and had a child, and was separated from his wife. He had a menial job in a local pizza parlor, and had moved back into the same family home he occupied while dating Brooks. Keefe was living with his mother.

Sergeant Cloud spoke with Walter about his profile. An intriguing detail jumped out at Walter from the old police file. An hour before the murder, Alfred Scott Keefe's pickup truck had been seen in a parking lot next to Roy Rogers. Unique among the personality subtypes, the anger-retaliatory killer stalked his prey. "From a distance, the AR builds and reaffirms his rage," Walter said. "When he begins to close the distance, the commitment to kill has been made."

"Congratulations," Walter told Cloud. "You've found your killer."

In September 1998, Sergeant Cloud noted a significant fact in Keefe's DUI, his only offense on record. When Keefe was stopped while driving under the influence, on the front seat of the car was a pack of cigarettes.

Keefe was a smoker; Newport Filters.

Thanks to the forensic savvy of VSM and medical examiner Hal Fillinger, who had performed the autopsy on Brooks fifteen years earlier, the police had DNA samples of the killer. Fillinger had carefully saved the hairs on Brooks's clothing, and the skin lodged under her fingernails during her desperate fight for life, having no way of knowing how useful the genetic material could be fifteen years later. The material contained the DNA of a male human, but was it the genetic material of Alfred Scott Keefe?

Early one morning in October, Keefe walked out of his mother's house in the one hundred block of Horseshoe Lane in Warminster Township—the historic burg where William Penn signed his treaty with the Indians—left a bag of garbage on the sidewalk, and returned inside. He was unaware that Warminster had been alerted not to pick up his trash that morning. Falls Township, twenty miles away on the Delaware River, would be providing the service.

Officer Nelson Whitney, who had been watching, quietly drove an unmarked car up to the curb on Horseshoe Lane, grabbed the garbage bag, and drove away. Back at the station, he and Sergeant Cloud were pleased to find a treasure in Keefe's trash.

It was a cigarette butt. A Newport Filter.

They sent it to the lab to test for the presence of DNA in dried saliva.

Walter chuckled when he heard. "Maybe cigarettes are bad for your health after all."

CHAPTER 48

INTERROGATION

Alfred Scott Keefe, a skinny man with nervous dark eyes, was sitting in a windowless interrogation room the size of a storage closet. The cops had taken him from the pizza parlor and he smelled faintly of mozzarella cheese, cigarettes, and body odor. He was seated in a hard wooden chair, with his back literally against the wall. Two pneumograph tubes crossed his chest. A cardio cuff clamped his arm. Galvanic skin electroplates pinched his fingers. The large shadows of Vidocq Society Members Bill Fleisher and Nate Gordon, sumo wrestlers in suits and two of the best polygraph examiners and interrogators in the world, were very close.

Keefe had volunteered to come in from his job making pizzas that afternoon to answer questions to clear himself. He'd agreed to take the lie-detection test. But now his whole body was vibrating as if the scientific instruments were medieval irons holding him fast, and the cool, mechanically repeated questions the incessant falling of a whip.

Gordon asked him if he had killed his fiancée, Terri Lee Brooks.

Gordon could make a man who had something to hide very nervous. Sitting directly in front of the wan Keefe, Gordon was a hulking man, bald with a white fringe of beard, a disarmingly high, quick voice, and hyperalert blue eyes. He had the bulk of an offensive lineman, a black belt in karate, a master's degree in criminology, was credited with numerous innovations in lie detection, and published in scholarly journals like *Radiology* articles such as "Brain Mapping of Deception and Truth Telling About an Ecologically Valid Situation: An MRI and Polygraph Investigation." He began his forensic lectures by shredding conventional assumptions with razor logic; he ended them by splitting a brick in half with his head.

Fleisher could play "good guy" to Gordon's "bad guy" if necessary. Fleisher could play it any way you wanted. With the FBI and Customs, Fleisher had literally written the federal book on detecting lies in the human face. Seated on Keefe's right, the Vidocq commissioner was dapper in his brown suit and neat gray Old Testament beard, leaning forward into the green glowing monitor of a computer, where the polygraph test whirred and dipped its digital judgments.

Were you engaged to Terri Lee Brooks? Did you cause the death of Terri Brooks? Do you know who killed Terri Brooks? Did you use a knife to kill Terri Lee Brooks? Where were you when Terri Brooks was killed? Gordon pounded the same question from a dozen different angles; Keefe volleyed back with terse, controlled denials. But the rest of his body was telling a different story.

For a guy who claimed to have done nothing wrong in his life but skimp on the pepperoni, his sympathetic nervous system was going haywire. His head shook like a bobble-head doll's. His hands were sweating like he was on a bad first date. Nothing was clipped to his eyebrows, which exploited their freedom by twitching.

Fleisher stared at the computer screen and quietly shook his head, a small, controlled motion of amazement. Keefe's physiological responses were charted immediately as waves moving across the green-glowing monitor, rising and falling like a miniature emerald sea. *Deception all over the lot,* he thought. In his decades conducting and teaching the polygraph in New York, London, Rome, Dubai, Keefe was a record breaker. His blood pressure was spiking. His breathing was slowing. His sweat gland activity was not what you'd expect of a bereaved fiancé. Homicide generates stronger emotions than any other crime, and Gordon and Fleisher were expecting big reactions. But this was something else—these were the biggest reactions they'd ever seen.

Keefe's nervous system was stirring up a perfect storm on the monitor. Whoever was watching behind the one-way observation glass was getting a show.

It was February 4, 1999, the fifteenth anniversary of Terri Brooks's murder. Richard Walter had read the tea leaves at the murder scene and predicted that Brooks's killer would be a man in his late thirties with an unkempt appearance who held a menial job and lived with his mother. Alfred Scott Keefe, pizza maker, age thirty-eight, lived with his mother.

In the hallway had gathered the combined powers of Bucks County law enforcement, waiting to pop the champagne on the biggest cold case in county history. The group included District Attorney Alan Rubenstein, a man with ambitions to be a judge, eager to crack what he called one of the "most brutal, heinous, and malicious homicides" he had ever encountered. There was Police Chief Arnold Conoline, the reformer hired to clean up a troubled department. One of his first moves had been to assign his detective sergeant, Wynne Cloud, to reopen the cold case. There was Cloud's ambitious young patrolman, Nelson Whitney II, working his first murder case, who scored the coup of quietly convincing the pizza maker to voluntarily come in for questioning from his job at the pizza parlor in Horsham, some twenty miles away. There was the deputy DA who had worked long hours on the case with Sergeant Cloud and Officer Whitney. VSM Ed Gaughan, the private eye and former Philadelphia homicide investigator, was on hand, eager to help crack the case he had brought to the Vidocq Society. The police had also invited VSMs Fleisher and Gordon with their polygraph equipment to assist in the interrogation if necessary. Though often challenged about its usefulness, the polygraph, in the hands of experienced examiners like Gordon and Fleisher, had been shown to be accurate in measuring truth versus deception better than 95 percent of the time. Few doubted its value as a tool to help pry loose a confession, or the fact that the Vidocq men were two of the most accomplished polygraph interrogators in the world. The men and women in the hallway behind the glass were confident he had done it, as confident as cops could be with DNA evidence in hand.

The DNA evidence was indeed damning. The trash that Whitney collected from Keefe's curbside had yielded a treasure: the Newport Filter cigarette butt was Keefe's brand. Testing of the dried saliva on the cigarette revealed male caucasian DNA—the same DNA found in the hair on Terri Brooks's clothes, in the blood on the knife protruding from her throat, and in the bits of skin from under her fingernails that she had clawed off her attacker.

But was it the DNA of the other male caucasian living in the house, Keefe's brother, Charles Keefe? Whitney tailed Charles Keefe to a restaurant, watched him smoke a cigarette, and retrieved the butt from the ashtray after Charles left the restaurant. Lab testing showed that Charles Keefe's DNA did not match the DNA found on Terri Brooks.

It was technically possible that there was some other male caucasian DNA in the universe matching Alfred Keefe's, and he was the wrong guy. But the odds were long—one in five quadrillion. If Keefe was going to find someone else to take the fall, a thousand new planets with five billion human beings on each would have to be discovered quickly.

Alfred Keefe was the killer.

All they needed now, after fifteen years, was a confession.

Whitney and another officer had started the interrogation shortly after 6 P.M., when Whitney brought Keefe in from the pizza parlor. As hours passed without a confession, Gordon and Fleisher had paced the hallway like caged beasts. Gordon lobbied the chief hard to let him and Fleisher go in with the polygraph. Keefe had had fifteen years to get his story together, and he had it down. He'd kept the interrogators at bay for hours with a cigarette and a sneer. Gordon and Fleisher believed the cops had not properly focused the interrogation, and squandered away the hours out of inexperience.

In Gordon's view, the young officers had let Keefe get too comfortable by taking an extraordinarily detailed statement from him—where he was born, his mother's name, and so forth. Keefe never felt pressured; interruptions didn't help. A technician came in, swabbed Keefe's cheek for additional DNA material, and left. Keefe was made to feel important, the center of attention, in control—not like the hunted man he was and needed to feel like to break.

Then the police began to run out of time. If the police didn't bring Keefe before a magistrate on charges within six hours, they'd have to let him go. But letting Keefe go, now that they'd showed him their hand, was unthinkable. He'd have time to think up a better story, time to go twirl pizzas in Patagonia.

In the hallway, Gordon was about to explode. The police interrogators weren't even detectives, Gordon thought. Patrolmen handed out traffic tickets, they didn't bust down killers. *What are you going to war with cavalry for when you got the fighter jets on the runway itching to attack?* he wondered. Finally the chief nodded to the Vidocq examiners to give it a try. Whitney left the interrogation room, and Gordon and Fleisher went in.

They'd been hammering away at Keefe now for more than an hour, watching the green digital sea whip into a frenzy, and Keefe was weakening. Fleisher looked over at Gordon and knew he was thinking the same thing: *The guy's bombing the test as bad as anyone,* and his guard was down.

Fleisher stared hard at Keefe. It was time to go in for the kill. "You blew it," he said. "Your charts are some of the clearest ever. And they got the DNA. You're doomed."

Confronted by Fleisher with the overpowering evidence, Keefe seemed to lose the last of his composure. He was off balance, ready to drop. *We could get a confession in two minutes,* Fleisher thought.

Fleisher glanced at Gordon, who nodded his assent. Despite their drive to nail Keefe, their honor as VSMs was more important: Their role was to provide advice and counsel, "not steal anyone's thunder." Both men abruptly stood, told Keefe to stay seated, and left the room to find the cops.

Chief Conoline agreed his men would take it from there, finish what they started. He told Whitney and his partner to go back in. Fleisher asked what they thought of Keefe's violent shaking when they watched through the observation window. The cops shrugged. They didn't think anything. Nobody had been watching at the observation window.

Minutes later, the police adopted a new strategy. Whitney and his partner were joined by a uniformed officer said to know Keefe personally, and the three cops marched Keefe out of the small interrogation room and into a large, comfortable conference room and shut the door. Gordon and Fleisher exchanged puzzled looks. Twenty minutes later, with no confession emerging from the new room, Gordon couldn't stand it any longer. He walked up to Chief Conoline and said, "I'm going in." The chief nodded OK.

As Gordon opened the door, he saw the problem right away. Four faces around a long conference table turned to the huge bald man with the intense blue eyes. *The room set-up is horrible,* he thought.

Keefe was sitting nonchalantly at one end of the table, leaning close to the table. He was calmly smoking a cigarette, with an ashtray in front of him. *He's too comfortable,* Gordon thought. *He looks like he's about to have dinner.*

Keefe was using the expanse of table as a barrier to protect himself. "There can be no barriers between you and the suspect," Gordon noted later. "You have to be in his face."

Whitney was seated at Keefe's left, going through a pile of photographs of Brooks's corpse. One by one the officer showed Keefe the gruesome photographs of the bloodbath, as if their horror held great power. He told Keefe the police thought he was involved. Keefe was calmly shaking his head no. The uniformed cop who knew Keefe was on his right side, sitting up on the table nodding. "We think you were involved."

The third cop sat opposite the suspect far across the long table, nodding his agreement, too.

Keefe drew on his cigarette, tipped it into the ashtray, and said coolly, "No, you got the wrong guy." His eyes went from man to man.

Gordon knew that Keefe couldn't be "induced by guilt and remorse into a confession." Walter had advised the Vidocq agents and police not to even attempt it. With an anger-retaliatory or AR, "all attempts to create remorse will fail spectacularly, just empowering the suspect ARs who aren't capable of guilt," Walter said. "They're not like you and me."

Walter gave the example of a classic AR case he had worked of a lovers'-lane killer in upstate New York. The murderer viciously attacked a young couple, raped the woman while the boyfriend watched, then pumped twenty-five bullets into both of them. Arrested within an hour of the slaughter, the killer was sitting in the back of the police car en route to the police station, drenched in his victims' blood, when he fell asleep. He was tired. "Anyone can understand it," Walter said sarcastically. "He'd been very busy. It was a long day. Typical AR—absolutely no guilt."

"You can't show them photos of the killing and expect to weaken them into tender remorse," Walter said. "These guys are euphoric half an hour to an hour after the killing! It's a big relief, and that hardens into a certainty that 'the bitch deserved it'! A guilt or shame-driven attack backfires. Lacking any such feeling he grows cooler and more powerful, more sure of his web of lies."

Walter thought police were "always too hyped up about getting a confession. I'd rather establish fifteen different points of inconsistency in a perp's story, fifteen lies, than one confession that can be overturned." Yet with an AR killer, "the trick to a confession is to attack their weakness, get them off guard, then incite rage—reproduce the out-of-control anger that led them to commit murder in the first place."

Gordon asked the cops to leave the room, then went to work. He walked swiftly to Keefe at the end of the table, grabbed a chair with one hand and plunked it down on the suspect's right side, invading his space. Keefe turned to face Gordon. The large bald head leaned in, inches way. Gordon's blue eyes looked fierce, and he talked fast.

"I just gave you the polygraph test, and you can tell them anything you want, but you and I both know you did it," he said. He let that sink in a moment. "I just have one question. Did you kill her for drug money, or was it a lovers' spat and she came at you with a knife and you defended yourself? The clock is running and you don't have any more time."

Keefe said, "Neither."

Gordon's eyes flared. "Listen, don't insult my intelligence."

"Neither."

Gordon scowled. "OK, if you're telling me it's neither, I know you're lying. Therefore I have to assume it's the worst-case scenario: You killed her for the drug money. There's no reason to talk to you anymore."

Gordon propelled his bulk from the chair, stood up, and walked out, shutting the door behind him.

As Gordon emerged, the chief sent Whitney and his partner back in. The young cops were itching to close the case they had worked so hard on. Meanwhile, Gordon conferred with Fleisher. It was time, the two Vidocqeans agreed, to use the technique Fleisher called "The Everything Must Go Sale." Getting a confession was the ultimate sales job, Fleisher said.

"You're convincing a guy that it's better to confess and go to jail for twenty years than to say nothing and walk free," he said. "It's the all-time sale. You're convincing him he needs the very last widget the company has made, when in fact there are seven million more gathering dust on the shelves. Time is everything. You gotta act now; the clock is ticking."

He and Gordon discussed possible approaches. "We have DNA evidence," Fleisher suggested, "and if you don't tell us what really happened by midnight, we're going to have to go with it. We're going to have to nail you."

Gordon looked at his watch. They had less than a half hour to go. Whitney and his partner were still in the interrogation room with Keefe, getting nowhere. Gordon grabbed the biggest guy in uniform he could find, a sergeant, and pulled him aside. "I want you to go into the room and say, 'Mr. Gordon came out, he says you did it, we don't want to talk to you anymore,' and walk out." The sergeant went in, made his announcement, and came out.

Less than a minute later, patrolman Whitney came out of the interrogation room, grinning widely. He'd gotten the confession. "Keefe confessed. It was a lovers' spat. He says he was trying to defend himself." The suits and uniforms congratulated him as cheers filled the hallway.

Gordon quietly pulled the young officer aside. "I want you to go back in and take his cigarettes from him, turn your chair so you're parallel at the table, right across from him, and tell him, 'Bullshit. There's no way a woman gets stabbed twenty times, suffocated, and beaten; it's not gonna work as self-defense.'"

Whitney returned to the room and three or four minutes later emerged with a report. "As soon as I turned the chair and sat across from him, his head went down, his body gave in, and he admitted he killed her for money to buy drugs."

Gordon nodded. "Good work. Now I want you to go back in and take a statement, name, birth, graduated, such and such—start from the beginning and then everything he did that night. I want it written down he's confessing of his own free will, no threats or promises of anything. Ask him, why did he confess? In court it'll be attacked—why would a person voluntarily give a confession against his own interests? So we need him to write down what his interests are—why did he confess?"

Whitney went back in. Minutes passed, the door stayed shut. The group in the hall fidgeted nervously.

Half an hour later he came out waving a handwritten confession and cheers went up in the hallway, louder now. The DA and deputy DA, the chief, Sergeant Cloud and his officers, and Gordon, Fleisher, and Gaughan were shaking hands, slapping backs, high fives all around. The Vidocq men felt excited to be part of the team. Rivalries and criticisms melted away instantly with success; they were all human, it was a natural part of the process. The VSMs said the cops had done a great job.

The charge would be first-degree murder, the DA said with an air of triumph. The deputy DA grinned as she studied the written confession.

"Didn't these cops do a great job?" she said.

Later that morning, the DA held a press conference to announce an arrest in the county's longest-running cold case. Surrounded by beaming cops, Rubenstein praised the police chief and his officers and their "dogged" and "high-tech" work. "These things don't happen by accident," he said. "It takes good police work. You can't imagine the man- and woman-hours put into this." Headlines in all the regional papers sung their praises. Betty Brooks said she was shocked but "relieved" and applauded the wonderful police work. *The New York Times* saw the arrest as nationally significant because of the use of a daring new technology; as the *Philadelphia Inquirer* wrote, "What really cracked the case were the DNA tests the police had done." Chief Conoline noted that coroner Halbert E. Fillinger Jr. was "a great pathologist" for having flawlessly saved the skin and hair samples that provided the DNA evidence. A week later, the Families of Unsolved Murders Victims, a local support group, honored Detective Sergeant Cloud, Officer Whitney, and Deputy District Attorney Lori Markle for their outstanding achievement. Rubenstein said he would seek the death penalty.

Nowhere was the Vidocq Society mentioned.

Sixteen months later, on June 5, 2000, Bucks County judge John J. Rufe sentenced Keefe to life in prison without parole for the murder of Terri Brooks. Keefe had pled guilty on the advice of his attorney, who said the evidence against him was so "overwhelming" the most they could hope for was to avoid the death penalty. Keefe refused to address Brooks's parents directly, who said they were not surprised, and were satisfied with the outcome. In a related civil case, the Marriott Corporation, owners of Roy

Rogers, paid Brooks's sister, the administrator of her estate, $675,000 in a wrongful death settlement; $276,322 of the settlement went to the attorneys.

Nowhere were VSMs mentioned.

Fleisher admitted his disappointment in a *Vidocq Society Journal* column, headlined, WE KNOW WHAT WE DO . . . AND DID.

He praised the Falls Township Police Department, and especially Sergeant Cloud, now a Vidocq Society Member, for its "great work." Yet, "It still hurts me that members who selflessly volunteer their time and expertise are not always publicly appreciated," he wrote. "Whoever said, 'Success has a thousand parents and failure is an orphan,' knew of what he was speaking."

Fleisher said the case was a reminder to VSMs to "stop and remember what we are really about in the Vidocq Society and who is our ultimate client. The client was, is, and will always be the truth. And our client is an unforgiving one."

He signed the column:

Bill Fleisher, VSM, Commissioner.

Veritas Veritatum ("Truth begets Truth").

CHAPTER 49

THE HAUNTING OF MARY

In the darkness before dawn in her Ohio home, Mary turned in the coils of a nightmare. When she opened her eyes she was sweating. She got up and went into the kitchen, but the nightmare followed her. Even in waking hours now, she couldn't escape it. She tried to calm herself, apply reason to the problem. She was in her fifties, a scientist, a Ph.D. chemist with a logical, orderly mind that had fueled an impressive executive career at one of America's largest pharmaceutical companies. "I was always good in the sciences," she said. "You can trust science. It yields up its secrets, if one keeps looking. Science can play tricks, but it doesn't lie." But this problem didn't respond to logic; it was at the farthest end of the spectrum from reason. She lived alone. It was terrifying. The horror had trailed her her whole life, but she'd managed to repress it. Now this demon of memory was demanding notice. The ghostly hollow eyes stared back, wherever she looked.

Before sunup, she picked up the phone and called her psychiatrist.

Early that morning of February 25, 2000, the psychiatrist called from his Cincinnati office to the Philadelphia Police Department and asked for homicide. He had a murder to report. Or rather, his patient, who had been wrestling with the memory in therapy for many years, had a murder to report, forty-three years after the fact. Her brother had been killed on February 25, 1957, by her mother. She had witnessed it, been an accomplice to it. She needed to unburden her soul.

The officer took the information. The report was filed with the hundreds of other leads that had come in, especially after the *America's Most Wanted* episode.

Kelly and McGillen were struck by the dates, surely more than coincidence. Mary called in her confession on the anniversary of the murder of the Boy in the Box. It was exactly forty-three years after the boy was killed. The memory of her brother was haunting her, she said. She wanted to talk to the police. Sergeant Augustine, and VSMs Kelly and Joe McGillen called the psychiatrist to see if the woman would come to Philadelphia. No. Perhaps the cops could travel to Cincinnati. No. Suddenly, the woman panicked. She said she couldn't talk about it. Not yet.

Kelly and McGillen kept in touch with the psychiatrist. They wrote on Vidocq Society stationery. They called. Not yet, the psychiatrist said. He refused to press his patient. She had to volunteer it, he said. She had to heal. It was a tremendous leap of faith to decide to go public. Suddenly the psychiatrist cut off all communication with the Vidocq Society; his patient was regressing. Kelly and McGillen were polite, understanding. Fleisher was stunned by their persistence, "classic shoe-leather stuff, great old-fashioned detective work." But like the previous half century of efforts on the case, nothing had come of it.

Mary needed more time, years more time, to sort it out.

CHAPTER 50

THE CASE OF THE MISSING FACE

When a weary Frank Bender picked up the phone in his studio and heard the voice of a young New York detective excited about an impossible murder case, he was tempted to say, "The wizard is not in. No miracles will be performed tonight." But Keith Hall, the twenty-five-year-old detective from Manlius, a small town outside of Syracuse, said that after banging his head against the impenetrable cold case for two years he'd just had a revelation. He knew that nobody on earth could solve the murder but Frank Bender of Philadelphia.

"My wife and I knew it as soon as we saw your work on *America's Most Wanted* the other night, a rerun of the John List case," Hall said. "I told Kathy, 'This guy's a genius. I'm going to call him in Philadelphia. He's our last hope.'

"Frank, we need you."

Bender was intrigued. He liked to be told he was an irreplaceable genius as much as the next guy, and he heard in Hall's voice "sincerity, a real good guy, a tremendous passion to solve the case." When Hall explained that his small police department couldn't pay Bender the $1,500 he now asked for his busts, not one cent, that about sealed it. Money was tight and Jan might not be pleased, but pro bono work appealed strongly to Bender's conviction that money shouldn't matter as much as art or justice.

"Tell me about the case, and we'll see."

The scant remains of a skeleton had been found in a shallow grave in woods that ran along a farm outside Manlius, Hall said. At first they thought it was a nineteenth-century farmer or Revolutionary soldier, but the corpse was dated as more recent, perhaps twenty years old. The skull had been smashed, and it was clearly a murder. They were the small bones of a female, possibly a victim of notorious serial killer Arthur Shawcross of Rochester who killed and mutilated eleven Rochester prostitutes from 1988 to 1990. The Genesee River Killer's reign of terror sent frightened Rochester hookers fleeing the ninety miles to Syracuse.

That was about it.

If Bender could reconstruct the skull and police could learn its identity, they might be able to track down the killer, Hall said.

"Can you mail me the skull?" Bender asked. Well, that was the problem, Hall said. He could mail a photograph, but there really wasn't a skull. The skull, such as it was, was a U-shaped collection of bones framing the face. But there was no face—no eye, nose, mouth, or cheekbones. It was a donut skull—mostly hole.

"Send me what you have," Bender said.

As soon as he saw the picture of the donut skull, Bender thought, *I can't do this*. How could he rebuild the surface of a face without bones? Not wanting to give up easily, he consulted with a physical anthropologist at the Smithsonian in Washington, D.C., for another opinion, then another expert at the National Center for Missing and Exploited Children. All agreed: It's impossible. Nobody can do it. Don't even try. If you try, the implication was, it'll be perceived as an act of stupidity or hubris; it'll make a mockery of the profession of forensic reconstruction. "It's impossible," Bender told Hall. But the young detective wouldn't hear of it. "Frank, I know you can do it."

"OK, you win," Bender said. "I'll do it, but I'll only ask for money if you make identification." Hall enthusiastically agreed.

On October 19, 2000, Detective Hall, a burly, fair-haired twenty-five-year-old, stood before the Vidocq Society luncheon at the Downtown Club. Up flashed a PowerPoint image of the Skull with the Missing Face on the screen. Bender beamed at Hall, a bright, outgoing, no-nonsense cop he liked even more in person.

Walter fairly gasped.

"Frank, what the hell are you thinking?" he hissed to his partner one seat away. "Or are you relying on your sixth sense instead of your brain on this one?"

Bender, sitting quietly with a loopy smile, ignored him. The artist loved a challenge, and this was shaping up as maybe his biggest ever. As he studied the photo, he could feel the sensation like an electric charge searching for ground—the nameless dead calling him. He lived for that feeling.

"I figure it's better to try something, Rich," he said, "than to try nothing at all."

"Frank, be honest. Are we playing God again?"

Bender grinned. "Rich, I forgot to tell you. Manlius asked for help from the FBI, and the bureau refused. They said there wasn't enough material to do a profile. They said it was impossible."

"Hmmm." Walter arched his left eyebrow, and his eyes shone with a fierce light. He looked up at the photo and down at the police report. In addition to the face, the left arm and hand, left pelvic bones, left leg and foot were all missing. He himself had seldom seen a case with less to go on. Perhaps it would be interesting, he thought, to profile a murderer based on tiny fragments of bone found in a grave many years after the crime, and nothing else. Perhaps it would be fun.

"This was an ideal place to hide a body," Hall said. The corpse was found buried in a shallow grave in an isolated patch of woods alongside an abandoned farm outside Manlius. Manlius, the wealthiest burg in Onondaga County, is a bedroom community of Syracuse with 31,000 people spread over a wide and picturesque rural area of hills, pastures, woods, and lakes. Named for Marcus Manlius Capitolinus, the consul of Rome in 390 BC, the prosperous town is comprised of three small villages, one of which, Fayetteville, has a proud history as the boyhood home of President

Grover Cleveland, as well as the first magazine publisher of *Uncle Tom's Cabin*, and the noted suffragist Matilda Joslyn Gage (whose son-in-law L. Frank Baum, author of *The Wonderful Wizard of Oz*, is said to have used her as the model for the Wicked Witch of the West).

Thus the town's first murder in a quarter century was shocking, unseemly, not what one expected of the good people of Manlius. It was not committed by or against one of them, they hastened to add, or even within the village limits. It was done by outsiders, "out there."

The grave was hidden in the woods some four and a half miles east of Fayetteville and an equal distance from either of the other two villages in an unincorporated area—a barren spot locals know as "the middle of nowhere." The nearest road was impassable in the snow and ice of winter, and in the summer a visitor had to walk through a cornfield to reach the woods. It was there that the ex-con Robert Updegrove, a transient, as locals were quick to mention, was hunting deer without a license on the morning of Saturday, November 29, 1997.

By midday, he was sitting on a log having a smoke, rifle on his knee, when he saw something small and white lying in the brush and leaves. He thought it was a cigarette, he later reported to police. But when he reached down to pick it up, it was hard; a bone, a fragment of a human skull. Updegrove had disturbed the grave.

Hall ordered the remains guarded overnight. After determining the grave was "nonhistorical," they began excavation the next morning, Sunday, November 30, in a murder investigation. The Manlius detective regarded Updegrove as an immediate suspect. To cover the fact that he was hunting illegally, the convicted felon concocted a story that he was looking for his lost dog, not for deer. Updegrove denied involvement in the murder, but Hall wasn't convinced. Updegrove rented a cottage on one of the abandoned farms, so close that Hall could almost see it from the grave site. Had Updegrove just discovered the bone fragment? Or had he put it there many years earlier and returned to memorialize the murder, enjoy his trophy, and flaunt it to cops?

Hall and his men dug up the grave with their hands for five days until their fingers were numb with cold, uncovering only a partial skeleton, indicating the work of animals or a depraved human.

The remains were so sparse they were extraordinarily difficult to identify. A Cornell University forensic anthropologist claimed to identify a raccoon bone. Another noted anthropologist said it was a child, before Dr. Anthony Falcetti at the C. A. Pound Human Identification Laboratory in Gainesville, Florida, identified the bones as belonging to a small, slight woman in her midtwenties to early thirties, probably of mixed race, about five foot five, 100 to 110 pounds. The bones indicated she had suffered from poor nutrition as a child. All of it supported Hall's hunch that the young woman was a prostitute—and possibly Shawcross's victim. Hall sent her description to all the national crime databases in the United States and Canada, including the National Center for Missing and Exploited Children. There were no matches. Two dozen police officers swept the area with metal detectors and rakes, examined nearby trees for bullet holes, and collected bird nests for possible hair samples woven in. They came up empty.

Hall was left reading fragments of clothing, a zipper, and a Virginia Slims Menthol 100s cigarette pack found in the grave for the story they might tell.

Hall was disappointed that the blue stamp on the cellophane pack had faded so badly the date sold could not be read, even in a forensics lab. But the manufacturing dates of the clothing—size ten or twelve Gitano jeans, size six Sergio Valente-brand underpants, and a small Cappacino-brand shirt—indicated the young woman was alive on June 15, 1986, and probably dead by April 1988. Those dates coincided with Shawcross's reign of terror. Paroled from prison after serving only fifteen years for the admitted rape and murder of a ten-year-old boy and an eight-year-old girl, Shawcross moved to Rochester and began killing in early 1988. He was arrested in January 1990, when police left his eleventh victim floating in a creek based on a psychological profile that suggested the killer would return to the scene. Shawcross was arrested masturbating as he sat in his car on a bridge over the creek. He confessed in custody, and his eleven victims were all identified. Maybe this was a twelfth?

The detective was deeply frustrated. He hadn't ruled Updegrove out, but he'd been unable to build a case against him or anyone else. He'd interviewed thirty-nine people who lived in the area around the crime scene during the suspected period of the crime and had since moved away. Nearly nine months after the grave was discovered, he led a team of police officers, state troopers with cadaver-detection dogs, and a state wildlife expert to search for other graves and for animal dens that might contain bones or artifacts taken from the grave. Nothing was adding up. He asked for help from the FBI Behavioral Sciences Unit in Quantico, Virginia, but the FBI "felt there was insufficient data for case profiling," Hall said. The Vidocq Society was his last hope.

Following the presentation, after Fleisher had given the Manlius police the ceremonial magnifying glass, "symbolizing the first scientific tool of detection," Walter approached Detective Hall. "The fact of the matter is," he said, "despite what our friends at the bureau say, a profile might be possible in this case. More than one may think is revealed by fragments of bone in a grave."

Killing a prostitute and dumping her body in the woods was a "classically efficient, practical, cold" crime that bore "the marks of a power-assertive killer," he said. Walter said he'd already formed "bits and pieces" of a psychological profile.

Of the dozen suspects the Manlius police had considered, he said, "only Updegrove fits the profile." Walter invited the Manlius officers to visit the Biddle House, his home in Montrose, Pennsylvania, to discuss it further.

"I believe," he added, "that we're looking at a serial killer."

"I don't think Updegrove did it," Bender blurted out from the circle of cops, his face reddening. The artist had been busy researching the crime, his first step of the process of reconstructing the bone fragments into a skull and face. But it was a gut feeling, rather than any particular research that told him Updegrove was innocent.

Walter rolled his eyes. "Frank, I appreciate your thoughts, OK, but you'd best stick to your day job. Don't let your emotions carry you beyond your pay grade." Walter admired his partner's extraordinary forensic art and intuitions, but did not appreciate it when those intuitions crossed onto his turf of psychological profiling of killers.

"Richard, you're good," Bender shot back. "But you're not always right."

"My dear boy, your thinking has no structure, no foundation," came the arch accent. "You pick up your primary ideas from TV shows. You're like a fart in a bathtub."

VSMs on the edge of the conversation tittered. A decade after their most famous case, the capture of mass murderer John List, Bender and Walter had become even more nationally prominent in their fields. They had collaborated successfully on Vidocq Society cases, and seemed closer-than-ever drinking buddies and brothers-in-arms. But their teamwork resembled the work of an anvil and hammer; the more productive they became, the more sparks flew.

Bender had taken to telling anyone who would listen that it was he, not Walter, who had the idea to put thick tortoiseshell eyeglasses on John List's face—a key detail that helped lead to the swift identification and arrest of the killer. Bender claimed Walter was stealing undue credit.

Exasperated, Walter patiently reminded his friend that indeed he had first suggested that List would be wearing thick-rimmed glasses "like mine" to convey power and authority. But he happily acknowledged that Bender had accomplished the crowning work, the "coup de grace," of finding an old pair of tortoiseshell glasses at an antique store that he put on the bust. They worked perfectly.

"So I suggested the concept, and you made it reality, which some might suggest is the harder and more praiseworthy part. I know it's hard to follow, but this is called teamwork, and in such instances, credit is shared."

Fleisher was beaming like a football coach watching his star players beating each other up at practice before a big game. The Case of the Missing Face was one of the most challenging cold cases ever brought before the Vidocq Society, he thought, and they needed this level of passion and commitment to solve it.

It was clear as Bender returned to his South Street warehouse studio in Philadelphia and Walter to his Victorian mansion in the Pennsylvania mountains that the partners would be simultaneously working together and competing, as only they could.

"I think Richard's got a good profile going, and there's nobody like Frank in giving name and face to the dead," Fleisher said. "There's nothing to go on but if anybody can do it it's this group, my friends." He grinned. "The question is: To whom will the bones talk?"

Stripped to the waist in his studio, Bender animated the dead with clay using unknown powers that frightened those who saw him as arrogant, a Dr. Faust making deals with the devil. These people never knew the deep humility that Bender brought to his work. As he began to build up a skull with clay he abandoned all ego, left the moorings of space and time, gave himself utterly to "enter the flow of nature. You start with the eye, nose, and mouth and you keep them all flowing at the same time. Beautiful or ugly, our features were made to harmonize together." Yet the Girl with the Missing Face was beyond humbling; with no nose, mouth, eyes, cheeks, or chin to go on, he called Hall up and repeated his fear: "This is impossible." After parts of three days mulling the gaping hole in the center of the skull, he still didn't know where to begin.

Frustrated, he returned to his high-profile commission sculpture *Unearthed*. He was sculpting two slaves—a man and two women—from their exhumed eighteenth-century skulls to make a memorial for the African Burial Ground in New York City. Working with a slave skull, he noticed the small sphenoid bone behind the eye was nearly the same width as the nasal bones. The Girl with the Missing Face still had a sphenoid bone and since she was believed to be partly African American . . . had he stumbled upon a way to gauge her nasal aperture?

He called a Howard University anthropologist working on the *Unearthed* project; the professor made a series of measurements on other skulls and said, "I think you're onto something." So Bender started with the nose. A broad coffee-colored face quickly appeared with soft brown eyes; the bones seemed to be telling him they did not belong to a *typical coldhearted prostitute. She was a warm person with the weight of the world on her,* Bender thought. It was a wild guess, he admitted, but it was somehow more than that. "I can feel it."

The unmarked police sedan came out of Manlius, New York, south on I-81, and down into the Appalachian ridge-and-valley country of Pennsylvania. It was a melancholy tumble of twisted forested roads and steep bluestone hills shadowing rocky streams. A hundred miles south, they reached the Biddle House at noon. Richard Walter answered the door himself.

He ushered them into the parlor, seated them in the nineteenth-century chairs. As they laid the case file on the antique cherry table, he offered them a spot of coffee or tea. "Would anyone like cookies? I bake them myself, chocolate chip and gingersnaps, with real butter in the old-fashioned way, and I don't fool around with the chemistry. They're quite wonderful recipes." Lieutenant Kevin Barry and his two officers said they'd love some cookies.

Over steaming coffee, Walter lit a Kool and said, "As a point of fact, there are only about five of us profilers in the world who know what we're doing. The rest who claim to be profilers are fucking charlatans and frauds."

The cops grinned. It was true that profilers were getting a bad name in some quarters.

"In truth, I prefer the term 'crime assessment' to 'profiling,'" Walter continued. "Now because of all the TV forensic dramas and the amateur hour on the nightly news the public thinks profilers are wizards who come out of caves with their fantastic visions or some Borborygmic grumblings, but you can't get there from here. The frauds read our stuff and give flip out-of-context assessments like, 'He's driving a blue car and hates women.' It doesn't work that way. Like anything else, it takes a lot of hard work. We're talking probabilities and years of experience with similar cases, and analyzing them through the psychological continuum as well as the crime scene continuum."

Walter tipped his chin and blew cigarette smoke to the ceiling. "Gentlemen, let me explain the case to you in terms of a crime assessment."

Many factors, he said, including the remote burial of the young woman's corpse, suggested the victim was a prostitute. Power-driven killers "love to kill prostitutes," and when they do they dump the body as if disposing of trash. This type of killer typically makes a bold assault to the head, a straight-on attack, and here "we find that the victim's skull has been smashed, the apparent cause of death."

The half of a zipper police found near the surface of the grave was a valuable clue. "With this type of killer," Walter said, "we often find that the clothing of the victim had been forcibly torn off." According to a police report, four teeth of the zipper were damaged. Detective Keith Hall led the painstaking effort to find and interview the zipper manufacturer and learned that "the damage appears to have been caused by the slider pulling out over the teeth when the zipper was forcibly pulled apart."

"Given these and other factors and probabilities, it's highly likely that the killer is in his early to midtwenties, an ex-con, very muscular, lifts weights, macho, emotionally primitive, arrogant, drives a pickup truck, has girlie magazines lying around."

"As it happens," he went on, "Updegrove fits the profile. That's not to say he did it. But it was a guy like him, happy brandishing guns or other weapons—a guy with a criminal record."

They left with pages of notes, and cookies in freezer bags.

· CHAPTER 51 ·

THE KILLER ANGELS

Women around the wealthy, seventy-one-year-old Alabama businessman had a nasty habit of disappearing. So when he called the police to report his second wife missing, he was a suspect. Thirty years earlier, he had murdered his former mother-in-law—strangled and then stabbed the dead woman thirty-seven times with an ice pick—then returned home and told his first wife, "Our life is going to change. I killed your mother." He had done only thirteen months in a reformatory, then received a partial pardon from Kentucky's governor.

"That's one for *Bartlett's Book of Perverse Quotations,*" Walter said. He was intrigued as the Alabama police presented Vidocq Society Case No. 112 at the August 2002 luncheon. He was afraid the suspect was a rich, brilliant, experienced psychopath too smart for the police. But he was more concerned that afternoon by his uncharacteristically glum partner. Bender had buried his eighty-nine-year-old mother, Sarah, in June. Bender had previously buried his father, Francis A. Bender, and taken the unusual step of participating in his father's autopsy. Holding his father's heart in his hands, Bender had tried to understand and make peace with him. Now his mother was gone, and Bender looked like he was holding her heart, too.

That summer Bender felt as if the other dimension was shadowing his daily life. He and Walter flew to Chicago to make a joint presentation, "Criminal Case Studies," to the Federal Bureau of Prisons national training program. After the lecture at the Chicago Hilton, two nuns who worked in prisons approached the artist and profiler with rosy praise, broad smiles on their faces.

"You two do the work of angels," one said.

"Killer angels, perhaps," Bender said.

Walter was taken aback. He was quite sure that if a God had made the world He would not have created Theodore Bundy, but he held his tongue and mumbled a polite thank-you. Though it made him profoundly uneasy, he had to admit the seraphs of God seemed to be following him.

At Christmas, he had received an unusual gift—a crystal obelisk depicting an angel—from a young Pennsylvania couple who had long suffered the agonies of grief, fury, and uncertainty over the unsolved murder of the wife's brother. He had met them at a convention of the National Organization of Parents of Murdered Children, and his heart went out to them, as it did all the woebegone men and women at POMC who called him, there was no getting around it, "the avenging angel."

Yet it was not merely vengeance the profiler peddled to the stricken; it was wholeness and health. He had volunteered his services in the name of the Vidocq Society to speak to parents about the unspeakable, to wield sword or soft words, whatever tool necessary to vanquish their demons. "Their tormentors are all in the mind," he said. "Either their own or the mind of their child's killer. It's a matter of bringing the darkness to light." Just he, it seemed, could explain it all.

Only at POMC conventions could one find a hotel conference room filled with fifty mothers whose children had been murdered. At the Cincinnati Westin they gathered to hear a talk on murderer subtypes, earnest faces turning to the tall, balding, bespectacled, thin man they had seen rushing through the hallways in his dark suit like a blade.

He began his lecture by asking jauntily, "How many of you folks have not heard my little talk before?" Hands went up. "Liars!" he bellowed, and they roared with laughter. He approached a woman in the front row with a small trash can. "Madam," he said, "if you are about to eat that butterscotch candy, please unwrap it and put it in your mouth now. I will not have plastic crinkling whilst I attempt to speak." They gasped and laughed again. They loved him. Blasphemous, courtly, reeking of smoke and profanity, they loved him. After the speech, one by one, the mothers filed into a small smoking room of the hotel for private meetings with Walter in his cloud of Kools. In gentle, ten-minute confessionals, each gave a capsule description of their child's murder, answering the detective's questions—was the body face up or down? Was the knife at the scene?—and one by one they left with palpable serenity, careworn faces smoothed in some sense of peace. "He told me why Brian died," an Asian woman said, leaving the confessional in Cincinnati. "For the first time I know. Now I can really grieve and heal."

Walter had the mind to discern and the heart to explain within the limits of human understanding why and how a heart of darkness took their child. He gave evil its place, however difficult, in the human family; saw shapes and forces at work that others did not. He was, one journalist said, the Stephen Hawking of the universe of the damned.

Bob Meyer, a retired Tampa doctor, and his wife, Sherry, told Walter they were devastated to the point of emotional breakdown by the senseless, vile murders of their daughter Sherry-Ann Brannon, a lovely thirty-five-year-old blonde, and grandchildren: Shelby, seven, and Cassidy, four. The murders had occurred in Sherry-Ann's large, new dream house with pool in Manatee County, Florida. There was no sign of forced entry. Meyer was convinced his son-in-law, Dewey Brannon, who had recently left the dream house and Sherry-Ann for another woman in the midst of a contentious divorce, was the killer.

Police also considered Brannon the main suspect. The most intense six-week murder investigation in county history had revealed that it was Brannon, estranged and banned from the house on Father's Day, who had called 9-1-1 for help on the morning of September 16, 1999. He told the dispatcher he'd found the bodies of his wife and older daughter and thought it was a murder-suicide, but then he saw that Cassidy was badly hurt, too.

He was cradling the four-year-old, dying from multiple stab wounds, in his arms.

"Sir. It's gonna be OK, all right," the dispatcher tried to calm him.

"It's NOT gonna be OK," he replied. "I've got two dead people here 'cause of me, all right. So just get somebody out here." Three little words—the colloquial for "because of me"—had the whole county convinced Brannon was the killer, reporters wrote.

But as the crime lab did its work, all the physical evidence at the scene pointed to Larry Parks, a forty-seven-year-old landscaper who had recently dug the family's pool. Parks's DNA was found in a piece of skin under Sherry-Ann's fingernail. Parks confessed that he was "mighty high" on cocaine and crystal meth that morning when, after a failed night of hunting hogs to sell for cash for more drugs, he knocked on Sherry-Ann's door with the ruse that his truck had broken down, and forced his way in intending, he said, to rob her. When she fought back, he stabbed her ten or more times with a kitchen knife, went upstairs and stabbed Shelby to death in her bedroom, then dragged Cassidy downstairs and stabbed her in front of her dying mother.

Even though Parks pled guilty in exchange for three life terms—to avoid the death penalty—Bob Meyer said the case was destroying his family. He wanted Larry Parks dead. His wife had tried to enter the courtroom for Parks's trial with a gun in her purse, an attempt at frontier justice all too common at POMC. His son-in-law, now exonerated, had plunged over the wooden railing to try to kill Parks. As deputies handcuffed him and took him away, his wife shouted toward the judge and Parks: "He killed our babies!"

Bob Meyer, boiling in anger and confusion and still suspecting his son-in-law, said he just wanted the truth: How and why could a human being do such things, and was it Parks, and why him, or his son-in-law? He asked for Walter to help. The Vidocq profiler studied the case file, and then flew to Tampa on Meyer's request to sit in on Parks's sixty-seven-minute confession to six attorneys and police officers. Afterward, Walter told Meyer that the killing, down to the last detail, was a perfect expression of Larry Parks's history, personality, and character. Parks was "absolutely the killer and the only killer. He's the purest, coldest power-assertive killer I've ever seen."

The Meyers continued on their imperfect path of healing, but Walter remained concerned about Bob and Sherry. Passionate about music and baking, Sherry no longer found pleasure in her hobbies. She was dropping weight, growing sickly. Grief, Bob said, was literally killing her. Walter returned to Florida and walked in the door demanding one of Sherry's "famous tangerine pies." She said she didn't feel like baking. "I want it now!" he insisted. She was out of tangerines, and the stores were closed. "Well, let's go find some damn tangerines." They drove country roads together until Walter spotted a tangerine tree behind a diner. The fruit was too high; laughing and scheming like schoolkids, they got a ladder. The pie was delicious. Late that night over Scotch, Bob confessed he was haunted by dreams of vengeance against Parks that sounded like something out of ancient Athens. "I'll deny it if you tell anybody," Meyer told the others, "but I want him blinded. I want Mr. Parks to live in prison not knowing what's coming at him for the rest of his life."

"As it happens, it's not uncommon for one to have such feelings," said Walter. "Indeed since the Greeks, it was deemed important to vent them in appropriate places—to the courts, to family, to friends, to one's god—until we find our way again." He left knowing there was still work to do.

Joy and Brian Kosisky also had a murder in the family that was ruining their lives. Joy's brother had been murdered in Greenville, Pennsylvania. In gratitude for his work in helping them understand the case, the couple had sent him the crystal obelisk for Christmas. As Walter turned the glass in the sunlight, there appeared in the crystal the delicate lines of an angel, acid-etched into the interior of the glass.

"An acid angel," he mused. "I quite like that."

Now the acid angel, ensconced in a cloud of cigarette smoke, sat in his Chicago hotel room the day after his presentation with Bender. Before him sat a pair of Urbana, Illinois, police officers with their bulky cold-case file. The police from the southern Illinois city had presented one of the most notorious and puzzling cold murder cases in the state's history to the Vidocq Society the previous spring, March 15, 2001. It was the 1988 murder of the wealthy, popular University of Illinois veterinary student Maria Caleel, a case that had earned Urbana police little but frustration and embarrassment for fourteen years.

After hearing Walter's luncheon theory on the murder, police sent him the case file. They had driven the 140 miles from Champaign-Urbana to meet him while he was in Chicago and hear his thoughts.

"Gentlemen, now that I've read the file," Walter said with a grim smile, "let me explain the case to you."

The file for the fourteen-year investigation had grown to more than 1,600 pages. Police had accumulated forty suspects, but never made an arrest. "I've read the 1,600 pages on the computer, so I couldn't make notations," Walter said. "Nonetheless, I eliminated thirty-nine of the forty suspects. In the course of events, one is the killer, who has flown all these years just below the radar."

"The killer was obviously someone Maria knew," he continued. Sometime after three o'clock in the morning on March 6, 1988, Caleel was asleep in her garden apartment in Urbana when someone knocked on the door, or perhaps entered using a key. Her attacker struck in the dark, grabbing her from behind and plunging a six-inch knife upward and deep, precisely nicking her heart, and fled. As Caleel crawled to an apartment across the hall, dying from a single stab wound, a female student called police and asked her, "Who did this to you?"

"I can't believe it," Caleel replied. "I just can't believe it." Those were her dying words. She never identified her killer.

The murder of the attractive, bright, gifted twenty-one-year-old vet student made headlines across the country. Her friends said that Maria's family dined with princes, yet they never knew she was wealthy. She had entered Brown University at sixteen, graduated with a biology degree, and was a straight-A student at the highly competitive Illinois vet school. Grounded in her love for animals, she rode her horse Tristan early on the day she died, and later that day tried to save the life of a prematurely born foal.

The police were "absolutely gobsmacked" by the murder, Walter said. It defied logic. There was no break-in, no robbery, no sexual assault. The popular young woman had no enemies who would want to kill her. The FBI was brought in to study the case, to no avail. Maria's parents, the prominent Chicago physician Dr. Richard Caleel, and former model Annette, hired private eyes, and personally provided most of a $50,000 reward.

As the years passed with no arrests, the Caleels did everything in their power to keep the case and their daughter's name alive. They donated a small fortune to create Maria Caleel funds and scholarships across the country—a Maria Caleel polo trophy at the Oak Brook Polo Club; Maria Caleel conferences on violence against women; a Maria Caleel University of Missouri journalism school award; Maria Caleel horse shows, equine research grants, a Maria Caleel prize for the best biology student at Brown. Finally, the Caleels asked their family-friend Lynn Abraham, the renowned Philadelphia district attorney and VSM, for advice. The DA recommended a Vidocq Society investigation.

Walter had sparred at times with Illinois investigators, using lines such as "I fully respect your constitutional right to be wrong, nonetheless . . ." But now his voice purred as he coolly described the killer as a young man in the vet school and friend of Caleel's who bore a psychopathological anger toward her for her "relatively innocent college student flirtations."

The signs of a murderer who killed neatly and efficiently "in a manner of disposing of trash" to correct a perceived wrong were evident at the scene. The killer's precision with the knife was no accident given his anatomical skill with animals. With a misogynistic hatred, Walter said, "His thought process was thus: I didn't realize she was a disgusting and despicable whore, but I'm responsible for her, and I'll clean up the mess. So he killed her." Walter raised an eyebrow. "With no one else among the forty suspects," he explained, "can one draw a straight line connecting the crime and pre-crime and post-crime behavior? This guy is the lemons falling into place—the jackpot."

At first skeptical, police grew enthusiastic and were finally stunned by the analysis emerging from billows of menthol smoke. They talked about zeroing in on the killer, now a prominent man with a wife and children, and unearthing his secret of fourteen years. It would not be easy, but the Vidocq Society would advise each step of the way.

"Are the police happy with our work?" Fleisher asked later when Walter called to report in.

The thin man began to laugh. "Oh, yes. They're as happy as a pervert with two dicks."

As Walter worked the Illinois murder, two of the oldest Vidocqeans reached Ohio on a Sunday night, pulling a big American sedan into a Cincinnati hotel in time for dinner. Bill Kelly and Joe McGillen had left Philadelphia that morning right after mass, with city homicide detective Tom Augustine sharing the wheel during the nine-hour drive. Time had not been kind to the Vidocq senior investigative team. VSM Sam Weinstein, the third retired Philly cop on the Boy in the Box team, was in Israel working with the Israel Defense Forces. The widower McGillen, fearless on a murder, was deathly afraid to fly, thus the 600-mile drive. Kelly had spent the long drive quietly praying for a break in the half-century-old case, fearful he too was running out of time. After another year of beseeching God for help, he'd attended the St. Joseph's Seminary annual retreat, the weekend that kept him sane. Steeped in prayer, he asked a sister to help him ask God for a solution to the case, and she replied that she had been asking. Her words haunted him: "Maybe God said no."

The next morning, the three of them were seated stiffly in a psychiatrist's office. The psychiatrist was a tall man with wavy white hair. None of the cops had ever been in a shrink's office. Kelly had teased McGillen in the car: "Maybe you want to confess this flying phobia of yours." Now, after setting some ground rules, the psychiatrist led them into an inner room, and introduced them to a middle-aged woman, sitting at a table, they would call "Mary." Mary was a tall, handsome woman with unusually broad shoulders and keenly intelligent eyes. She seemed nervous, yet also distant. She demanded her identity be protected; she was an executive at one of the largest drug companies in the world, and "they mustn't know." The old cops nodded their promises. She breathed deeply to compose herself. "Oh, God," she said, "this is so hard."

Two years after her psychiatrist first contacted the police, and fifty years after witnessing the horrors that had scarred her for life, Mary was finally willing to talk about the murder of her brother Jonathan, the Boy in the Box.

"No one outside our house could have imagined what went on. . . . My parents did not have normal sexual desires. My father molested me. . . . My mother didn't just silently let it happen, the usual scenario. She was enthusiastic about it, even joined in. The agreement was that my father let her indulge her taste in little boys. She preferred them to adult men because she thought them purer, somehow. . . . One night a little boy came into our lives. . . ."

It was a hot August night, she remembered. "I was thirteen when my mother took me in the car to get him."

Kelly bent his head to his maker and the weight of the words, and scribbled notes on a pad.

Between them, Kelly and McGillen had nearly a century of investigative experience, and as Mary rambled on, both men felt in their guts she was telling the truth. Mary was highly credible and had no reason to lie. This was the real story, at last. It was horrifying, Augustine thought. It was a story that even Hitchcock would have been afraid to film.

On the surface, as Mary told it, her childhood in the 1950s on the Main Line of Philadelphia was one of comfort and privilege. She lived in a house in Lower Merion, a lovely, affluent town, an only child of highly educated, well-respected parents. Her father was a teacher at the high school, one of the better public schools on the East Coast. Her mother was a librarian. The students loved her parents; "I bet my parents autographed a thousand yearbooks," she said.

But in the privacy of their home, life was a horror from which Mary could not awaken. At thirteen, Mary knew in her heart something was wrong, but she was unable to fully face it, couldn't begin to understand it. That August night when her mother parked in front of a row house in Philadelphia, she rang the bell, gave the woman an envelope apparently filled with money, and was handed a baby who had peed his diapers. Mary, excited, confused, scared, held the baby in the car. She didn't mind the smell; she felt a sudden sympathy for the helpless child. She could feel that "this baby, this little human being, needed me. Needed somebody."

She asked her mother, "Can he be my brother?"

"Sure," her mother said. "Only we can't keep him upstairs."

Her mother put the baby in the basement in a small room that used to be a coal bin. He had a box to sleep in, some blankets, and heavy dishes like dog dishes. A drain was his toilet. Mary thought, *It's just like we got a new puppy.* Her mother called him Jonathan. She went down to visit Jonathan and play with him. She took food and water down to him. He always had coal dust in his hair. She got him to laugh once. Jonathan never said a word. She realized he was retarded.

Her mother said, "Don't go down there."

Jonathan's hair grew long, like a girl's. His parents never cut it. They never took him outside. When Mary was fifteen, feeling weighted now with a terrible secret, her mother dragged Jonathan upstairs for a bath, "cursing . . . his feet going *thump, thump, thump* on the steps as she dragged him along." She put him in a bath that was scorching hot and he started screaming. She took him out of the tub and he was crying and stamping his feet. She put him back in the water and he threw up their baked-beans dinner. "My mother shrieked like I'd never heard before. She yanked him out of the tub and slapped him. I mean hard." He cried but she kept slapping until he fell and hit his head on the bathroom floor and then she was punching him all over with her fists. "My mother's head was shaking from side to side, she was swinging so fast."

Jonathan was still. "I could tell he was dead. His eyes were open but not seeing. There was sadness in his face. If I live to be a hundred, I will never feel as sorry for a human being as I did for Jonathan right then." His parents chopped his hair short; Mary was ordered to trim his fingernails. "I tried to be gentle," she said. The next morning her mother lifted Jonathan from the tub, where he'd been kept all night. They wrapped him in a blanket and carried him out a side door in the basement that faced the driveway, hidden by a hedge, and put him in the trunk of the car. Her mother drove past a church and down a country road and stopped by a patch of woods. A car came by as her mother opened the trunk, and she told Mary, "Don't say a word." They carried Jonathan into an overgrown field. Her mother found an empty box near the road. "Oh, good," her mother said. "Tilt it." Mary tipped it and her mother slid Jonathan into it and made sure he was out of the rain. "Did it matter?" Mary wondered. They stopped at a diner on the way home and Mary had a donut. She threw it up in the car. Her mother was very angry. "Then we went home and tried to act like everything was normal." Her father died years ago from a heart attack, her mother died after that at a nursing home in Florida. She never told anyone but her psychiatrist.

As they drove back to Philadelphia, Kelly could hardly contain his excitement. He recalled that the Good Samaritan saw a young boy wearing a raincoat standing next to a woman—the tall, wide-shouldered Mary said she was wearing a raincoat, and she easily could have been mistaken from behind for a boy. Kelly and McGillen agreed the route Mary described to the field made sense.

Her account of the boy vomiting baked beans was intriguing; the autopsy, not widely reported, noted a brown residue in the boy's esophagus.

Mary gave the address of the family's house on the Main Line, and Kelly and McGillen raised their eyebrows. The address matched an earlier tip the society believed to be reliable and had never made public. To pick a matching address in a metropolitan area of more than five million people seemed more than coincidence. Kelly and McGillen confirmed the existence of the house, and of Mary's late parents, a teacher and librarian. They were stunned by what she witnessed and suffered, and amazed at how she struggled to make her life a success.

As Augustine listened to Mary, he kept thinking, *Why does she hate her parents so much, to tell a story like that?* He didn't believe Mary, and even Fleisher was skeptical of the story. Augustine pointedly asked the psychiatrist why he didn't have any notes confirming Mary's story. The therapist was offended. "I don't need notes. My job was to help Mary unlock the memory, series of memories, and free herself from them. . . . And I can tell you . . . her account has been consistent from the start. What you heard is what I've been hearing for thirteen years now, long before there was a Web site about this case. I believe Mary is telling the truth."

Later that summer, on Philadelphia's top-rated TV news station, *Eyewitness News* reported that according to confidential sources the Vidocq Society had achieved a breakthrough in the case "that has tormented Philadelphia police for more than four decades."

Augustine remained unconvinced. "It may be true. It may not be true. Hell, there's just no corroboration for any of it," he said. Bruce Castor, the Montgomery County district attorney, said the information was "sketchy and unreliable." He said Mary's story is "akin to Martians coming down and marching somebody off in a spaceship."

But within days Kelly and McGillen located Mary's old house. The white-haired cops walked up and down the street interviewing neighbors. Several neighbors recalled the couple who once lived there, a very conservative, conventional teacher and librarian, and dismissed the lurid story as ludicrous. None of them ever saw a boy come out of the house.

Kelly and McGillen knocked on the door of Mary's old house. Kelly explained the situation and politely asked the current owner if they could see the basement. No, she said firmly. But Kelly and McGillen figured it was a good start. It was just their first conversation. They would be back.

They wanted to see if there was a coal bin.

· CHAPTER 52 ·

THE GHOST

The fax arrived at the nineteenth-century brownstone head-quarters of the Vidocq Society, on Locust Street in Philadelphia, at midday. Fleisher walked down the hall and crossed the large red Oriental rug in the waiting room, past the mantelpiece with the Vidocq bust and the cadaver skull, to the fax closet. He barely read it as he brought it back, scowling, to the "war room," where he was meeting with Bender and Walter. It was the winter of 2002, and the commissioner of the Vidocq Society should have been happier. Before Christmas, the society had heard one of his favorite cases. VSM Richard Walton, a California investigator, had come east to describe his thirteen-year effort that led California to exonerate American Indian Jack Ryan, wrongly framed for a celebrated 1920s double murder in Humboldt County.

"Redemption is the sweetest human event," Fleisher said. He had just been named one of the seventy-six finest minds in Philadelphia by *Philadelphia* magazine. He and Nate Gordon had recently published a book, *Effective Interviewing and Interrogation Techniques,* exploring his favorite subject, the historic search for truth. New tips on the Boy in the Box case were pouring in since VSM George Knowles, a New Jersey volunteer, had created an "America's Unknown Child" Web site; Knowles had been haunted by the case since he went to his local police station in central New Jersey to register his new bicycle at age eleven, and saw the police "Information Wanted" poster—"my first exposure to death."

Even the planned Vidocq Society movie was getting media attention now, helping attract more cases, more chances to help the helpless. The movie "will be full of thrills, murder, mayhem, and disgust," Walter told a Binghamton, New York, newspaper. "A typical day for me."

But Fleisher's optimistic view of human nature had been challenged that fall by the terrorist attacks of September 11, 2001. A number of VSMs answered the call, including forensic dentist Haskell Askin, a leader of the identification effort in the New York medical examiner's office, and Utica College forensic anthropologist Thomas A. Crist, who worked night shifts at the Fresh Kills Landfill sorting human remains from other materials and rubble brought by barge and spread over seven acres. Richard Walter was contacted by shadowy figures in American intelligence asking if he could profile Osama bin Laden. "Why of course, said I," he related. "He, like Stalin and assorted other monsters of history, is a malignant narcissist. He is all about power; religion is a guise. Ultimately he will be defeated because he can't take a step backward."

Fleisher said America and other nations must "find the evil animals responsible for this horrific act . . . and dispatch all of them back to Satan. However, it's critical for the global community to acknowledge that true Muslims around the world are good, religious people who equally abhor what these traitors to true Islam have done." He issued a fresh call in the *Vidocq Society Journal* for VSMs "to live by our motto, Veritas Veritatum, and help protect ALL innocent people from prejudice and hate."

Now as he reentered the war room, he looked down at the fax and his face brightened. "Good news. The suspect confessed to killing Lorean Quincy Weaver, the Girl with the Missing Face that Frank identified." Fleisher threw the paper fax on the table, and Bender and Walter took turns studying it. The police dispatch warmly congratulated Walter for his profile.

"Richard's profile was right on the money," Fleisher said with pride, as Walter smiled graciously, and Bender's face fell. "Way to go, Richard."

The killer was a macho ex-con known for carrying weapons, and he'd struck Weaver in the head, just as Walter predicted. But the killer wasn't Robert Updegrove, the ex-con who found the grave and Walter said also fit the profile.

"I knew it wasn't Updegrove!" Bender said. "Rich, you're not always right."

Walter rolled his eyes, wondering how to fend off the coming attack. For once, he wished his partner would be satisfied with the remarkable role his forensic art had played in bringing a killer to justice.

"Frank, you're going to push me only so far."

The Vidocq Society had lost track of the case in the two years since Bender completed his facial reconstruction. The department had transmitted the image widely to police departments and the media, with no results. Keith Hall, the officer who led the investigation, had left the small department to become a detective with the Onondaga County sheriff's office, taking his passion with him. The case had gone nowhere.

Then in September 2001, Thaddeus Maine, a bright, young Manlius officer, was ordered by his commander to throw out hopeless cold-case files, including that of the Girl with the Missing Face.

But as Maine looked over the old files, he was intrigued. He had guarded the grave five years ago, and had hung a photograph of Bender's bust on his office wall. It was still there, staring down at him, a coffee-colored woman with a broad nose and lips, close-set eyes, and a high forehead fringed with short curly hair. He saw decency, and a world of pain, in those eyes. They chilled him. He liked the woman, whoever she was, and felt sorry for her.

Maine decided to make a few phone calls. A respected investigator, he had been given permission to look into any worthwhile cases one last time before shredding them, but he had been asked to do it quietly. He began to interview residents of nearby farms, asking about itinerant laborers who had passed through the area more than ten years before. Hundreds of phone calls later, he came across the name of Roland Patnode, an American Indian carpenter from Massena, New York, on the Canadian border who had rented a cabin on a farm within sight of the grave—the same cabin Updegrove rented years later.

Patnode quickly became Maine's chief person of interest. The six-foot-four, 230-pound man, a great high school athlete who'd earned a wrestling scholarship to college, had served time for a 1986 murder committed within the likely range of time the Manlius victim had disappeared. While working as a carpenter in Syracuse, Patnode was convicted of murdering a transvestite prostitute. At the July 1987 trial, Patnode claimed he'd stabbed David McLaughlin, twenty-two years old, to death in the throat after discovering the slim figure in a dress giving him oral sex was "not a female, it was a man."

The jury, apparently sympathetic to his lawyer's claims that a "sleazy homosexual transvestite . . . duped this poor country boy," found Patnode innocent of murder and convicted him of manslaughter. After serving only four years in prison, he'd violated parole and fled to Canada. Rochester police, Maine learned, considered Patnode a possible suspect in the disappearance of several prostitutes, including a missing person from 1986 named Lorean Quincy Weaver.

Following routine procedure, Maine got a copy of Weaver's mug shot from Rochester. As he studied the young black woman's short hair, wide mouth, and soft eyes, he literally felt a jolt running through him. While the faces were not identical, he felt certain it was the same young woman who was staring at him from the bust on the wall. He ran down the hall to two superior officers with the photographs and his gut feeling; they all felt the same thing. When they "compared the photo to the bust prepared by Mr. Bender," a police report later said, "we were certain we had identified the victim."

It was Lorean Quincy Weaver, twenty-six years old; when her

mother saw a photo of the bust she said, "I always wondered what happened to Lorean." DNA from Lorean's relatives matched DNA taken from bone marrow in the scattered remains. Police were amazed that Bender had captured her personality in the bust, as well. Lorean, they learned, was a sweet young woman who never wanted to be a prostitute but started as young as fourteen, and never made much money. Her story was the rare one that touched the cops. "She was unlucky," said Manlius Sergeant William Becker, "right up to getting in the car with the wrong man." She had last been seen alive getting into a pickup truck in late 1986 with Patnode.

In February 2002, two Manlius detectives went to interview Patnode at the Downstate Correctional Facility in Fishkill about the murder of Weaver. Patnode, thirty-nine, had just been picked up on his parole violation from an Indian reservation in Canada, expecting to serve only a few months on the minor infraction. Then the interrogators put Weaver's picture in front of him, and his eyes filled with tears. "She's my ghost," he said. He confessed to the murder twelve minutes into the interview.

Patnode admitted to killing her in late August or early September 1986. As Walter reviewed the confession, he saw that the crime was a "classic" fit for the profile. Patnode went looking for a prostitute after drinking in a downtown bar, he told detectives, and picked up Weaver and paid her twenty dollars for a sexual encounter in his pickup truck. When that was done, he told her he was breaking up with his girlfriend and wanted a second, more extended sexual encounter, but Weaver objected. Patnode began to force her and she slapped him. He slapped her back hard, four or five times in the face, and then began punching her. She drew a small knife and cut him in self-defense.

"She kept trying to fight me off, but I was much bigger than her," Patnode said. "I then grabbed her around the neck with both of my hands and started squeezing. I couldn't stop, and I was feeling so angry. She was trying to get out of my grip, and I kept squeezing her neck. I don't remember how long I squeezed her neck for, but she slowly stopped moving, and she went limp."

Patnode began to drive home, wondering what to do with the body, when suddenly Weaver moaned and tried to sit up. Patnode said he grabbed a framing hammer from the center console of his truck and struck her on the head four or five times until she stopped moving. In a three-page confession, he also admitted to sexually violating the corpse before burying her at the edge of a field off Salt Springs Road in Manlius.

The Manlius detectives realized that Richard Walter's profile was correct in another respect—Patnode was a serial killer. It was a month after killing Weaver on October 1 that Patnode picked up transvestite prostitute McLaughlin and killed him, and he was a likely suspect in other murders.

Weaver's body went undetected for eleven years. Patnode had all but gotten away with two murders, and might never have been brought to justice if he'd buried Weaver deeper than eleven inches—and if Bender hadn't been willing "to take a long shot rather than no shot at all." In October 2002, Patnode was convicted of the murder. As Patnode wept and apologized, Judge Anthony Aloi sentenced him to the maximum penalty of twenty-five years to life in state prison for committing "an unbelievably heinous, atrocious, and cruel act."

"Lorean Weaver may have been your ghost, Mr. Patnode, but she was a human being. She was a daughter. She was a sister. She was a mother. She was a memory to her family. She was a crack in their broken hearts for all those years. . . . Mr. Patnode," he said, "you should remain in prison for the rest of your life."

Lorean's daughter, Schmillion Weaver, an infant when her mother disappeared, thanked the police for bringing justice to the killers. "I feel closure now," she said.

"I knew it wasn't Updegrove!" Bender repeated. "Rich, you got the wrong guy."

"Frank," Walter said wearily, "I've told you a thousand times a profile is not a suspect. It's a description of the traits of the likely suspect based on a crime assessment, including the signature at the crime scene and a series of other probabilities. The profile was on the mark."

But Bender, his eyes shining with glee, seemed not to understand or care about the distinction. The Girl with the Missing Face, the case everyone said was impossible, had turned into one of his greatest triumphs. And Walter had named the wrong guy.

If God had made Lorean Quincy Weaver the first time, Bender had re-created her in clay the second time, and he would never let Walter forget it.

· CHAPTER 53 ·

THE NINTH CIRCLE OF HELL

The crowns of great trees made shadowy tracings on the moonlit peak, but the upstairs windows of the Greek Revival were black. Hedges hid the downstairs panes in shifting walls of darkness. The only light came from the far rear of the house, the orange glow of a cigarette floating under the proscenium arch of the music room. Sitting at his beloved 1926 Chickering grand, a classic American piano he had "stolen from a fool quite ignorant of its value," the thin man placed the cigarette in the ashtray on the lid of the piano and his hands over the keys. He let his mind go, free as the cigarette smoke wending lazily in the faint moonlight by the spray of ostrich feathers in a black vase on the lid. The thin man, so disciplined to the cold beauty and rules of order, was consciously summoning chaos.

Of its own impulse a finger struck middle C.

He had started at dusk with a variation on Tchaikovsky's Concerto No. 1, gloriously filling the house with music as it drained of light. Now, from the single key, a song of his own creation leaped into existence, spontaneous and brilliant. "I play my mood," he said. He let his mood soar mightily, exalted in the knowledge that he was creating something new that would never fall on ears other than his own and he would never play again.

He had been a musical prodigy as a youth before the opera of the streets turned his head. Music was his joy, but also a discipline he practiced to enter the labyrinth of the criminal mind. "I do not know a great detective without musical sense," he once said. "The problem the police often have is that one cannot analyze human behavior with merely logic. You can't do it. Man is a creature of associative thinking."

In the thrall of the creation he no longer sensed the darkness beyond the piano, the moonlight on the windowsill, the cigarette smoke bending in the soft breeze from the garden.

Walter was a proud scientist, disdainful of things of the spirit, who lived by strict rules of evidence, the logical assessment of a crime scene bathed in the unsparing light of deduction. Among murder investigators he was often reputed to be the coldest mind in the world. He worshipped the god of reason. Yet his was a classical mind finely tuned to the Doric columns and classical harmonies of his house, stubbornly resistant to modern illusions. Many in our time have forgotten, he said, that "reason is born of twins—rational thinking and emotion. When one denies emotion, it's still there—we're animals—and it bites you in the ass, expressing itself now as anger and vehemence. The Greeks struck this balance best."

The warring Greek gods—Apollo, the sun god of order, forms, and rationalism; Dionysus, the wine god of revels, chaos, ecstasy—shared the same temple and space in men's hearts, forever in conflict. "As it happens," he said, "Apollo was the Greek god of detectives; Dionysus was the god of murder." A man could not think clearly without recognizing both sides of his nature, could not unite them without art or music.

As he played he closed his eyes and saw a boy materialize. He was a small boy in a dark wood on a winter night and he was very cold. He was tied up, perhaps to a tree. The boy was shivering and naked but did not cry anymore. There was an old church in the distance and maybe the boy heard its bells ringing. The night was clear and filled with stars. He felt terrible pain but even stronger were things he could not name, fear, confusion, sweet pleading love, anger, degradation, terror. Maybe he tried to speak but it's not likely he could get a word out by then. He was not alone. The person who loved the boy the most, who had always taken care of him, who bathed him and dressed him, was there with him now, too. He could smell him close, a large shadow smiling in the darkness, near enough now to blot out the stars. The boy might have screamed then but it was not likely.

This was what happened. Walter was certain of it. The hidden story told by the condition of the body and the crime scene was incontrovertible. Dozens of good men had gone to their graves, afraid to face it. That was OK. It was natural. This darkest of shadows was death itself and men could only live by turning away. "The truth is, the cops just didn't want to know."

He saw into the present. He saw the old killer living alone on the edge of a city, a decrepit shell of wantonness and stale pleasure. He saw the old man who had committed the most diabolical of crimes, an especially depraved and merciless child sex murder that would shake any decent person's soul. No doubt he was considered a little aloof or odd by his neighbors, a "funny old man," it was a shame he had no family on the holidays, one of those old bachelors who stank of alcohol and cigarettes and showered once a week, not pleasant but nothing to worry about—if they only knew! It was many years later now and the old man had nothing left but his memories. Walter could see him in his dim row house turning the yellowed and crumbling newspaper pages with appalling arrogance to read about himself once again, reliving the sweet memory of the killing when he was young, the zenith of his power and achievement, the high point of his life! What kind of society allowed such a monster his freedom for nearly fifty years, while the nameless and innocent child, he would be a father now, perhaps a grandfather, moldered unknown and unmourned? Walter was offended to the core of his sense of decency. The old killer had exulted over his dark triumph for too long. It was time to go get him.

The piano thundered. This new creation of his seemed to

summon shades from every corner of the parlor. It was thrilling to make but it was good he would never hear it again. It was the song of the beast.

Lost in his music, Walter didn't detect the soft, dissonant tympanic beat in the darkness of the great house, the click of the door against the jamb.

A thick-shouldered man stood in the gloom. He had shining black eyes and the glint of a gun at his hip. His smile was brilliant.

The mighty music stopped, and the echoes faded in the lower rooms. A big hand clapped Walter on the shoulder.

"Nice!" the thin man exclaimed with a hoarse laugh. "I could have had a heart attack! I assumed I'd be enjoying libations alone. The least you could do is call."

"I did! You were too busy being Beethoven to answer the phone."

"I think not," Walter shot back.

Stoud. Walter walked into the parlor turning on lights, and tossed a Hallmark-style card to Stoud with a smirk. It was the invitation to the fifth anniversary of the reburial of the Boy in the Box, also known as America's Unknown Child, in his prominent new grave at Ivy Hill Cemetery. Stoud hadn't been able to go; Walter had brusquely declined the invitation.

Inside was a drawing of a baby being sung up to heaven and a poem, "Little Angels"; Stoud snorted. "Your cynicism is apt, check this out," Walter said, reading: "From this day forth he becomes a symbol for every child in America who has paid the ultimate price for abuse."

The thin man took a long drag on his cigarette. "Fleisher thinks my heart has finally turned to stone. OK, he may be right." He smiled wickedly. "But first they bring him toys, fetishizing the joys of a childhood that was spent six feet underground. Now they're quite happy to ignore what really happened to him."

His eyes flared. "The child is not a symbol of anything. He was not a trendy victim of 'child abuse.' He was murdered, tortured and murdered. He was prey to the darkest, most complicated murdering personality type the human race has produced, and since we can't bring a dead boy back to life, it's not our job to imagine him playing second base. It's our job to go get the S.O.B. who did it."

Stoud grinned. There was nothing quite like Richard Walter reaching for the sword.

"AE," the state trooper said. It was a statement, not a question. The boy had clearly been murdered by the fourth and most diabolical type of killer—the anger-excitation killer.

"Of course," Walter said, as he spun the triple-digit combination of his silver attaché on the coffee table in front of him. Stoud watched the thin fingers carefully lift out an eight-and-a-half-by-eleven piece of paper.

"The Helix," Walter said, holding it up. "The map to the bottom, the black hole at the end of the continuum."

Walter was loath to discuss the Helix, and was downright paranoid about showing it to anyone, even his protégé. When murder descended to the fourth personality subtype, AE, Walter's schemata described a murderer who killed not for any tangible achievement— money or power or revenge—but simply for the unmatched excitement and pleasure of killing. The AE or sadistic killer murdered and tortured strangers, killed purely for secondary sexual enjoyment, and couldn't stop. The complex pleasures of sadism drove him insatiably to kill and kill again until he was caught and incarcerated, was killed himself, or died of old age. It was the kind of killer responsible for the dark legends in all cultures of human beasts like Dracula and the werewolf—and in modern times men like Pedro Alonso Lopez, "The Monster of the Andes," arrested in 1980 after killing more than three hundred women. Yet it was a monster rare enough in American civilization until the 1960s and '70s, until it went by the names Bundy, Gacy, Boston Strangler, Night Stalker, Green River Killer, and dozens of others. Now the FBI said there were sadistic serial killers operating in every state.

The Helix was a hand-drawn illustration of a swirling spiral cone, marked all along its length by tiny neat handwritten legends in black ink.

"Richard," Stoud teased. "Turn on that computer yet? Revolutionary papers in forensic journals are generally not handwritten."

Walter scoffed at the idea he would publish it. "I do not even want to expose it to a hacker, or leave its impressions on a typewriter ink ribbon."

Walter was right to be paranoid about the Helix and keep it locked away in the steel-ribbed attaché, Stoud thought. The thin man sounded grandiose when he described it as "the most dangerous knowledge in the world." But he had a point. While it didn't teach a man how to build a nuclear bomb, it showed him something more perilous—how to release the darkest evil in himself.

"I have to be careful," Walter said. "The sadists are the first ones to attend my lectures, to order reprints of my papers. Like everyone, the sadist is eager to find out who he really is, how to achieve his dream. In the wrong hands, the Helix is a self-help guide for a serial killer or a mass murderer." Once, when making his speech in Marquette, Michigan, "Sadistic Acting Out: A Theoretical Model," at a forensic convention, Walter saw a suspected rapist in the audience.

Sadists take their work seriously, he said. Sexual sadists, like Ted Bundy, represent the class of criminals with the highest IQ, an average of 119. They are often very bright, charming, and utterly normal and trustworthy—until, being master manipulators, they get an unsuspecting victim alone, and the monster emerges. The learning curve is complicated and absorbs all the senses—touching, viewing, smelling, tasting, hearing. It's difficult and time-consuming to figure out exactly what to do next. In Kansas, Walter spent a day consulting with the Wichita police helping them piece together a series of murders that police believed were caused by one man. That afternoon as he was about to lecture on sadism to the First World Meeting of Police Surgeons and Police Medical Officers, "a detective came up to me and said, 'I just kicked the suspect out of your audience.'" The suspected serial killer had been prepared to take notes.

As one of the founders of modern criminal profiling, Walter was widely known for describing the four personality subtypes of killers with Keppel. He was the first to deeply analyze the psychology of bite-mark evidence left by murderer-rapists. He pioneered a system for analyzing pre-crime, crime, and post-crime behavior of murder suspects. But the Helix, containing his theory of sadism, was his greatest contribution to criminology. When FBI agent Robert Ressler heard him lecture on it in the mid-1980s, he immediately invited Walter to Quantico to lecture to the bureau's Behavioral Sciences Unit profilers, and the two profilers began a lifelong friendship. Walter teased Ressler that "the bureau still doesn't understand sadism. Bob, the FBI hasn't had a new idea since 1978."

Unlike the first three personality types of killers, for whom murder is the goal, murder is not the motivation for the anger-excitation killer; the process of killing itself is the pleasure and the goal—prolonged torture that sparks the killer's fantasy life. While other murderers acted as deeply flawed or evil human beings, the sadist's indoctrination and transformation was so thorough he or she seemed no longer human. Once a murderer reached the complex fury known as anger-excitation, it was as if a trapdoor opened beneath him, with eight steps down to the very bottom, the worst killers of humankind. Based on thousands of interviews with sadists and other murderers as well as the testimony of cops in the field, Walter's Helix charted those eight steps with psychological and behavioral precision.

It was a time-honored path of self-discovery pointing toward annihilation blazed by the Marquis de Sade, the seventeenth-century father of sadism, and all who follow. The journey could also be seen as the precise opposite of the hero's journey, the timeless climb to redemption, the soul's climb to enlightenment or God; in ages past it was known as the downward journey, to the Father of Darkness. The medieval imagery was apt. It was the wasteland of the soul. Although visually the Helix resembled Francis Crick and James Watson's DNA double helix representing the code to life, it functioned more like Dante's fourteenth-century map of the underworld, leading through increasing human sins, betrayals, and monstrosities to the bottom, the Ninth Circle of Hell.

"Sadism is a crime of luxury," Walter said. "Not everybody can afford it. It takes time, investment, it takes a covert life, it takes a whole series of learning requirements—it's like a Ph.D. There's a sequential learning pattern for them; you just don't wake up one day and you're a sexual sadist. It's the growth curve of evil."

But like other arts that were once the exclusive province of the aristocracy, sadism is now within the reach of the masses. Once a man needed wealth, power, position to have the luxury of time and access to victims. Now all he needed, Walter said, was "a minimum-wage job, a studio apartment, a cheap panel truck, cable TV to instruct him, and his full suite of constitutional freedoms." Sexual sadists are rarer in repressive societies; they are a dark fruit of democracy.

In the Helix, Walter charts an inexorable eight-step pattern of increasing depravity that leads to the sadistic killer and beyond, to the very depths of human evil.

"If I locate a developing sadist on the Helix, I know where he's been, and I know where he's going."

In the beginning, the developing sadist, lured by the temptation of his own obsessions, is drawn to a self-destructive fetish, such as "pornography, a lust for women's shoes or teens' underwear, or whatever. All sexual sadists have fetishes, usually three or four operating at one time. All fetishists don't become sexual sadists."

Once snared by his fetish, however, the potential sadist has entered the Helix. And once inside, there is no way out. Walter spoke of it as if it were a "House of Sadism." "A man enters a room," Walter said, "and the door closes behind him. Men make choices, and there are doors that close permanently. There is no going back." He may never progress to step two, but that is the only direction available—downward, to the depths of the pathology.

The pathology is insatiable. When the fetish no longer satisfies, the next step is voyeurism. The voyeur can be highly specialized. "I had a case where the voyeur was a Peeping Tom specializing in Army lieutenants' wives," Walter said.

The following step, when the voyeur needs more, is frotteurism. "We've all been victims of frotteurs," Richard Walter said. "These are the people who get sexual gratification from anonymously rubbing against you in a crowd." As an adjunct professor at Michigan State University, Walter investigated two students, homosexual twins, who wore tight jeans every Saturday and waited for the 72,000 faithful to pour out of Spartan Stadium after football games, touching and feeling as they worked unseen against the crowd.

The sadist is now on a path to achieve intimacy and sexual gratification without vulnerability, making the wrong choice endlessly depicted in the oldest stories, taking without giving his heart. Unable to form authentic relationships, he becomes a "master at manipulating others to get what he wants. Sadists even go through marriages, but by and large unless the person has something they want, they just don't count." Many achieve normal sexual relations with wives, husbands, or lovers, but after a time that level of emotional vulnerability becomes intolerable. It's "far more satisfying to target potential victims and imagine or later actualize out the relationship with them in the total control position."

Fetishists, voyeurs, and frotteurs choose and control their victims from an emotional distance. But in subsequent steps the sadist crosses a dangerous divide. Fantasy or limited touching or striking is no longer enough; he desires the more intimate relationship, and approaches the victim with punishing control in mind: dominance, submission, bondage, and discipline.

"He can't bond, he can't achieve sexual satisfaction by being honest and legitimate, can't emotionally invest in anybody else, is totally exploiting, so he finds secondary sexual gratification by dominating a victim utterly. It's a systematic way to feed and empower himself through fantasies by creating a sense of dread and dependency in the victim. Their thrill comes from the feeling

'I own you. You don't eat unless I say so. You live and breathe at my request. Your life is not your own.' It gives them a messianic sense of importance."

When bondage no longer satisfies, the developing sadist inevitably becomes a devotee of picquerism. A picquer derives from the French, meaning to penetrate, cut. "Picquers derive sexual satisfaction from stabbing, cutting, slicing, rendering human flesh. It's the people who cut leather coats in stores as a second skin, a practice skin. They're freeway snipers firing rifle shots into the victim, like the Tower Killer, or lovers'-lane killers like the Son of Sam."

The final descent is to full-blown sadism. One becomes a sadistic killer, deriving sexual satisfaction from a complex ritual of torturing and murdering a victim. Bundy, who said pornography started him onto the path of the Helix, ended here.

The Bundy-type killer has prepared extensively for this moment. He has taken health classes so he will not contract AIDS or another illness. He becomes expert on the universal methods of saving his victim's life—again and again—to prolong the pleasure of torture. He strangles her to within an inch of death, stops to apply Red Cross–approved mouth-to-mouth. He strangles her again, this time with ligature, a pleasure of a different shade, and moments before death revives her again with mouth-to-mouth resuscitation.

Then it's on to the bathroom, where he holds her head under a full tub of cool water and drowns her to within an inch of her life yet again. This is a subtly different pleasure entirely; while instructing police worldwide on the varieties of sadistic experience, Walter tells them to fill a bucket with cool water and hold a large sponge underwater with both hands, allowing themselves to feel the tingles on the small hairs along the arm, the awakening of an erogenous zone. Then they realize why so many female strangling victims are found near or in water or bathtubs—it's not, as police commonly assume, to destroy the evidence. The water heightens the killer's sensitivity and pleasure.

The horrors are limited only by the sadist's imagination. The endgame, always, is sexual gratification produced by constantly exposing the victim to dominance, degradation, and dread. Walter has interviewed a few extremely lucky and rare women who survived twelve hours at the hands of a sexual sadist and somehow escaped. "They were begging to die," he said.

Even during the torture and murder, the killer cannot expose himself emotionally to the victim. Only after he takes body parts back to his lair can he feel enough in control to open up sexually. Through more than forty victims, this was Ted Bundy's raison d'être. His souvenir was the head. In the privacy of his home, he masturbated on the young woman's head, then burned it in a fireplace.

When taking souvenirs doesn't gratify anymore, the sadistic killer knows three final, descending options: necrophilia, or sex with the dead, historic vampirism—the ancient practice of blood draining, driven by sexual sadism—and finally cannibalism. Eating human flesh is the sadist's ultimate sexual union, the ultimate intimacy without vulnerability: "I own you entirely."

This was Jeffrey Dahmer's final stop, the subfloor of the house of sadism. The centuries of fables about an angry man who must open his heart to love, to the vulnerability of life, or face psychological death—the tale of beauty and the beast—are not without meaning. Dahmer was simultaneously gratified and mocked by the insatiable hollowness and evil of his choice—a literal feast of death. For him, cannibalism was only the beginning. He literally could eat all he wanted, but he'd never be satisfied. "The desire is insatiable."

The eight steps led to the abyss, the root of the myth of Dracula and the reality of Hitler, the grotesque killing forms Walter called the "ultimate nightmare." Walter was an atheist, but despite his Christian metaphors Dante had done a fine job of portraying evil, Walter said.

The thin man went to the shelf and pulled down a beaten old copy of *The Inferno,* which he hadn't read since college. He was intrigued to see the fourteenth-century poet had done similar work, apportioning hell into nine concentric circles, the last of which had four zones.

"The Ninth Circle of Hell is impressive," he said. It was the lake of ice known as Cocytus, where betrayers of humanity were frozen for eternity, each encased to a different depth, from the waist down to total immersion. Walter admired the many excellent forms of vengeance portrayed, such as Count Ugolino beating the head of Archbishop Ruggieri, who had imprisoned and starved him and his children. At the center of the lake is Satan, waist-deep in ice, a huge, terrifying, winged beast with three heads. The three mouths each chew on traitors such as Brutus and Judas Iscariot. The six eyes weep tears that mix with the traitors' blood. The six wings beat to escape but send an icy wind that further imprisons all. Judas suffers the most, his head in the mouth of Lucifer, his back forever skinned by Lucifer's claws.

"I quite like it," Walter said. "A little overdramatic, perhaps. But perps haven't changed much, nor their just desserts."

Stoud saw the photographs of the boy covering the trestle table. His studied the old police photos from 1957. Walter pointed to the cuts and bruises all over the body. He saw evidence of burning, cutting, spanking, and ligature marks. There were signs of starvation and dehydration. The anus had been sodomized, evidently with all manner of instruments. One hand and one foot were severely withered, a process caused by overexposure to water.

The burn scars on the torso showed perhaps where cigarettes had been put out. There was evidence needles had been inserted here and there. The narrow head squeezed in on the sides by some terrible pressure, probably a vise.

As soon as he saw the photographs, Walter realized that the police, led by the late Remington Bristow, had built much of four decades of investigation on the wrong premise. Bristow's sentimental attachment to the idea the boy had been accidentally killed by loving parents was absurd.

"It's sadism," Walter said. "Now we see that what Mary told

Kelly and McGillen in Cincinnati makes perfect sense." Mary's mother had an ideal setup to enjoy her exploitation of the boy, he said. The irony of being a respected librarian, working with school-children on the prestigious Main Line of Philadelphia, would have excited her. It was the 1950s, when the world of suburban mothers and children was portrayed by June Cleaver standing in the kitchen in her apron saying with a frown, "I'm worried about the Beave." And the Beaver saying, "Gee, Wally, that's swell!"

The boy's secluded basement prison was a perfect cover for her. Emotionally drained after her attacks, she could clean herself of blood or hair, lock the boy back down in his box, and reassume her roles in society. Neighbor. Friend. Librarian. Wife. Mother. She'd become more rigid, sadism would change her personality, but she'd handle it far below the radar, a few more Bloody Marys with her husband, a few more appearances at church.

She would have thrilled with the sense of power of dominating her secret, far different world.

"She didn't need to cover up in front of her husband or daughter; they were thoroughly terrified of her, totally submissive," Walter said. "Guilt was nonexistent. She was comfortable with the facts—this is who I am. While everyone else is searching for who they are, she knows the truth."

The torture would have proceeded slowly and escalated over the months and years. "The fancy term for the cuts and bruises we see is polymorphic perverse—all over the body, equidistant, no one particular preference. Keep in mind this boy's penis is not going to give this woman any satisfaction, what's going to give her satisfaction, in this heaviest and most complicated of subtypes, is in the process of killing. So therefore one administers torture in a sys-tematic way that then gets them off. Each time she's injuring him she's fantasizing the ultimate death, but she's trying to maximize the experience of emasculation over time."

She probably read to him. Hansel and Gretel would have given her pleasure. The fairy tale, stale and locked in a children's book in the library, was one she brought to life in her own house.

*"Get up, you lazy bones, fetch water and cook something
for your brother," the witch cried. "When he's fat I'll eat
him up."*

*Gretel cried and cried for she could do nothing to save
Hansel.*

The appeal of Jonathan was to snuff out a man when he was
just developing. Destroying him will be the ultimate sexual pleasure, but she prolongs it by slowly degrading him. "She has him
dependent, fearful, degraded, she's created an image of him and
now she's trying to destroy the image, and he just becomes a prop.
Everything that went wrong in her own life, she had a wonderful
whipping boy."

The narrow misshapen head indicates "she did a lot of head
pressure, squeezing his head real tight with hands or implements or
a vise, keeping him immobile in a head harness. She probably had
a fair amount of bondage, tying up, whipping him, taking him out
of the box, someplace where he was unseen. She had sex with him.
She's getting off as she's doing this."

She despises him for his innocence, youth, and his failure. "He's
likely retarded, has surgical scars from his first year of life so he's
damaged goods. He was told by his parents, he's trash, a throw-
away child. She knew what she wanted. She knew she needed a sex
toy, and instead of choosing a dildo or a plastic doll, which they
didn't have then, she could have a real live one and it didn't make
any difference. Now you see how they view other people. Other
people simply don't exist."

When the nightmarish headlines begin about the Boy in the
Box, she follows it closely, getting high from it. At the library and
in church she says, "Isn't it terrible about that boy?" Her power
feels ever more expansive; she is aggressing not only against the
boy but the police department, the entire community of Philadelphia, and the Main Line especially.

By the time of the boy's death, Mary's mother had moved
deep into the Helix and was on the high cusp of bondage and

discipline. "He's bonded in the basement, chained down, secured in that box." Advancement down the scale is unpredictable; it can take weeks, years, or mere hours. The puncture scars on Jonathan's body indicate that the next phase was starting—picquerism—when suddenly on an afternoon in 1957 the mother became a murderer. It was clear to Walter that the mother, having teased out her pleasure over years and then suddenly discovered the exhilarating rush of killing, "would have chosen another victim in short order, and dispatched him much more quickly."

The Main Line librarian, he believes, was a serial killer in the making.

The hatred of innocence continued unabated, of that there is powerful evidence. Shortly before her death, the aging mother asked her daughter, now a young woman, if she could share her bed sexually one more time. The daughter refused, engendering rage from the old woman.

"So the mother was the perfect killer," Walter said. "There's only one problem with this scenario." He took a long draw on a Kool.

"She didn't do it."

He smiled coolly in the gloom of the parlor.

"But I know who did."

CHAPTER 54

DEATH IN THE TIME OF BANANAS

Late one Sunday night, the week before Christmas 2004, Walter was drinking wine and watching ultimate fighting on cable when he received a call from the police department in Hudson, Wisconsin (population 8,775), a small town on the St. Croix River west of Minneapolis–St. Paul. Was it too late to call? The officer sounded nervous.

"Not to worry," Walter said.

"Erickson is dead."

"You're *kidding* me."

"They found him at the church."

Walter listened quietly. He had visited Hudson two weeks ago to consult with the police on the biggest cold case in the small town's history—the double murder at the O'Connell Funeral Home nearly three years earlier.

On February 5, 2002, funeral director Dan O'Connell, thirty-nine, one of the town's leading citizens, and his assistant, college intern James Ellison, twenty-two, were found shot to death in the funeral home in broad daylight. The police were astounded. It was as unthinkable as a spaceship landing in the river and little green men swimming ashore. In Hudson, folks only saw such things on TV, or read about them in the city newspaper.

The victims were respected people with no known enemies

who hadn't engaged in any risky behavior, such as drug dealing, that could have set them up for murder. O'Connell was one of Hudson's most prominent businessmen, a leader of the Catholic Church, a paramedic, and active in the Rotary Club, the Boy Scouts, and YMCA fund-raisers. He had been named King of the North Hudson Pepper Fest. Ellison was an upstanding young man with few local ties. There was no robbery, no motive for the double murder in the quiet small town.

As the police struggled to find suspects, O'Connell's sister, Kathleen, heard from a friend about the Vidocq Society in Philadelphia. The local *Star Tribune,* in Minneapolis, said they were a group of "volunteer super sleuths" and "cold-case cowboys" who tackled murders that "stymied local law enforcement across the nation" and solved 80 percent of them. Willing to "grab on to anything for answers," Kathleen O'Connell e-mailed the Vidocq Society in Philadelphia, pleading for help. She received a formal reply that, out of respect for local police, the society would not consider a murder case until it was at least two years old. On the second anniversary of the slaying, with the Hudson police still thwarted, she wrote again, and was approved. "The Murder of Daniel O'Connell and James Ellison" went on the Vidocq docket as Case No. 133. The society paid for Hudson lieutenant Paul Larson to present the case in the Downtown Club over lunch on April 15, 2004. The case "had Richard's name all over it," Fleisher said, and indeed Walter took an immediate interest and flew out to Hudson to assist.

Fleisher was convinced the case had attracted a strong collective commitment, the passionate heat "absolutely required" to solve a cold murder. "There's a family very interested in their loved one's case, a police department willing to go that extra distance, a prosecutor who's willing to cooperate to get the job done, and the media willing to pay attention to the case," he said. "You need all of it to get the job done."

The famous profiler from Philadelphia arriving in Hudson was front-page news in the weekly *Hudson Gazette.* Walter was pictured grinning and standing alongside the young cops he quickly took under his wing. He used the story to plant seeds of doubt in the suspect. "We know more than the killer thinks we do," he said, employing one of his favorite lines. "If I were him, I wouldn't buy any green bananas."

In the first two days Walter read the case file, interviewed the cops, and considered the seven suspects of some interest to the police, none of whom stood out in their minds after two years. As the young cops trailed him around town, they, too, began smoking Kools.

"Gentlemen, it's plain to me," he announced. "It's the priest."

The suspect was Roman Catholic priest Ryan Erickson, thirty-one years old, who had a powerful motive to silence O'Connell. The funeral director, a leader of the Catholic Church, had confronted the priest the day before the murders about his alleged sexual abuse of boys. O'Connell didn't like Erickson, whose tenure in the church had been disappointing, and threatened to force him out of the church if the charges were true. Walter advised the police to bring the Reverend Erickson in for questioning, and interrogated the priest himself. During questioning by the police and Walter, the priest had been reduced to tears. "He's our guy," Walter said afterward. "The double murder is executed just this way, all power, the removal of a threat."

But now on the telephone, the officer sounded anxious. After Erickson told people that the police considered him a suspect, the priest had killed himself. Parishioners found him that Sunday morning, December 19, before early mass at St. Mary of the Seven Dolors Church in Hurley, Wisconsin, a town of 1,800 people near Lake Superior, where Erickson had been transferred to lead the parish. Churchgoers were confronted with the sight of the priest in full vestments hanging from the porch of the rectory.

Walter let out a low whistle.

Case manager Fred Bornhofen would record Case No. 133 in Vidocq Society records this way: "Investigation revealed that a Roman Catholic priest became a prime suspect and R. Walter assisted in an interview and a confrontation. . . . Fr. Erickson was found hanged in front of his church. . . . Erickson was suspected to be a pathological liar, embezzler, gun enthusiast, and a pervert." Case closed.

But it wasn't so simple. Erickson had left a suicide note in which he denied killing anyone. Investigators didn't have anything on him, he wrote in the note. "None of my guns matched, no DNA of mine was found, and no one saw me leaving the funeral home."

"Hmmmm," Walter said. "It sounds less like the plea of an innocent man than a criminal defense argument. He's unwittingly admitting guilt. It seems the supposed man of God lived a divided life between his professed image and his rather tawdry personal secrets. When events threatened to expose the charade, he refuses to take responsibility, killing to silence it, and when that doesn't work, committing suicide."

"Any thoughts on what we should do?" The police considered Erickson the prime suspect, but they were concerned about the ramifications of his suicide before he was charged, tried, or convicted. The department wanted to somehow resolve any questions and close the case. Walter had the novel idea of bringing the case to court posthumously.

"But first things first—good riddance to bad rubbish."

The officer smirked. The Hudson police had never worked with anybody like Walter.

"By the way, Richard, we found a bunch of ripe bananas in the priest's apartment. But we know he didn't like bananas."

Walter chuckled. The priest had read the newspaper, he said, and risen to the challenge.

"He used them as a timer, and as it happens I was right. He shouldn't have bought any green bananas."

· CHAPTER 55 ·

THE MIRACLE ON SOUTH STREET

Bender was walking along a remote lake on a sunny day. In woods along the shore he saw an old white Cadillac overgrown with vines, the trunk open. He went to investigate. The car had a vintage Jersey plate, the color of yellowing teeth, with the 1930s-style black block letters, GARDEN STATE. The license number swam away as he tried to read it. The trunk was empty, but he saw clearly the blood-stains on the carpeted face of the wheel well. He walked back to the lake and out onto a narrow wooden dock over the shallow blue-green water. Just under the surface a man was floating on his back, naked, his skin a rotted gourd, his black hair swirling in the current, the red dot of a bullet hole through his forehead. His eyes were wide open, bright blue. The lips were moving.

"Help me," the lips cried. "Help me."

Bender startled awake from the dream. An hour later, a New Jersey coroner called, a friend, looking for help in identifying a body. It was a new one.

"A wet one?"

"How'd you know?"

"I had a dream. A man in the water. I'll let you know what I find out." *What I find out when I talk to him again.*

Bender walked with the dead in his dreams. He felt comfort-able with them, embraced, at home. They called to him, shielded him, welcomed him. But mostly they pleaded. It was a gift and he didn't ask its source. He submitted to it without question. You had to do what you were made to do; this was why, in his youth, he was repulsed by art hanging on walls. He was the advocate of the dead, the voice for the voiceless who walked between worlds.

He told Walter about the man in the water. His partner scowled. "Frank, I'm not often intrigued by mob killings. I like challenges. Mob hits are all the same, all power, as nuanced as a tire iron to the head." The dream of the man in the water stopped. But others came—the girl in the steamer trunk, the man hanging in the tree, the boy shot through the temple—crowding his nights and pushing into his days.

Now in his late sixties, Bender was increasingly sensitive to the shadowy realm of dreams. He felt like an instrument being finely tuned with age. Yet he was also more modest and wary of his gift. It spooked him sometimes that he just didn't know how he knew things. Once, while sculpting a statue of a policeman standing heroically in a New Jersey park, a memorial to the courage of fallen officers, he had reluctantly included on the statue the badge number of the young officer he used as a model. "I warned him against it. It was a memorial statue, and it just felt like bad karma." Shortly afterward, the young officer was killed.

Bender never used the word "psychic"; admit to that and he'd never work again. Cops and forensic intellectuals like Walter were the ultimate hypocrites: They mocked seers, except when they used them to spectacular result. Bender was more fully immersed in the world of the flesh than anyone he knew, but somehow it wasn't his purpose.

That summer he found himself praying to God for the first time in his life. He had been given a single hard flame of purpose. Jan had been diagnosed with a fatal cancer, and Bender had abandoned all his other projects for the single task of keeping her alive.

The nonsmoker's lung cancer had rapidly metastasized. Jan had left her job, and stopped chemotherapy after one session, saying it wasn't worth the pain. Doctors at two city hospitals performed numerous tests and said she had weeks, perhaps months, to live. Bender held her through long sleepless nights of screaming pain; the morphine wasn't helping. She was making plans to move into a hospice.

Bender's partners were devastated for him and for Jan. Fleisher wept. All of them were feeling mortal. The Vidocq Society, now seventeen years old, was beginning to lose its old lions. Renowned pathologist Halbert E. Fillinger Jr., seventy-nine, said by many to embody the highest virtues of the Vidocq Society, died in June 2006 of complications from Parkinson's disease. Fillinger, who worked as a pathologist for more than forty years, performed more than 50,000 autopsies, and helped solve hundreds of homicides, was nationally mourned in the forensics community. He was still working as the Montgomery County coroner the week before he died.

In May 2004, Detective Samuel Weinstein, the first officer on the scene at the Boy in the Box crime in 1957 and head of the Vidocq Society team still investigating the death, became the latest in a long blue line to follow the boy. Fleisher eulogized him as a "man among men," a World War II combat Marine who served as a Philadelphia police detective for thirty-five years and voluntarily served with honor seven times with the Israel Defense Forces, including the tank division, making parachute jumps with the IDF while in his seventies. "Rest in peace, my friend," Fleisher said. "You are in a far better place."

Ressler, one of the FBI's pioneers of modern criminal profiling, suffered from a rapidly advancing form of Parkinson's disease. Walter was distraught. With Ressler in a wheelchair and unable to come to the phone, and his coauthor Keppel slowed by major heart surgery, his peers in the first generation of great American profilers were seriously ill or dying. "Who will I have to talk to?"

Fleisher had blacked out while at the wheel, with his wife and two daughters in the car, going sixty miles an hour on an expressway in upstate New York. He came to just in time, but was increasingly worried about his health and his weight. Walter lost days every winter to lung ailments. The training of Stoud took on a new imperative, as he felt his decades of heavy smoking closing in.

Walter was especially moved by Frank and Jan's plight.

"Frank, I won't pray for you," he said, "because that's not what I do. But I will bake some cookies and come down to Philadelphia and we will smoke and drink and enjoy life together. We will all have a marvelous time."

That morning in July 2007, Bender returned to the only job he had allowed himself while supporting Jan through her battle with cancer. It was, ironically, a death mask, one of the crowning works of his career.

Bender had been commissioned by the Roman Catholic Church to sculpt the death mask for Saint John Nepomucene Neumann, the nineteenth-century Bishop of Philadelphia and the first American male saint. Neumann had died in 1860 and was buried in the basement of St. Peter's Church at the corner of Fifth Street and Girard Avenue. The body was being fitted with new vestments, a new Episcopal ring, pectoral cross, and the new mask to mark the bicentennial of the Archdiocese of Philadelphia.

The body of the saint, now 147 years old and wearing the bishop's miter and white robes, lay in a brightly lit glass case beneath the altar of the old Baroque stone church. Thousands of people from around the world visited the national shrine, pressing their hands against the glass and praying for intercessions, for favors and miracles. It was the intact skeleton of the saint, except for small bones that had been reverently removed many years before and cut into tiny pieces and set in very small, glass-covered containers that priests carried, sometimes set in crosses. These were the relics of the saint.

Bender, feeling a bit like Michelangelo, who had labored for popes, had to be approved by the Vatican itself to perform the sacred act of touching the body of a saint. Cardinal Justin Rigali, the Archbishop of Philadelphia, oversaw the opening of the saint's casket and the exchange of the Episcopal garb. Bender was rebuilding the face from a single nineteenth-century photograph of Neumann.

That morning he gently caressed the plaster contours of the face again, and felt the familiar sense of awe and mystery he found hard to describe. Surely it was not the face of God he was touching, but to millions of people around the world, it was the next best thing.

He was pleased with his work. The Redemptorist Father Kevin Moley, the pastor of St. Peter's, was coming to visit the studio that day to inspect his progress. Bender loved to talk to Father Moley about the amazing miracles attributed to the saint.

Within days of Bishop Neumann's death at age forty-eight in 1860, devoted Catholics began coming to the church and praying at the tomb for special favors. Word spread that favors, even miracles, were being granted. Epidemics of typhoid and cholera that killed thousands of Philadelphians between 1891 and 1900 did not claim a single parishioner of Bishop Neumann's church.

According to Father Moley, the first of the three documented miracles that led to sainthood occurred in 1923 in Sassuolo, Italy. Eva Benassi, eleven years old, beyond medical help with acute peritonitis, was given the last rites, as doctors said she could not survive the night. While praying over Benassi, a nun touched the girl's abdomen with a picture of Neumann; that night the peritonitis disappeared.

The second miracle occurred in Villanova, Pennsylvania, on the Main Line of Philadelphia in 1949. On July 8, Kent Lenahan, nineteen years old, was standing on the running board of a moving car when it struck a telephone pole. His skull was crushed, his collarbone broken, a lung punctured. He was admitted to Bryn Mawr Hospital in a coma, and doctors said nothing could be done. Kent began his recovery after his parents prayed at the shrine of Neumann, and then touched him with a relic, a piece of cloth from the bishop's cassock. A month later, he left the hospital on his own power.

In 1963, Michael Flanigan of Philadelphia, six years old, was dying from Ewing's sarcoma, a usually fatal form of cancer.

Doctors said the boy had little hope of recovery. His parents took him to Neumann's tomb, where a parish priest blessed the boy and touched his body with a crucifix containing a relic of the bishop, a chip of bone from the bishop's remains. Another chip of bone, encased in glass, was pinned to the boy's clothing. Six weeks later, all traces of the disease had disappeared.

Father Moley arrived on South Street that afternoon with a young priest. Bender showed them the death mask, nearly complete. The project had taken nearly a year of planning by the church, and now Father Moley was thrilled. "It's magnificent," he said.

Jan appeared, and Frank introduced her.

"My wife has cancer," Bender said.

"May I pray for her?" Father Moley asked.

He looked at Jan, who nodded. "Please," Bender said.

His assistant priest placed on her the saint's relic, a tiny peice of Neumann's bone. Father Moley gently laid his hand on Jan's head and said the prayer to Saint John Neumann. It is a prayer for his intercession to bring a miracle from Jesus Christ that ends, "May death still find us on the sure road to our Father's House with the light of living Faith in our hearts."

Jan felt a warmth coursing through her body. "It's not like a bolt of lightning. It's soft," she said.

Within days, the pain began to fade. Jan rose from bed and returned to work. Six weeks later, test after test confirmed the inexplicable: She was completely clear of cancer. Doctors were baffled; the local NBC station reported the "medical miracle." The Benders were awed. Jan wept with joy with Frank; she believed his devotion to her and to his work with Saint John Neumann had saved her. Father Moley said, "Maybe Saint John Neumann wanted this intercession as a gift" to the artist for his magnificent work. Fleisher jubilantly shared the news with the Vidocq Society.

Walter, ever skeptical, didn't believe it. He saw Bender talking about his wife's illness in a firestorm of publicity. It didn't work for him. It didn't seem right.

CHAPTER 56

KNIGHTS OF THE ROUND TABLES

Richard Walter, the thin man in black tie, was nearing the end of a Chardonnay and his patience, listening to a society woman prattle on about this and that. The Pen Ryn mansion, 250 years old, glowed with yellow light on the west bank of the Delaware River, America's first mansion row. Music and laughter floated out into the darkness over the broad lawn down to the river. Ladies were greeted by a string quartet, a flute of champagne, and a rose from a smiling federal agent who specialized in busting drug lords. Men had tucked Berettas and Glocks into the jackets and pants of tuxedos; women swapped DNA and blood sample kits for gowns and pearls.

Suddenly without a word Walter pirouetted and walked away from the woman, the back of his starched-proper figure disappearing swiftly into the crowd. She flapped her mouth open and closed like a magnificent egret.

"My God! He walked away right in the middle of my sentence!"

"Oh, it's OK," said the woman standing next to her. "He does that to everyone."

No ball was quite like it: the Vidocq Society annual black-tie fête, event of the year for men and women dressed to kill.

"Where else can you see Frank Bender in a tux?" asked Bill

Fleisher, magnificent in black tie with the bronze Vidocq medal around his neck on the tricolor ribbon. He raised a glass of champagne, toasting Bender's remarkable identification of Colorado Jane Doe, fifty-five years after the young woman's corpse was discovered by hikers in a Boulder canyon in 1954. The Vidocq Society's latest triumph had unearthed another possible victim of Los Angeles's "Lonely Hearts Killer" Harvey Glatman. Fleisher impulsively grabbed Bender and gave him a hug.

Walter stood to the side, frowning at the public display of affection. In his classic tuxedo, Walter looked like a gaunt double for Holmes in the original Sidney Paget illustrations of Arthur Conan Doyle's stories in *The Strand* magazine in the 1890s. But no one had the courage to tell him.

The round tables in the great hall were crowded with detectives from the United States, Europe, and the Middle East on this Sunday in October 2009. Bottles of wine and sprays of alstroemeria lilies had replaced crime-scene photos and autopsy reports de rigueur the rest of the year. This one night of the year, the Murder Room, a portable feast, was decorated for butter, not guns, for celebration and sheer joy.

Commissioner Fleisher prepared for the event as if for a State of the Union address. After the prime rib and salmon, the cake and the coffee, and as the wine and whiskey made extra rounds, Fleisher would emcee the awards ceremony for the coveted Vidocq Society Medal of Honor. The ball was the moment to take stock; a chance to look back and ahead. For nearly twenty years now Fleisher had done so with pride, excitement, and keen anticipation of what was to come. He had watched the society grow from a social luncheon club for detectives to a crime-fighting organization with a global reach.

The Vidocq Society family had grown from three men at lunch to 82 full members, one for each year of E. F. Vidocq's life, to more than 150 total members, including associates. They had investigated more than 300 unsolved murders, solving 90 percent, offering advice and counsel and the name of the killer. There were more tangible results: arrests, convictions, and depression, and perhaps suicide prevented among families haunted by murder. Truth was their client. It was Aeschylus who said the words of truth are simple, and so it was with the Vidocq Society's achievements: the lost found, the nameless named, the guilty punished, the innocent set free. VSMs were helpmates to the living, heroes to the dead.

Fleisher, Bender, and Walter sat separately at the round tables, honoring the democratic fellowship. But even the casual views of them standing together in the great hall, draped in the bronze relief medals of E. F. Vidocq cast by Bender, their own Medals of Honor for meritorious service, were powerful affirmations of their unique partnership, the heart of the Vidocq family.

It was a family that kept growing. Jim Dunn, now a tricolor-pinned VSM, shared news that he said was "music to my ears"—his son's killer was denied parole until 2013. Walter said in a letter to the Texas Parole Board that by refusing to reveal what happened to Scott's body, Leisha Hamilton showed that "for her . . . the murder is not over!" She was an unrepentant psychopath with an "insatiable desire for stimulation and conquest" who would seek new victims: "If and when [Hamilton] is reviewed again for release, it is suggested that you re-read this letter."

Dunn and Walter would continue to battle to keep her in prison the full twenty years, until 2017. But time and Dunn's wife were steering him toward Walter's wisdom that a man lets the fires of fury and righteousness burn down.

Walter's wisdom was for others. He burned with the desire to put away a third killer of Scott Dunn who had "flown beneath the radar all these years."

"I reminded Jim I'm a graduate of the Evelyn Woods School of Revenge. I'm in this for the long haul."

It was a night for stories, family stories. Walter was full of them. He had received a strange package from a man in New Jersey some years ago, Mike Rodelli, who claimed to have solved the most famous unsolved serial killer case in modern American history. He'd learned the name of the Zodiac Killer, the unknown

assailant who had killed five Californians in 1968 and 1969, taunt-
ing the police with letters and cryptograms. Walter had been skeptical, but he'd worked with the amateur sleuth for years, coaching
him, and now he was convinced the man was right—the Zodiac
Killer was still alive, an elderly and quite wealthy man in California, still living off the pleasure of his iconic murders. Few doubted
Walter. He'd also worked for years with another amateur investigator, Ohio trucker Robert Mancini, whom Walter believed
had finally cracked the case that Eliot Ness couldn't. Years after
the Vidocq Society studied the case, Mancini had identified the
Butcher of Cleveland. The killer was a long-dead sexual sadist
who'd worked for the railroads. Justice was a different matter in
both cases; justice always was.

"Did I tell you about the time I killed a prosecutor?" Walter
asked. He had gone to Oklahoma on a Vidocq Society case to confront the state attorney on a double murder the prosecutor refused to
investigate for political reasons, and demanded he file murder charges.
The prosecutor told him, "Screw yourself and leave the state." Walter replied, "I could go through you as easily as around you, but I'd
prefer to give you a chance to grow wiser. I will call you three days
after Thanksgiving, and if you have not changed your mind, you
and I will have a man-to-boy chat." The prosecutor died of a heart
attack before Thanksgiving. "Good!" Walter told the prosecutor's
office. "Whom do I have to deal with next?" Fleisher called the governor of Oklahoma, a friend of his, and the result was "an extremely
cooperative new prosecutor," Walter said. "We solved the case."

Walter was nearly seventy years old and suffered winter ailments now of greater duration. But he hadn't slowed down.

"Did I tell you about the time I killed a priest?" Walter asked.

The solving of the double murder in Hudson, Wisconsin, had
become one of his favorite stories. After the suicide of Catholic priest Ryan Erickson, whom Walter had named as the prime
suspect, the police had taken the profiler's unusual advice to try
to establish the dead cleric's guilt in court. In a remarkable October
2005 "John Doe" hearing, St. Croix County circuit judge Eric

Lundell determined the priest had committed the double murder to avoid exposure as a pedophile. The priest's lawyer refused to attend, maintaining his deceased client's innocence. There was no jury.

The prosecution presented fifteen witnesses. A young man testified that Father Ryan served him alcohol and sexually assaulted him repeatedly as a teenager in 2000 and 2001. An eyewitness described a car similar to Erickson's parked outside the funeral home at the time of the killings. Detectives testified that Erickson knew crime scene details only the killer would know, such as how many bullets were fired into the victims (three) and where they struck (in the head). A church deacon testified that Erickson confessed the killings to him. Erickson was looking out a window when he blurted out, "I done it, and they're going to get me. . . . Do you know what they do with young guys in prison, especially priests?"

Judge Lundell wrote, "I conclude that Ryan Erickson probably committed the crimes in question. On a scale of one to ten, I would consider it a ten." The Vidocq Society awarded the Medal of Honor to several members of the Hudson Police Department for solving the double murder at the O'Connell Funeral Home.

Fleisher was especially proud of their work on the tragic case of Marie Noe, convicted of killing eight of her babies. Three months after her arrest, Marie Noe, then seventy years old and walking into the courtroom with a cane, pleaded guilty in June 1999 to smothering eight of her ten children beginning in 1949. The case drew national attention, forcing police and medical professionals to rethink many cases long believed to be sudden infant death syndrome or "crib death" as possible murders.

Marie's husband, Arthur, sat shaking his head as the names of the eight children were read aloud, and the prosecutor described his wife as "as much a mass murderer as Ted Bundy."

Noe's lawyer, David Rudenstein, said Marie did not have "the heart of a killer. This is one of those situations that make us human. Some things happen in life that we cannot understand."

The court treated Marie more like a sad old mother than a psychopathic killer. She would serve no jail time for mass murder.

By the conditions of her plea bargain, which took into account Arthur's frail health, she was given twenty years of probation, the first five under home confinement, with at least a year with an electronic monitoring ankle bracelet. She was also ordered to undergo treatment sessions with a psychiatrist; her brain was said to be important to study for clues to the root causes of infanticide. Marie told detectives, "All I can figure is that I'm ungodly sick."

The Vidocq Society had awarded Medals of Honor to *Philadelphia* magazine writer Stephen Fried and Philadelphia homicide Sergeant Larry Nodiff for their work on the Noe case.

Even amid celebration, Fleisher had regrets. "I'm Jewish," he said. "I always have regrets."

Near the top of the list was Carol Ann Dougherty, the nine-year-old raped and murdered in a church in 1962. The Bristol police investigation had gone nowhere. DNA testing advised by the Vidocq Society was "inconclusive." In 1997, Chief Frank Peranteau told the Vidocq Society that "he considers the matter over as the Grand Jury had identified a possible suspect who has been convicted of another murder in another state," O'Kane wrote in the Vidocq case log. "The investigation appeared to clear the suspect priest, but he could not explain the ligature," the strangulation marks that matched a priest's cincture. No arrests were made.

But thirteen years after the Vidocq Society called the priest the prime suspect, a Philadelphia grand jury in 2005 named Father Sabadish one of sixty-three pedophile priests that the Archdiocese of Philadelphia had allowed to prey on their flocks in the past fifty years. The archdiocese was accused of routinely transferring molesters to keep hundreds of abuse allegations from surfacing.

Joan McCrane testified to the grand jury that Sabadish molested her when she was seven years old in 1960, two years before Carol was murdered, at St. Michael the Archangel in Levittown. It started with "tickling," she said. "He'd put his hands on my shoulders. Then, on my chest. Then, down my pants. . . . He told me that it was our secret and that I was never to tell anyone or we'd both go to hell. I never said anything because I was a little girl and I was scared to death."

Transferred to St. Mark's in 1962, Sabadish molested her for two more years, then started abusing her ten-year-old brother, Bill Henis. Sabadish's assaults on the siblings occurred at the rectories at St. Mark's and St. Michael's, the priest's home, his car, and his mother's home, often weekly.

"I hated the guy and I was afraid of him," Henis said. "He didn't like kids. He'd slap you around, call you stupid. You never knew what would set him off. . . . Sabadish said this is how he showed his love for me. He'd always give me candy. The glove compartment of his car was always filled with it. He'd tell me candy fairies had put it there."

Sabadish didn't live to see his secret exposed. After serving as chaplain of the Norristown church, he was appointed in 1994 to the fifteenth parish of his career, as the parochial vicar of St. Stanislaus in Lansdale, Pennsylvania, before retiring. He died in 1999 at the age of eighty-one. He was eulogized by another priest as a man who "touched countless souls, especially those of children."

Fleisher remained confident the VSMs were right, and the police had missed it. "It was the priest all along," he said. "The guy was a monster."

Forty-seven years after her murder, the Carol Ann Dougherty murder case remained cold.

As the great hall filled, a crowd formed around Bender. The sculptor was, as he often had been, the man of the moment. His ID of Colorado Jane Doe, which would make national news, helped crack the oldest case the Vidocq Society had ever worked on in the field.

Fleisher had just learned that the Boulder County sheriff's office had identified the unknown corpse found by hikers along the banks of Boulder Creek on April 8, 1954, as Dorothy Gay Howard, an eighteen-year-old blond woman reported as missing from Phoenix, Arizona.

VSMs had worked the case since 2004, when the sheriff's office reopened it. The Vidocq Society sent two nationally renowned forensic scientists to exhume Jane Doe's grave—VSM Dr. Walter Birkby, a forensic anthropologist at the Human Identification Laboratory in Tucson, Arizona, and forensic pathologist Dr. Richard Froede, the former U.S. Defense Department chief medical examiner.

Dr. Birkby had appeared in the Discovery Channel documentary *Mummies: Frozen in Time,* and been part of a scientific team that uncovered the remains of Colorado cannibal Alfred Packer and the five gold prospectors he killed and ate in 1874 (their bones showed "an insatiable hunger").

Jane Doe's grave had collapsed in half a century, crushing the skeleton, and forcing the two VSMs to work painstakingly for two days recovering her remains. Dr. Birkby spent three to four weeks at the Human Identification Laboratory just piecing together the many shattered pieces of the woman's skull before Bender could build a face on it. Bender's bust appeared on *America's Most Wanted,* adding to an avalanche of publicity that prompted Michelle Marie Fowler to contact the sheriff's office, saying she thought Jane Doe was Howard, her great-aunt. A DNA sample from another great-aunt—Roberta Marlene Howard Ashman, a surviving younger sister of Howard—matched the DNA that Drs. Birkby and Froede had recovered from the grave. The mystery that had haunted the family was over, Ashman said. They could "begin the journey of healing and closure that has eluded our family for the past fifty-six years."

Howard's ID was so new that the Boulder sheriff's office would not announce it until three days after the Vidocq ball, in a press release that didn't mention the Vidocq Society by name. But Boulder sheriff's detective Steve Ainsworth—the lead detective on the case—said, "Frank gave Jane Doe a face and a personality. The likeness was uncanny."

Bender seemed to grow more amazing as the years went by. Yet this evening was shadowed by the fact that his wife was too ill to attend. Her cancer had come back. Jan believed her husband's love and divine intervention had allowed her to beat the prognosis for more than a year. But recently she had quit her job as a law firm receptionist. The exhaustion and pain were too much. She was planning for hospice care. Doctors did not expect her to live another year. Bender was trying to remain positive. "Jan's beat it once, and the doctors couldn't explain it. If miracles can happen once, they can happen again."

Ella, his longtime Girlfriend No. 1 and art assistant, was his date for the evening. Tall and blond, with her hair done up over a black dress, she looked on with tenderness and pride as he received a stream of well-wishers and kudos.

Bender still felt the loss of legendary medical examiner Hal Fillinger, the old lion of the Vidocq Society who died in 2006, and who had launched Bender's career in the Philadelphia morgue in 1977. In those thirty-two years, Bender's forensic art had changed the face of American crime and criminology. The FBI, after years of slighting Bender and experimenting with computer forensic busts, had returned to old-fashioned art by human hands—to doing it like Frank did it.

His powerful assist to the marshals in bringing in their number one Most Wanted fugitive in 1987, Cosa Nostra kingpin Alphonse "Allie Boy" Persico, had shaken up the Joseph Colombo crime family in New York City. Persico was the older brother and right-hand man of Carmine "The Snake" Persico, the godfather of the Colombo family.

On September 12, 1989, two years after his arrest, Allie Boy died of cancer of the larynx at the age of sixty-one while serving a twenty-five-year sentence at the federal correctional facility in Lompoc, California.

Mass murderer John E. List, whose capture two decades earlier brought Bender international notice, had also recently died in prison. On March 21, 2008, List, an inmate at New Jersey State Prison in Trenton, succumbed to complications of pneumonia. He had enjoyed the largesse of New Jersey taxpayers until the ripe old age of eighty-two.

List lived eighteen years behind bars, nearly the same amount of time he spent as a fugitive. He outlived the family he murdered by thirty-seven years. In a 2002 television interview with ABC's Connie Chung, List said he killed his family out of fear they would be destroyed by debt and fall away from their Christian beliefs. List prayed aloud for their souls as he laid the bodies of his wife and children under the Tiffany dome skylight in the ballroom. Walter pointed out that if List had simply sold the Tiffany, he could have erased his debts instead of his family.

Until his death List corresponded monthly with the ninety-three-year-old Lutheran pastor he knew as a young man, who believed God had forgiven List for killing his wife, mother, and three young children. The Newark *Star-Ledger* begged to differ. "If the hell John List so strongly believed in exists, surely he is there today."

The New York Times told its worldwide readers that a producer at *America's Most Wanted* had asked "Frank Bender, a forensic sculptor, and Richard Walter, a criminal psychologist," to help capture the fugitive mass murderer. For the previous eighteen years, "dozens of FBI agents and investigators from Union County, New Jersey, found no trace of Mr. List in the United States or overseas." Bender's bust led to List's arrest in eleven days.

John Walsh, the host of *America's Most Wanted*, was widely quoted crediting Bender's List sculpture for launching *AMW* as a phenomenon. "I call Frank with the tough cases," Walsh said. Bender's legacy as a crime-fighting artist was secure.

The *Times* described his work in admiring detail. "Studying photographs of Mr. List when he was in his mid-40s, Mr. Bender imagined how he might look in 1989, his face sagging with time," the newspaper wrote.

But the sculptor was apoplectic when he read the next sentence in the *Times:* "Mr. Walter theorized that Mr. List would still be wearing horn-rimmed glasses, to make him appear successful." Although the newspaper had gotten it mostly right, Bender grew more determined to extinguish Walter's small but important contribution from the record. He talked about suing media organizations that made the same mistake. "Frank, are you nuts?" Walter replied.

But the thin man let his own fires tamp down. "If he's nuts, he's our nut. Frank's my partner, for better and often for worse."

Just a month before the Vidocq banquet, on September 10, Bender's thirty years of forensic work came full circle. John Martini, the mob hit man and serial killer who murdered Anna Duval at the Philadelphia airport in 1977, Bender's first case, died in New Jersey State Prison in Trenton, also the jailhouse of John List.

Martini, seventy-nine, New Jersey's oldest death row inmate, was confined to a wheelchair, ill, obese. Depressed, he told his attorneys in 1991 that he wanted to drop appeals and be put to death rather than eat bad prison food and live in "horrible" conditions. The week before he was to be executed, a nun working as a prison chaplain got him to change his mind, and the execution never occurred.

The long suffering of Marilyn Flax, the widow of business executive Irving Flax, kidnapped and murdered by Martini in 1989, reminded Fleisher of the passion that still drove him to help America's victims of crime, who still were often victimized by the justice system as well.

For years the widow was afraid to go to the bank where she withdrew their entire $25,000 savings to pay the ransom to Martini (who shot her husband anyway). She had negotiated with the kidnapper herself, a "horror," looked into his ice-cold eyes at the drop-off. For years she slept three hours a night, terrified Martini would fulfill his threat to "have somebody kill me."

She still wore the first diamond pendant her husband gave her, kept his pajamas, socks, and ties in a dresser in her bedroom, carried the first note he ever sent her, "Miss you already."

"We were madly, madly in love," she said of her husband. "I couldn't wait to wake up in the morning to see him. He felt the same way." When she realized she would never have the satisfaction of seeing Martini die by lethal injection, she wrote him a letter on death row.

"You took away the love of my life," she wrote. "They say God is a forgiving God . . . but I am certain that Heaven's doors are not open to you. Just to think that your soul will be tormented forever and ever—what a comfort that gives me. Enjoy hell."

Walter and Bender were still tight as warring brothers. They had gone up to Manlius, New York, together to be honored at the Manlius Police Benevolent Association banquet for joint work in solving the murder of Lorean Weaver, the Girl with the Missing Face. After the banquet, they celebrated at the crowded hotel bar in what seemed a competition to drink the most vodka. At four in the morning, they were the only two standing. Later, they lectured together to a high school criminal justice class in Manlius taught by Kathy Hall, wife of detective Keith Hall (who'd first called Bender and the Vidocq Society in on the case, and received the Vidocq Society Medal of Honor for his work).

As he talked to the students, Walter realized that despite their differences he and Bender shared a rare bond, a sense of mystery. Bender told the students the trick to "putting a face on a faceless skull" was to feel the invisible harmonies in the universe. Walter told them, "Once you have crawled inside the soul of the criminal and heard some of the just evil people do, it has an effect. It can put the cold water to innocence. There're lots of things if I didn't have to know, I'd rather not." The thin man said that when one faced these things as he and his partner did, when one acknowledged true evil, life became very precious.

"Remember, life is grand," he told the students. "Life is wonderful!"

It wasn't long before Bender was telling everyone he met that Walter had named the wrong suspect in the Manlius murder.

At the podium Fleisher called for quiet. It was time.

In past years, the Vidocq Society had also honored the famous forensic anthropologist William Bass, for founding "The Body Farm" at the University of Tennessee, which revolutionized the study of human decomposition; FBI special agent John S. Martin, America's top Soviet spy catcher, who investigated the 1964 murders of three civil rights workers in Meridian, Mississippi; and Dr. Henry Lee, who investigated the JonBenet Ramsey and Laci Peterson murders, and O. J. Simpson's alleged slayings of Nicole Brown Simpson and Ronald Goldman.

The first two winners this year were Vidocq Society stalwarts.

Philadelphia district attorney Lynn Abraham was known for unflinching toughness and integrity and her relentless pursuit of French fugitive killer Ira Einhorn. Haskell Askin, one of the nation's top forensic dentists, had worked on a string of major cases from the Megan Kanka trial to the 9/11 terrorist attacks.

Abraham spoke movingly about her determination to become a lawyer after medicine, her first choice, was denied to her as a woman and a Jew. Askin, to the surprise of those who hadn't seen him lately, had gone from a hearty man in the prime of a brilliant career to a frail, smiling, wistful man at the podium, shrunken by terminal cancer. Surrounded by family and friends, he thanked his VSM colleagues with courage and humor and the air of a noble farewell.

It was the first surprise in an evening of unexpected revelations.

Finally, Fleisher bestowed the Vidocq Society's highest honor, the Halbert Fillinger Lifetime Achievement Award, reserved for an illustrious forensic investigator at the end of a long career.

The award went to Frank Bender.

Frank Bender thanked his late mentor, Hal Fillinger, for introducing him to corpse No. 5233 in the morgue thirty years ago. He said it was a shock to feel the cold gray flesh—"You know I like bodies warm." He grinned, his silver incisor winking in the lights, and there was laughter.

The tuxedo couldn't conceal Bender's fit boxer's body or sense of vigor. Sixty-eight years old, balding with a white goatee, he looked like a man at least a decade younger, the envy of younger men, capable of chasing muggers and drawing justice for years to come. His eyes gleamed with energy, like a bulb too bright for the fixture. He looked like a man women would always love.

He said he felt the great forensic pathologist was with him, watching him now. Fillinger had said, "Once you get bit by the forensic bug, you're hooked forever. And he was right." Looking back on his career, Bender loved being a part of the Vidocq Society because it gave him a feeling of camaraderie he had experienced only once before, in the Navy.

He wanted to do more with Vidocq; there weren't enough cases that needed his art. He always wished he could do more.

He smiled again and thanked everybody, and the applause rang through the great hall. They were still cheering him when he sat down. He was Frank, a cad among moral men, a hero among mortals, the incarnation of the wild Vidocq, and they loved him. He could say anything to them.

Walter scowled. What had Bender—the same age as him—accomplished to deserve such crowning recognition? Others thought it was odd. It was strange hearing Frank look back fondly on his career when he was smack in the middle of it, fresh from one of his greatest cases, Colorado Jane Doe. Strange, too, when Fleisher introduced "my great friend Frank Bender" in an emotional speech that summed up their decades together, and then gave Frank a sloppy bear hug. No one burned with more passion for the work than Bender, the all-night iron horse. No one lived more in the moment and less in memory.

After the speech, Bender, Fleisher, and Walter walked together out onto the patio overlooking the river. The founders were joined by other men in tuxedos, with cigars and port, Cockburn's Special Reserve, and women tippy in high heels and gowns with light throws. The autumn evening was unseasonably warm. They stood looking out at the river rolling by in darkness. Pushing the bank, it looked joined to the flat landscape, the rough stitching between two states.

Frank said, "I feel great right now. And it's now that counts, right?" His smile, like his voice and his eyes, was electric, joyful.

His partners nodded. "Yeah, sure, Frank. It's great." They knew. Some others knew but Frank had not wanted to share it widely.

Frank Bender was dying.

Walter stared at Fleisher, who laughed nervously. "Yeah, it was a last-minute thing. We weren't going to give Frank the award, but then we found out he's dying. We gotta give it to him."

Walter glared. Bender roared with laughter.

In recent days he'd learned that he had pleural mesothelioma, the cancer brought on by exposure to asbestos. The cancer was extremely rare, a thousand times rarer than lung cancer caused by heavy smoking. Only about one in a million people worldwide developed it. And it was deadly.

Mesothelioma took twenty to fifty years to develop after exposure. Bender was exposed to asbestos in the Navy, having fled the art establishment and an art college scholarship, knowing only that he didn't want his art to hang only in museums. The Navy had offered to make him a photographer, but he refused. He wanted to work in the engine room, a mechanic like his dad, although he still couldn't stop pencil-sketching the other mechanics. He spent three years in the late 1950s and early 1960s in the engine room of the destroyer escort U.S.S. *Calcaterra*, loving it. "I not only worked with asbestos," he said, "I slept with it."

The cancer filled his torso. "It's bigger than a baby's head," the doctor said. The image made him feel bitterly miraculous, like he was giving birth to his own death. Radiation could ease the pain, but it wouldn't save him. Chemotherapy could shut down his kidneys. "Surgery would be fatal," Bender said, "because the cancer is already around my heart and lungs like a spiderweb. I have no options."

Shaken, he had taken his partners into his confidence. He asked Fleisher to read the medical reports for him and give his impression. "It looks very grim, Frank," Fleisher said sadly. Then Fleisher let out a small laugh.

"It's just like you, Frank. There could be a movie on your life, and you kick the bucket. The big check comes, and you won't be here to cash it."

Bender laughed. They had been friends forever and Fleisher could do no wrong, ever. Bender loved life and he was going to keep at it. He wasn't frightened. He was Frank.

The pain was very bad at night. The doctors gave him morphine, but he wouldn't take it.

"Vodka and orange juice works much better," he said. A screwdriver eased the hurt more smoothly, and it was still sexy. It was hard to pick up a woman after you did morphine.

"His biggest worry," Fleisher told Walter, "is he still wants to have sex."

Walter rolled his eyes. "Typical Frank."

"I don't think he has as much sex as he says he does," Fleisher said. "I think he just likes to say it."

Walter agreed. He didn't even completely believe that Bender had cancer. The fact was, he hadn't believed it when Bender had crowed to the media rooftops about the divine "miracle" of Jan's cancer disappearing, and Jan's cancer came back. Had it ever really gone? Or was Frank just addicted to getting his name in the paper, exposure that might mean work? It was a harsh thought, but in Walter's world, such psychopathic deceptions and worse happened with every dawn. But deep down, Walter knew his cold reaction was largely a defense.

He didn't want Frank to be sick. He didn't want him to die.

"Richard, if you don't believe me I can show you the medical report," Bender said at the next Vidocq Society meeting.

"Not necessary," Walter said, grabbing his friend's arm. "Come with me." He dragged Bender over to talk with Dr. Maryanne Costello, distinguished VSM and former chief medical examiner of the state of Virginia. Dr. Costello was one of the nation's most esteemed forensic pathologists. The living Sherlock Holmes was investigating, searching for evidence.

"Tell Dr. Costello what your doctors told you."

Bender launched into detail about his cancer, and the two of them were going back and forth, "using a lot of words I didn't understand," Walter said.

Dr. Costello said, "How long did they give you?"

Walter lowered his head. "I knew then that this was real," he said.

Bender said, "Eight to eighteen months. It's already destroyed one of my ribs."

Walter arched an eyebrow. "I've got an extra rib," he said.

Bender stared at him.

"Really. Do you want it?"

"No, thanks, I'm watching my weight."

They laughed.

"You see, doctor, he's all about vanity to the end."

Bender was determined to make his time with Jan sweet time. He knew they'd always been meant to be together, and now he felt it in a deep soul way. He remembered when he was eight years old, standing on the stoop of his row house at 2520 Lithgow Street. A young couple carrying a baby knocked on the door of number 2518 next door, the Schwartzes' house. The door opened and the Schwartzes excitedly welcomed the couple. Frank saw them carry the baby into the house. Many years later he learned the Schwartzes were Jan's aunt and uncle. The baby was Jan, on the day of her christening. "I saw my wife when she was just born," Frank marveled. "Now *that's* having history."

Now they were dying together. The doctors had them going at almost the exact same time. It stunned him, like the plot of an opera. "It's kind of romantic, in a way."

Frank poured his energies into taking care of Jan. Sixty-one and very tired, with nerve damage from chemotherapy, she said, "I'm like a fuse that burned out at the tip." He was still a forensic artist, willing to take on any assignment, hoping the Vidocq Society would need him. But it was harder than ever to find work in a recession.

Bender took up the brushes that had started him in the art world. He began painting again. A watercolor of Jan as a smiling ghostly presence floating above a green field; a stark Gothic sketch of a black-and-gray wasteland above which triumphantly rises a tall church (St. Peter's Church, the shrine of Saint John Neumann, the miracle worker); a man making love to a young woman on a train.

He'd made seven paintings inspired by Jan when she first got sick, and put them on his Web site with a one-line legend: "And she survived!"

On Halloween 2009, the couple that had had their wedding reception in a graveyard celebrated their thirty-ninth anniversary with the gusto of a first date. They drank and danced to "Nobody Does It Better."

"They've had a rich life," their daughter Vanessa Bender,

thirty-eight, told the *Philadelphia Inquirer*. "We wish they had more time."

Frank said he wasn't afraid of death. "I can't say, 'Wow, I wish I had done this or that,' because I realize what I've done. If I go in eight months, I'll still feel fulfilled." Death wasn't something foreign; he'd had his hands on the Reaper for years. And there was a lot of good karma waiting for him wherever it was he was going.

"My father would rather see a victim identified than make money," their daughter Lisa Brawner, forty-four, told the *Inquirer*. "It drives my mother crazy, but I know when he gets to heaven, people will be lining up to thank him."

"In all my dreams," he said, "the dead protect me."

That night in the mansion, with the lights and the music floating out over the river, it still all seemed like a dream to him. A friend, VSM Barb Cohan-Saavedra, the former assistant U.S. attorney, warmly congratulated him on his award. She said she always thought of him as a wizard.

"We always knew you were Merlin," Fleisher quipped. "I'm glad somebody announced it officially from the podium tonight."

A speaker had told them that men, and now women, had met at round tables to battle evil for a thousand years. There was evidence for a historical King Arthur. Yet, why, he asked, had the Arthurian tales featured three men? Why had these archetypes lasted for ten centuries? Looking at Fleisher, Bender, and Walter, he said there was always in the old stories a wounded king struggling to save the wasteland; his right-hand knight to destroy evil; and the wizard, Merlin, a seer who introduces the life of the spirit, transcendence of good and evil, but is bewitched and finally entrapped by women. Bender grinned, and laughter rippled in the room.

Why did the king keep the seat next to him empty? It was the Perilous Seat, fatal to all but a knight worthy of the journey, who could claim the Holy Grail. More laughter. Fleisher, they knew, kept the seat next to him at the round table empty as a memorial to his late brother-in-law Sal. "That was Sal's seat, and I loved him. There was nobody like Sal."

"It's *perfect!*" Cohan-Saavedra said. "Frank *is* Merlin. Richard is Lancelot, and Bill is the Fisher King." She turned to Bender. "Frank, next year you'll have to come dressed in a long robe and a tall wizard's hat."

"If I make it next year."

She hadn't heard. He told her his news, and she didn't hesitate a second. "Frank, you'll make it."

Two men stood nearby, at the edge of the conversation. One short, one tall, both white-haired. Kelly and McGillen were quiet that night. Their table felt empty. Weinstein was gone, having died quietly in his sleep on his seventy-eighth birthday, and Earl Palmer, too. The Vidocq Society Boy in the Box investigative team was the two of them now. Life was pills, prayers, grandchildren, great-grandchildren. They were slowing down. But they didn't stop.

There was a gentle wistfulness about the two old Irishmen, but they were ironweed stubborn. They declined to share the police skepticism about Mary. They had finally talked to the owner of Mary's old house, who was terrified about what her children and the neighbors would think, into letting them see the basement.

On a fall day when the children were at school, Kelly, McGillen, Detective Augustine, and two police crime technicians arrived at the house in two unmarked cars. The basement walls, floor, and drain seemed just as Mary described. So did the side door that led outside, blocked by shrubs as it opened onto the driveway. Kelly took pictures and the crime tech measured everything. "Those beams show where the coal bin used to be," said Kelly, who'd tended a coal furnace as a child. "Do you see?" Extra ceiling beams formed a rectangle that looked like it once supported the walls of a coal bin. Augustine said they could go ahead and dig into oil company or real estate records to see if the house once had a coal furnace, but it didn't matter if they proved that, too. It just didn't add up. The police closed the case. The old men of the Vidocq Society smiled and nodded, but they knew in their hearts that Mary told the truth.

"We see the boy in three weeks, Bill," Kelly reminded Bill Fleisher. "The fifty-second year."

It was just the three of them now at the grave every Veterans Day, the anniversary of the reburial. The park cemetery was gray in the fall, but they brought armfuls of bright flowers. They stood at the tombstone and said a few words to one another and to God. Then they took pictures standing together behind the stone. There were years of pictures like a family album, once five and now three of them standing with the boy in their fedoras and military caps and autumn smiles, guardians of something nameless. It was a private ceremony; the media and public were not invited. They were carrying on Rem Bristow's thirty-seven years of work, the blue unbroken line. Sometimes Kelly went alone, an errand of joy. The old man leaned down and kissed the stone. "I'll see you soon, Jonathan."

Fleisher wasn't convinced that Mary had told the truth. But he believed "we're going to get it. The case is solvable."

Walter wrinkled his nose, as if he smelled sentimentality. "I know who killed the Boy in the Box," he said, "and Mary's mother isn't it." Walter said it was the young college student who discovered the boy but delayed reporting it for days because the cops had already been hassling him about being a Peeping Tom. The cops at the time couldn't have understood the significance of the sexual perversion, the signs of the pathology in the suspicious man who discovered the body.

The student admitted he'd spied on the unwed mothers of the Good Shepherd Home, Walter said, and the newspapers in the 1950s didn't publish the rest of the story: Hidden behind the tree line the young man masturbated as he watched the women across the street. "First, the guy's an admitted liar and he's a pervert. The police gave him a rough time about the peeping, but nothing came of it." With his sexual perversion, he had already entered the Helix, the "House of Sadism." He was on the growth curve of the sadistic killer.

"This is the guy who found the body," Walter said. "I don't believe in coincidences. As it happens, he's still alive. He's in his eighties. He's had a long time to revel in the memory of raping and killing the boy. In fact, he's still taking pleasure from it. The murder isn't over until the murderer says it is."

Fleisher looked over his shoulder to make sure no society women or laymen were in earshot. The Murder Room had unexpectedly rematerialized in the foyer of the Pen Ryn. Sexual sadism hadn't been on the menu.

"Joe, I've got a job for you." Walter turned to his friend Joe O'Kane, the burly, bearded crooner, poet, and federal agent. "I know where the killer lives. Are you game?"

O'Kane tonight had been singing sad Irish songs he wrote himself to a lovely blond woman, singing with a power that caused her to hold his hand, close her eyes, and tremble with the ancient trails of the O'Kanes. His eyes gleamed with Tullamore Dew, "the milk of my race."

"I'm there," O'Kane said in his strong tenor.

Walter had a simple plan. They'd park the Crown Vic on the crowded block in the small eastern Pennsylvania city. He saw it in his mind's eye. He and the hulking O'Kane would knock on the row house door. An old man, living alone, would peek over the chain, white-haired, probably decrepit and smelling of booze, face tight.

The killer would most assuredly refuse to invite them in. With O'Kane behind him, Walter would set aside his Victorian manners. There was a child to remember, a child who would be a man of fifty-five now, probably a husband and father. It didn't matter how many years had passed, who forgot or remembered that the boy had ever existed, what the movies and TV news said, who cared or who didn't. There was fundamental decency at stake. "One is never too old to do the right thing." He would push his way in, decline a seat if offered. His face would become stone, the prison stare he'd developed in Michigan long ago. Unsmiling, his eyebrow raised up like a blade, he would say, "My dear fellow, it's high past time you and I had a man-to-boy chat."

"Rich, can I come with you?" It was Bender.

Walter startled. Bender had already taken one of his well-publicized long shots in the case, and missed. His speculative bust of what the boy's father might look like had gone out on *America's*

Most Wanted and a thousand other media outlets like a note in a bottle. It had been a decade, and nothing came back.

"Frank, what the hell you talkin' about? You'll be haunting me soon. Even more than you do now."

Bender stared at him, grinning like a cat, a cat with a secret. He said nothing.

Walter flushed. "See," he said, turning to the commissioner, the judge of truth and lies. "What'd I tell you? He's such a flim-flam artist I won't believe he's sick until he's in the grave. He's the type who would make a deal with the devil and beat it."

"You guys." Fleisher smiled and shook his head. "The greatest show on Earth."

The three of them stood in the parking lot. The night was overcast, no stars. From the great house came the sound of voices, men talking. The lights were going out. The river was black, indistinct, an inky mass with land and sky. When the moon flickered on the water you could see it, wide and slow, moving in the dark.

Bender said he'd gotten full veteran's benefits now from his time with the Navy, just as if he'd retired from it, because of the cancer.

Fleisher grinned. "Frank, with your fucking luck, you'll get recalled to Afghanistan."

They all laughed.

Fleisher looked up. He felt a touch of winter. "A beautiful night."

Bender's voice was reverent. "It's the form of nature. Can you see it, the harmony?"

"Bah." Walter blew cigarette smoke into the night air.

"I'll pray for you, Frank." Fleisher and Michelle were getting in the car. "We all will. We love you."

"Thanks, Bill." He waved.

It was just the two of them, still standing.

The thin man coughed. Bender looked pale to him in the moonlight.

"I still won't pray for you," Walter said. "But I'll cross my fingers."

The *Murder Room* is a history of the pro bono crime-fighters of the Vidocq Society of Philadelphia, focusing on the federal agent, forensic psychologist, and forensic artist who founded the society and more than a dozen murder cases Vidocq Society Members (VSMs) investigated from 1990 to 2009. The story is drawn from hundreds of interviews with homicide detectives, federal agents, forensic pathologists, anthropologists, dentists, and many other forensic scientists; police and court records; newspapers, magazines, television, radio tapes and transcripts, diaries, Web sites, e-mails, books, and theses, published and unpublished. In a story as complex as this one, my debts are great.

My deepest gratitude goes to federal agent, private eye, and Vidocq Society commissioner William Fleisher; forensic artist Frank Bender; and forensic psychologist and criminal profiler Richard Walter. *The Murder Room* is the story of the Vidocq Society but it is also a partial biography of these three men, the society's founders. With Fleisher, leading the way as commissioner, Bender and Walter gave me unprecedented access to the Vidocq Society, including its luncheon investigations in the Murder Room, board meetings, case files and archives, and discussions not open to the public. The three men made themselves available for more than a thousand hours of interviews across more than five years.

With Fleisher and Walter, I attended a forensics-law enforcement program at Albright College in Reading, Pennsylvania, featuring two days of lectures by Vidocq Society Members, including Haskell Askin on forensic dentistry, Fleisher on truth detection, and Walter on the personality subtypes of sex murderers—a lecture I heard Walter give many times, to universities, at forensic conferences, and to more than a hundred prosecutors at the Philadelphia district attorney's office. The three founders also gave me access to their personal lives, from Christmas dinners and New Year's Eve parties to the people closest to them. Special thanks for the time and recollections of Michelle Fleisher and Elizabeth Fleisher; Gloria Alvarado, the Vidocq Society's office secretary; Jan Bender; Ella Portnova; the gifted editor Vanessa Bender; Nan and Morris Baker; Beverly Fraser; and Richard Walter's extended family.

I am in debt to the Vidocq Society board of directors for its support, especially former U.S. Customs special agent Joseph M. O'Kane; former assistant U.S. attorney Barbara Cohan-Saavedra; polygraph examiner Nathan J. Gordon; and former Philadelphia major-crimes homicide detective Ed Gaughan. Gordon and Gaughan, Fleisher's partners in the Keystone Intelligence Network detective agency, were particularly helpful in reconstructing old cases. Board chairman Frederick A. Bornhofen, the former naval intelligence officer, gave generously of his time explaining the history of the society, as did O'Kane. William Gill III, the former U.S. Treasury agent and supervisor, former IRS inspection agent Benjamin Redmond, ex-Philadelphia chief inspector of detectives John Maxwell, and English professor and former hostage negotiator Donald Weinberg were also generous with their time and recollections.

I would like to especially acknowledge the contributions of the late Dr. Halbert Fillinger of Philadelphia, aka "Homicide Hal." One of America's great forensic pathologists, he was the old lion of the Vidocq Society and his presence pervades this book.

I'd like to thank all the members of the Vidocq Society (VSMs) for their help and forbearance as I watched them investigate murders and chatted with them over lunch. Being in the Murder Room for an afternoon of cuisine and crime is like attending a symphony orchestra, and this book is the story of all VSMs. I'd especially like to thank the society's chaplain, Bill Kelly, a retired Philadelphia Police Department latent fingerprinter, and Joe McGillen, the retired Philadelphia medical examiner's investigator, for their recollections of the Boy in the Box; Frank Friel, the Philadelphia homicide captain and police chief of Bensalem, Pennsylvania, for his memories of numerous cases and police investigation in general; Philadelphia captain of detectives Laurence Nodiff for his recollections of the Marie Noe case; California cold-case investigator Richard Walton, for taking me through his reconstruction of a 1920s murder; former U.S. Customs agent Frank Dufner for his remarkable memory of numerous federal cases; document examiner Robert J. Phillips for his frank discussions about JFK's handwriting; Arizona forensic pathologist Dr. Richard Froede for describing his autopsy of CIA Beirut station chief William Buckley, kidnapped, tortured, and murdered by Hamas and Islamic jihadists.

Thanks to former FBI agent and VSM Robert Ressler, and Washington State investigator and forensic professor Robert Keppel. These two prominent members of the first American generation of criminal profilers, colleagues of Richard Walter, gave generously of their time and insights into crime assessment and profiling. VSM Steve Stoud, a profiler with the Pennsylvania State Police, put into clear perspective Walter's theories in the history of profiling—and Walter himself, to the furthest extent humanly possible.

The story of the Vidocq Society was lodged mostly in memory and oral history, but the efforts of the society's former publicity director Richard Lavinthal, English professor Weinberg, science officer Dr. Jolie Bookspan, and her husband, Paul Plevakas, have led to publication of the excellent quarterly *Vidocq Society Journal*, now converted to digital format by editor Plevakas. It was an important source for the book.

In many hours of interviews, Jim Dunn shared with me his passion and years of effort to find the killers of his son, Scott, culminating in Jim's relationship with Richard Walter that secured justice. Homicide detective Keith Hall, now with the Onondaga County (New York) sheriff's office, was an important source of his work on the Case of the Missing Face with the Manlius (New York) Police Department, as was officer Thaddeus Maine. Homicide detective Tal English of the Lubbock (Texas) Police Department gave invaluable help on the Dunn case. Amateur investigators Robert Mancini of Ohio and Mike Rodelli of New Jersey, both mentored by Richard Walter, shared their research on two of America's most notorious unsolved serial killer cases—the Butcher of Cleveland and the Zodiac Killer, respectively.

My thanks go to Nancy Ruhe, executive director of the National Organization of Parents of Murdered Children (POMC), who helped me understand the formidable issues facing families victimized by murder. With Richard Walter, a former POMC board member, I attended a POMC national convention in Cincinnati, and saw firsthand a scale of suffering not widely known or imagined. Retired Tampa doctor Bob Meyer and his wife, Sherry, shared with me their anguish and their bravery in facing and solving the murders of their daughter Sherry-Ann Brannon, thirty-five years old, and grandchildren Shelby, seven, and Cassidy, four. California forensic pathologist and POMC leader Harry Bonnell also helped me understand this tragic American underground.

I had the good fortune to meet Dr. Richard Shepherd, leading forensic pathologist in London and Liverpool and author of *Simpson's Forensic Medicine*, at the American Academy of Forensic Sciences (AAFS) convention in Chicago. At the AAFS convention, I also met and interviewed John DeHaan of Vallejo, California, the premier fire, arson, and explosions investigator in criminal cases around the world and author of *Kirk's Fire Investigation*, and Vernon J. Geberth, retired lieutenant-commander of the New York City Police Department and author of the detective's bible, *Practical Homicide Investigation: Tactics, Procedures, and Forensic Techniques*. All three men contributed significantly to my understanding of cold-case investigations.

Thanks to Betty Smith of Montrose, Pennsylvania, for walking me through the history of the Susquehanna County seat, particularly the presence of the Biddle family of Philadelphia. Tom

DeTitto, Cushman and Wakefield's project manager and archivist for the Philadelphia Navy Yard redevelopment, helped me understand the history of the Navy Yard and the Officers' Club where the Vidocq Society first met, including pictures and elevations of Building 46. Douglas C. McVarish was also helpful.

Special thanks to Larry Biddison, emeritus professor of English at Mansfield University in Mansfield, Pennsylvania, for helping me sort out the unexpected presence of the Arthurian archetypes in the Vidocq Society. The professor walked me through Jessie L. Weston's classic *From Ritual to Romance,* Tennyson's *Idylls of the King,* and T. S. Eliot's *The Waste Land,* writings that echoed themes I first discovered in *The Grail Legend* by Emma Jung and Marie-Louise von Franz. Thanks also to English professors Tom Murphy of Mansfield University and Nelljean Rice of Coastal Carolina University for providing inspiration. Sue Cummings of the Native Bagel in Wellsboro, Pennsylvania, sustained me as well as offered a clean, well-lighted reading, writing, and interviewing place.

Sabrina Rubin Erdely's November 2003 *Philadelphia* magazine story on Bill Kelly and the Boy in the Box was a useful resource.

As I came down to the home stretch, I was lucky that Tom French, Pulitzer Prize–winning *St. Petersburg Times* reporter-turned-Indiana University professor, turned his remarkable narrative eye on this story one night over beers, and came up with several great suggestions. Tom was my teacher when I went back to school to the inspiring MFA program at Goucher College in Towson, Maryland, where Patsy Sims also deserves thanks for her support and encouragement. Maryland always seems to be a place to recharge, thanks to my friend Jeff Leen of *The Washington Post,* and the incredible faculty and students at the University of Maryland's Philip Merrill College of Journalism—Eugene Roberts, Jon Franklin, Ira Chinoy, and especially Dean Tom Kunkel, author, journalist, and now president of St. Norbert College in De Pere, Wisconsin. Thanks, too, to my attorney and magazine partner George Bochetto, Dave

Tepps, Tucker Worthington, Denise and Pete Boal, Steve Sonsky, Peggy Landers, Christopher Boyd, Bruce Boynick, Matt Walsh, Richard Strauch, Barb Madden, Gus Ciardullo, Theresa and Stanley Banik, Mark and Jessica Banik, Ron and Jackie Patt, John and Ruthann Gasienski, Stephen and Lisa Banik, Christopher Banik, Greg Banik, Kim Achilly, Michael and Mary Ann Banik, and Mohammad and Kathleen Sanati.

My publisher, the brilliant William Shinker, founder and president of Gotham Books, was passionate and unwavering in his support and vision for the book. The book is dedicated to my wife, Teresa Banik Capuzzo, one of the most tireless and gifted editors and wordsmiths I know. Now Bill Shinker knows it, too, having formally worked with Teresa on this book. It would not have happened without them—or without the great editing support of Gotham executive editor Lauren Marino and her all-star lineup including Erin Moore, Brett Valley, Brendan Cahill, who first saw the story's potential, Cara Bedick, Sophia Muthuraj, and Beth Parker, who shared it with the world. Thanks also to Eric Rayman, for his keen eye as both publishing attorney and former magazine publisher. Thanks to New York literary agents Robert Gottlieb and David McCormick for their irreplaceable roles in the selling and nurturing of this book and this author. A special thank-you to Douglas C. Clifton, the great newspaper editor of *The Miami Herald* and *Cleveland Plain Dealer*, who introduced a then-twenty-year-old intern from Northwestern University to the power of narrative.

The following is a partial record of the sources I consulted while writing *The Murder Room*, offered to provide readers additional sources of information. In addition to police records, court records, interviews with investigating police officers, prosecutors and Vidocq Society investigators, and hundreds of magazine and newspaper articles, I read and consulted dozens of books on crime and murder. These books, written by or about Vidocq Society Members, were valuable sources:

Botha, Ted. *The Girl with the Crooked Nose: A Tale of Murder, Obsession, and Forensic Artistry.* New York: Random House, 2008. The story of Frank Bender's remarkable career.

Dunn, James, and Wanda Evans. *Trail of Blood: A Father, a Son, and a Telltale Crime Scene Investigation.* Far Hills, NJ: New Horizon Press hardcover, 2007; Berkley True Crime paperback, 2007. A father's search for his son's killer ends with the Vidocq Society.

Gordon, Nathan J., and William L. Fleisher. *Effective Interviewing & Interrogation Techniques.* San Diego: Academic Press, 2002. The classic text by the Vidocq Society founder and board member.

Pettem, Silvia. *Someone's Daughter: In Search of Justice for Jane Doe.* Lanham, MD: Taylor Trade Publishing, 2009. By the Colorado journalist whose work brought the long-dormant Colorado Jane Doe case to public and police attention and to the Vidocq Society.

Ressler, Robert K., and Tom Shachtman. *I Have Lived in the Monster: Inside the Minds of the World's Most Notorious Serial Killers.* New York: St. Martin's Paperbacks, 1997. The murder cases and forensic adventures of VSM Ressler.

Ressler, Robert K., and Tom Shachtman. *Whoever Fights Monsters: My Twenty Years Tracking Serial Killers for the FBI.* New York: St. Martin's Paperbacks, 1992. More cases of VSM Ressler.

Stout, David. *The Boy in the Box: The Unsolved Case of America's Unknown Child.* Guilford, CT: The Lyons Press, 2008. VSMs Bill Kelly, Joe McGillen, Fleisher, and others pursue the legendary child murder case.

The numerous murder cases described in *The Murder Room* are true stories, with only slight changes in names and circumstances in order to protect the privacy of various individuals. To avoid confusion by those readers interested in other books about Vidocq Society cases, I have used the same pseudonyms of some of the true-life characters in these books: *The Girl with the Crooked Nose* (Laura Shaughnessy); *The Boy in the Box* (John Stachowiak and Frank Guthrum); and *Trail of Blood* ("Jessica").

Several other books were especially helpful, and I recommend them for readers interested respectively in the history of Philadelphia crime and the John List murders:

Avery, Ron. *City of Brotherly Mayhem: Philadelphia Crimes & Criminals.* Philadelphia: Otis Books, 1997.

Sharkey, Joe. *Death Sentence: The Inside Story of the John List Murders.* New York: Signet, 1990.

I also recommend the *Philadelphia* magazine investigative stories of author and National Magazine Award–winning journalist Stephen Fried, who broke open the Marie Noe case (see www.stephenfried .com). Fried's reporting and personal recollections are reflected in the chapters about Marie Noe and in my understanding of the history of the Vidocq Society. The books and articles written by forensic psychologist Katherine Ramsland, especially in the *Vidocq Society Journal* and truTV Crime Library, also were very helpful.

I read hundreds of newspaper and magazine stories on Vidocq Society cases or the Vidocq Society itself. Most stories about the society are general histories with a smattering of case and character information, often based on a reporter spending a couple hours over lunch and being asked to leave before the investigation began. These include accounts in *The New York Times, Los Angeles Times, USA Today,* Associated Press, *Harper's Magazine, Reader's Digest, London Telegraph, Montreal Gazette, The Philadelphia Inquirer, Miami Herald, St. Petersburg Times, Philadelphia* magazine, *The Pocono Record,* and *The Philadelphia Lawyer.*

Important sources for major cases included: the *Lubbock Avalanche-Journal* and *Plainview* (Texas) *Daily Herald* coverage of the police investigation of Scott Dunn's murder and two trials, Dunn's diary, travel itinerary, and other notes, tapes, photographs, and personal materials including the prepublished manuscript of his book; the *Syracuse* (New York) *Post-Standard* coverage of the Manlius murder, The Case of the Missing Face; articles in the *Trentonian* newspaper of Trenton, New Jersey, *UPI, Philadelphia Inquirer, Philadelphia Daily News,* and *Bucks County Courier Times* on the murder of Terri Lee Brooks; the *Rocky Mountain News, Denver Post, Boulder Daily Camera, North Platte Telegraph, USA Today,* and Boulder County sheriff's office on the Colorado Jane Doe case; the *Atlantic City Press* and the CBS *48 Hours with Dan Rather* documentary "Murder on the Menu" reported by Richard Schlesinger for the Zoia Assur case; AP, *UPI, Philadelphia Inquirer, Philadelphia Daily News,* Drexel University archives on the murder of Deborah Lynn Wilson; numerous sources on John List including the *New York Times,* Newark *Star-Ledger,* truTV Crime Library, and an *America's Most Wanted* episode. Thank you to J. D. Mullane of the *Bucks County Courier Times* for his excellent reporting and guidance on the Choir Loft Murder, based on his six-part series on the subject.

The Boy in the Box case has been extensively documented for more than half a century. The national coverage includes a July

1958 *Saturday Evening Post* story ("A Box, a Blanket, and a Small Body"), a 1957 *Front Page Detective* magazine story ("Who is the Boy in the Box?"), articles in *American Way* magazine, an October 1998 *America's Most Wanted* episode, and a CBS *48 Hours* transcript. While interviews with many Vidocq Society Members on the case were most helpful, I read more than a hundred articles dated from 1957 to the present in *The Philadelphia Press*—all that I could find—mostly in the *Philadelphia Inquirer* and *Philadelphia Daily News* but also the *Philadelphia City Paper, Northeast Times,* and *Frankford News Gleaner.* Other sources included the Associated Press, KYW-TV Channel 3 Philadelphia, and Fleisher's obituary of Detective Samuel Weinstein published in May 2004 by the Philadelphia area chapter of Shomrim, the national Jewish law enforcement association.

Frank Bender may be the best-known VSM outside of FBI agent Robert Ressler. In addition to an avalanche of newspaper and magazine coverage from Paris to Philadelphia, several books, an *Esquire* profile, and a *60 Minutes* profile, I read reams of Frank's personal materials including an unpublished autobiography. I read about Frank in sources as diverse as *Harper's Magazine; ArtForum* magazine; *Frieze* magazine—London's "leading magazine of contemporary arts and culture"—the transcript of an NPR/*Weekend Edition* interview with Frank; "Inside Corrections: The Quarterly Newsletter of the New Jersey Department of Corrections," about the death of one of his captured fugitives (not in the book); and *Rockhound News,* the newsletter of the Memphis Archaeological and Geological Society on the "Ice Man." Richard Walter contributed thick files of press and personal material, plus his professional publications from such sources as the *International Journal of Offender Therapy and Comparative Criminology.* In addition to Bill Fleisher's book on interrogation, highlights of his U.S. Customs career were covered by the Philadelphia newspapers and wire services; Fleisher and Bender did an NPR "Talk of the Nation" interview in February 2009.

FBI Uniform Crime Reports since 1950 were a source of

crime statistics. For historic weather, in addition to press accounts and interviews, I purchased National Oceanic and Atmospheric Administration Local Climatological Data weather charts for Lubbock, Texas, and Philadelphia, Pennsylvania, and consulted weather data on the Web from the Franklin Institute in Philadelphia and the Weather Underground. The Web was useful in hundreds of ways, from the Boy in the Box Web site—americasunknownchild.net—and its treasure trove of information to the Camelot Project at the University of Rochester.

Selected other book sources:

Aeschylus. *The Oresteia: Agamemnon; The Libation Bearers; The Eumenides.* New York: Penguin Classics, 1984.

Alighieri, Dante. *The Divine Comedy: Volume 1: Inferno.* New York: Penguin Classics, 2003.

Badal, James Jessen. *In the Wake of the Butcher: Cleveland's Torso Murders.* Kent, Ohio: The Kent State University Press, 2001.

Black, Joel. *The Aesthetics of Murder: A Study in Romantic Literature and Contemporary Culture.* Baltimore: Johns Hopkins University Press, 1991.

Campbell, Joseph. *The Hero with a Thousand Faces.* New York: MJF Book, 1949.

Campbell, Joseph. *The Mythic Image.* Princeton, NJ: Princeton University Press, 1974.

Campbell, Joseph. *The Power of Myth with Bill Moyers.* New York: Doubleday, 1988.

Capote, Truman. *In Cold Blood: A True Account of a Multiple Murder and Its Consequences.* New York: Random House, 1965.

Collins, Philip. *Dickens and Crime.* Bloomington, IN: Indiana University Press, 1968.

Dostoevsky, Fyodor. *The Brothers Karamazov*. New York: Farrar, Straus, and Giroux, 2002. Translated by Richard Pevear and Larissa Volokhonsky.

Douglas, John, and Mark Olshaker. *The Anatomy of Motive: The FBI's Legendary Mindhunter Explores the Key to Understanding and Catching Violent Criminals*. New York: Scribner, 1999.

Doyle, Sir Arthur Conan. *Sherlock Holmes: The Complete Novels and Stories, Volume 1*. New York: A Bantam Classic, 1986.

Doyle, Sir Arthur Conan. *Sherlock Holmes: The Complete Novels and Stories, Volume 2*. New York: A Bantam Classic, 1986.

Edwards, Samuel. *The Vidocq Dossier: The Story of the World's First Detective*. Boston: Houghton Mifflin Co., 1977.

French, Thomas. *Unanswered Cries: A True Story of Friends, Neighbors, and Murder in a Small Town*. New York: St. Martin's Paperbacks, 1992.

Friel, Francis, and John Guinther. *Breaking the Mob: The Gripping True Story of a Dedicated Cop Who Led the Fight That Put an Entire Mafia Family out of Business*. Lincoln, NE: Excel Press, 2000.

Gardiner, Eileen, ed. *Visions of Heaven & Hell Before Dante*. New York: Italica Press, 1989.

Hare, Robert D. *Without Conscience: The Disturbing World of the Psychopaths Among Us*. New York: The Guilford Press, 1993.

Hugo, Victor. *Les Misérables*. New York: Modern Library, 1992.

Jeffers, Paul H. *Who Killed Precious: How FBI Special Agents Combine Psychology and High Technology to Identify Violent Criminals*. New York: Pharos Books, 1991.

Johnson, Paul. *A History of the American People*. New York: Harper Perennial, 1999.

Jung, Emma, and Marie-Louise von Franz. *The Grail Legend*. Princeton, NJ: Princeton University Press, 1998.

Keppel, Robert D., with William J. Birnes. *Signature Killers: Interpreting the Calling Cards of the Serial Murderer.* New York: Pocket Books, 1997.

Kessler, Ronald. *The Bureau: The Secret History of the FBI.* New York: St. Martin's Paperbacks, 2003.

Leeming, David Adams. *The World of Myth.* New York: Oxford University Press, 1990.

McVarish, Douglas C. *Warships and Yardbirds: An Illustrated History of the Philadelphia Naval Shipyard.* Philadelphia: Kvaerner, 2000.

Michaud, Stephen G., with Roy Hazelwood. *The Evil That Men Do: FBI Profiler Roy Hazelwood's Journey into the Minds of Sexual Predators.* New York: St. Martin's Paperbacks, 1998.

Nickel, Steven. *Torso: The Story of Eliot Ness and the Search for a Psychopathic Killer.* Winston-Salem, NC: John F. Blair, Publisher, 1989.

Ruehlmann, William. *Saint with a Gun: The Unlawful American Private Eye.* New York: New York University Press, 1974.

Sade, Donatien Alphonse François de. *The Marquis de Sade: Three Complete Novels: Justine, Philosophy in the Bedroom, Eugenie de Franval and Other Writings.* New York: Grove Press, 1966.

Scott, Gini Graham. *Homicide: 100 Years of Murder in America.* Lincolnwood, IL: Roxbury Park Books, 1998.

Tennyson, Alfred Lord. *Idylls of the King.* New York: Penguin Classics, 1989.

Vidocq, Eugène François. *Memoirs of Vidocq: Master of Crime.* Oakland, CA: Nabat/AKPress, 2003.

Weston, Jessie L. *From Ritual to Romance.* Mineola, New York: Dover Publications, 1997, republished from Cambridge University Press first edition, 1920.